W9-CAV-572

THE BASEBALL CHRONICLES

THE BASEBALL CHRONICLES

Edited by David Gallen
Introduction by Mark Harris
Afterword by Peter Golenbock

Galahad Books · New York

Published in 1994 by

Galahad Books
A division of Budget Book Service, Inc.
386 Park Avenue South
New York, NY 10016

Galahad Books is a registered trademark of Budget Book Service, Inc.

Published by arrangement with Carroll & Graf Publishers, Inc.   .

Library of Congress Catalog Card Number: 94-75060
ISBN: 0-88365-851-8

Printed in the United States of America

Acknowledgments

I want to extend my gratitude to Peter Golenbock for the idea, Kent Carroll and Herman Graf for the opportunity, Kevin Adler for his time and editorial expertise and the entire staff of the National Baseball Hall of Fame Library, particularly Mike Wendell, for all their research help. To Michael Bertolini for his spirited negotiations and ebullient humor I offer my special thanks, and to Peter Skutches for his keen insights, effervescence and friendship.

Finally, I thank Henry, Jon, Jill and Richard Gallen who have endured gracefully through far more of my shenanigans than I had ever intended and whom I love very much.

Permissions

1)   Lou Gehrig: The Man and The Legend by Jack Sher, October 1951, *Sport* Magazine. Reprinted by permission of Petersen Publishing Co.

2)   The Emancipation of Jackie Robinson by Milton Gross, October 1951, *Sport* Magazine. Reprinted by permission of Petersen Publishing Co.

3)   This Is The Truth by Shoeless Joe Jackson, October 1949, *Sport* Magazine. Reprinted by permission of Petersen Publishing Co.

4)   Dizzy Dean: The One and Only by Jack Sher, March 1948, *Sport* Magazine. Reprinted by permission of Petersen Publishing Co.

5)   John McGraw: The Little Napoleon by Jack Sher, January 1949, *Sport* Magazine. Reprinted by permission of Petersen Publishing Co.

6)   Always On The Spot by Tom Meany, April 1942, *Sport* Magazine. Reprinted by permission of Petersen Publishing Co.

7)   Walter Johnson: The Big Train by Shirley Povich, January 1950, *Sport* Magazine. Reprinted by permission of Petersen Publishing Co.

8)   Sophistication of Sandy Koufax by Bill Libby, September 1963, *Sport* Magazine. Reprinted by permission of Petersen Publishing Co.

9)   Roberto Clemente: Man of Paradox by Arnold Hano, May 1965, *Sport* Magazine. Reprinted by permission of Petersen Publishing Co.

10) Baseball and The American Character, October 17, 1975, Speech by Bart Giamatti. Reprinted by permission of Mrs. Toni Giamatti

11) Next To Godliness by Red Smith, 1947, *The Red Smith Reader*, Vintage Books. Reprinted by permission of Alfred A. Knopf, Inc.

12) Winning By Striking Out by Red Smith, 1941, *The Red Smith Reader*, Vintage Books. Reprinted by permission of Alfred A. Knopf, Inc.

13) Hub Fans Bid Kid Adieu by John Updike, October 22, 1960, *New Yorker* Magazine. Reprinted by permission of Alfred A. Knopf, Inc.

14) The Day Bobby Hit The Home Run by Roger Kahn, October 10, 1960, *Sports Illustrated*. Reprinted by permission of Roger Kahn.

15) Streak of Streaks essay by Stephen Jay Gould, 1988 Nyrev, Inc. Reprinted by permission of Stephen Jay Gould.

16) The Ups and Downs of Old Pete by Jack Sher, April 1950, *Sport* Magazine. Reprinted by permission of Petersen Publishing Co.

17) Red Sox: 68 Years and Counting by George Vecsey, October 26, 1986, *New York Times*. Reprinted by permission of George Vecsey.

18) The Grey Eagle by Gordon Cobbledick, July 1952, *Sport* Magazine. Reprinted by permission of Petersen Publishing Co.

19) Mickey Mantle: The Twilight of a Hero by Arnold Hano, August 1965, *Sport* Magazine. Reprinted by permission of Petersen Publishing Co.

List of Illustrations

Contents

Introduction

By Mark Harris

Hey, Jackie Brandt, how are you? Where are you? Fancy meeting you here. Where have you been? Haven't seen you in ages.

Haven't seen him in fact for more than thirty years. It was 1959. He was playing baseball for the San Francisco Giants and I was covering the Giants for an article for *Life*. Jackie was a blond fellow— boy, man, twenty-five years old, handsome chap, neither friendly nor unfriendly, ready to speak, I suppose, if he were spoken to, and so was I. I was a stranger in the clubhouse. We nodded. We never spoke.

I remember him on that day as one whose demeanor belied the logic of the moment. He appeared glum when he should have been happy. He had just won a game for his team with a home run. He hit twelve home runs that year. Not bad, right? Hadn't he every reason to be a happy man? He was a big-league baseball player. Nobody could ask for more than that.

Now here he is again, just today, on a page of this book. He is no longer in the uniform of the Giants but of the Baltimore Orioles. For Baltimore he is playing center field.

The game is at Boston in the bottom of the first inning. Ted Williams, who has walked on four pitches, has arrived at third base, whereupon another Bostonian—at any rate one Lu Clinton, a player for Boston—

sends a fly ball to Jackie Brandt in center field. "Williams tagged up and ran home," says the author. "As he slid across the plate, the ball, thrown with unusual heft by Jackie Brandt, the Oriole center fielder, hit him on the back." It didn't hurt. Williams scored the run.

That day's game, written up by John Updike in this volume, was the occasion of Ted Williams's last appearance as a player. Williams had played more than two thousand games. Lu Clinton, who hit the fly ball, had played less than a hundred. I hadn't thought about Jackie Brandt in thirty years. Every thirty years we meet. He was up, he played, he was gone. I don't know where he is now. Maybe someone will write me a letter and tell me.

Today I see him once again for a moment through Updike's eye, hurling that ball with "unusual heft" into Ted Williams's back. Does Jackie Brandt remember that moment? Does Ted Williams remember that moment? There were an awful lot of ball games to remember. "Bangin' around the way I was," says Satchel Paige in the pages of this book, "playing for guarantees on one team after another that I never heard of, in towns I never seen before, with players I didn't know and never saw again, I got lonesome."

In my lifetime at college I met two students whose late fathers had been big-league baseball players. Both students were women. Both fathers (this is a marvelous coincidence, don't you agree?) had been catchers for the same team, though in different years. Both catchers were obscure. They did not catch much. You will not have heard of their names even if I tell you.

These two fathers possessed in common the memory of their unique craft, and the pale taint of their obscurity offset by their fame in the minds of their daughters. It is their daughters' idea that their fathers played much longer in the big leagues than they did, that they were more illustrious than they were. Perhaps these young women heard these things from their mothers. Mothers do not always tell their daughters the truth of the past.

Of course, with the *The Baseball Encyclopedia* at my elbow, I could have corrected the memories of those daughters. "Dear girl, your father was an obscure player—you could look it up."

No, I would never say such a thing. We are obscure. The planet is crowded and fierce. However famous we may be to ourselves, to our heirs, to our family, to our descendants, we endure only for a limited term in the minds of the living, as Jackie Brandt in mine, as two dead catchers in the minds of their daughters.

Almost everyone inflates his career, doesn't he? Some people have told me they played baseball in the big leagues, but I cannot find them in the

Encyclopedia. Everyone contends that he really did it all a little better than perhaps he did. Nobody feels that he quite got a fair shake—the memorable error he once made, which cost his team the game, the pennant, the world, should never truly have been scored as an error: consider the extenuating circumstances, the bad hop the ball took, the wind, the sun, the bad condition of the turf.

But what we have here in this book exceeds customary reality. These few men of baseball could hardly have been exceeded even in their own imaginations. They are who they are and they did what they did beyond question or cavil or dispute. Their achievements are clear and unclouded. They are not doubtful figures, furtive or shrouded, but players on a scene whose every act was open and observed. Everyone may see every pitch and catch or hit or out. Baseball players "cannot hide from clear responsibility," the late Comissioner Giamatti writes in these pages, "as in football or Congress."

These men were physically so tough they could play this aching game of baseball even when they were broken into pieces. Mickey Mantle required his friends to hoist him out of taxicabs. He played with steel pins drilled through his collarbone, and a wide assortment of injuries to his knees, thighs, shoulders, and groin—according to Arnold Hano, "a lifetime of pain." Mantle said to Hano, "I think I've been real lucky, but I can't help wondering how far I'd have gone with two legs." John McGraw, struck by a taxicab, walked around unknowingly for days with a broken leg. Lou Gehrig, "The Iron Man," played 2,130 consecutive games and died all in a day at thirty-eight. Dizzy Dean, struck in his big toe by a batted ball, ruined his arm compensating for his toe. The scientist Satchel Paige analyzes his own arm. "I just explained to the gentlemen that the bones running up from my wrist, the fibius, which is the upper bone, and the tiberon, which is the lower bone, was bent out, making more room for my throwing muscles to move around in there. I attributed most of my long life, and so on and so forth, to them two bones. The gentlemen was amazed to hear about that."

This is a lively book.

Some of these men were unspeakably fierce, like Ty Cobb, McGraw, Durocher, or they were essentially gentle like Honus Wagner and Walter Johnson.

Hear how the savage Cobb exploited Johnson's gentleness:

I had to figure Johnson out. I realized quickly that he wasn't a vicious pitcher, despite all that speed. I saw him wince when he fired one close to somebody's head, and he used to tell me that he was afraid someday that he would kill a man with that fireball. So I used to cheat. I'd crowd that plate so far that I was actually sticking my toes on it when I was facing Johnson. I knew he was timid about hitting a batter, and when he saw me crowding the plate he'd steer his pitches a little bit wide. Then with two balls and no strikes, he'd ease up a bit to get it over. That's the Johnson pitch I hit. I was depending on him to be scared of hitting me.

Where have all the young men gone? Ted Williams has gone to the Hall of Fame. Jackie Brandt has joined the less exclusive company of the *Encyclopedia*: he shares his little space with the thirteen thousand men who have played at least one pitchworth in the major leagues of baseball.

Ty Cobb played twenty-four years, mainly for the Detroit Tigers, immediately preceded in the *Encyclopedia* by Joe Cobb, who played one game for the same team, in 1918, batted once, drew a walk, and that was all. Ty Cobb is immediately *followed* in the *Encyclopedia* by Dave Coble, who came to bat twenty-five times in fifteen games for the Philadelphia Phillies in 1939, stroked seven safe hits (one a double), and scored two runs. Fate deals unevenly. Babe Ruth hit 714 home runs. Jim Rutherford, who follows Babe Ruth in the *Encyclopedia* lineup, played one game, hit no home runs.

One section of *The Baseball Chronicles* is devoted to "great games, feats, moments in baseball history." The thought occurs to me that the indelible moments of baseball are associated in general with players often unremembered except in the context of their isolated moments of triumph or chagrin: Merkle's omitting to run to second base, Mickey Owens's dropping the third strike, Ralph Branca's fateful pitch, Bobby Thomson's home run, Bruckner's error, Lavagetto's hit, Sandy Amoros's miraculous catch, Wambsganss's unassisted triple play, John Vander Meer's back-to-back no-hit games, Don Larsen's perfect game. These were good players—nobody plays in the big leagues who is not a good player—but the superstars of this book, Ruth, Cobb, Gehrig, Speaker, Paige, DiMaggio, appear to be remembered for their lives as a whole, for lifetime performance, rather than for isolated moments of their play.

In Stephen Jay Gould's learned essay, "The Streak of Streaks," Gould examines the other side of the "capricious character" of those events I have just mentioned. "Single moments of unexpected supremacy . . . can occur at any time to almost anybody," he writes. "But a streak must be absolutely exceptionless; you are not allowed a single day of subpar play, or even bad luck. . . . Thus Joe DiMaggio's fifty-six game streak is both the greatest factual achievement in the history of baseball and a principal icon of American mythology . . . one sequence so many standard deviations above the expected distribution that it should not have occurred at all. . . . DiMaggio's streak is the most extraordinary thing that ever happened in American sports."

Hey, Leo, what's up?

Leo don't answer. He's too tough and gruff. I had the feeling he didn't like me.

Somebody on the bus mentioned Babe Ruth. Leo had once been a teammate of Babe Ruth. Mention Babe Ruth and Leo promptly tells of the time he picked a clubhouse fight with Ruth, who was twice his size.

Hey, Leo, remember when we rode a bus together? He don't remember. Who am I that Leo should remember me? Nevertheless it happened. One day late in cold January of 1966 I rode in a bus somewhere south of Chicago with Leo and Ripper Collins and several Chicago Cubs baseball players. It was a ticket-selling promotional tour arranged by the Cubs in their own behalf. The front office was represented by Charlie Grimm.

Leo sat up front beside the driver, huddled in his overcoat, staring at the treacherous road ahead. In the back of the bus Ripper Collins smoked his cigar. Durocher hated Collins's cigar and made him sit in back. I had thought a man called Ripper would be fierce, but Ripper no longer ripped. He sat in back. The years had tamed him. In the center of the empty, hollow bus the baseball players played cards.

On the following morning we boarded the bus for another day's tour. One of our players was missing. He had been out bowling late last night and was therefore a little slow getting started today. We would fall behind schedule. Late to leave meant late for the luncheon. Late for the luncheon meant late for the dinner. People were waiting for us. Wasn't anyone worried? The players in the bus were not worried. They broke out the cards. Leo assumed his seat up front, Ripper Collins fired up his cigar in the back, and Charlie Grimm's impassive face told me all I needed to know. He could not worry. Give Charlie several baseball players and one of them is bound to have been up too late last night. This had always been so, and it was not less likely to be so this winter morning. Charlie Grimm had been playing this game, boy and man, player, coach, manager and front office since 1916—exactly half a century—and he knew that the baseball player was immortal, that his species endured, that he repeated established patterns. There was always going to be one baseball player up too late last night, and nothing in the world Charlie Grimm could do about it.

Hey, Old Pete, there you are. Do you remember me? I punched you in the stomach once—how can you not remember?

Grover Cleveland Alexander had been wounded in World War I. He drank thereafter and suffered a variety of afflictions of body and mind. He had earned money at baseball but saved none of it.

When his career ended he lived marginally on small sums earned for humble work or taken as gifts. He appeared for a while, half celebrity half freak, for a so-called museum or flea circus on Times Square in Manhattan. Manhattan had been a scene of triumph for him. He had pitched two complete games for victories for the St. Louis Cardinals against the Yankees in 1926. In the seventh game he came to the mound as a relief pitcher in the seventh inning with the bases loaded and two men out. He struck out Tony Lazzeri to end the inning, pitched two scoreless innings beyond, and saved the World Series for the Cardinals.

The Times Square flea circus attracted boys like me, drawn to the scene by promises of marvels. I paid my way in. Grover Cleveland Alexander's name meant nothing to me. He had been gone from baseball for almost a decade, too long for my memory, and he was featured instead by a shrewd management not as the exceptional baseball player he had been but as a man with an iron stomach whom any boy could punch for a price.

I was not yet sensitive to other people's dignity. I punched him in the stomach. He had won 373 big-league baseball games. Only two men in the history of baseball had won more games than he.

What a gang here in this book we hold in our hands! All pals of mine so briefly met.

Hello, Jack. Long time no see but think about a lot.

For example, a year ago something suddenly came to my mind. I was playing Sunday softball—Slow Pitch, that's me—with university associates, teachers, students, men and women. Several of our players were black. One morning we were warming up, throwing back and forth when my epiphany hit. It was this. I had never thrown a baseball to a black man, nor had any black man ever thrown a baseball to me, though I had played hundreds of baseball games in the town where I was raised. I was a boy not indifferent to the beauty of equality, for I cared myself to be thought equal by others, and over the years my sense in this respect had deepened and strengthened until it had become an obsession, a political and social imperative.

I was a newspaper reporter in St. Louis when the great news came: the Brooklyn Dodgers had signed Jackie Robinson. The year was 1946. I ran up and down the halls of the *Star-Times* telling everyone, but not everyone rejoiced like me. A newspaperman said to me, "No nigger will ever set foot in Sportsman's Park." In Sportsman's Park the Browns and Cardinals played. The newspaperman offered to bet, but I wasn't a betting man. I was a writing man, and I wrote a little piece about my sensations of that day.

I had "scouted around," I wrote, "to find out what St. Louis people thought about Brooklyn's new shortstop. Some people did not have any opinions at all . . . Other people, however, asked a question instead of answering mine, the way some people do. They wanted to know how I would like it if my sister married Jackie Robinson. They even hinted that such a union was imminent."

Martha, my sister, lived then in Mt. Vernon, N.Y. She was in the sixth grade at the Wilson School, on the playground of which I had played so many of my lily-white baseball games. She was twelve years old. Robinson was twenty-six. She was left-handed, the spiritual model for a novel I was soon to write called *The Southpaw*. Left-handed, she wrote me a letter.

In her letter, written in reverse slant on blue-lined notebook paper, she hinted that she is now in love with Raymie Carucci . . . Martha was in love with Billy Pelkus when I was home. During the winter, however, he smacked her in the eye with a snowball, putting an end to what had been, at best, a one-sided affair. I do not believe Martha has ever heard of Jackie Robinson. . . . I am certain my mother will not permit her to marry before she has completed junior high school . . . And my sister's present attachment to Raymie Carucci appears to be a determined thing. If Raymie backs out there's always Billy Pelkus. The whole thing is out of the question.

And the face of the game was changed.

In his chapter on John McGraw, Jack Sher writes in these pages, "It annoyed McGraw that baseball was not always considered the most important thing in American life, on a par with the scientific discoveries that were changing our nation and the policies that were being formed in the White House." In search of the most important thing the people of the United States of America have ranged among options.

Baseball has competed among the options for our affection. We have sentimentalized it and we have commercialized it, and it persists.

How fitting that baseball's late, brief commissioner should have been a man so erudite and so humane as Mr. Giamatti of Yale! He treasured the game in spite of impurities not likely to have been observed by Mr. McGraw.

We are a nation of immigrants, Giamatti said, always migrating in search of home . . . The hunger for home makes the green geometry of the baseball field more than simply a metaphor for the American experience and character; the baseball field and the game that sanctifies boundaries, rules, and law and appreciates cunning, theft and guile; that exalts energy, opportunism, and execution while paying lip service to management, strategy and long-range planning, is closer to an embodiment of American life than to the mere sporting image of it.

My own hope is that baseball, with all its impurities, will prevail among the options. Conquerors, warrior-presidents, tyrants, mad leaders of nations and tribes, arrogant liberators, and self-appointed saviors, take heed. Stop. The humblest man in *The Baseball Encyclopedia* will have done more for humankind than you. In all the history of the big-league game only one man (Ray Chapman of the Cleveland Indians, struck in the head by a ball pitched by Carl Mays of the New York Yankees, in 1920) was ever killed at play. One in thirteen thousand men in *The Baseball Encyclopedia*! I can almost say with Pete Rose, "I can't think of a single thing wrong with the game of baseball."

PART ONE

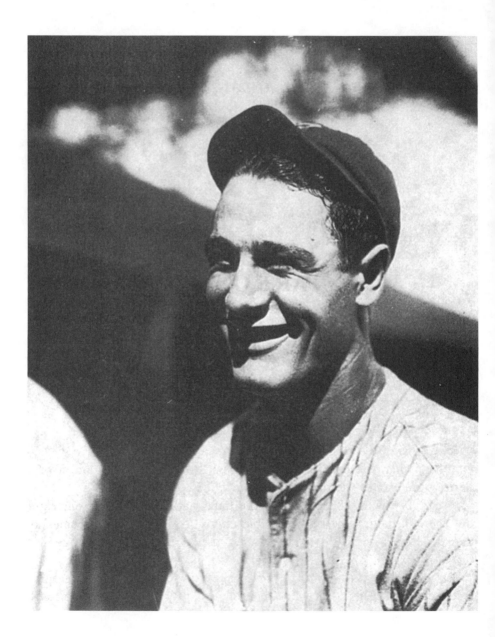

Lou Gehrig

LOU GEHRIG

The Man and the Legend

Sport Magazine   October 1948

Jack Sher, who worked on the 1942 film biography of Lou Gehrig, **Pride of the Yankees,** *produced this tribute to the Iron Horse 10 years after the slugger's death.*

By Jack Sher

Along with the folk legends that are native to America—tall tales of the bravery of Davey Crockett and the strength of Paul Bunyan—there is also one about a seemingly indestructible baseball player who was called "The Iron Horse." His name was Henry Louis Gehrig. The incidents of his life are best remembered during early October, when the bright, blue days begin to grow shorter and World Series time excites the nation.

"Yeah, it was in '28, see? I seen the Babe walk up and paste one right out there in them same right-field bleachers. And then Gehrig comes up and he dumps another one right under the scoreboard there in center. Geez, it was too bad about Lou. He was a strong guy."

He was strong, all right. He was a giant of a man in the American tradition. But the fans remember him most poignantly as a weak and broken man, his body wasting away, standing in Yankee Stadium, a white handkerchief held to his face, crying softly. It was July 4th, 1939, and the words Gehrig had just spoken into a microphone had created the most heart-breaking moment in sport. He had said, "I may have been given a bad break, but I got an awful lot to live for." Pause. "I consider myself the luckiest man on the face of the earth."

Lucky? Well, Lou Gehrig was never a lucky man. But, at that moment, he must have been a supremely happy one. For from then on, until the wretched, creeping disease snuffed him out, Lou had the one elusive thing he had always wanted most—the wholehearted love of baseball fans and people everywhere in the world.

"You have to get knocked down to realize how people really feel about you," Gehrig said to me in an interview late in 1940, shortly before he died. "I've realized that more than ever lately. The other day, I was on my way to the car. It was hailing, the streets were slippery and I was having a tough time of it. I came to a corner and started to slip. But before I could fall, four people jumped out of nowhere to help me. When I thanked them, they all said they knew about my illness and had been keeping an eye on me."

All through his playing days, Gehrig never seemed to kindle much enthusiasm or regard in the fans. He was laughed at as "Old Biscuit Pants" and "Piano Legs." While Ruth was slamming those prodigious homers, Lou's great hitting was called "monotonous!" After the Babe bowed out, the graceful, easy style of Joe DiMaggio captured the imagination of spectators and Gehrig became merely a "fixture" in the line-up.

He was characterized by fans and sportswriters as a quiet plugger. But his former teammates will tell you that Gehrig's constant stream of peppy chatter on the playing field kept alive the famed Yankee spirit during the days when they were so invincible.

Bucky Harris, present manager of the Yankees, who played against Lou year after year, rated him on a par with Ruth as a terror at the plate. "Listen," Bucky told me recently, "when that guy came to bat, all you could do was hold your breath. When you consider everything, the number of games he played, the way he hit, his reliability, and his drive, he was, for me, the greatest first baseman of all time!"

There were several sportswriters listening in on this conversation in Bucky's dressing room. One of them grinned and said, "Billy Terry ain't gonna like you when he reads that, Bucky."

"I'll still take Gehrig," Harris said, his face serious. "Everyone keeps picking Sisler and Chance and Terry, but maybe they ought to take a look at Lou's record. He didn't seem very fancy around first base," Bucky went on, "but in seven World Series, his average was .997—and who ever did better than that? Young fella," he turned to me, "don't write a line about Gehrig until you study his record."

Ruth hit 15 Series home runs to Gehrig's 10, but Lou did better with his World Series batting average, hitting .361 to the Sultan's .325. It isn't necessary to list Ruth's World Series records. It has been done many times. Lou Gehrig's records have seldom seen print other than in baseball's official books.

Lou holds the record for batting in the most World Series runs, a total of 35. He made the most homers in three consecutive games, four in 1928. He tied with Ruth for the most runs scored in one Series, nine in 1932. He batted in the most runs by any player in one Series, nine in 1928. That same year he whacked the most four baggers in a four-game series, four.

The tragedy of Gehrig's tremendous records and stunning career was not only that he lacked the flashy showiness so popular during the era in which he played, but that he always seemed to rise to his greatest heights at the precise time when it would be least noticed. And no matter what he did, that wonderful, flamboyant, cussed but naturally beloved Babe Ruth seemed to have been born to outshine him and dim the glory that should have been Gehrig's.

No more bitter epitaph to Lou Gehrig's powerful slugging has been penned than the one written by columnist Franklin P. Adams: "He was the guy who hit all those home runs the year Ruth broke the record."

Bitter and true. Lou's lifetime batting average was .340. Babe Ruth's was .342. That's the way it always went. Gehrig's greatest World Series play was against the Cards in 1928, when he set three all-time records. He had the unbelievable batting average in that Series of .545. The fantastic Babe went absolutely superhuman in that same Series and got 10 hits in 16 times at bat for a .625 average!

Every school kid knows the story of how the King of Swat slaughtered the Cubs in the World Series of 1932. The score tied in the fifth inning of the third game, the Cubs jeering, Ruth pointed at the center-field fence and then teed off to dump the ball beyond the barrier. It was his second home run of the game. But another player, Lou Gehrig, also got two home runs that day, and the final score was 7 to 5 for the Yankees.

Only a few know that Lou Gehrig also called his shot that afternoon. He didn't do it in the dramatic way the Babe did. As Ruth jogged home, Lou was waiting for him at the plate, a smile on his face. Babe gripped his hand briefly and said, "You do the same thing I just done, kid."

"I will," Gehrig said, simply.

And he did. He hit the first pitch that came to him into the right-field bleachers. It was just another home run.

By the Yankees, Gehrig was always referred to affectionately as "Buster." The nickname suggests a big, awkward kid who can bust 'em. When he took his cuts, he stood up there almost motionless, waving his bat a little, planted like a rock on his oversized legs. His unusually wide shoulders were always hunched slightly forward. When he took his lashing swing at the ball, there was little grace in the movement. In later years, he learned to pull his hits and loft the ball. But at his peak, he was a line-drive hitter whose homers were punched into the stands or over the fence like a lightning right cross in the prize ring.

His amazing endurance record, for which Lou Gehrig will be most remembered, was hung up at frightful cost in pain and punishment. He played with fractured hands, doubled over with lumbago, woozy from being hit in the head by wild pitches. He performed in every Yankee game for 14 years. He played in 2,130 consecutive games, not counting World Series contests, and there isn't a ballplayer alive who won't tell you that this record will stand forever.

Even the hard-headed, unsentimental Ed Barrow, who was then General Manager of the Yanks, was deeply affected by Gehrig's passion to keep his record intact. One morning, as Lou's consecutive-game run was approaching the 2,000 mark, Gehrig was so sick he couldn't get out of bed. As game time approached, a cloud appeared in the sky. Barrow cancelled the game. Not one drop of rain fell that afternoon.

"Say Ed," a reporter asked Barrow the next day, "you really didn't think it was going to rain, did you?"

"Damn it, of course I did!" Barrow snapped. And then he added, "Gehrig will be able to play today."

In the 1936 World Series against the Giants, Gehrig came as close to becoming a headline hero as he had ever been. Ruth's career had ended. That year Lou copped the home-run title, smashing out 49 round trippers. He was voted the most valuable player in the American League for the fourth time. As the Series opened, the spotlight began to focus on him. The Yankees jumped off to a 2-1 lead in the Series, but in the fourth game they faced the Giants' speedy ace, the great Carl Hubbell.

It was anybody's ball game until the third inning. With a man on base, Lou came to the plate, took that characteristic hitch at the top of his swing, and blasted one of Hubbell's fast balls into the center-field stands. The crowd really went berserk that day, cheering the way they had for the Bam. The Giants never recovered from that blow. The Yanks won the game 5-2 and went ahead 3 to 1 in the Series. For 24 hours, Lou Gehrig was elevated to almost Ruthian heights of acclaim.

But it didn't last long. The next day, in the most crucial moment of the game, Gehrig fluffed a chance to score. He had singled, then gone to third when Mel Ott muffed the ball in the outfield. Bill Dickey hit a screaming ground ball to the infield. The play was at first, Gehrig started for home, then stopped. He stood there, undecided, then started for home again. Dickey was thrown out, the ball was whipped to the plate, and Lou was tagged out. The Giants won the game 5-4 and the fans went away mumbling about "Bonehead Lou."

The Yanks won the Series, but Gehrig, who had turned the tide for them in the fourth game, was just another player on a winning team.

One of the most shocking revelations I ran into as I quizzed players and managers and scouts and authorities about the life and times of Gehrig, was that not one of them mentioned the greatest day Lou ever had on a ball field June 3, 1932, in Shibe Park against the Philadelphia Athletics.

Those in the stands that day saw Lou Gehrig hit *four home runs in four consecutive times at bat.* He hit two of them into the center-field stands, and two over the right-field fence. In the ninth inning, Lou sent another one screaming toward the fence. Al Simmons, the Philly outfielder, made an incredible leap into the air and speared it with one hand.

"Well Lou," the usually taciturn manager Joe McCarthy said, patting the number 4 on Gehrig's back. "Nobody can take today away from you."

But somebody did. That afternoon was the one in which the immortal manager, John McGraw, chose to announce his retirement from baseball. This was the news that made the newspaper headlines across the country.

Gehrig yearned for his rightful share of fame. But he was hopelessly inept when it came to the magic touch that would get it for him.

Late in his career, Gehrig went all out in an attempt to become a hearty, social, colorful sort of guy. He hired a manager, fell prey to publicity stunts, even took to holding parties for the press and slapping the astounded newspaper boys on the back. The reaction of the columnists and baseball writers was that Lou was being ill-advised and hypocritical, and had better just stick to being himself.

There has always been a great deal of mystery over how Gehrig felt about Ruth and vice versa. There are those who will tell you that the two were close pals. Others say that bad feeling existed between them. Neither statement is fact. When Gehrig first came up, the rawest of rookies, he idolized the Babe. The King was friendly toward him. He gave him tips on batting and how to conduct his life. At times there was some slight rivalry between them, but it was never serious.

The truth is that Gehrig never considered himself the equal of the Babe—and neither did Ruth. He was often generous to Lou and lavish in his praise, but they were never, as many have suggested, close friends.

When they toured the country on exhibitions together in 1929, Gehrig spoke of his travels with Ruth as, "the most wonderful education I've ever been given. I don't mean in books. I mean in getting the most out of life, in learning how to meet people and having a good time and really seeing all there is to see.

It was on this trip, during which they covered 8000 miles in 21 days, that the sportswriters began referring to Gehrig in relation to Ruth as the "Crown Prince." Actually, Lou behaved more like a trusted servant, or a bodyguard to the King. One night at a dinner in a Midwestern city, the Babe, feeling in an expansive mood, chose to deliver one of his lectures to Lou before a crowd of admirers.

"You've got 10 years ahead of you in the big leagues, Lou," the Babe said, puffing a cigar. "Save your dough. Start one of those trust funds. Every dollar you save will be one more laugh when your home-run days are over."

A few months over 10 years from that day, Gehrig's life as a home-run hitter was finished. He *did* save, although his salary never approached what Ruth collected each year. The highest Lou ever received was $37,000 in 1937, not even half of the Bam's fabulous $80,000 top. Gehrig's lifetime earnings from the Yanks totalled $316,000. Considering that he was in there every day, giving all he had, he was hardly overpaid.

One Summer, to augment his salary, Lou became an insurance salesman. The first customer he went after was the Babe himself. Lou spent days chasing Ruth around a golf course, trying to convince him that he should take out a policy. Finally, in exasperation, Ruth threw down his clubs and signed up for a huge amount. "Thanks, Babe," Gehrig said earnestly. "You'll never regret this."

Unlike Ruth, the steady, sincere, and sentimental Gehrig needed roots. He was always uncomfortable in strange surroundings. His love for his mother, that large, stolid, self-sacrificing woman, was overwhelming. For years, his sole purpose in life, other than playing baseball, seemed to be devotion to her. In 1928, using his profits from two World Series, he bought his parents a small but lovely house in New Rochelle, New York.

Some of the reporters and ballplayers used to try to get him dates. They'd rib him about his shy and even terrified attitude toward females his own age. He would blush, this six-foot, one-inch, 205-pound giant. Rubbing a bony wrist with a huge paw, he'd remark, "Aw, guys, you oughta know my mother makes a home comfortable enough for me. I don't need much else."

Lou loved the movies. He was absolutely gone on them, because in the safety of a darkened theater he could experience secondhand all the romantic yearnings he felt without the danger of seeming awkward or gauche, or getting hurt for expressing himself. He was probably one of the most widely read of any of his contemporary players. He was an avid opera fan. He liked poetry. He also liked comic strips, kids, and animals.

It was grown-up people, light conversation, sophistication, and gayety that frightened him.

"After I announced that I was through," he told me in his last interview, "I was able to tell the fans how I had felt about them and the way they treated me through the years. Their letters came pouring in. There were about 30,000 of them. Can you imagine that?

Although he spent two years at Columbia University, when he came up to the major leagues he was as raw and countrified-looking a rookie as you could find anywhere. He carried a cheap paper suitcase, stumbled all over himself, and cheerfully took the unmerciful and unceasing wisecracking and riding of rival players and teammates.

"I'll never forget the first time I saw him," Johnny Schulte, one of his Yankee contemporaries said. "He was a big lumberjack type. He didn't look like a ballplayer. With that barrel chest, piano legs, wide rump, and those rolls of fat, he looked more like a wrestler."

Gehrig forgave them all their jests. The only man who ever aroused him to serious and deadly anger was the ferocious and spiteful Ty Cobb. Although Cobb hated almost every rival, he seemed to have a special distaste for Gehrig.

Gehrig stood it for months. Then, one day, as he passed the Tiger dugout, Cobb let fly with a barrage of unusually distasteful epithets. Lou lowered his head, clenched his fists, and charged down into the opening to annihilate Ty. He traveled like a locomotive toward Cobb, who nimbly stepped out of the way. Gehrig's skull cracked into an iron stanchion and he fell to the ground, stunned. He got up a few seconds later and went after Ty again like a punch-drunk fighter, but the players managed to hold them apart. The next day, Cobb was willing to call off his feud and the inherently decent Gehrig shook hands with him.

Possessed of terrifying strength, the massive Gehrig could have used it to scare half the players in the American League out of their wits. But there wasn't an ounce of bully in him. The diminutive Bucky Harris, half apologetically, told how, when he was with Washington, he once caused Lou to boot a ball game by stepping on his toe.

"With the score tied 2-2 in the eighth inning and a man on third, I bunted down the first base line. Lou fielded it and ran for the bag. I came down hard on his toe. I've never seen a man look so surprised and hurt. When the man on third broke for home, Gehrig threw the ball way over the catcher's head and we won the game."

Gehrig took a terrific riding from the sportswriters for booting the game, but he never said a word about what Bucky had done to him. All that season, Harris waited for Lou to get even with him—to give him the hip or spike him. "He never did," Bucky said. "Every time I came down to first, he just looked at me as though to ask me how could I do such a thing to him. I got to feeling so ashamed of myself that I finally apologized to him. You should have seen him light up!"

Without his brute strength and his fanatical determination to learn how to control his muscles, Lou Gehrig would probably never even have been able to hang on to a position in the minor leagues. Little Miller Huggins, his first manager, almost went out of his mind trying to drill baseball savvy into Gehrig. "Only this kid's willingness and lack of conceit will make him a ballplayer," Huggins once said despairingly. "That and those muscles are all he has."

"Some ballplayers have natural-born ability," Lou reminded me that year before he died. "But I wasn't one of them. You take a player like Joe DiMaggio," he said, his eyes lighting up. "Now there's a natural. Baseball comes easy to him. He instinctively knows the right thing to do and does it. Charlie Gehringer is another one. Sometimes I wonder how in the world I was ever able to make it."

Lou was one of the common herd, a fat boy from the congested upper regions of Manhattan, one whose inheritance was drabness and poverty, whose young eyes knew only littered streets, grimy rooms with paint chipping off the walls and wornout carpets on the floor. His only luck in those days was that he was healthy enough to stay alive. The brother and sister who preceeded him had been sickly; they died in infancy.

Henry Louis Gehrig was the son of German immigrants. His mother was a domestic worker, his father a handyman, tinsmith, butcher, and itinerant mechanic. He was born June 19, 1903, on a hot night in the Yorkville section on the upper East Side. From then on, the family moved all over uptown Manhattan, always living in the poorest sections. But Lou's mother scrubbed and slaved and somehow managed to stuff food down her son. Louis was going to be strong. Louis was not going to be taken away from her, weak and lifeless, the way her other children had been.

Heinrich Gehrig was never a steady provider. He tried his best, but it was Lou's mother who was the backbone of the family. It was from her that Lou got, not only his physical strength, but the moral courage that held him together through the hardship of his early life, his playing days, and up to the very end. Gehrig's worship of his mother went beyond the bounds of reason. In some ways, it was even harmful, because for many years of his life he seemed to be living only for her. She was, until he married, the only person with whom he could be completely at ease.

Lou began his endurance record early in life. His grade-school teachers remember him as a chubby-faced, fat-bodied boy who plugged doggedly away at his school work, and refused to stay home even when he was sick. His grades were fairly high, earned by steady attendance and hard work. One fear clung to him all of his days—the fear that if he ever once took his nose off the grindstone, he would fall by the wayside.

His wife, Eleanor, mentioned this to a reporter after his death. "No matter what his achievements," she said, "he was dogged by a sense of failure and a need, constantly, to prove himself. Success brought Lou no sense of attainment, no relaxation. It was like something ephemeral to be clutched with both hands. He was afraid if he loosened his grip for a moment, everything he had struggled for would slip away from him."

As a kid, Gehrig's life outside of school was not very different from that of most street urchins. He played ball on the vacant lots, swam in the filth of the East River, teased cops, made tar balls on roofs, idolized baseball heroes, and worked. At eight and nine, his round chunky legs pounded the streets on errands for merchants. He did odd jobs and dutifully brought home his pennies and nickles to his mother. He never got into trouble. He was average in every sense of the word, almost pitifully so.

When Lou was in seventh grade, his mother took a job as a cook at the Sigma Nu fraternity house on the Columbia campus. Heinrich, her husband, tended the furnace and did odd jobs. Lou hung around the backyard in his spare time, tossing a baseball back and forth with the amused fraternity brothers who called him "Little Heinie." He envied them.

Sometimes, sitting on a chair in the kitchen, watching his mother at work over the stove, he would listen to the soft voice coming from the sturdy, work-bent body. "You'll go to college like these boys, Louis. You'll see," she said, in her precise, immigrant's English. "We will manage it. Your father will get a better job and you will go."

The Gehrigs left the Sigma Nu job and moved downtown to the outskirts of Greenwich Village, in to a cheap flat. Christina got a job doing housework in New Jersey, and Heinrich found temporary work as a tinsmith. Lou entered the High School of Commerce, his mind set on becoming an accountant.

At 15, when he was in his junior year in high school, he had his first taste of fame. It was overpowering. It worked on him like a drug. It gave him an ambition to be great that he never relinquished. It happened at Wrigley Field in Chicago. The High School of Commerce team had won the New York City championship and was sent to Chicago for an intercity game with the Windy City's Lane Tech.

Coach Harry Kane sent "Henry," as he called him, to the plate in the seventh inning with instructions to "Hit one out of the park."

It was a fantastic request. Nobody imagined that a high-school kid could hit one out of bounds in a major-league ball park. The youngster weighed 230 pounds then, but there were layers of fat over the muscles. He looked ludicrous and bulging in the tight-fitting uniform.

The 15-year-old Gehrig, legs wide apart, caught a pitch squarely. To the amazement of those in the ball park, it sailed on and on and out of sight beyond the fence. It created quite a stir in the press. HIGH SCHOOL BOY ANOTHER RUTH? the headlines asked. Lou came back to Commerce High something of a hero.

Gehrig historians, swayed by this extraordinary feat, often make the error of referring to Lou as a sensational high-school athlete. He wasn't. With the exception of that one mighty clout, his hitting was under .200 and he was a very clumsy specimen around first base. It was his football playing, that earned him a chance to go to Columbia University.

The athletic director of Columbia, a Sigma Nu man, was scouting the high schools looking for football talent for Columbia. He was quite impressed with the way a big, beefy fullback named Gehrig bulled through the lined for Commerce High. As he stood on the sidelines, a small man with a graying mustache touched his sleeve.

"Pardon me," the man said, "but I am Heinrich Gehrig. The boy out there playing is my son."

The college man looked at the old fellow in bewilderment.

"Don't you remember," Gehrig's father went on. "I used to tend furnace. That's little Heinie. Don't you remember?"

A light dawned in the athletic director's eyes. "That kid—the little fat boy—" he pointed at the playing field in amazement. "That's him?"

After the game, the Sigma Nu man approached Gehrig as he came out of the showers. Lou remembered him. Unlike Ruth, he remembered almost everyone he ever met. They talked over old times, the days when Lou hung around the fraternity house and the athletic director was a college boy. It ended with the college man going home with Lou. Together, they told Christina that her son would be able to go to Columbia with the help of the athletic department and spare-time jobs. Her reaction to the news was to break down and cry.

When Gehrig left Columbia in his junior year to play professional baseball, Christina cried again. She would always remind the reporters who came to the house in Morningside Heights, and later on in New Rochelle, "My son went to Columbia University. He was a college man. He was very good in his studies and I did not want him to leave the university."

At Columbia, Gehrig was a guy in an old gray sweatshirt and unpressed pants, a hard-working student, the way he had been in grade and high school. He took up engineering and, if he had not been obligated to turn out for athletics, he probably would have spent his time trying for an engineering degree.

As a tackle on the Columbia Lions, Gehrig was again average. "They stomped all over Lou," one of his teammates said, "but they could never crush his grin or spirit. And anyone who ran into him head on never felt quite the same afterward."

On the baseball diamond, Lou was clumsy, unpredictable, and slow at fielding. His throws were as apt to wind up in the stands as they were in the hands of a receiver. But he hit!—knocking windows out of buildings over 400 feet from home plate—reached the ears of big-league talent seekers.

"The first time I saw Lou Gehrig play was against Rutgers," scout Paul Krichell said. "He was playing the outfield. He didn't know what he was doing out there, but the moment I saw him hit one, I knew he would eventually be a great ballplayer. I've been with the Yankees 28 years," Krich grinned, "and I'd like to find just one more like him."

Krichell also saw Gehrig perform as a pitcher for the Lions. The big southpaw threw the ball with such blinding speed that Columbia batters, in practice games, refused to take their licks at the plate. Gehrig was dangerously wild. Those he didn't strike out, he walked. "He would have learned control," Krichell commented. "He was the sort of boy who could learn anything, given enough time and patience."

It was not widely known, but Gehrig played pro baseball while he was still going to school. He had a tryout with the Giants and was sent to Hartford, where he played one Summer under the name of Lewis. In 1923, he was approached by a number of major-league scouts and offered some very juicy contracts. He turned them all down, stubbornly insisting that he wished to complete his education. He meant it. Then his mother came down with pneumonia and his father became desperately in need of an operation.

"When I left school to play baseball," Gehrig once said, "it was a case of necessity. There were hospital and doctor bills to pay. My family needed the money."

He took the Yankee contract because his father needed to go to the hospital immediately and Colonel Ruppert offered a $1500 cash bonus if he would sign. His salary that first year was $3000. Only a few hundred dollars of it was spent on himself.

Gehrig played 13 games with the Yankees before he was sent to Hartford, then an independent team which had player agreements with major-league clubs. In 1924, he played 10 games with the Yanks and was sent down again. His first time at bat in New York uniform, as a pinch hitter, Hollingsworth of the Senators struck him out on three pitched balls. The second time at bat, again as a pinch hitter against St. Louis, he got a double.

Lou played his first full major-league game against Washington in 1923, over the protest of Bullet Joe Bush. The veteran Yankee pitcher had his heart set on winning 20 games that year.

"Don't put that dumb rookie in, Hug," he begged the Yankee manager. "He'll gum up the ball game."

Gehrig began by living up to the Yankee hurler's prophecy. In an early inning, with a Senator on first and third, crafty Joe Judge dropped a perfect bunt down the first-base line. Lou ran in and scooped it up, then stood there holding the ball, dazed. The runner scored from third.

Bush was apoplectic.

The big first baseman blinked and stumbled back to first base. He suffered silently until the seventh inning. Two Yankees got on base. Then the Washington pitcher walked Ruth to get at the rookie Gehrig. The score was 5-2, the bases loaded. Bush looked wildly at Huggins as Gehrig hesitantly reached for a bat.

"Hey, Hug," Bush said. "You ain't gonna let that kid hit in this spot? I want to win this one!"

Huggins looked at the nervous Gehrig. "Go on out there and hit the ball," the Yankee manager snapped.

Gehrig swung at the first ball thrown to him and drove it against the right-field fence for a solid double. A few minutes later, a single brought Lou home and the Yanks won, 6-5. When the game was over, Bush walked over to the locker where Gehrig, still trembling, was undressing.

"Listen, kid," Bush grinned, "thanks for the game. You may be stupid with that glove, but you can sure pound that ball."

That game-saving double didn't keep Gehrig up in the big time. The aging Wally Pipp was still too classy around first base for Lou even to hope to replace him. Gehrig was sent to Hartford, with instructions to manager Paddy O'Connor from big boss Ed Barrow to put Gehrig on first base and keep him there.

Paul Krichell laughed: "Paddy was sure moaning. 'What can this guy do?' he yelled over the phone. 'He can't field, he can't hit his hat, he throws 'em where they ain't. Tell Barrow I got to get rid of him!' "

Krichell was as adamant as Ed Barrow. "He'll hit," he told Paddy, "Just keep him in there."

Early in September, Gehrig's batting average was .062 and O'Connor had reached the bursting point. There was a vital Labor Day series beginning on Saturday, and Lou had struck out three times the day before. That night, O'Connor sent a long telegram to Barrow stating how terrible Gehrig had been and asking permission to remove him from the lineup.

It was one of the few times in his life that Lou got a break. Barrow didn't come into his Yankee office that Saturday. Paddy had to leave Gehrig in for the three-game series. That Saturday, afternoon, Gehrig poled one over the fence to win the ball game. On Sunday, in a double header, he broke loose with tigerish fury and won both games almost singlehanded.

O'Connor called Barrow on Monday and told him to forget the wire, saying gleefully, "Gehrig has finally come out of the closet." He pitched, played first base, and closed the year hitting .304. He wound up the season with 24 home runs in the basket.

There were good reasons why Lou Gehrig couldn't seem to get going the first time he was sent down to Hartford. He was lonely. He was worried about his folks. He was always broke. Harry Hesse was Lou's roommate at Hartford in 1923, the first baseball player to really get to know him.

"I was playing first base when Lou came to Hartford," Hesse recalled, "so they moved me into the outfield. I had been rooming with him for several days before I realized the guy didn't have a dime. Not a dime. After his father got over that operation, Lou sent them on the first vacation they ever had. To do it, he had to strip himself down to nothing.

"He didn't have money for clothes," Hesse went on. "He looked like a tramp. He was a guy who needed friends, but didn't know how to go about getting them. He'd get low and sit hunched over and miserable and it was pretty tough to pull him out of it."

During his early days in baseball, Gehrig was utterly naive, completely unaware of his rights as a big-league ballplayer. When in trouble, Dan Daniel, the baseball writer so told me about meeting him one day in 1924 on a street in New Orleans. Gehrig who had come down to take Spring training with the Yankees, was, as usual, hatless and coatless.

"What's the trouble, Lou?" Dan inquired.

"Things are pretty tough, Dan," Lou said, shaking his huge head. "I can't seem to find a job, not even washing dishes."

"A job!" the amazed Daniel said. "You belong to the Yankees; you're a ballplayer. You're not supposed to be looking for a job. If you're broke, go see Huggins."

"Oh, I couldn't do that," Gehrig said.

And Gehrig wouldn't. Daniel went to Miller Huggins and told him about meeting Lou and what he'd said. Hug called Gehrig in, gave him a $100 advance, and told him to stop looking for outside work. During the interview, Huggins learned that Lou had arrived in New Orleans with exactly $12 and had been trying to get along on that amount for two weeks!

On June 1, 1925, Gehrig was sent in to pinch hit for Pee Wee Wan-

ninger in the eighth inning of a game against the Senators. That day,
officially, marked the beginning of the magnificent consecutive-game record of the Yankee Iron Man. The following day, the veteran first-baseman, Wally Pipp, was struck on the side of the head during batting
practice. In the locker room, Huggins saw Pipp swallowing a couple of
aspirin tablets.

"Take a rest today, Wally," Huggins said. "I'm going to start young
Gehrig in your spot."

When the Yankee manager told Lou that he was going to start him in
the game and, if he made good, There were tears in his eyes as he stumbled up the stairs to the dugout. Huggins was right behind him, saying,
"Now take it easy, boy. Don't get rattled. If you muff a few, nobody's
going to shoot you."

He booted plenty of ground balls that year. Often he looked like an
overgrown sandlot player around first base. But Hug kept him in the
lineup. He stayed in there because at the plate he followed the pattern he
established in that first game, connecting for a double and two singles.

"In the beginning, I used to make one terrible play a game," Gehrig
told Quentin Reynolds in 1935. "Then I got so I'd make one a week, and
finally I'd pull a bad one about once a month. Now, I'm trying to keep it
down to one a season."

There was never any doubt in Gehrig's mind that the Bam was the
greatest home-run hitter of all time. In practice, he would often try to
copy the Babe's swing, but this change in style caused him to miss the
ball by a foot. In 1927, he told reporters, "The trouble with me is that
I'm trying to be a home-run hitter like Babe. Now I'm going to forget
those homers and just hit the ball."

It was that year that Ruth reached the pinnacle, clouting the big 60 to
Gehrig's 47. In the years that followed, baseball fans held their breath
while these two fence busters battled it out for home-run honors. But
year after year, it was almost as if Lou Gehrig were playing a previously
rehearsed role in winding up second to the Babe.

Gehrig never did top Ruth in home runs. For four seasons, he was
runner-up in circuit clouts to the Bambino. In 1931, he tied him with 46
four baggers. That year was a heart-breaker, for a bonehead piece of
business by Gehrig himself and another Yankee robbed him of the crown.

The incident is referred to as the "home run that didn't count." Lyn
Lary was on base when Gehrig teed off and hoisted one over the right-
field barrier. For some inexplicable reason, Lary thought that the rival
fielder had caught Lou's blast. Two were away, so Lyn left the base path
as he rounded third and trotted into the Yankee bench. Lou trotted on
around the bases, unthinkingly passing the spot where Lary had left the

base path. This caused Lary to be ruled automatically out. It ended the inning and crossed Gehrig's homer off the books.

In 1934, when Ruth was in Yankee uniform only occasionally, Gehrig won his first home-run title, hitting 49. That same year, for the first and only time, he also won the American League batting championship with a .363 average. Before, he had been nosed out of this honor by a few points almost every year since coming into the majors.

After Ruth left, Gehrig was appointed captain of the Yankees. He made heroic attempts to become a colorful, off-hand, likeable, and popular character. But the glare of the spotlight which made Ruth glow and sparkle, only befuddled, confused, and made ludicrous the quiet and retiring Gehrig.

He was voted the most valuable player of the American League four times, but nobody seemed to notice it. The records he was setting, like driving in the most runs of any player of his time, did not excite the interest of many fans. The few times he stumbled into the national limelight, off the playing field, it was for things he'd done that made him look sad and ridiculous.

There was that classic live appearance on the radio. The makers of a breakfast cereal named "Huskies" hired Lou for a one-shot air appearance to boost their product. Lou was interviewed at great length about his career with the Yankees. Then the announcer led up to the pay-off line with: "Tell me, Lou, to what do you owe your tremendous hitting strength and fine condition?"

The nervous Gehrig, not heeding the script, gulped and answered: "Wheaties."

It brought the house down. Laughter shook the nation for weeks. Lou felt wretched about his mistake. He even sent back the fee he had been paid for his appearance on the program. The breakfast food company wouldn't accept it, however, because the publicity, at Gehrig's expense, was worth a fortune.

Gehrig followed that one up with a fling at the movies. While the sportswriters snickered, Lou's manager, Christy Walsh, posed the big fellow in a leopard skin and announced that he was going to replace Johnny Weissmuller as the new Tarzan. Lou took it all very seriously.

This was the childhood dream. This was what he must have yearned for when he sat in the darkened movie theaters, a fat, little boy, a mediocrity, unnoticed and unloved. But he should have known that it was never in the books for him to spring to glory like a meteor. The Tarzan episode brought him only ridicule. In 1937, he did star in a horse opera called "Rawhide," which the movie critics panned and the fans ignored.

It is somewhat ironic that one of the most successful motion pictures ever made, "Pride of the Yankees," was based on Lou Gehrig's life. He would have been thrilled by that movie. It would have meant more to him than anything else in the world. He was an honest guy. He wanted and needed the love of the common people from whom he came. He yearned to be known and appreciated and remembered.

In 1933, at the age of thirty, Gehrig married Eleanor Twitchell, the warm-hearted, loyal, and wonderful woman who was to mean so much to him during the twilight of his life. She was the opposite of Lou—a vivacious, brown-eyed, auburn-haired girl who had money and social position and a talent for being able to mix easily with people.

It took four years for the bashful Gehrig to reach the point, with her help, of stumbling through a proposal of marriage. He first met her at a party in Chicago in 1929. He sat with her for quite a long time, but could think of nothing to say. He met Eleanor again at a friend's house in 1932. Again he was tongue-tied. One night, many months later, he called her long distance and talked a little more easily. In 1933, Eleanor was visiting a friend in Long Island, and Lou began to drop in to see her. One night, shortly before she returned to Chicago, Eleanor guided him through the necessary words that constitute a proposal.

"It began," she related long after they were married, "with talk about baseball. Even when proposing, in stating his qualifications as a potential husband, Lou spoke disparagingly of himself as a ballplayer. It finally got around to my asking him if what he was trying to say was that he wanted to marry me. He nodded his head, and told me that was it. Then he kissed me and ran for the door."

On the day the engagement was announced, Eleanor was in the stands watching Lou play. He hit a home run for her, and waved to her as he crossed the plate. It was one of the happiest days of his life and, for once, nothing jinxed it. The fans and players and reporters were very decent about it. Nobody kidded him or made him feel uncomfortable. Even Lefty Gomez, who often made him the butt of his gags, said, "Well, guy, I wish you a lot of luck. You deserve a nice girl."

The marriage was planned for the 30th of September, but Lou couldn't face the thought of the formal ceremony that was being arranged. The day before it was to come off, he talked Eleanor into calling in the mayor of New Rochelle and marrying them quietly. She agreed. They were married in the presence of a few friends and the carpenters and painters and decorators who had been hired to dress up the house for the big event.

"Less than an hour after we were married, Lou was on his way to the Stadium to play baseball," Eleanor said.

Almost from the moment they were married, Eleanor Gehrig went on a campaign to build up her husband's self-confidence. She knew that he worked too hard, worried constantly about his playing, and felt that what he had accomplished was slight and unimportant. But no amount of effort or love could change the pattern of years. Pointing out his accomplishments, holding little parties, thinking up frivolous stunts to make him laugh, provided only temporary relief for a man trapped by this poignant sense of his personal inadequacy.

The Iron Horse continued to drive himself. His incredible record kept mounting. Hits crashed off his bat with machinelike regularity. When it was over, he had driven in close to 2,000 runs, made 2,721 hits, 1,190 of them for extra bases! He had crossed the plate 1,888 times and poled 494 home runs. For eight years, he played in more games than any man in the league. In seven of those years, he drove in more than 150 runs.

Perhaps Gehrig's greatest thrill, the one he talked the most about after his retirement, was the home run he hit off Dizzy Dean in the 1937 All-Star game. The steady, reliable quiet, workhorse facing the most quixotic, brash, and colorful player since the days of Ruth. It was a pitiful and tragic afternoon for the Great Diz, the one in which he was struck by a line drive, the afternoon he wrenched that magnificent arm. Lou seemed to have a knack of being around when tragedy struck.

"Gehrig will go on forever," the sportswriters said. "Short of being hit by a locomotive, nothing will stop him."

What stopped him was deadlier than any man-made machine. It was a tiny virus, so mysterious and elusive that it has not yet been seen by microbe hunters after centuries of search.

During the latter part of the 1938 season, the disease began to work on Gehrig. He began to lose his great strength, his tremendous energy and drive. Sometimes his hand would tremble as he held a coffee cup and he would drop it. On the baseball field, he would be overcome by lethargy. His coordination—the thing he had worked so hard to learn—would fail him. Only his great willpower enabled him to muster the energy to get through a game.

"Please give yourself a rest, Lou," his wife pleaded with him. "Your record is safe. You need a rest."

"I've got to go on playing," he said. "I've got to work myself out of this."

He went on, game after game, ashamed of the way he looked out there. He told Johnny Schulte that every time he went to bat, he felt that all the fans in the stands could hear him creak.

Spring training in 1939 was a nightmare for Gehrig. The ball slipped out of his fingers or went through his wobbly legs. He would swing with a superhuman effort, but even when he connected it would be a scraggly sort of pop fly. His legs would give way suddenly. A frightened look would come over his face. He'd look like a kid who had been unexpectedly slapped.

The season opened with Gehrig still in the line-up. After a day at the park, he would come home looking weak, stunned. He was afraid, terribly afraid. Eleanor, was pleading with him to quit so that they could find out what the trouble was, couldn't get through to him.

"Sometimes he would break down and cry," she said. "But he would be back at the ball park the next day, trying harder."

The players on the Yankees suffered with him. One of them told how Lou, stooping over to tie his shoe one day before the game, fell flat on his face. Everyone pretended not to notice it. When he floundered around on the field, tripped over his own feet, fell down when walking to the plate to take his cut, they all felt his pain and embarrassment and shriveled up inside. Manager Joe McCarthy didn't take him out of the line-up. He knew that would really break Lou. He knew, and the players knew, that they were witnessing a terrible private contest.

He played eight games in 1939. He played his last game against the Washington Senators on April 30, 1939. On May 2, he stopped manager McCarthy in the lobby of a Detroit hotel. His face was pale, his hands shook, but he got the grin up.

"You'd better take me out, Joe," he said. "I guess that's all."

That afternoon in Briggs Stadium Babe Dahlgren was at first base for the Yankees. An epic had ended. An immortal had stepped down. Sportswriters on copy desks across the country, men in small towns who had never even seen him play, read the wire services release and felt a lump in their throats.

That June, on his thirty-sixth birthday, Lou left the Mayo Clinic where he had gone for an examination.

"He is suffering from amyotrophic lateral sclerosis. This type of illness involves the motor pathways and cells of the central nervous system and in lay terms is known as a form of chronic poliomyelitis (infantile paralysis). The nature of this trouble makes it such that Mr. Gehrig will be unable to continue his active participation as a baseball player. . . ."

It also meant that he had only two or three years to live. Gehrig was never told this. His wife zealously kept this knowledge from him to the end.

Lou returned to the Yankees. As the captain of the team, he walked to the plate before every game and handed the umpire the line-up. The applause of the fans was thunderous. For the first time, he was able to realize the extent of his achievements. He was deeply moved and extremely grateful. "In his own way," his wife said, "he was happy."

The Yanks voted Lou a share of their 1939 World Series money.

In December, 1939, the Baseball Writers of America waived the ruling that a baseball player must be out of play for a year before he can be eligible for baseball's Hall of Fame. They voted Lou Gehrig a permanent spot at Cooperstown.

They knew how short his time was.

The last time this writer saw Lou Gehrig alive was at his Centre Street office when Lou was doing a job as a member of Mayor LaGuardia's New York City Parole Commission. He understood and had deep compassion for those who, like himself, had grown up in squalor and poverty. Few men so well understood frustration and loneliness and deprivation.

He was a man who believed in working for everything he got. He could have taken the hundreds of offers that came in, of cushy jobs at fancy salaries. He was paid $5,700 a year as a Parole Commissioner and he took it only after three months of study had convinced him that he could do some good on the job.

Late in 1940, it became impossible for him even to move around, and he had to give up his position. He remained at his home in Riverdale, where his wife read to him by the hour, because he could no longer hold a book in his hands. He was humorous and sheepish about it. There was almost no self-pity, but now and then he would smile wistfully and remark to his wife, "I wonder what the guys at the ball park would think of me now."

The way his life ended was so different from the way it had begun. The childish eyes had seen only drabness and want. Now the gay, the wise, the wealthy, the flashy, the brilliant and talented citizens of the land came to his house. As life began to flow out of him, his wife, Eleanor, did all she could to keep him amused and unaware of the fact that the game would soon be called because of darkness.

"The house was like a circus," Eleanor Gehrig said, "but they were all welcome. I wanted to keep Lou busy, and I wanted to keep him entertained. All the activity kept me from thinking too."

By the end of May, in 1941, he became too ill to see his friends. On the morning of June 2, he passed into a coma. At 10 o'clock that night, the big body was lifeless.

Crowds gathered that week on a New York street to pay tribute to Lou Gehrig. Gangs of kids were clustered on the sidewalk in front of the funeral parlor. A long, black limousine pulled up and Babe Ruth climbed out. As always, the kids rushed the Babe, begging for autographs. For once in his life, the Babe shook his head, brushed by them, and went inside to have a last look at another "kid" who had shared some very special and wonderful days with him.

Christina Gehrig was there. She had outlived all of her children, even the one who had grown up to become so strong and famous.

Babe Ruth

BABE RUTH

As I Knew Him

In addition to his playing exploits, part of Babe Ruth's appeal was the way in which he was a very human hero, comical in appearance as well as action. This profile by teammate, roommate, and fellow Hall-of-Famer, Waite Hoyt, caught the lighter side of the Babe.

By Waite Hoyt

I met Babe Ruth for the first time in late July, 1919. I had just reported to the Boston Red Sox and was escorted around the clubhouse meeting all the boys. McInnis, Shannon, Scott, Hooper, Jones, Bush and the rest. Ed Barrow, the manager, was making the introductions and when we reached Ruth's locker, the Babe was pulling on his baseball socks. His huge head bent toward the floor, his black, shaggy, curly hair dripping downward like a bottle of spilled ink.

Ed Barrow said, "Babe, look here a minute."

Babe sat up. He turned that big, boyish, homely face in my direction. For a second I was startled. I sensed that this man was something different than the others I had met. It might have been his wide, flaring nostrils, his great bulbous nose, his generally unique appearance—the early physical formation which later became so familiar to the American public. But now I prefer to believe it was merely a sixth sense which told me I was meeting someone beyond the usual type of ball player.

He casually said, "Pretty young to be in the big league, aren't you, kid?"

Knowing something of his history, I replied, "Yep—same age you were when you came up, Babe." By that time Ruth had turned back to dressing. I was talking to the back of his head.

In those formative years with the Red Sox, Ruth's antics were looked upon as huge jokes. His utter failure to remember places, people and incidents was refreshing material for humor in the clubhouse. The ball players told with glee how in the 1918 World Series against the Cubs, Ruth was ordered to "brush off" Leslie Mann, a rugged right handed batter. Ruth not only forgot the identity of Leslie Mann but went the orders one better. He hit little Max Flack with a pitched ball, and later told his manager, "I got Mann for you, didn't I?"

Not long after I had joined the Red Sox, Ruth was assigned to one of his already infrequent hurling chores. He was to pitch against Ty Cobb & Co., of Detroit. In the clubhouse before the game, Ed Barrow called a meeting to study the weaknesses of the Detroit batting order. Barrow handed Ruth the score card and waited for Ruth to begin his analysis. Ruth looked over the Detroit batting order. Bush, Veach, Cobb, Heilman, Jones—they all got one and the same treatment. Ruth chanted in a rapid monotone, "I'll pitch high inside and low outside. High inside and low outside. High inside and low outside."

Barrow ended the tortuous ritual in a hurry saying, "Aw, forget it, Babe. Just go out and beat 'em." Babe did.

Such was Ruth. He was not an ordinary ball player.

I came to know him intimately for twenty-nine years, first as a teammate, then as an opponent, and finally as a friend. It seemed to me Ruth's entire life was predestined. How else can you explain the meteoric rise from anonimity at St. Mary's Industrial School to heights never before or since attained by a baseball player?

Babe Ruth was Champion of Champions.

His history was not merely a list of baseball feats, but one which, served first to revive a game looked upon after the 1919 Black Sox scandal with nasty suspicion. Secondly, the force of his bat, and the power of his personality revolutionized the industry, bringing baseball out of the stereotyped doldrums into the flash and brilliance of a high-level entertainment loved by men, women and children alike.

In Boston, Babe began his development, not only as the slugger supreme, but expanded physically and mentally and culturally as well. It was as if the whole structure of the man began some sort of metamorphosis. With each home run he gained new confidence—new stature.

Even his body began to change. As a pitcher he had weighed about 185 pounds and stood six feet two inches. He took on weight. His wrists grew stronger. His biceps enlarged. His physical endowments changed to suit the new pattern.

No one I have ever met looked like Babe Ruth. His moon face was in itself an advertisement. Very few people have considered the facial contours of the Babe, yet it was one of his most important assets. His homeliness was classic. No one failed to recognize Ruth, no matter where he was. He was the cartoonists' dream and, of course, profited thereby. The name "Babe" fitted him like a lastex girdle. "Babe" was an easy word to roll out, coupled with "Ruth" was easy on the ears, eyes and tongue. His actions were in perfect keeping with his name.

If anyone had explained the value of a dollar to the Babe the explanation was wasted. Money and fame came too quickly, and in the beginning, Ruth was wholly at a loss to understand how to deal with the pressures this fantastic fame was forcing upon him. He was like a kid who has never been allowed candy and is suddenly presented with a truckload. Baseball was the instrument which pried off the lid to his treasure chest. And he just wasn't prepared for it. He made mistakes. Some serious. Some silly. But his progress was always forward.

Before Babe Ruth, home runs had been a scarce commodity in baseball. Ruth began supplying the item with astonishing regularity. Word of the new sensation spread. Sports writers stared at the records as Babe's totals mounted. The historians discovered that Ed Williamson of the Chicago Cubs of 1884 had blasted 27. Gabby Cravath of the Phils had clouted 24 in 1915. By September, Ruth had passed the twenty mark and was creeping up on Cravath. Soon he was by Gabby and sneaking up on Williamson.

Part of Babe's charm during that period was his utter unconsciousness of the sensation he was causing. In the clubhouse he was the practical joker, sawing off bats, clowning, telling wild tales of his excursions the night before.

After he hit his twenty-sixth homer, and seemed likely to tie and pass all major league marks in that department of slugging, the City of Boston, in co-operation with the Knights of Columbus, decided to give him a "day."

September 20th, 1919, was the day set aside for the honoring of the youngster who was standing the baseball world on its ears. A double header was scheduled with the famed Chicago White Sox, a great ball club, with Jackson, Collins, Schalk, Risberg, Weaver, Cicotte, Kerr and Williams. Williams was a left-handed pitcher, a good one, a fellow who could thread a needle with any pitch. Pants Rowland selected him to pitch the first game.

The first game was tied when the ninth inning came up. Williams retired the first two Red Sox batters.

Ruth strode to the plate. The fans were calling for a home run. It was one of the first occasions on which fans exhibited a real belief in the potentiality of their hero. Fans had always called for home runs but most of the time their demands had been born of desperation rather than hope.

Ruth justified their faith that day by walloping a long home run over the LEFT FIELD FENCE off Williams, a LEFTHANDED PITCHER. The magnitude of that feat will be lost on the newer fans today, but back in 1919 it was nothing short of colossal. Left-handed batters just did not hit home runs off lefthanded pitchers over the left field wall. After the game, the Chicago White Sox players, who had not yet been touched by the taint of crookedness, crowded the Boston clubhouse shaking hands with Ruth, yelling congratulations, shouting, "How'd you do it, big boy? Where'd you get that drive?" Even the losing pitcher, Lefty Williams, came in to express his horrified disbelief to the Babe.

In the winter of 1919–1920, Harry Frazee, the Boston owner, short of cash for his theatrical enterprises, sold Babe to the Yankees for about $108,000, in those days, a king's ransom for a baseball player. Ruth at first objected to the transfer. Ruth always said New York cost him so much dough he couldn't afford to live there. A $20,000 season's contract changed his mind.

So Ruth became an opponent of mine for a year. In that 1920 season on July 25th, I faced Ruth in the Polo Grounds. I had reasoned the only way to stop him was to make him supply his own power. I threw him a high looping slow ball. Today, Rip Sewell of the Pirates calls the same pitch the "blooper ball." Ruth booped my scientific pitch high into the upper deck of the right field grandstand.

The first wave of hero worship engulfed him in New York. He was the recipient of a flood of gifts, fan mail and telephone calls. Ruth was busy from the time he awoke until the dreamy hours of morning. They said his pace was too fast. He wouldn't last. The Babe didn't agree. And at the end of the 1920 season he was a bigger hero than ever.

The Yankees did not win the pennant in 1920, and Miller Huggins the manager decided to strengthen the club further. He raided the Boston Red Sox again, and brought down McNally, Harper, Schang and me.

Close to the Babe again, I immediately noticed the change. In Boston he had been a surprised young man—hardly able to assimilate the extravagance of success. Now he was sure of himself. He was developing poise, demanding respect when it was slow to appear voluntarily.

He requested special considerations in the clubhouse. A pay telephone was installed. There was a waste basket by his locker—his private mail box. Thousands of letters went unanswered, but Ruth liked the receptacle there as a mute testimonial to his popularity.

But true to the legend that was Ruth, his excesses only fed his ego. Never in Ruth's baseball career was he tormented by conscience, or by the physical distress excesses bring to others. Among baseball players Ruth's hardiness in face of late hours and over indulgence was more talked about than his home runs.

When Marshal Foch, the Commander of all the Allied forces of World War One, visited here in 1921, he was received in New York with open arms. The usual reception at City Hall. Ticker tape and confetti floated from the office windows. It was summer, and Marshal Foch had been persuaded to attend his first baseball game. The Yankees were then still tenants of the Polo Grounds and it was the Yankee team which was to play host to the world-famous hero. At two forty-five, the motor cavalcade bearing the Marshal drew near the Polo Grounds. The park was bedecked with French and American Flags. The stands were crowded. The line of autos came through the center field gates. The band played the Star Spangled Banner and the Marseillaise. The crowd rose to its feet. As Marshal Foch alighted from his motor car and stepped into Col. Ruppert's private box, the players lined up at attention to one side of the Yankee bench. He was attired in a powder blue French uniform, with myriad battle ribbons and insignia pinned to his chest. The ball players, were to have the privilege of shaking hands with the great French Marshal. Babe Ruth was to make the speech of welcome on behalf of the ball players.

When it was time for Ruth to speak, the crowd was hushed. Marshal Foch bent over to catch Ruth's words. They were slow in coming, as the Babe was flustered. Finally he managed to blurt, "Hey Gen., they tell me you were in the war."

A similar incident occurred at the Yankee Stadium later in the twenties. Cal. Coolidge was President of the United States. Just before one game, word reached the bench that President Coolidge was arriving. Once again we were to line up to meet a dignitary. Once again Ruth was to speak for the ball players. We filed by shaking hands with Mr. Coolidge. Babe Ruth finally arrived in front of the quiet mannered President. Ruth again was flabbergasted. He whipped out a big, red bandana handkerchief, mopped his face and snorted, "Hot as hell, ain't it Pres.?"

The clubhouse telephone was always busy. One particular phone call was the tip-off to Babe's lack of memory and complete unconcern about famous folk. After the 1921 season Ruth had been invited to make a motion picture in Hollywood. Ruth made the film and in the process met Mary Pickford and Douglas Fairbanks. They had promised to get in touch with Babe when they reached New York. One afternoon the clubhouse telephone rang. Ruth went to the phone and "yeahed," and "sured" for a while, then said, "Sorry, can't make it. I gotta see a party." Ruth hung up abruptly. "Who was that?" I asked. Ruth snorted as he loped off, "Oh a coupla actors I met in Hollywood. They wanted me down for dinner. A guy would go crazy goin' out for dinner every night."

Ruth lived at the Ansonia Hotel in New York. It was rather a Bohemian existence. His suite was shared with the first Mrs. Ruth, an adopted daughter, Dorothy, and anyone who cared to drop in. Babe was paying all the checks, wandering about making promises he never kept, entering business deals he forgot ten minutes later. He hit 59 home runs in 1921 and was most instrumental in helping the Yankees win their first American League pennant.

Two incidents that season bore out the man's infinite capacity for ballplaying efficiency under duress. The Yankees ran into a flock of doubleheaders. We were terribly short of pitchers; finally, manager Miller Huggins called a clubhouse meeting and asked, "Who shall we pitch today? There isn't anyone left."

Ruth spoke up. "I'll pitch, Hug."

The Yankee players looked at him in astonishment. Ruth hadn't pitched an inning in over two years. Detroit was our opponent. Cobb, Heilman and the rest. One of the best hitting ball clubs in baseball.

Huggins astonished us further by agreeing, "All right Babe, you try it."

Babe Ruth pitched six or seven innings. He struck out the great Cobb twice, and retired only after he'd begun to weaken. We won the game.

In late September, we Yankees, leading the league, were ahead of Cleveland by the slim margin of a game and a half. The Indians arrived at the Polo Grounds for a crucial four-game series, and won the first and second games and lost the third. The final game of the series came up. If we could beat the Indians in that final game, it was almost certain we would win the pennant.

The Yankee pitchers that day weren't particularly effective, and Cleveland jumped out in front. The Yankees tied the score, then went ahead. Pitchers were parading in and out of the box like tin soldiers. The Polo Grounds fans were in a frenzy. Cleveland would score runs, always one short of tying the score. Twice in the game Ruth saved us with home runs. We won that game 8-7. It is established fact that two spectators died in the grandstand during the contest, one of the wildest games ever played.

We came into the World Series of 1921 against the Giants with Ruth on the injured list. He had developed a serious infection in one elbow. He played five games, but had to bow out after the fifth because the pain was too much for him. Whether or not the result would have been different, no one can say, but the series went to eight games, with the Giants winning, five games to three. I remember one amusing incident in the series. The Giants were giving the Babe an unmerciful riding, ridiculing his broad nose and his looks in general.

In the clubhouse after one game, Ruth was burned to a crisp. "Those lousy so and sos. I'll get them. In fact I think I will right now." Ruth, with Bob Meusel as a second, invaded the Giant clubhouse. There was a wild scene with the Babe challenging little Johnny Rawlings. Pancho Snyder and others of the Giants jumped in to defend Rawlings. It was touch and go for a few seconds, then Babe calmed down. Recognizing the futility of the argument, Babe finished lamely, "I don't mind you guys calling me a —— —— ——, and a dirty ——, ——. That part's all right. But when you start mentioning my looks, that's a different matter. I don't mind the cuss words but you gotta cut out them personalities."

In the early twenties Ruth got along well with the rest of the team except pitcher Carl Mays. Carl had the unfortunate trait of expecting perfection from his infielders and outfielders, and when one made a mistake behind him, Mays told him all about it. Ruth, who had played with Mays in Boston, didn't go for Carl's comments on the abilities of his mates. There were many clubhouse arguments between the two, but the fight never came off. Mays knew, I believe, that Babe had reached such an unassailable position that any big fight with him would have brought about Mays' release.

Little Miller Huggins, the Mite Manager of the Yanks, was in those days hamstrung between two official forces. Col. Ruppert, the majority stockholder of the Yanks, liked Huggins. Col. Til' Huston did not. But Huston liked Ruth.

Huggins, who weighed but 145 pounds, had many an oral bout with Ruth, who now weighed well over two hundred. The arguments usually developed when the Yankees were on the road. They would start with Huggins questioning Ruth's whereabouts on the previous night.

Ruth would say, "If you don't like it, why don't you send me home?"

Hug would answer, "If you don't want to play for this ball club, why don't you go home?"

Ruth would retort, "You won't be here next year. It will be either you or me, wait and see."

Of course Hug was there until he died. Ruth came to love the little guy, and Huggins eventually loved Ruth.

Ruth on the road, was an incurable sightseer. And no one knew where he went nights. It was enough that he was at the ball park every day, walloping his home runs. Ruth's roommates became an object of discussion. They were basking in the Ruth limelight—or so everyone thought. The colorful Italian, Ping Bodie, was once asked how it felt to room with such a hero. Ping replied, "I don't know. I only room with his suitcase."

Ruth had many roommates before the Yanks consented to park him alone. There was Bodie, Fewster, Roth, Hofmann, and Jimmy Reese. Before long, all of them were released. Ruth had nothing to do with it— but word got around that it was a jinx to room with the Babe.

By this time none of us called him "Babe." He was known as either the Big Bam, George, or more commonly "Jidge." "Jidge" was really "Gigge"—a contraction of his first name George.

At the end of the '22 season, the Yankees had moved to their own park, the Yankee Stadium. Sports writers dubbed it, "The House That Ruth Built." It was true enough—for despite Babe's unpredictable escapades, he was ever the Sultan of Swat, the world's greatest ball player. The Stadium opened in 1923—and Ruth immediately christened the right field bleachers with a home run, helping to win the game from the Red Sox for Bob Shawkey.

The "Sultan" had a locker right next to the clubhouse entrance, jammed with mementos fans had sent him. Its floor was littered with letters. Doc Woods, the trainer, opened all the envelopes which bore business addresses. We opened the blue and pink ones. It from ladies quite frank in their invitations, and often we experienced fleeting pangs of envy for Babe's home run prowess. It was well known on our club that a year or two before, Babe, in his rush to sample the tasty delights of life, had merely torn up his mail. Doc Wood pieced a lot of it together and discovered over six thousand dollars in checks Ruth had destroyed, checks for endorsements and royalties.

Back in 1923, one summer's day at the Stadium, Miller Huggins shuffled up to the batting cage. Strolling behind him, was a broad shouldered, good looking kid. Huggins said, "Let this youngster hit a few."

The kid looked shy and awkward. We stepped aside. Ruth stood with one foot on the batting cage rail. The boy picked up Ruth's pet bat, a 46-ounce weapon. Babe grunted. "Don't use that one, son."

Then as an afterthought, he hurriedly corrected himself. "Go ahead, you can't hurt it. I got others."

The youngster hit at a couple of balls and did not do so well. He rolled them to the infield. Suddenly, he uncorked a drive high up into Ruth's favorite parking space, the right field bleachers. He walloped another, then another. The Babe looked interested. Not many American League sluggers had hit the ball in his private domain. Who was this powerful young kid?

The name was Lou Gehrig.

The big bam had begun to take on polish. His manner in the presence of strangers and upon introduction was one of as much grace as his limited education permitted. He was better tailored. Better shod. He struggled to be the courtier.

They tell one story concerning his new manner, but I can't vouch for its authenticity. In Florida one winter, he supposedly pulled his big automobile into a gas station. Babe was out of the car while the attendant was gassing up. A Rolls Royce pulled alongside Ruth, and a dignified member of the Palm Beach colony, a well upholstered dowager, leaned out of the window to inquire, "May I ask if you are not Mr. Babe Ruth?"

Babe, now able to recognize quality in something other than a hickory bat, replied, "You are quite correct, Modom."

Modom continued, "Mr. Ruth, is your car equipped with hydraulic brakes or are they mechanical?"

Ruth gave a courtly bow and said in his most cultured tone, "Modom, I haven't the slightest consumption."

It was inevitable that when the Yankees reached Knoxville on their northern trek each spring, Mr. Ruth, would need a loan. It was always $1500. Joe Dugan would turn to me and say, "How do you feel about it —wanna loan the Bam some dough?"

That part of it was a foregone conclusion. Ruth had raised the standards of players' salaries. We, as players, owed the Big Fellow a lot. Dugan and I would sit down and write out checks for $750 each. We knew we would get it back the first pay day. We not only got our money back—Ruth added six percent interest as well. Babe had heard it was right to pay interest on any loan he had made. He gave us six percent, although he had had possession of the money just over a month.

He was like that in all money matters. No one ever cheated the Babe— no one wanted to. If he borrowed from you, he paid up. If you borrowed from him, he forgot how much he had loaned you and was forever surprised at the repayment. He just wasn't interested in petty cash. His earning capacity, it seemed to him, was limitless and eternal.

His home run productivity fell off in 1923 and 1924—and his personal life was disintegrating. Helen Ruth finally decided it would be better if she and the Babe separated. Helen retired to a friend's house in Boston, little Dorothy went with her. On trips to Boston, Ruth had them stay at the hotel with him. He idolized Dorothy, but he just hadn't the necessary time to allot to the role of loving father.

With Babe and Helen separated, Babe's momentum increased. In his own specialized department, the Bambino rivaled John Barrymore. But his antics didn't always seem spontaneous now, and he was beginning to overdo it. The ballplayers sensed Ruth's tension, realized that something frightening was happening within that gigantic legend that Ruth had become. His fabulous personal escapades were shaded with pathos, for the Babe was no longer sampling life. He was wolfing it down in immense, oversized doses. Although we all recognized his undiminished baseball genius, we knew we were witnessing a gradual disintegration of Ruth, the man.

About that time an incident occurred in Washington which led to a two year breach in the Babe's relations with me. I had pitched the third of a four-game series, and Miller Huggins had given me permission to return to New York ahead of the team.

Babe, in his growing, formless anxiety, considered my early return a personal affront to his station. I went over to ask the big guy about it, but Babe was short and adamant.

"Skip it," he said, "you and I are through."

I said, "That's okay with me. It's mutual."

So we didn't speak for two years, except for one brief flurry. One afternoon, while I was pitching, the Bam missed a catch in right field. It didn't strike me that he had made a special effort to get the ball, and I struck a critical pose in the box—hands on hips—a sign that ball players will understand.

The Babe was first into the clubhouse after the game and opened up on me right away.

"You lousy bum," he began, "you're not going to show me up!"

"What do you figure to do about it?" I said.

"I'll punch you in your . . . nose," yelled Babe.

"You fathead," I shouted back.

At that point we both rushed at each other, fists flying. Huggins jumped in between us. And Huggins, little Huggins, was the guy who was punched. The rest of the boys pulled us apart, and the feud continued.

About a year after that fracas, the Yanks were on a night train out of St. Louis. We were all sitting in the men's wash room when Ruth walked in with a few bottles of beer he'd bought to give the gang. He offered me a bottle, and I said "No thanks, Babe."

"Aw, go ahead," Babe said. "It's all over—that argument—a lot of damn fool nonsense anyway. Forget it."

I was quick to forget it. I really liked the big fellow.

1925 was a tough year for Babe Ruth. His batting average fell below .300 for the first time, he appeared in only 99 games and hit but 25 homers. He had made involved business commitments. He was deep in debt. He was wrangling continuously with Miller Huggins. Besieged on all sides, Ruth met the situation the only way he knew; he fought with everyone, indulged in maudlin self-pity. And he blamed everyone but himself. It was the lowest point in Ruth's career.

In the meantime, Manager Huggins was having his own troubles. The Yankees, champions in 1921, '22 and '23, had blown the 1924 pennant to Washington. In 1925, Huggins was frantically trying to build a new machine, the nucleus of which was supposed to be Ruth. The blow-off finally came in St. Louis between them.

I was to pitch that day, and as was my habit, had delayed going out to the field. Huggins was sitting there in the corner, knees bobbing nervously as they always did when he was overwrought.

The Babe was late for batting practice. This is the exact conversation that took place.

"You don't have to dress today, Babe," said Huggins.

"Yeah? And why not?"

"Because I have suspended you," continued Huggins. "I am fining you five thousand dollars and I am sending you back to New York."

"Suspending me!" Ruth snorted. "That's great stuff. What for?"

"You know what for, Babe."

"Why you little runt!" The Babe was yelling now. "You'll never get away with this."

Huggins, who had already discussed the problem with Col. Ruppert, smiled grimly. "That we shall see."

Ruth didn't go to New York. He went to Chicago to see Commissioner Landis. Landis was not in to the Babe. He stormed back to New York and went up to his hotel apartment on the Concourse Plaza. His chauffeur had been in an accident. A process server was waiting in the lobby. So were a dozen sports writers. He shoved his way through the scribes, sent the process server flying over a nearby desk and stamped to his rooms alone, like an injured child.

The Yankees finished the season without the Big Bam and wound up in seventh place. The great, wonderful world had come crashing about him and no one could convince him that the chaos was entirely self-made.

It was his manager, Christy Walsh, who finally pulled the Babe out of his shattering doldrums. He arranged a big banquet for the reporters, at which Mayor Jimmy Walker made his famous speech that concluded: "The dirty-faced kids in the street look up to you, Babe. Don't fail them!"

When the Big Bam got up to speak, his eyes were brimming with tears. He realized that he was absolutely wrong. He told them he hadn't meant to mistreat all his friends. He said all he wanted to do now was live a decent life and play baseball.

Babe Ruth was to keep his promise.

If the sports writers were suspicious at first, Babe's actions soon had them convinced. He did a complete about-face, and was welcomed back into the fold like the prodigal son.

The year 1926 began another bombastic succession of Yankee pennants, with Babe Ruth as the key man. In spring training, the team had looked hopeless. One scribe wrote that we were merely a collection of isolationists working out on the same diamond and predicted we would finish in seventh place again. Maybe eighth. The truth is, we looked that bad. Then came the trek north, with a series of exhibitions against the Dodgers, and we beat the Brooklyn team in six straight games.

Riding back to the hotel with Dugan and me, the Bambino made one of his careful predictions. "If we can take every game from the Dodgers," he said, "we'll win the pennant." We beat them—twelve straight—and we won the pennant hands down.

Ruth, in his new role of baseball player, business man and goodwill ambassador was a wonderful guy. He was still a big kid; but his habits had moderated. His automobiles were still enormous, but the colors were subdued. His suits were smartly cut and stylish. In the old days, he used to wear a huge diamond horseshoe pin as his Tuxedo button. The new Ruth discarded that as bad taste. Indeed, the Babe had become one of the best dressed men in America.

And he was sublimely happy in those days. Christy Walsh had taken over the entire financial burden. Ruth didn't collect his checks—they went into a special fund from which Babe drew expense money. Ruth was turning into an executive.

I was in Ruth's room in Chicago when the advertising director of a big department store phoned him. Babe had endorsed some line of underwear. The store was planning to put it on display. The guy was trying to pressure Babe into standing by the underwear counter in the store each morning of his stay in Chicago.

Ruth said: "I can't say anything without consulting my business manager. You'll have to call him in New York. No. No. I'll tell you now, it's gonna cost you a thousand dollars an hour." The conversation was over, but in twenty minutes the phone rang again. Same man. Ruth was paid the unprecedented sum of one thousand dollars an hour to stand next to a pile of underwear.

Babe Ruth's life was now running like satin. His playing was at peak form. He worked with the rest of the boys, improved mediocre batters beyond their wildest ambitions. He made baseball playing look so easy. It has been said that the Bambino never made a mistake on a ball field. Of course that's exaggerated, but for the life of me, I can't personally recall a single boner the big guy ever pulled.

Everything the Babe did was fabulous. One day, in Boston, with a strong wind blowing toward the plate, he hit a high towering fly. The left fielder came running in to get it and kept coming. He never got near it— the ball landed in the infield, nearly beaning the shortstop. The ball had been hit so high, that Ruth was able to gallop all the way around the bases for a home run. Probably the first and last infield home run in history.

In the same Fenway Park he pulled another stunt, but this one will never show on the records. He was up at bat with two strikes against him. Just as the pitcher started his windup, a pigeon swooped down from center field and flew directly over the plate. Babe swung and missed, and started to walk away. The umpire called him back, and gently told him he'd struck out swinging at a bird.

The most fabulous story circulated concerns the time in the 1932 World Series when Ruth pointed to the center field bleachers and hit the next ball right to that spot. The feat made history, but we Yankees saw the Babe pull that one earlier.

There used to be a horrible drunk named Conway who haunted Boston's Fenway Park. The ball players knew him fairly well, since he was a regular and most vociferous fan. One day, after striking out his first two times at bat, Ruth was ushered to the batter's box with a stream of Conway's invectives heard all over the Park. Babe backed away from the plate and pointed to the right field seats. As usual, the Babe was up to the occasion. A deep home run followed. When he reached the plate after rounding the bases, he stopped, turned toward Conway and made a deep, courtly bow. Then he had Conway thrown out of the place. That was five years before the Chicago incident, and I always thought the memory of that day prompted Ruth to pull the later stunt against Charlie Root.

Those were the days that Ruth was obeying orders. When Huggins told Ruth to "push one to left" against the Athletics one afternoon, he pushed it to the left field bleachers for a block-busting home run.

In Cleveland, the right field wall of League Park was heightened by a tall wire screen. Ruth hit many balls over that screen. One fine day he hit one *through* it. The Cleveland players sadly shook their heads.

In Detroit, Babe had some of his biggest days. One homer he hit in Navin Field, carried over the right center field bleachers. It rolled down a street which ran at right angles to the avenue behind the right field fence. A boy chased it for blocks on a bicycle. The sports writers could see that from the press box. "It nearly went downtown," they wrote.

In St. Louis, the King of Swat was in a terrible batting slump. He took up a "fungo stick." A long thin underweight bat, used to knock flies in practice. He clouted a homer on the roof of the right field stand and snapped his slump.

In Chicago, they renovated Comiskey Park. They added a second tier to the right field stands. The architects said, "No one will ever hit a ball on that roof. Not even Ruth." The first time at bat, Ruth hit a home run over the newly constructed grandstand.

The Yankees won the pennant in 1926, but they lost the World Series to a fine Cardinal team. That was the classic in which Grover Cleveland Alexander starred, striking out Tony Lazzeri with the bases filled. I had started the game.

Ruth was criticized for trying to steal second in the ninth inning with two out. Bob O'Farrel, the Cardinal catcher made a perfect peg to second. Ruth was the final out. The game was lost, but despite the murmurs from the fans, the Yankee players never blamed Ruth; they all knew it was good baseball to try to get the tying run on second.

Ruth, always the individualist, was picking up exotic habits. He had become a user of snuff—his daily diet was two boxes—and his regular sneezes almost blew the spectators out of the grandstands. Like all ballplayers, Ruth was highly superstitious. But Ruth's superstitions passed all standard bounds.

The Big Bam entered the clubhouse one afternoon holding his stomach.

"Woody," he said to our trainer, "I got a pain in the gut. What shall I do?"

Woody answered, "Try a little bicarb."

Ruth groaned, "What's bicarb?"

Woody explained, "Just a little powder you mix in water. It'll relieve that congestion." This seemed like a pretty sound idea.

Ruth said, "Fix up a jug of that stuff."

The bicarbonate of soda must have had the desired effect, for the Great Stomach Ache was relieved. That afternoon Ruth swatted a home run. He must have attached some significance to it for, after that, he never missed his mug of bicarbonate of soda before he went on the field. Ruth called it "milk."

Then another afternoon he bounced in the clubhouse proclaiming a terrific hunger. Woody recommended a quick visit to the kitchens of the Stadium caterers, Harry Stevens & Co. Ruth was back soon with a pair of hot dogs which he downed in four gulps. In the ball game that day, Babe stroked another homer.

Now his luncheon menu was complete. Before each game a couple of hot dogs followed by a wash of bicarbonate of soda. His before-game-snack became part of the Ruthian ideology.

Babe's civilian ensemble became the camel's hair coat, the camel's hair cap. The coat he never fully donned. He wore it like an opera cape—loosely draped over his massive shoulders. In truth, it was becoming. He must have borrowed the idea from a New York theatrical magazine.

The public had now discovered the new Ruth. He retained many of his old habits in moderated form—acquired new ones more satisfying to himself and his public. He partook of the flowing bowl quite freely but, in keeping with his enormous capacity for all types of intake, Ruth suffered no repercussions. His health was always good. His eyes clear. His senses bright.

The usual crowd of hero snipers say Babe Ruth was a good-time-Charlie, a night club denizen. Nothing could be farther from the truth. The Babe used to go out—sure—but usually to a couple of favorite spots at which he was assured privacy.

One was a tavern in New Jersey, Donohue's. Mr. Donohue went so far as to build a private entrance to a private room for Ruth. He didn't do it for the money Babe spent there. Babe's parties never numbered more than four or five, if that many.

In St. Louis, Ruth haunted a place operated by a rotund German woman. She cooked the most wonderful spareribs this side of Heaven, and the Babe could eat sparcribs three meals a day. Many times when the Yankees had to hit the road out of St. Louis right after a game, Ruth would order twenty-five to thirty racks of spareribs from her to be delivered right to the train. The team used to occupy an entire sleeping car, so the Babe set up shop in the ladies' room, selling the ribs at a quarter a rack—plus all the home brew you could drink.

On the road, Babe never had the usual hotel room. The Yankee officials installed him in a sumptuous suite, as befitted the King of Diamonds. Immediately after games, Ruth retired to his suite. He changed to a red moray dressing gown and red moroccan slippers. A long sixty cent cigar protruded from his lips, for all the world like the Admiration Cigar trademark. The king was in the throne room. His subjects were permitted audience. And the subjects came in droves. I have seen as many as two hundred and fifty people visit the Babe in a single night.

One Ladies' Day in St. Louis, the girls were swarming around the clubhouse like stagedoor Jills. The team had to push through the crowd to reach the door, a flimsy affair, half frosted glass, half wood. Suddenly, the surging crowd leaned with all its collective strength on the barrier and it just gave way. The door flew open revealing the team in various phases of undress with the Babe in the center of the stage.

The great Babe Ruth, who feared no pitcher, climbed out of a tiny window that day to escape the assemblage. The sight of that huge bulk squeezing his white-flanneled rump through an undersized dormer is something I will never forget.

The Yankees were riding high in 1927, sweeping through the American League like a flight of jet bombers. Ruth, reaching for his own record of 59 homers (hit in 1921) which he hadn't approached since. When the last game of the season rolled around, the Bam had just 59. We were playing Washington, with wise old Tom Zachary scheduled to pitch against us. Zach wasn't too fast, but he had the type of queer stuff which bothered the sluggers. In the clubhouse before the game, Ruth was holding forth on the possibilities of making a homer. "I'll bet anyone ten bucks I hit one," he said. There were no takers. When Ruth gave voice to one of his inspired hunches, we knew what to expect.

And he got his home run, breaking the record with his last at-bat of the season.

Just before the World Series that year, we had our clubhouse meeting to decide allotments of the Series money. There was a question of what share one youngster would receive. He hadn't been particularly instrumental in winning the flag, and opinion was divided.

"You fellows are yapping about losing some two hundred bucks apiece," Ruth argued. "If we beat Pittsburgh, we'll get about six thousand bucks each. But even if the series only lasts four games, I'll be *losing* four thousand. I can get twenty-five hundred a game in exhibition work —it costs me dough to play in the series. Now what are you kicking about?" The kid got a full share.

It was Miller Huggins who used to describe Babe Ruth's value in the lineup as "the most destructive force ever known in baseball." He didn't mean the force of Ruth's homers alone. The mere presence of the Babe created a disastrous psychological problem for the other team. Even when he wasn't hitting, the opposition was fearful that he might start. We won the 1922 pennant because the last month the opposing pitchers kept walking Ruth to get to Wally Pipp, and Pipp was hitting over four hundred at the time.

Ruth became embroiled in politics for the first time in 1928. Al Smith was running against Herbert Hoover for President, and Babe was a great friend of Smith's. At the time, Babe was bylining a regular syndicated article appearing in Republican and Democratic newspapers alike. The column was carefully nonpartisan.

Late in the summer, however, Babe was caught in the fray. We were playing in Washington and arrived to find the field ablaze in red, white and blue bunting. We knew some big wheel was going to be at the game, and were very impressed by a battery of cameras that had been set up in front of the box.

Ruth volunteered some explanation. "There's a guy coming out to the game. I gotta have my picture taken with him." The guy turned out to be Herbert Hoover.

Dugan decided to give the Babe a little riding. "Jidge," he said solemnly, "you better be careful, Jidge—you're a buddy of Smith's, and he wouldn't like that."

"I never thought of that," said Ruth soberly.

Soon a messenger arrived from the Washington bench to tell the Babe that all the photographers were ready. "I changed my mind." Babe informed him. "Tell Hoover if he wants to meet me I'll be glad to get together with him under the stands. But not in public. I'm a friend of Al's."

In 1930, I left the Yankees on a trade to the Detroit Tigers. It was tough leaving the team on which I had enjoyed so many happy years. A reporter once asked me to what I owed my pitching success. I had a ready reply: playing with Babe Ruth on my side.

After a year with Detroit, I was again traded, this time to the Philadelphia Athletics, the club of Grove, Simmons, Fox, Cochrane and Earnshaw. Connie Mack's outfit. The day came when I was selected to pitch against my old teammates. I wanted to win, of course, just as they wanted to beat me. That's baseball. I did fine for six innings. In fact, I had a shut-out. In the seventh, with two out, the Babe came to the plate. He was leaning in, and I figured to handcuff him with an inside fast ball. Behind the right field wall, in Philadelphia, there's a street. On the far side of the street stand a row of houses, and behind them another row of houses and still another street. Somewhere along that street they found my carefully planned inside fast ball where the Babe had put it. As I watched the big guy rounding the circuit, I thought to myself: "I've seen you hit over six hundred of those homers, big boy, but I *still* don't know how you do it."

To other biographers I leave the tales of Babe Ruth's declining days, the coming of Joe McCarthy, the sad period Ruth spent with the Boston Braves. I prefer the lighter side of the Babe's career. Like the tense conferences held in the enemy camp, on strategy in pitching to the big fellow: I remember a day in May, 1935. I remember the last home runs hit by the Big Bam. Ruth was with the Boston Braves, his power ebbing, his eyes and legs failing. He had consented to make one last road trip with the Braves, and we met again in Pittsburgh where I was playing with the Pirates.

Before the game, Pi Traynor, Pirate manager, held his pow-wow on pitching strategy. He held the score card in hand, running down the Braves line-up to analyze batting weaknesses. Red Lucas was scheduled to pitch, and he had one question. "How do we pitch to Ruth?"

I spoke my piece. "The best way to pitch to Ruth," I told them, "is to pitch behind him. He has no weaknesses except deliberate walks. You have your choice—one base on four balls, or four bases on one ball."

The boys were peeved. I assured them I wasn't kidding.

Guy Bush, once a great pitcher for the Cubs, said, "I pitched against him in the '32 series. I got him out throwing sinkers."

"So did Charlie Root," I answered. "Charlie threw the Babe a sinker that the Babe dropped into the center field bleachers."

The meeting ended without reaching a formula, and Lucas went out to the mound. Ruth came up the first inning as the crowd rose in a mighty ovation. He took his familiar pigeon-toed stance and waited. Lucas scratched, pawed the ground with his spikes, took a long windup and pitched. Ruth hit a tremendous home run over the roof of the right field pavilion.

On the players' bench, I nudged Cy Blanton. "What did I tell you, Cy? He should have pitched behind him."

When Ruth came up to bat for the second time. Lucas was soaping in the showers and Bill Swift was pitching. Babe connected with a fast ball and hit it far into the center field seats. In the seventh inning, when Ruth was up again, Guy Bush, the Mississippi Mudcat, was pitching. The sinker specialist. He put on a big show whipping two strikes past the big fellow. Bush was hot. He bounced up and down as if his knees were all springs. Sort of a free-wheeling effect. His third pitch came after a fancy, exaggerated windup to throw Ruth off balance. Ruth hit it for his third home run of the ball game.

For some years before his retirement, the Babe had found domesticity a pleasant retreat from the constant pressure of the spotlight. Christy Walsh was partly responsible for the change, but more so was Claire Hodgson Ruth, his wife who had given up a promising career as an actress to marry Ruth in 1929, months after the tragic death of his first wife, Helen.

I haven't heard enough compliments on the way Claire Ruth managed her husband. She guarded the minimum of privacy the Babe needed. She watched the exchequer. She ran the home. Ruth for once in his life, subordinated his impulses to his love for his wife. And make no mistake —Claire could talk baseball on equal terms with any major leaguer. After Christy Walsh surrendered Babe's business management, Claire took over those chores too. She was not only a fine wife, she was Babe's buddy.

Several years after the Babe retired, I had the opportunity of studying the domesticated King in his new domain. I had a favor to ask of the big fellow, and telephoned for an appointment. Claire told me to come right up. Mrs. Hoyt and I spent a pleasant evening in the well known Riverside Drive apartment. One of the rooms had been set apart as a combination trophy room and study. There, in a heavy leather armchair, we found the Sultan of Swat, puffing slowly on an oversized pipe. To one side sat Mrs. Ruth, occasionally interrupting the conversation to scold Babe mildly when he forgot a name or date. Babe was talking about his pictures, caps and deer heads. He never *pointed* to a prize—merely blew a shaft of smoke in the direction of the special object. I followed a blue ribbon of smoke to a large frame.

"That's what I'm proudest of," said Ruth. "You see there a picture of every one of the sixty balls I hit for home runs in 1927. There's not another picture like it in the world. Every ball has written on it the date it was hit and the name of the pitcher it was hit off. What tickles me most is that I hit the last home run the last time at bat on the last day. Remember?"

He puffed silently for a moment. "See that picture over there?" he continued suddenly. "That was taken in Manila." It was a picture of the Babe shaking hands with half a dozen or so Filipinos.

"We had a time over there. Those Hawaiians tried to give me the business."

"Filipinos, Babe," said Mrs. Ruth.

"Yeah—Filipinos. Well, anyway, there must have been 30,000 people out there that day. All you could see was heads jammed together. They tried to tell me there were only 10,000 in the park. I stood to lose a bundle of dough. I said, 'no money—me no play.' I've been looking at crowds all my life. I know 30,000 when I see them. So this Hawaiian says . . ."

"Filipino, Babe," said Mrs. Ruth.

". . . Filipino says, 'me no un'ers'an.' I picked up my glove and started for the gate. The guy understood that all right. We played and got paid."

"Who'd you play?" I asked.

"We wanted to split our troupe up," explained the Babe, "five or six major leaguers on each side with the rest local talent. But out of the stand rained cushions, bottles, straw hats—everything. They didn't want us to split up. So we played an all star team and beat them 35 to nothing, or something. That's what they wanted, a slaughter. Tough people, those Hawaiians."

"Filipinos," said Mrs. Ruth.

"Aw, what the hell," Babe said. "Make it Eskimos. We beat 'em!"

I saw another picture on the wall, Babe being interviewed. It reminded me of a time in Nashville during an exhibition game. I guess it was the shortest interview on record. Ruth was sitting idly watching pre-game batting when some cub reporter parked himself beside The Bam and announced that he was a roving columnist doing a series of articles about the opinions of famous people on world events.

"I have selected the Chinese situation for you," he said. "Mr. Ruth, what do you think of the Chinese situation?"

The Bambino gave him the answer sublime. "The hell with it," he said.

His biggest disappointment was the failure of baseball to give him a chance at managing. He raised salaries, made baseball the national pastime. He deserved the chance. Some said he should start in the minors and work up. That really rankled.

"I was as big as any of them," Babe told me. "Did Frisch start in the minors before he managed the Cards? Or Hornsby? Or Terry? Or Ott? Or Traynor? What a line."

Baseball missed the boat on that one. Babe might have failed. If he had, the baseball world could always have been able to say that he had been allowed to try. He had been part of the game all through its growing pains, part of its very heart. Even as a player he'd helped develop hidden talent among his teammates. Any way you look at it, the Babe should at least have had his chance.

Ty Cobb

TYRUS

The Greatest of 'Em All

The American Magazine   May 1915

Best known for his sports fiction, Ring Lardner uses his storytelling powers and mastery of the vernacular to give a feeling for how Ty Cobb awed major leaguers. And that intimidating presence, as much as raw batting or base-running marks, was Cobb's legacy.

By Ring W. Lardner

S it down here a while, kid, and I'll give you the dope on this guy. You say you didn't see him do nothin' wonderful? But you only seen him in one serious. Wait till you been in the league more'n a week or two before you go judgin' ball players. He may of been sick when you played agin him. Even when he's sick, though, he's got everybody I ever seen skun, and I've saw all the best of 'em.

Say, he ain't worth nothin' to that club; no, nothin'! I don't know what pay he's gettin', but whatever it is, it ain't enough. If they'd split the receipts fifty-fifty with that bird, they wouldn't be gettin' none the worst of it. That bunch could get along just as well without him as a train could without no engine.

He's twicet the ball player now that he was when he come up. He didn't seem to have no sense when he broke in; he run bases like a fool and was a mark for a good pitcher or catcher. They used to just lay for him when he got on. Sully used to tell the pitchers to do nothin' but waste balls when he was on first or second base. It was pretty near always good dope, too, because they'd generally nail him off one base or the other, or catch him tryin' to go to the next one. But Sully had to make perfect pegs to get him even when he knowed beforehand that he was goin'. Sully was the boy that could make them perfect pegs, too. Don't forget that.

Cobb seemed to think they was only one rule in the book, and that was a rule providin' that nobody could stay on one base more'n one second. They tell me that before he got into the South Atlantic League he was with a club down there in Georgia called the Royston Rompers. Maybe he thought he had to keep on rompin' up here.

Another thing was that he couldn't hit a left-hander very good. Doc W'ite used to make him look like a sucker. Doc was a fox to begin with, and he always give you just what you wasn't lookin' for. And then, his curve ball was somethin' Ty hadn't never saw before and it certainly did fool him. He'd hand Cobb a couple o' curves and the baby'd miss 'em a foot. Then, when he was expectin' another one, Doc'd shoot his fast one right past his chin and make a monkey out of him.

That was when he first come up here. But Ty ain't the guy that's goin' to stay fooled all the time. When he wises up that somebody's got somethin' on him, he don't sleep nor do nothin' till he figures out a way to get even. It's a good thing Doc had his chancet to laugh when he did, because Cobb did most o' the laughin' after a couple o' seasons of it. He seen he couldn't hit the curve when it was breakin', so he stood way back in the box and waited till it'd broke. Then he nailed it. When Ty'd learned that trick, Doc got so's he was well pleased when the balls this guy hit off'n him stayed in the park.

It was the same way with every pitcher that had his number when he first busted in. He got to 'em in short order and, before long, nobody was foolin' him so's you could notice it. Right now he's as good agin left-handers as he is agin regular fellas. And if they's any pitcher in baseball that's got him fooled, he's keepin' the fact well concealed.

I was tellin' you what a wild baserunner he was at first. Well, he's still takin' chances that nobody else takes, but he's usin' judgment with it. He don't run no more just for the sake o' runnin'. They was a time when the guy on the base ahead of him was afraid all the time that he'd get spiked in the heels. But no more o' that. They's no more danger of him causin' a rear end collision, providin' the guy ahead don't blockade the right o' way too long.

You may not believe it, but I'll bet most o' these here catchers would rather have somebody on second base when Ty's on first base than to have him on first base alone. They know he ain't goin' to pull no John

Anderson and they feel pretty safe when he can't steal without bumpin'
into one of his own teammates. But when the track's all clear, look out!

All my life I been hearin' about the slow, easy-goin' Southerner. Well,
Ty's easy-goin' all right—like a million-dollar tourin' car. But if South-
erners is slow, he must be kiddin' us when he says he was born down
South. He must of came from up there where Doc Cook pretty near got
to.

You say you've heard ball players talk about how lucky he was. Yes, he
is lucky. But it's because he makes his own luck. If he's got horseshoes,
he's his own blacksmith. You got to have the ability first, and the luck'll
string along with you. Look at Connie Mack and John D. and some o'
them fellas.

You know I ain't played no ball for the last few years, but I seen a lot
of it played. And I don't overlook no chancet to watch this here Tyrus.
I've saw him agin every club in the American League and I've saw him
pull more stuff than any other guy ever dreamed of. Lots o' times, after
seein' him get away with somethin', I've said to myself: "Gosh, he's a
lucky stiff!" But right afterward, I've thought: "Yes, and why don't nobody else have that luck? Because they don't go out and get it."

I remember one time in Chi, a year or two ago. The Sox was two to the
bad and it was the ninth innin'. They was two men down. Bodie was on
second base and somebody hits a single to center field. Bodie tries to
score. It wasn't good baseball to take the chancet, because that run
wasn't goin' to do no good without another one to put with it. Cobb pegs
to the plate and the umps calls Bodie out, though it looked to everybody
like he was safe. Well, it was a bad play of Bodie's, wasn't it? Yes. Well
then, it was a bad play o' Cobb's to make the throw. If Detroit hadn't of
got the best o' that decision, the peg home would of let the man that hit
the ball go to second and be planted there in position to score the tyin'
run on another base hit. Where if Ty had of played it safe, like almost
anybody would, the batter'd of been held on first base where it would
take two base hits or a good long wallop to score him. It was lucky for Ty
that the umps happened to guess wrong. But say, I think that guy's
pretty near smart enough to know when a umpire's goin' to make a
rotten decision.

O' course you know that Ty gets to first base more'n anybody in the
world. In the first place, he always manages to hit better'n anybody. And
when he don't hit safe, but just bounds one to some infielder, the bettin's
2 to 1 that the ball will be booted or throwed wild. That's his luck, is it?
No, sir. It's no such a thing. It's his speed. The infielder knows he ain't
got no time to spare. He's got to make the play faster'n he would for
anybody else, and the result is that he balls it all up. He tries to throw to

first base before he's got the pill to throw, or else he hurries the throw so much that he don't have no time to aim. Some o' the ball players round the league says that the scorers favor Ty and give him a base hit on almost anything. Well, I think they ought to. I don't believe in handin' a error to a fella when he's hurried and worried to death. If you tried to make the play like you do for other guys, Ty'd beat the ball to first base and then you'd get a hot call from the bench for loafin'.

If you'd saw him play as much baseball as I have, you wouldn't be claimin' he was overrated. I ain't goin to come right out and say he's the best ever, because they was some old-timers I never seen. (Comiskey, though, who's saw 'em all, slips it to him.) I just want to tell you some o' the things he's did, and if you can show me his equal, lead me to him and I'll take off my hat.

Detroit was playin' the Ath-a-letics oncet. You know they ain't no club that the Tigers looks better agin than the Ath-a-letics, and Cobb's more of a devil in Philly than anywheres else. Well, this was when he was battin' fourth and Jim Delehanty was followin' him. Ty singles and Del slips him the hit and run sign on the first ball. The ball was pitched a little outside, and Del cuts it down past Harry Davis for a single to right field. Do you know what Cobb done? He scored; that's all. And they wasn't no boot made, neither. Danny Murphy picked the ball up clean and pegged it to Davis and Davis relays it straight home to Ira Thomas. Ty was there ahead of it. If I hadn't o' been watchin' close, I'd o' thought he forgot to touch two or three bases. But, no, sir. He didn't miss none of 'em. They may be other guys that could do that if they tried, but the diff'rence between them and Cobb is that he done it and they didn't. Oh, I guess other fellas has scored from first base on a long single in the hit and run, but not when the ball was handled perfectly clean like this one.

Well, here's another one: I forget the exact details, except that the game was between the White Sox and Detroit and that Tannehill was playin' third base at the time, and that the score was tied when Cobb pulled it. It was the eighth innin'. He was on first base. The next guy hits a single to left field. Ty, o' course, rounds second and starts for third. The left fielder makes a rotten peg and the pill comes rollin' in. Ty has the play beat a mile and they ain't no occasion for him to slide. But he slid, and do you know what, he done? He took a healthy kick at that rollin' ball and sent it clear over to the grand stand. Then he jumped to his feet and kept on goin'. He was acrost the plate with the winnin' run before nobody'd realized what he'd did. It's agin the rules, o' course, to kick the ball a-purpose, but how could the umps prove that this wasn't a accident? Ty could of told him that he thought the play was goin' to be close and he'd better slide. I might o' thought it was a accident, too, if that had of been the only time I seen him do it. I can't tell you how many times he's pulled it, but it's grew to be a habit with him. When it comes to scorin' on kicks, he's got this here What's-His-Name—Brickley—tied.

I've saw him score from second base on a fly ball, too; a fly ball that was caught. Others has did it, but not as regular as this guy. He come awful near gettin' away with it agin a little while ago, in Chi. They was also somebody on third when the ball was hit. The guy on third started home the minute Bodie catched the ball and Ping seen they was no chancet to get him. So he pegs toward Weaver, who's down near third base. Cobb's at third before the ball gets to the infield. He don't never hesitate. He keeps right on goin' for the plate. Now, if Weaver'd of been able to of intercepeted the ball, Ty'd of been out thirty feet. But the throw goes clear through to the third baseman. Then it's relayed home. The gang sittin' with me all thought Ty was safe. I don't know about it, but anyway, he was called out. It just goes to show you what this guy's liable to do. You can't take no afternoon nap when he's around. They's lots of other fast guys, but while they're thinkin' about what they're goin' to do, he's did it. He's figurin' two or three bases ahead all the while. So, as I say, you don't get no sleep with him in the game.

Fielder Jones used to tell us: "When that bird's runnin', throw the ball somewheres just's soon as you get a-hold of it. I don't care where you throw it, but throw it somewheres. Don't hold onto it."

I seen where the papers says the other day that you outguessed him. I wasn't out to that game. I guess you got away with somethin' all right, but don't feel too good about it. You're worse off now than you was before you done it because he won't never rest till he shows you up. You stopped him oncet, and just for that he'll make you look like a rummy next time he plays agin you. And after he's did it oncet and got even, he'll do it agin. And then he'll do it agin. They's a lot o' fellas round this league that's put over a smart play on Tyrus and most of 'em has since wished they hadn't. It's just like as if I'd go out and lick a policeman. I'd live to regret it.

We had a young fella oncet, a catcher, that nailed him flat-footed off'n first base one day. It was in the first set of a serious. Ty didn't get on no more that day, but he walked the first time up the followin' afternoon. They was two out. He takes a big lead and the young fella pegs for him agin. But Tyrus was off like a streak when the ball was throwed, and about the time the first baseman was catchin' it, he was slidin' into second. Then he gets a big lead off'n second and the young catcher takes a shot for him there. But he throws clear to center field and Ty scores. The next guy whiffs, so they wouldn't of been no run if the young guy hadn't of got so chesty over the precedin' day's work. I'm tellin' you this so's you won't feel too good.

They's times when a guy does try to pull something on this Cobb, and is made to look like a sucker without deservin' it. I guess that's because the Lord is for them that helps themselves and don't like to see nobody try to show 'em up.

I was sittin' up in the stand in Cleveland one day. Ty was on second base when somebody hits a fly ball, way out, to Birmingham. At that time, Joe had the best throwin' arm you ever see. He could shoot like a rifle. Cobb knowed that, o' course, and didn't feel like takin' no chancet, even though Joe was pretty far out there. Ty waits till the ball's catched and then makes a bluff to go to third, thinkin' Birmy'd throw and that the ball might get away. Well, Joe knows that Cobb knows what kind of arm he's got and figures that the start from second is just a bluff; that he ain't really got no intention o' goin'. So, instead o' peggin' to third, he takes a quick shot for second, hopin' to nail Cobb before he can get back. The throw's perfect and Cobb sees where he's trapped. So he hikes for third. And the second sacker—I don't think the big Frenchman was playin' that day—drops the ball. If he'd of held it, he'd of had plenty of time to relay to third and nail Ty by a block. But no. He drops the ball. See? Birmy'd outguessed Ty, but all it done for him was to make him look bad and make Ty look good.

Another time, a long while ago, Detroit needed a run to win from the Sox. Ty gets to first base with one out. Sully was catchin'. Sully signs for a pitch-out and then snaps the ball to first base. Ty wasn't lookin' for it and he was caught clean. He couldn't get back to first base, so he goes for second. Big Anderson was playin' first base and he makes a bum peg. The ball hits Cobb on the shoulder and bounds so far out in left center that he didn't even have to run to get home. You see, Sully'd outguessed Ty and had pulled a play that ought to of shred the game. Instead o' that, it give the game to Detroit. That's what hurts and discourages a fella from tryin' to pull anything on him.

Somtimes I pretty near think they's nothin' he couldn't do if he really set out to do it. Before you joined the club, some o' the boys was kiddin' him over to Detroit. Callahan was tellin' me about it. Cobb hadn't started hittin'. One o' the players clipped the averages out o' the paper and took 'em to the park. He showed the clippin' to Ty.

"You're some battin' champ, Ty," he says. "Goin' at a .225 clip, eh?"

Tyrus just laughed at him.

"I been playin' I was one o' you White Sox," he says. "But wait till a week from to-day. It'll be .325 then."

Well, it wasn't. No, sir! It was .326.

One time, in 1912 I think it was, I happened to be goin' East, lookin' for a job of umpirin', and I rode on the train with the Tigers. I and Cobb et breakfast together. I had a Sunday paper with me and was givin' the averages the oncet over.

"Read 'em to me," says Ty.

"You don't want 'em all, do you?" I says.

"No, no. Just the first three of us," he says. "I know about where I'm at, but not exactly."

So I read it to him:

"Jackson's first with .412. Speaker's second with .400. You're third with .386."

"Well," says Ty, "I, reckon the old boy'd better get busy. Watch me this trip!"

I watched him, through the papers. In the next twenty-one times at bat, he gets exactly seventeen hits, and when the next averages was printed, he was out in front. He stayed there, too.

So I don't know, but I believe that if Jackson and Speaker and Collins and Lajoie and Crawford was to go crazy and hit .999, this Cobb would come out on top with 1,000 even.

He's got a pretty good opinion of himself, but he ain't no guy to really brag. He's just full o' the old confidence. He thinks Cobb's a good ball player, and a guy's not to think that way about himself if he wants to get anywheres. I know a lot o' ball players that gets throwed out o' the league because they think the league's too fast for 'em. It's diff'rent with Tyrus. If they was a league just three times as fast as the one he's in and if he was sold up there, he'd go believin' he could lead it in battin'. And he'd lead it too!

Yes, sir, he's full o' that old stuff, and the result is that lots o' people that don't know him think he's a swell-head, and don't like him. But I'm tellin' you that he's a pretty good guy now, and the rest o' the Tigers is strong for him, which is more'n they used to be. He busted in with a chip on his shoulder, and he soon become just as popular as the itch. Everybody played him for a busher and started takin' liberties with him. He was a busher, too, but he was one o' the kind that can't take a joke. You know how they's young fellas that won't stand for nothin'. Then they's them that stands for too much. Then they's the kind that's just about half way. You can go a little ways with 'em, but not too far. That's the kind that's popular.

Cobb wouldn't stand for nothin'. If somebody poured ketchup in his coffee, he was liable to pick up the cup and throw it at the guy nearest to him. If you'd stepped on his shine, he'd of probably took the other foot and aimed it at you like he does now at the ball when it's lyin' loose on the ground. If you'd called him some name on the field, he'd of walloped you with a bat, even if you was his pal. So they was all stuck on him, was they not?

He got trimmed a couple o' times, right on his own club, too. But when they seen what kind of a ball player he was goin' to be, they decided they'd better not kill him. It's just as well for 'em they didn't. I'd like to know where their club would of finished—in 1907 and 1908, for instance—if it hadn't of been for him. It was nobody but him that beat us out in 1908. I'll tell you about it later on.

I says to him one day not long ago, I says:

"You wasn't very strong with the boys when you first come up. What was the trouble?"

"Well," he says, "I didn't understand what was comin' off. I guess they meant it all right, but nobody'd tipped me that a busher's supposed to be picked on. They were hazin' me; that's what they were doin', hazin' me. I argued with 'em because I didn't know better."

"You learned, though, didn't you?" I says.

"Oh, yes," says Ty, "I learned all right."

"Maybe you paid for your lessons, too," I says.

"Maybe I did," he says.

"Well," I says, "would you act just the same way if you had it to do over again?"

"I reckon so," he says.

And he would, too, because if he was a diff'rent kind o' guy, he wouldn't be the ball player he is.

Say, maybe you think I didn't hate him when I was playin' ball. I didn't know him very well, see? But I hated him on general principles. And I never hated him more'n I did in 1908. That was the year they beat us out o' the big dough the last day o' the season, and it come at a time when I needed that old dough, because I knowed darn well that I wasn't goin' to last no ten years more or nothin' like that.

You look over the records now, and you'll see that the Detroit club and us just about broke even on the year's serious agin each other. I don't know now if it was exactly even or not, or, if it wasn't, which club had the best of it. But I do know one thing, and that is that they beat us five games that we'd ought to of copped from 'em easy and they beat us them games for no other reason than that they had this here Georgia Peach.

The records don't show no stuff like that, but I can remember most o' them games as if they was played yesterday; that is, Cobb's part in 'em. In them days, they had Crawford hittin' third and Cobb fourth and Rossman fifth. Well, one day we had 'em licked by three runs in the seventh innin'. Old Nick was pitchin' for us and Sully was catchin'. Tannehill was at third base and Hahn was switched from right to left field because they was somethin' the matter with Dougherty. Well, this seventh innin' come, as I was sayin', and we was three runs to the good. Crawford gets on someway and Cobb singles. Jones thought Nick was slippin', so he hollered for Smitty. Smitty comes in and pitches to big Rossman and the big guy hits one back at him. Smitty had the easiest kind of a double play starin' him in the face—a force play on Crawford at third and then the rest of it on Rossman, who wasn't no speed marvel. But he makes a bad peg to Tannie and the ball gets by him. It didn't look like as if Crawford could score, and I guess he was goin' to stop at third.

But Tyrus didn't pay no attention to Crawford. He'd saw the wild peg and he was bound to keep right on comin'. So Crawford's got to start home to keep from gettin' run over. Hahn had come in to get the ball and when he seen Crawford startin' home, he cut loose a wild peg that went clear to the bench. Crawford and Cobb both scored, o' course, and what does Ty do but yell at Rossman to follow 'em in, though it looked like sure death. Sully has the ball by that time, but it's just our luck that he has to peg wild too. The ball sailed over Smitty, who'd came up to cover the plate. The score's tied and for no reason but that Tyrus had made everybody run. The next three was easy outs, but they went on and licked us in extra innin's.

Well, they was another game, in that same serious I think it was, when Big Ed had 'em stopped dead to rights. They hadn't no more business scorin' off'n him than a rabbit. I don't think they hit two balls hard all day. We wasn't the best hittin' club in the world, but we managed to get one run for the Big Moose in the first innin' and that had ought to of been a-plenty.

Up comes Cobb in the fourth and hits one that goes in two bounds to Davis or whoever was playin' short. If he could of took his time, they'd of been nothin' to it. But he has to hurry the play because it's Cobb runnin', and he pegs low. Izzy gets the ball off'n the ground all right, but juggles it, and then Ty's safe.

They was nobody out, so Rossman bunts. He's throwed out a mile at first base, but Ty goes all the way to third. Then the next guy hits a fly ball to Hahn that wouldn't of been worth a nickel if Cobb'd of went only to second on the sacrifice, like a human bein'. He's on third, though, and he scores on the fly ball. The next guy takes three swings and the side's out, but we're tied up.

Then we go along to the ninth innin' and it don't look like they'd score agin on Big Ed if they played till Easter. But Cobb's up in the ninth with one out. He gets the one real healthy hit that they'd made all day. He singled to right field. I say he singled, because a single's what anybody else would of been satisfied with on the ball he hit. But Ty didn't stop at first base. He lights out for second and whoever was in right field made a good peg. The ball's there waitin' for Ty, but he slides away from it. Jake thought he had him, but the umps called him safe. Well, Jake gets mad and starts to kick. They ain't no time called or nothin'. The umps turns away and Jake slams the ball on the ground and before anybody could get to it, Cobb's on third. We all hollered murder, but it done us no good. Rossman then hit a fly ball and the game's over.

I remember another two to one game that he win from us. I don't recall who was pitchin'—one o' the left-handers, I guess. Whoever it was had big Rossman on his staff that day. He whipped him twicet and made him pop out another time. They was one out in the eighth when Cobb beats out a bunt. We was leadin' by one run at the time, so naturally we wanted to keep him on first base. Well, whoever it was pitchin' wasted three balls tryin' to outguess Tyrus, and he still stood there on first base, laughin' at us. Rossman takes one strike and the pitcher put the next one right over and took a chancet, instead o' runnin' the risk o' walkin' him. Rossman has a toe-hold and he meets the ball square and knocks it clear out o' the park. We're shut out in the ninth and they've trimmed us. You'll say, maybe, it was Rossman that beat us. It was his wallop all right, but our pitcher wouldn't of wasted all them balls and got himself in the hole if anybody but Cobb'd of been on first base.

One day we're tied in the ninth, four to four, or somethin' like that. Cobb doubled and Rossman walked after two was out. Jones pulled Smitty out o' the game and put in Big Ed. Now, nobody was lookin' for Ty to steal third with two out. It's a rotten play when anybody else does it. This ain't no double steal, because Rossman never moved off'n first base. Cobb stole third all right and then, on the next pitch, Rossman starts to steal second. Our catcher oughtn't to of paid no attention to him because Walsh probably could of got the batter and retired the side. It wasn't Sully catchin' or you can bet no play'd of been made. But this catcher couldn't see nobody run without peggin', so he cut loose. Rossman stopped and started back for first base. The shortstop fired the ball back home, but he was just too late. Cobb was acrost already and it was over. Now in that case, our catcher'd ought to of been killed, but if Tyrus hadn't did that fool stunt o' stealin' third with two out, they'd of been no chancet for the catcher to pull the boner.

How many did I say he beat us out of? Five? Oh, yes, I remember another one. I can make it short because they wasn't much to it. It was another one o' them tied up affairs, and both pitchers was goin' good. It was Smitty for us and, I think, Donovan for them. Cobb gets on with two

down in the tenth or 'leventh and steals second while Smitty stands there
with the ball in his hand. Then Rossman hits a harmless lookin' ground
ball to the shortstop. Cobb runs down the line and stops right in front o'
where the ball was comin', so's to bother him. But Ty pretends that he's
afraid the ball's goin' to hit him. It worked all right. The shortstop got
worried and juggled the ball till it was too late to make a play for Rossman. But Cobb's been monkeyin' so long that he ain't nowheres near
third base and when the shortstop finally picks up the ball and pegs
there, Cobb turns back. Well, they'd got him between 'em and they're
tryin' to drive him back toward second. Somebody butts in with a muff
and he goes to third base. And when Smitty starts to pitch agin, he steals
home just as clean as a whistle.

The last game o' the season settled the race, you know. I can't say that
Tyrus won that one for 'em. They all was due to hit and they sure did hit.
Cobb and Crawford both murdered the ball in the first innin' and won
the game right there, because Donovan was so good we didn't have no
chancet. But if he hadn't of stole them other games off'n us, this last one
wouldn't of did 'em no good. We could of let our young fellas play that
one while we rested up for the world's serious.
    I don't say our club had a license to be champions that year. We was
weak in spots. But we'd of got the big dough if it hadn't of been for
Tyrus. You can bet your life on that.
    You can easy see why I didn't have no love for him in them days. And
I'll bet the fellas that was on the Ath-a-letics in 1907 felt the same toward
him, because he was what kept 'em from coppin' that year. I ain't takin'
nothin' away from Jennin's and Crawford and Donovan and Bush and
Mullin and McIntire and Rossman and the rest of 'em. I ain't tryin' to
tell you that them fellas ain't all had somethin' to do with Detroit's
winnin' in diff'rent years. Jennin's has kept 'em fightin' right along, and
they's few guys more valuable to their club than Crawford. He busted up
a lot o' games for 'em in their big years and he's doin' it yet. And I
consider Bush one o' the best infielders I ever see. The others was all
right, too. They all helped. But this guy I'm tellin' you about knocked us
out o' the money by them stunts of his that nobody else can get by with.
    It's all foolishness to hate a fella because he's a good ball player,
though. I realize that now that I'm out of it. I can go and watch Tyrus
and enjoy watchin' him, but in them days it was just like pullin' teeth
whenever he come up to the plate or got on the bases. He was reachin'
right down in my pocket and takin' my money. So it's no wonder I was
sore on him.
    If I'd of been on the same club with him, though, I wouldn't never of
got sore at him no matter how fresh he was. I'd of been afraid that he

might get so sore at me that he'd quit the club. He could of called me anything he wanted to and got away with it or he could have took me acrost his knee and spanked me eighty times a day, just so's he kept on puttin' money in my kick instead o' beatin' me out of it.

As I was sayin', I enjoy seein' him play now. If the game's rotten or not, it don't make no diff'rence, and it don't make a whole lot even if he's havin' a bad day. They's somethin' fascinatin' in just lookin' at the baby.

I ain't alone in thinkin' that, neither. I don't know how many people he draws to the ball parks in a year, but it's enough to start a big manufacturin' town and a few suburbs. You heard about the crowd that was out to the Sox park the Sunday they was two rival attractions in town? It was in the spring, before you come. Well, it was some crowd. Now, o' course, the Sox draw good at home on any decent Sunday, but I'm tellin' you they was a few thousands out there that'd of been somewheres else if Cobb had of stayed in Georgia.

I was in Boston two or three years ago this summer and the Tigers come along there for a serious o' five games, includin' a double-header. The Detroit club wasn't in the race and neither was the Red Sox. Well, sir, I seen every game and I bet they was seventy thousand others that seen 'em, or better'n fifteen thousand a day for four days. They was some that was there because they liked baseball. They was others that was stuck on the Red Sox. They was still others that was strong for the Detroit club. And they was about twenty-five or thirty thousand that didn't have no reason for comin' except this guy I'm tellin' you about. You can't blame him for holdin' out oncet in awhile for a little more money. You can't blame the club for slippin' it to him, neither.

They's a funny thing I've noticed about him and the crowds. The fans in the diff'rent towns hates him because he's beat their own team out o' so many games. They hiss him when he pulls off somethin' that looks like dirty ball to 'em. Sometimes they get so mad at him that you think they're goin' to tear him to pieces. They holler like a bunch of Indians when some pitcher's good enough or lucky enough to strike him out. And at the same time, right down in their hearts, they're disappointed because he did strike out.

How do I know that? Well, kid, I've felt it myself, even when I was pullin' agin Detroit. I've talked to other people and they've told me they felt the same way. When they come out to see him, they expect to see him do somethin'. They're glad if he does and glad if he don't. They're sore at him if he don't beat their team and they're sore if he does. It's a funny thing and I ain't goin' to sit here all night tryin' to explain it.

But, say, I wisht I was the ball player he is. They could throw pop bottles and these here bumbs at me, and I wouldn't kick. They could call me names from the stand, but I wouldn't care. If the whole population o' the United States hated me like they think they hate him, I wouldn't mind, so long's I could just get back in that old game and play the ball he plays. But if I could, kid, I wouldn't have no time to be talkin' to you.

The other day, I says to Callahan:

"What do you think of him?"

"Think of him!" says Cal. "What could anybody think of him? I think enough of him to wish he'd go and break a leg. And I'm not sore on him personally at that."

"Don't you like to see him play ball?" I says.

"I'd love to watch him," says Cal, "if I could just watch him when he was playin' Philadelphia or Washington or any club but mine."

"I guess you'd like to have him, wouldn't you?" I says.

"Me?" says Cal. "All I'd give for him is my right eye."

"But," I says, "he must keep a manager worried some, in one way and another; you'd always be afraid he was goin' to break his own neck or cut somebody else's legs off or jump to the Fed'rals or somethin'."

"I'd take my chances," says Cal. "I believe I could even stand the worry for a few days."

I seen in the papers where McGraw says Eddie Collins is the greatest ball player in the world. I ain't goin' to argue with him about it, because I got nothin' but admiration for Collins. He's a bear. But, kid, I wisht McGraw had to play twenty-two games a year agin this Royston Romper. No, I don't, neither. McGraw never done nothin' to me.

Shoeless Joe Jackson   Photo credit: National Baseball Library/Cooperstown, N.Y.

SHOELESS JOE JACKSON

This Is the Truth!

Sport Magazine　　　October 1948

Produced in the style of **True Stories,** *another magazine then owned by the publisher of* **Sport,** *this is one of many tell-all pieces by Black Sox players in the 1930s and 1940s. Furman Bisher, long-time sports editor and columnist for the* **Atlanta Constitution** *and* **Atlanta Journal,** *helps Joe Jackson tell a more upbeat story than legend has it.*

By Shoeless Joe Jackson
As Told to Furman Bisher

When I walked out of Judge Dever's courtroom in Chicago in 1921, I turned my back completely on the World Series of 1919, the Chicago White Sox, and the major leagues. I had been acquitted by a twelve-man jury in a civil court of all charges and I was an innocent man in the records. I have never made any request to be reinstated in baseball, and I have never made any campaign to have my name cleared in the baseball records. This is not a plea of any kind. This is just my story. I'm telling it simply because it seems that 30 years after that World Series, the world may want to hear what I have to say.

If I had been the kind of fellow who brooded when things went wrong, I probably would have gone out of my mind when Judge Landis ruled me out of baseball. I would have lived in regret. I would have been bitter and resentful because I felt I had been wronged.

But I haven't been resentful at all. I thought when my trial was over that Judge Landis might have restored me to good standing. But he never did. And until he died I had never gone before him, sent a representative before him, or placed before him any written matter pleading my case. I gave baseball my best and if the game didn't care enough to see me get a square deal, then I wouldn't go out of my way to get back in it.

Baseball failed to keep faith with me. When I got notice of my suspension three days before the 1920 season ended—it came on a rained-out day—it read that if found innocent of any wrongdoing, I would be reinstated. If found guilty, I would be banned for life. I was found innocent, and I was still banned for life.

It was never explained to me officially, but I was told that Judge Landis had said I was banned because of the company I kept. I roomed with Claude Williams, the pitcher, one of the ringleaders, they told me, and one of the eight White Sox players banned. But I had to take whoever they assigned to room with me on the road. I had no power over that. Sure, I'd heard talk that there was something going on. I even had a fellow come to me one day and proposition me. It was on the 16th floor of a hotel and there were four other people there, two men and their wives. I told him:

"Why you cheap so-and-so! Either me or you—one of us is going out that window."

I started for him, but he ran out the door and I never saw him again. Those four people offered their testimony at my trial. Oh, there was so much talk those days, but I didn't know anything was going on.

When the talk got so bad just before the World Series with Cincinnati, I went to Mr. Charles Comiskey's room the night before the Series started and asked him to keep me out of the line-up. Mr. Comiskey was the owner of the White Sox. He refused, and I begged him: "Tell the newspapers you just suspended me for being drunk, or anything, but leave me out of the Series and then there can be no question."

Hugh Fullerton, the oldtime New York sportswriter who's dead now, was in the room and heard the whole thing. He offered to testify for me at my trial later, and he came all the way out to Chicago to do it.

I went out and played my heart out against Cincinnati. I set a record that still stands for the most hits in a Series, though it has been tied, I think. I made 13 hits, but after all the trouble came out they took one away from me. Maurice Rath went over in the hole and knocked down a hot grounder, but he couldn't make a throw on it. They scored it as a hit then, but changed it later.

I led both teams in hitting with .375. I hit the only home run of the

Series, off Hod Eller in the last game. I came all the way home from first on a single and scored the winning run in that 5–4 game. I handled 30 balls in the outfield and never made an error or allowed a man to take an extra base. I threw out five men at home and could have had three others, if bad cutoffs hadn't been made. One of them was in the second game Eddie Cicotte lost, when he made two errors in one inning. One of the errors was on a throw I made trying to cut off a run. He deflected the ball to the grandstand and the run came in.

That's my record in the Series, and I was responsible only for Joe Jackson. I positively can't say that I recall anything out of the way in the Series. I mean, anything that might have turned the tide. There was just one thing that doesn't seem quite right, now that I think back over it. Cicotte seemed to let up on a pitch to Pat Duncan, and Pat hit it over my head. Duncan didn't have enough power to hit the ball that far, particularly if Cicotte had been bearing down.

Williams was a great control pitcher and they made a lot of fuss over him walking a few men. Swede Risberg missed the bag on a double-play ball at second and they made a lot out of that. But those are things that might happen to anybody. You just can't say out and out that that was shady baseball.

There were supposed to have been a lot of big gamblers and boxers and shady characters mixed up in it. Well, I wouldn't have recognized Abe Attell if he'd been sitting next to me. Or Arnold Rothstein, either. Rothstein told them on the witness stand that he might know me if he saw me in a baseball uniform, but not in street clothes.

I guess the biggest joke of all was that story that got out about "Say it ain't so, Joe." Charley Owens of the Chicago *Daily News* was responsible for that, but there wasn't a bit of truth in it. It was supposed to have happened the day I was arrested in September of 1920, when I came out of the courtroom.

There weren't any words passed between anybody except me and a deputy sheriff. When I came out of the building this deputy asked me where I was going, and I told him to the Southside. He asked me for a ride and we got in the car together and left. There was a big crowd hanging around in front of the building, but nobody else said anything to me. It just didn't happen, that's all. Charley Owens just made up a good story and wrote it. Oh, I would have said it ain't so, all right, just like I'm saying it now.

They write a lot about what a great team the White Sox had that year. It was a good team. I won't take that away from them. But it wasn't the same kind of team Mr. Connie Mack had at Philadelphia from 1910 to 1914. I think that was the greatest team of all time. Our team didn't have but two hitters high in the .300's, Mr. Eddie Collins, as fine a man as there ever was in baseball, and me. It wasn't a hard-hitting team, not the kind they make out it was.

It was sort of a strange ball club, split up into two gangs. Collins and Chick Gandil were the two leaders. They played side by side at second and first, but they hadn't spoken to each other off the field in two seasons. Bill Gleason was the manager, but Collins ran the team out on the field. Cicotte was the best pitcher in the league, next to Walter Johnson, I guess. They called Williams the biggest and the littlest man in baseball. He had a great big neck and shoulders, but a small body. He had only been up two or three years when he was kicked out. Looked like he would have been a real fine pitcher.

They hadn't thought much about Dickie Kerr in the World Series, at least not for the sort of pitching he did. Red Faber was the relief man mostly. We had Swede Risberg at short and Buck Weaver at third, me and Hap Felsch and Nemo Leibold in the outfield, and one of the smartest catchers ever, Ray Schalk. It was a good ball club, but not like Mr. Mack's.

I'll tell you the story behind the whole thing. The trouble was in the front office. Ban Johnson, the president of the American League, had sworn he'd get even with Mr. Comiskey a few years before, and that was how he did it. It was all over some fish Mr. Comiskey had sent Mr. Johnson from his Wisconsin hunting lodge back about 1917.

Mr. Comiskey had caught two big trout and they were such beauties he sent them to Mr. Johnson. He packed the fish in ice and expressed them, but by the time they got to Chicago the ice had melted and the fish had spoiled. They smelled awful and Mr. Johnson always thought Mr. Comiskey had deliberately pulled a joke on him. He never would believe it any other way.

That fish incident was the cause of it all. When Mr. Johnson got a chance to get even with Mr. Comiskey, he did it. He was the man who ruled us ineligible. He was the man who caused the thing to go into the courts. He did everything he could against Mr. Comiskey.

I'll show you how much he had it in for him. I sued Mr. Comiskey for the salary I had coming to me under the five-year contract I had with the White Sox. When I won the verdict—I got only a little out of it—the first one I heard from was Mr. Johnson. He wired me congratulations on beating Mr. Comiskey and his son, Louis.

I have heard the story that Mr. Comiskey went to Mr. Johnson on his deathbed, held out his hand and asked that they let bygones be bygones. They say Mr. Johnson turned his head away and refused to speak to him.

I doubt if I'd have gone back into baseball, anyway, even if Judge

Landis had reinstated me after the trial. I had a good valet business down in Savannah, Georgia, with 22 people working for me, and I had to look after it. I was away from it about a year waiting for the trial. They served papers on me which ordered me not to leave Illinois. I finally opened up a little place of business at 55th and Woodlawn, across from the University of Chicago. It was a sort of pool room and sports center and I got a lot of business from the University students.

I made my home in Chicago, but I didn't follow orders completely. I sneaked out of Illinois now and then to play with semi-pro teams in Indiana and Wisconsin. I always asked my lawyer, Mr. Benedictine Short, first, and he told me to go if I could get that kind of money.

They kept delaying the trial until I personally went to the State Supreme Court judge, after which he ordered that the case be heard. They tried me and Buck Weaver together, and it took seven weeks. They used three weeks trying to get a jury, and I was on the witness stand a day and a half. After it was all over, Katie, my wife, and I went on back to Savannah, settled down there, and lived there until we came back to Greenville to bury my mother in 1935.

I have read now and then that I am one of the most tragic figures in baseball. Well, maybe that's the way some people look at it, but I don't quite see it that way myself. I guess one of the reasons I never fought my suspension any harder than I did was that I thought I had spent a pretty full life in the big leagues. I was 32 years old at the time, and I had been in the majors 13 years; I had a lifetime batting average of .356; I held the all-time throwing record for distance; and I had made pretty good salaries for those days. There wasn't much left for me in the big leagues.

All the big sportswriters seemed to enjoy writing about me as an ignorant cotton-mill boy with nothing but lint where my brain ought to be. That was all right with me. I was able to fool a lot of pitchers and managers and club owners I wouldn't have been able to fool if they'd thought I was smarter.

I guess right here is a good place for me to get the record straight on how I got to be "Shoeless Joe." I've read and heard every kind of yarn imaginable about how I got the name, but this is how it really happened:

When I was with Greenville back in 1908, we only had 12 men on the roster. I was first off a pitcher, but when I wasn't pitching I played the outfield. I played in a new pair of shoes one day and they wore big blisters on my feet. The next day we came up short of players, a couple of men hurt and one missing. Tommy Stouch—he was a sportswriter in Lancaster, Pennsylvania, the last I heard of him—was the manager, and he told me I'd just have to play, blisters or not.

I tried it with my old shoes on and just couldn't make it. He told me I'd have to play anyway, so I threw away the shoes and went to the outfield in my stockinged feet. I hadn't put out much until along about the seventh inning I hit a long triple and I turned it on. That was in Anderson, and the bleachers were close to the baselines there. As I pulled into third, some big guy stood up and hollered:

"You shoeless sonofagun, you!"

They picked it up and started calling me Shoeless Joe all around the league, and it stuck. I never played the outfield barefoot, and that was the only day I ever played in my stockinged feet, but it stuck with me.

When I started out in the majors a fellow named Hyder Barr and me reported to the Athletics in the middle of the season. We got in right close to game time one day, so we checked our bags at the station and went straight to the park. They were playing the Yankees, and I hit the first pitch Jack Warhop threw me for a double. I got a single later and had two for three.

But I didn't stick around Philadelphia long then. I went back to the station to get my bag that night, and while I was waiting for it I heard the station announcer call out: "Baltimore, Washington, Richmond, Danville, Greensboro, Charlotte, Spartanburg, Greenville, Anderson" and so on. I couldn't stand it. I went up to the window and bought a ticket to Greenville and caught that train.

Sam Kennedy came after me on the next train. He found out I'd gone from Barr. I was supposed to get Barr's bag, too. He was quite a ladies' man and he'd taken up with some girl while I went for the bags. When I didn't come back, he came after me and found out I'd gone.

That was just the first time. I went back with Sam Kennedy, after he offered me more money. But I came home three other times before that season was over. It wasn't anything I had against Mr. Mack or the ball club. Mr. Mack was a mighty fine man, and he taught me more baseball than any other manager I had. I just didn't like Philadelphia.

I was traded to Cleveland later on and I liked it there. Charley Somers, who owned the Indians, was the most generous club owner I have ever seen. We couldn't play Sunday ball in Washington then, and when we were playing the Senators over a weekend, we'd make a jump back to Cleveland for a Sunday game, then back to Washington Sunday night. There never was a time we made that jump that Charley Somers didn't come down the aisle of the train and give all the players $20 gold pieces.

He was a generous man when it came to contracts, too. The first year I came up to Cleveland, in 1910, I led the league unofficially in hitting. When I went to talk contract with him for 1911, I told him I wanted $10,000. He wasn't figuring on giving me more than $6,000, and he wouldn't listen to me.

"I'll make a deal with you," I told him. "If I hit .400 you give me $10,000. If I don't, you don't give me a cent."

It was a deal, I signed the contract, and I hit .408. But I still didn't win the American League batting title. That was the year Ty Cobb hit .420. I was hitting .420 about three weeks before the season was over and Mr. Somers called me in to pay off, told me I could sit it out the rest of the season. I told him to wait until the season was ended and I wasn't quitting. I wrote my own contract the rest of the time I was at Cleveland.

Babe Ruth used to say that he copied my batting stance, and I felt right complimented. I was a left-handed hitter, and I did have an unusual stance. I used to draw a line three inches out from the plate, from the front to the back of the plate every time I went to bat. I drew a right-angle line at the end next to the catcher and put my left foot on it exactly three inches from the plate. I kept both feet together, then took a long stride into the ball.

They say I was the greatest natural hitter of all time. Well, that's saying a lot with hitters like Wagner, Cobb, Speaker, and Ruth around. I had good eyes and I guess that was the reason I hit as well as I did. I still don't use glasses today.

I have been pretty lucky since I left the big leagues. No man who has done the things they accuse me of doing could have been as successful. Everything I touched seemed to turn to money, and I've made my share down through the years. I've been blessed with a good banker, too—my wife. Handing money to her was just like putting it in the bank. We were married in 1908 when I was just 19 and she was 15, and she has stood by me through everything. We never had any children of our own, but we raised one of my brother's boys from babyhood.

He never was interested in baseball, but they used to tell me he would have been a fine football player. He didn't get to go to college. The war came along and he went into the Navy as a flier. He was killed accidentally a couple of years ago when a gun he was cleaning went off. Katie and me felt like we'd lost our own boy.

I hadn't been able to do much work for a year until last Summer because of liver trouble. A good doctor in Greenville took my case when I thought my time was about here, and he brought me back to good health. I went back to my liquor store last July and I'm running the business now myself. I had leased it out while I was sick. I've been doing about $50,000 to $100,000 a year business.

Some people might think it's odd, but I still have a connection in baseball, sort of a judicial connection, I guess you'd call it. I am chairman of the protest board of the Western Carolina Semi-Pro League. I think that is an indication of how I stand with my own people. They have stood by me all these years, the folks from my mill country, and I love them for their loyalty.

None of the other banned White Sox have had it quite as good as I have, I understand, unless it is Williams. He is a big Christian Science Church worker out on the West Coast. Last I heard, Cicotte was working in the automobile industry in Detroit. Felsch was a bartender in Milwaukee. Risberg was working in the fruit business out in California. Buck Weaver was still in Chicago, tinkering with softball, I think. Gandil is down in Louisiana and Fred McMullin is out on the West Coast. I don't know what they're doing.

I'm 61 years old now, living quietly and happily out on my little street close to Brandon Mill. I weighed 186 and stood six feet, one inch tall in my playing days. I'm still about the same size.

There never were any other ballplayers in my family that went to the big leagues. I had five brothers, but only one, Jerry, played pro ball long. He was a pretty good minor-league pitcher, they tell me. Jerry's 48 years old now and he's one of my umpires in the Western Carolina League.

Well, that's my story. I repeat what I said when I started out—that I have no axe to grind, that I'm not asking anybody for anything. It's all water over the dam as far as I am concerned. I can say that my conscience is clear and that I'll stand on my record in that World Series. I'm not what you call a good Christian, but I believe in the Good Book, particularly where it says "what you sow, so shall you reap." I have asked the Lord for guidance before, and I am sure He gave it to me. I'm willing to let the Lord be my judge.

Tris Speaker Photo credit: National Baseball Library/Cooperstown, N.Y.

TRIS SPEAKER

. . . *The Grey Eagle*

Sport Magazine   July 1952

Tris Speaker's defensive feats will always set the standard by which centerfields are measured, **Sport** *informed DiMaggio-era fans.*

By Gordon Cobbledick

A man could tell the story of Tris Speaker, the old Grey Eagle, in a lot of different ways, but never with a tear in the eye and a catch in the voice. It isn't that kind of story. The element of heartache and tragedy is lacking. Not since, as an eight-year-old kid, he was thrown from a fractious bronco and suffered a broken right arm, has anyone referred to Tristram Speaker as "Poor Tris." And even then, in his impatience to get back to the serious business of life, he choked off the sympathy at its source by learning to throw a baseball left-handed.

The world has done all right by Tris Speaker. He knew what he wanted and he got it, with a minimum of frustration and disappointment along the way.

In a career that spanned 22 years in the American League he batted and fielded and fought and thought his way into the center of baseball's all-time outfield, flanked by Ty Cobb and Babe Ruth. His talents brought him fame and a comfortable fortune. He was well-paid in his baseball lifetime (he saw to that!) and he didn't gamble away his money like Hornsby nor drink it up like Grover Cleveland. He didn't die in the prime of life like Matty and Gehrig. He never, as Cobb did, soured on the game that made him and that he helped so greatly to make. He lives with his wife, Frances, in a fine home in one of Cleveland's better residential suburbs, drives expensive cars, dresses quietly and well, belongs to a few good clubs. Seeing him at luncheon with a group of obviously solid citizens, a stranger might identify him as a banker with a taste for the outdoors. The same stranger would guess his age in the mellow middle 50's. He is 64.

To say that Tris Speaker has a host of friends in Cleveland would not, perhaps, be strictly accurate. But most of the friends he has are of long standing and they are intensely loyal. In the main, they date back more than a quarter of a century to the days when he was playing center field and managing the Cleveland Indians.

Tris is actively engaged in the steel brokerage business, but his major interest is baseball. He serves the Indians as a sort of consulting coach. And he remains what he has been since his retirement from active play in 1928—one of the few dedicated fans to be found among the ex-ballplayers of any generation. If he ever gives out with a blast at modern baseball, which is unlikely, it will carry the weight of authority—the authority of a man who has witnessed hundreds of big-league games in the last 20 years with the eager eye of a knothole-peeping kid and the sober judgment of a lifelong student.

The life of Tris Speaker could be a dull success story if it weren't so full of drama and excitement.

The emphasis which history has placed on Speaker's attainments as a defensive outfielder—probably the greatest who ever hounded a fly ball until it became discouraged and gave up—has tended to obscure his position as one of the four or five most distinguished all-around performers in baseball. Look, for a moment, at the record:

Only two since the turn of the century (Cobb and Hornsby) have surpassed his lifetime batting average of .344. Only three others, Dan Brouthers, Willie Keeler and Ed Delahanty of an earlier era, have topped that mark. Speaker is one of the seven players who have made more than 3,000 hits in the majors, and his total of 3,515 is second only to Cobb's 4,191. In total bases, Tris trails only Cobb and Ruth. His record of 793 doubles has never been seriously challenged. Still isn't. Only Sam Crawford, Cobb and Wagner hit more triples.

He wasn't a home-run hitter, but his total of 115 was by no means substandard for his era. He held the season home-run record for a Cleveland player until Earl Averill shattered it in 1929. In sacrifices, he was second only to Eddie Collins. His 433 stolen bases put him well up among the leaders and his 1,146 bases on balls gave him fourth ranking behind Ruth, Gehrig and Collins. He struck out only 222 times in 22 seasons and 10,207 times at bat!

It has been argued in some quarters, chiefly in New York, that the time has come to revise the all-time outfield, to relegate Speaker to the mythical ball club's bench and to install Joe DiMaggio in center field. DiMaggio was great—by all odds the greatest of his day—but a comparison of the records serves only to accentuate Speaker's own greatness.

Speaker played nine more seasons than DiMaggio and took part in 1,053 more games. He scored 491 more runs and made 1,301 more hits. He hit 404 more doubles and 93 more triples and stole 361 more bases. Only in the matter of home runs does the record give the advantage to DiMaggio (351 to 115), but DiMaggio never batted against the dead ball of the pre-Ruth era. Speaker had only a few seasons against the lively ball. Fielding statistics are notoriously fallible as indicators of a player's true defensive worth, but even a generous allowance for error leaves Speaker with an impressive edge. He had a lifetime total of 461 assists. DiMaggio had 153.

Speaker has been credited with revolutionizing outfield play, but that is less than true. The word revolution suggests followers, and few outfielders were capable of following Speaker's pattern. He played the shallowest center field ever seen before or since his time. His habitual station was so close behind second base as to make him, in effect, a fifth infielder. He turned literally hundreds of singles into outs, and his second-baseman and shortstop never had to range into his territory after the shortest pop flies. And yet the longest hitters seldom succeeded in driving a ball over his head. A contemporary critic attributed to him "the greatest sense of baseball flight ever conferred on man."

Twice in one month Speaker executed unassisted double plays at second base—by collaring low line drives and outracing the retreating baserunners to the bag. At least once he figured as the pivot man in a routine infield double play. A favorite trick of his was to sneak in from short center to take a pickoff throw from the catcher and retire a runner at second. He devised and employed for many years a unique defense against a sacrifice with runners on first and second. Standard practice in such a situation is for the first-baseman to charge the plate, for the pitcher to break in and toward the third-base line, for the third-baseman to go part way in, but to be prepared to retreat to the bag to take a throw if the ball is handled by the first-baseman or pitcher, for the shortstop to cover second and the second-baseman to cover first. Speaker's defense sent the first- and third-basemen, as well as the pitcher, charging in to field the bunt. The shortstop covered third and the second-baseman covered first. Protecting second base was the Grey Eagle himself.

In later years, after Babe Ruth had demonstrated that there was gold in home runs and the jet-propelled baseball came into use, Speaker was obliged to retreat a few yards deeper into the outfield, but to the day of his retirement he still played an amazingly shallow position, still caught those low line drives that would have dropped as singles in front of any other center-fielder in the game, and still ranged deep to pull down the long flies.

"It was a matter of percentage," he explained recently. "I saw that a lot more games were being lost by singles that dropped just over the infield than by triples that were hit over the center-fielder's head. I recognized that I could save more games by cutting off some of those singles than I would lose by having an occasional triple fall behind me."

It is a matter of record that few triples ever fell behind him.

Dozens of Cleveland fans of ancient vintage still recall a catch made by Speaker in September of 1920 as perhaps the most magnificent single bit of outfielding the game has ever seen. Some say it won the pennant for the Indians.

Their perfidy in the 1919 World Series still unrevealed (although dark rumors were being heard even then), the Chicago White Sox were pressing the Indians hard. Also in contention were the New York Yankees, a mere whisker behind and fighting to win their first pennant in a league which they later were to dominate for more than 30 years. In the deciding game of three played in Cleveland's old Dunn Field, the Indians were nursing a one-run lead. The White Sox had two men on the bases with two out when Joe Jackson smashed a screaming liner, such as only Jackson could hit, toward right center. Speaker streaked toward the exit gate, timed a tremendous leap and made the catch as, with both feet off the ground, he crashed into the concrete wall. He fell and lay unconscious for several minutes, but they had to pry the ball out of his hand.

It was an inspiring play by an inspired player and leader, and it came at a moment when the Indians were badly in need of inspiration. Stunned by the tragic death of their brilliant shortstop, Ray Chapman, felled by a bean ball a short time before, they were slumping badly. Something out of the ordinary was needed to lift them up, and in that single play Speaker supplied it. They went on to win the pennant and the world championship.

As playing manager, and he was always a playing manager, his leadership was of the same order as that with which, 23 years later, another playing manager, Lou Boudreau, was to give Cleveland a pennant-winner.

For historical purposes, Speaker's big-league career divides naturally into two phases—the Boston phase, lasting nine years, and the Cleveland phase, which covered 11. There followed a season at Washington and another at Philadelphia which are not significant, although he played 141 games and batted .327 for the Senators in 1927. Wounded by an abortive scandal, he was only playing out the string after he left Cleveland, writing a graceful finish to the story. About the scandal, which Commissioner Kenesaw Mountain Landis found to be no scandal at all, more later.

But back before the Boston phase was the Texas phase.

Tristram Speaker was born in Hubbard City in eastern Texas, April 4, 1888, the only boy in a family of seven children. Thirty years later, when he had reached the pinnacle of his fame, the neighbors remembered him as a "wild" boy with a rare gift for getting into trouble and talking and smiling his way out.

"Never bad, you understand," said lumberman Wiley Johnson, "but wild. When he wasn't much more'n 12 years old, he packed a six-shooter as big as he was. Used to worry the life out of the town marshal, but I never heard of him getting into any real scrapes."

To one of his six sisters, Mrs. Pearl Scott, the kid brother's success in baseball remained a source of wonder. "Not that he wasn't always good at it," she explained, "but baseball just seemed to me to be too tame to hold him long. Why, that young one used to ride high-spirited horses without a saddle or bridle when he wasn't much more than a baby.

"I'll say this much for Tris," said Col. J. C. Mecklin, editor of the weekly Hubbard City News, "he may have been a little wild, but he wasn't a loafer. I guess he couldn't hold still long enough to loaf properly.

John Walker, who later became the proprietor of Hubbard's only drug store, was the first-baseman of the first uniformed team Speaker ever played with. "He was so small the other teams always kidded us about using a mascot in the lineup," Walker remembered, "but the kidding usually stopped about the first time he came to bat."

In Hubbard High School, Tris played football as well as baseball, but when, at 17, he enrolled at Fort Worth Polytechnic Institute. It was in the summer following his sophomore year at Polytech that Speaker was pitching for a store team in Corsicana in 1906 when Doak Roberts, owner of the Cleburne club of the North Texas League, stopped off to scout an outfielder on the same semi-pro outfit. Tris won the game, and he hit two home runs. Roberts forgot about the outfielder he had come to look at and asked Speaker how he would like to play professional baseball.

Two weeks later, Speaker met the clubowner at the railroad station in Hubbard. "I want you to join my team in Waco tomorrow," Roberts said. Here's a dollar for your railroad fare."

Speaker hopped a freight and saved the dollar.

The second morning afterward, Roberts alighted in Waco to find Mickey Coyle, his second-baseman, waiting for him at the platform. "You'd better get rid of that kid left-hander you sent up from Corsicana," Coyle announced. "He's cussed out Manager Benny Shelton and challenged everybody on the ball club to fight, including me."

Setting out to investigate, Roberts found Speaker at breakfast in the hotel. "What's the idea of insulting Shelton?" he demanded.

"Who insulted him?" Tris replied. "All I said was he was a splay-footed, butter-fingered tramp that ought to pay his way into the ball park. He booted an easy grounder that made me lose my game yesterday. And that monkey-faced second-baseman"—glaring at Coyle—"stuck his nose into it and I told him I could lick him. Which I can."

"Son," Roberts said softly, "come upstairs with me. We've got business to talk."

Their conference resulted in Speaker's agreeing to a contract to play for Cleburne for $50 a month, the only condition being that he apologize to Shelton. The manager accepted, more or less graciously. The next day he started Tris again and made him stay the full nine innings while the opposition piled up 22 runs.

"That convinced everybody, including me, that I was an outfielder if I was anything," Speaker recalled years later.

An outfielder he was and, considering his contentious beginning as a member of the Cleburne team, a remarkably peaceful one. His only fight was a one-punch affair in which he knocked a big catcher named Bill Powell through a railroad coach window.

Roberts transferred his team to Houston the next year, becoming a member of the fast Texas League. A series of exhibition games with the St. Louis Browns brought Speaker to the attention of Jim McAleer, the Browns' manager. "He isn't ready yet," McAleer told Roberts, "but I'm asking you to wire me when he is."

It was barely midseason when the wire was dispatched. "SPEAKER READY (STOP) YOU CAN HAVE HIM FOR FIFTEEN HUN-DRED."

No reply was forthcoming and Roberts tried again. "I OWN TWO HUNDRED ACRES GOOD TEXAS BLACK LAND," he telegraphed to McAleer. "WILL DEED TO YOU IF SPEAKER DOES NOT MAKE GOOD."

Still no answer.

The next day, George Huff, a scout for the Red Sox, bought Speaker's contract. The price: $800.

But here an unforseen obstacle appeared. Tris was a minor and his father's consent had to be obtained to sign the contract. Jennie Speaker sent her regrets and refused. "I've never been so insulted in my life," she said. "I will not have my boy sold like a . . . a long horn steer."

Thirteen years later, as the final out of the seventh and last game of the 1920 World Series was made, Tris fought his way through the mob that had surged out of the Dunn Field stands and overflowed the field. Straight to the field box where Jennie Speaker was seated, crying a little and beaming a lot, the manager of the world champions made his way. "This was what I meant, Mom," he said as he embraced her. "This was why I had to go away and play ball."

Speaker appeared in only seven games for the Red Sox in the fall of 1907, and his undistinguished batting average of .167 meant neither much nor little. However, it became apparent that he had made no very deep impression on Boston.

The Red Sox trained in Little Rock in 1908—a fact which wrung nothing but yawns from the Arkansas populace. A considerable deficit had been incurred, the main items of which were a hotel bill and rental for the Little Rock ball park. The Red Sox treasury was short of cash—a chronic condition with ball clubs of that day—and what could be mustered barely satisfied the innkeeper. There remained the tab for the use of the grounds.

To Mickey Finn, owner of the Little Rock club, a proposition was submitted. Would Mr. Finn accept a player in lieu of a check for the rent?"

"What player?" he asked.

"We could," said the Red Sox spokesman, "let you have that young outfielder, Speaker."

The deal was agreed to, and before a month was gone it was clear that Mickey Finn had got a bargain. Speaker was the sensation of the Southern League. He batted .350 and his defensive play rocked the Ozarks. By midseason, the scouts were swarming about the place. Finn could have sold his prize to the Giants, the Pirates, the Senators, but he felt he owed an obligation to the Red Sox, and Boston bought Speaker back for $500.

He played 31 games for the Sox in the waning season and batted only .220. But the following year he came into his own with a .309 performance. That was also the year a fleet young outfielder named Harry Hooper joined the team. In 1910, George Edward (Duffy) Lewis came up.

For six years, the Boston outfield of Speaker, Lewis and Hooper was recognized as the best in the major leagues. It still rates a mention when the great all-time outfields are under discussion. Speaker patrolled the middle reaches, Hooper roamed the spacious right field and Lewis developed a positive genius for playing Fenway's short but tricky left, with the steep hill that slanted up to meet the high board fence.

One torrid midsummer, several members of the Red Sox, Lewis among them, had their hair clipped to the scalp—ostensibly in the interest of comfort but in reality as a gag. Later, they regretted it and some, including Lewis, refused to remove their hats or caps except in the privacy of their homes. One afternoon, in full view of the several hundred early-arriving fans at Fenway, Speaker snatched the cap from Lewis' head, revealing the embarrassed Duffy in all his tonsorial nakedness. Furious, Duffy threw a bat at his tormentor and Speaker, painfully hurt, had to be carried off the field. For the rest of that season their nearest approach to conversation was an exchange of "I got it" and "Take it" in the outfield. By the following spring, They forgot their anger.

Ill feeling between Speaker and a fresh rookie named George Herman Ruth had a longer life. Tris was a veteran of five full seasons and one of the game's brightest ornaments when the brash Ruth joined the Red Sox in 1914. Speaker's bosom pal was Smokey Joe Wood, the great pitcher whose 34 victories against five defeats won a pennant and world championship for the Sox in 1912. Wood's arm was never the same after his Gargantuan labors of that season, and by the time Ruth arrived on the scene, he was no more than a so-so pitcher.

The Babe, who was never famed for his reticence, addressed a contemptuous remark to Wood and Smokey Joe invited him to fight. No blows were ever struck and the quarrel was, in any case, strictly between Ruth and Wood. But Speaker took his roommate's part and treated the Babe with icy coolness from that time forward. Although their careers overlapped by 13 years, no warmth ever appeared until they met at the dedication of the baseball Hall of Fame at Cooperstown in 1939.

By a neat bit of irony, it was Ruth who elevated Speaker to the managership of the Indians in 1919.

Spoke—he picked up that nickname early in his career in Boston—had a tremendous year in 1912, playing 153 games, batting .383 and stealing 52 bases. In the feverish World Series against the Giants the teams were tied with three victories apiece. One game, the second, had resulted in a deadlock after 11 innings. Tied, too, was the deciding game at the end of the ninth. Then the Giants scored against Joe Wood in the tenth and took a 2 –1 lead. It seemed to be all over. But Clyde Engle, a pinch-hitter who started Boston's last-ditch stand in the bottom of the overtime period, was saved when Snodgrass incredibly dropped his lazy fly. After Hooper had been retired, Steve Yerkes walked. Speaker lifted a simple foul fly between the plate and first base and Chief Meyers and Fred Merkle of the Giants meekly allowed it to fall between them. Tris then lined a single to center that scored Engle with the tying run and put Yerkes on third. A long fly by Larry Gardner did the rest.

Again in 1915, Speaker was largely instrumental in bringing a pennant to Fenway, followed by another World Series victory, this time over Philadelphia. The Phillies won the opener behind Grover Cleveland Alexander's pitching, but the Red Sox came back with four straight, the first three of them by 2–1 scores.

It was a magnificent catch by Speaker that saved the second game and perhaps prevented the Phils from taking a two-game advantage that might have changed the complexion of the whole Series.

The Red Sox went into the ninth inning nursing their slender 2–1 lead, but in a desperate attempt to tie up the game the Phillies' Dode Paskert hammered a long shot toward the centerfield seats. Speaker, caught up with the ball just as it was about to fall among the customers and made the catch as he tumbled headlong into the seats. Even Mr. Wilson lost some of his monumental dignity in his approval of the play.

Relaxing in Hubbard the following winter, Speaker was first incredulous, then angry when he ripped open an envelope bearing the stamp of the Boston American League Baseball Club. It contained a contract calling for $9,000 to be paid for his services in 1916. He had anticipated a generous increase on the basis of his work in the last two seasons. This was a replica of his 1914 and 1915 contracts.

He quickly sent Lannin his answer. He would sign a contract for $15,000 but not for a dime less. Lannin was stubborn, but so was Speaker. Caught in the middle, Bill Carrigan, the Red Sox manager, was miserably unhappy. He didn't believe he could win another pennant without Speaker and he knew his employer too well to think he could talk him into meeting Spoke's demands. Carrigan devised an ingenious compromise—or one, which, at any rate, seemed ingenious to him. He arranged with his star outfielder to train with the Red Sox at Hot Springs, Arkansas, and to travel north with them, playing in exhibitions at a fixed fee per game. It was Carrigan's rather transparent hope that if he once got Speaker into his uniform the man's lust for baseball would keep him there at any wage.

In the springtime games over the long road between Hot Springs and Boston, Speaker played in a manner to convince Lannin that he would be the bargain of the ages at $15,000.

But in the meantime, Lannin, without the knowledge of either the player or the manager, was sounding off for publication. On the Saturday before the opening of the season, a brief Associated Press story dropped on the desk of Ed Bang, sports editor of the Cleveland *News*. It quoted Lannin that he meant to trade Speaker if a suitable deal was proposed.

Grabbing a telephone, Bang called Robert McRoy, general manager of the Indians, in his office at League Park. "Bob, we can get Tris Speaker and I think we ought to do it," Bang said. "I know Lannin and I know he'll sell any player he owns if he's offered enough money."

Jim Dunn had become president of the Indians only a few weeks before and was anxious to make an impression by a spectacular deal. Late that Saturday afternoon, he talked with Lannin by telephone, but with no result beyond a promise of further discussion the following day.

Speaker knew that Lannin was in the stands at Ebbets Field in Brooklyn when he went to his position for an exhibition game with the Dodgers on Sunday. The Red Sox and Dodgers were tied going into the ninth. Speaker stepped to the plate against Rube Marquard, swung mightily and drove a home run over the right-field wall that broke up the game. Lannin was waiting for him when he entered the runway to the clubhouse.

"Great stuff, Spoke," he beamed as he threw an arm across Speaker's shoulders. "You win. We'll sign when we get to Boston tomorrow."

Hours later in his hotel room, Tris was packing for the last leg of the trip when the telephone rang. "This is Bob McRoy, general manager of the Cleveland club," the voice at the other end of the wire said "if you're not too busy I'd like to talk to you."

Speaker knew McRoy only by reputation and could think of no reason why the Cleveland executive should want to see him, but common courtesy required that he invite the other to his room. They talked baseball generalities for a few minutes. Then McRoy said: "How would you like to play for Cleveland, Tris?"

Speaker was taken aback, but he didn't have to grope for an answer. "Frankly," he said, "I wouldn't. Not in any circumstances."

McRoy asked his reasons. "You've got a bad ball club," Tris said, "and you're in a bad baseball town. Why would I want to go to Cleveland?"

McRoy hesitated before he broke the news. "I wish you didn't feel that way," he said. "We've made a deal for you. We've bought you."

Speaker protested that there must be some mistake. Lannin had assured him only that afternoon that their differences were at an end, that they would sign the contract in the morning. McRoy said yes, he knew all about it. But Dunn and Lannin had come to terms by telephone after the game.

If Doak Roberts had been there he might have recalled the evening years earlier when Jennie Speaker had refused flatly to allow her boy to be sold like—"like a longhorn steer." Her boy's face set the same stubborn lines. "I won't go," he said angrily. "I'll quit baseball first. Don't announce the deal. You'll just make yourselves look foolish."

"It's in the papers already," McRoy said. "It's the biggest deal in the history of baseball. We've paid the Red Sox $55,000, plus two players. That's big news, Tris."

The two players thrown in by Cleveland were the original Sad Sam Jones, a pitcher who was to make a fine mark in 22 American League seasons, and Freddie Thomas, a rookie infielder.

Speaker reflected. McRoy was right; it was big news. And $55,000 was a big bale.

"I'll go to Cleveland on one condition," he said. "I want $10,000 of the purchase money."

McRoy pointed out that the purchase money was Lannin's and that any deal for a split must be between Lannin and Speaker. Reached by phone, the Boston owner refused, but when Tris reassured him that unless the $10,000 was forthcoming he would catch the next train to Hubbard, Lannin agreed to the player's demand.

Speaker arrived in Cleveland on the morning of Opening Day and called Jim Dunn at once. He hadn't received Lannin's check, he said, and wasn't playing until he did. Dunn sighed and said he would pay the $10,000. But Tris was adamant. The obligation was Lannin's. Only when Ban Johnson, the president of the American League, assured Speaker that he would order the Boston owner to forward a check at once did the Grey Eagle consent to play in the opening game.

The city of Cleveland was, of course, elated over the acquisition of the man who, with the single exception of Cobb, was the greatest ballplayer in the world. The Forest City hadn't had a major baseball hero since the incomparable Frenchman, Napoleon Lajoie. There was not then and is not now another city which demands a diamond god as insistently as Cleveland.

With Lajoie's decline, the fortunes of the Indians (they were the Naps then) had hit bottom. They had suffered Cleveland's only cellar finish, in 1914, and had barely managed to climb to seventh in '15. In spite of Speaker's dazzling .336 batting, they could get no higher than sixth in his first season in Cleveland uniform. But from there on, things began to look up. They soared to third in 1917, to second in '18 and '19. It was in mid-July, 1919, that Babe Ruth promoted Speaker to the managership.

Lee Fohl was a stout, plodding, colorless man who had done a sound if unimaginative job of leading the Indians. He had welcomed Speaker as a member of the rank and file. For more than three years his tactical decisions had been, as often as not, the result of daily conferences with his able lieutenant. Their relationship had never been disturbed by any hint that Speaker was, like Caesar, ambitious.

It was inevitable, however, that the stolid Fohl should be overshadowed in the minds of press and public by the dynamic center-fielder. To the people of Cleveland, Speaker was the Indians' "big man;" Fohl was a nobody. Ruth made the status official on July 18, as the Red Sox undertook to snap a string of nine straight defeats at the hands of the Indians.

Cleveland was leading, 7–3, going into the ninth, mainly because of a base-cleaning triple by Joe Harris in the eighth. The Red Sox scored once in the ninth against Elmer Myers and had the bases loaded with two out. The batter? Who else? The mighty Babe! Ruth was poison anywhere, but in no other ball park was he a more virulent dose than in Dunn Field with its right-field foul line only 290 feet away from the plate. Three pitchers were warming up in the Cleveland bullpen. Two were right-handers, one a southpaw, Fritz Coumbe.

Fohl looked to center field and Speaker raised his right arm. Fohl hesitated momentarily and then, as if asking himself "Who's managing this ball club, anyhow?" signaled to the bullpen with his left hand for Coumbe. Speaker shouted one anguished "No!" from the outfield, then shrugged and took his station in deep right center. Not even the Grey Eagle played shallow with Ruth at bat.

Coumbe completed his warmup and pitched to the Babe, a curve ball waist-high over the center of the plate. Ruth swung and missed, but catcher Steve O'Neill called time and went into an earnest conference with his pitcher. "Don't," he begged, "throw another one like that. Keep it low and away. Walk him if you have to. Force in the run. But don't give him another one like that!"

Coumbe nodded. He pitched again. It was a duplicate of his first curve, waist-high and over the middle. Some witnesses say the ball cleared the low frame buildings on the far side of Lexington Avenue and skulled a taxpayer puttering in his backyard garden. Ruth romped around the bases behind three teammates and the Red Sox won, 8–7.

Fohl hurried through his post-game toilet and disappeared. Speaker, as was his custom, dressed slowly. Only a few straggling players were around when the clubhouse boy brought a message. "Mr. Dunn wants to see you upstairs," he said.

"Fohl has resigned, Tris," were Dunn's first words. "I want you to take over as manager."

Spoke considered briefly. "I'd rather not. I'd rather play under Fohl."

"There's no question of playing under Fohl. He doesn't work here anymore. He's quit. It's you or somebody else. I want it to be you."

Again Tris thought it over. "I want it to come from Lee," he said, finally. "If he asks me to take the job, I'll do it. But I don't want him or anybody else to think I applied for it."

Fohl, reached by telephone, confirmed Dunn's story. He hoped Speaker would succeed him. He wished Speaker luck.

The Indians were in third place, five and a half lengths behind the White Sox, one behind the Yankees. Under Speaker's leadership, they won 40 games, lost 22 and finished second, three and a half games behind Chicago.

With the cares of the managership on his shoulders, Speaker slumped at bat and wound up the season with his first (and until 1928, his only) sub-.300 average. It was .296. But it was the last time his play ever was noticeably affected by his added responsibilities. He bounced back with a mighty .388 to lead the Indians to the pennant the next year and followed it in successive seasons with .362, .378, .380, .344 and .389.

Speaker had recommended trades which brought two former Red Sox teammates to Cleveland. Smokey Joe Wood had lost his smoke, but he was a hard hitter and became a successful outfielder for the Indians. Larry Gardner gave Cleveland four fine years at third base. In the Gardner deal, the Indians got Charley Jamieson, a 26-year-old outfielder. He played 17 years for Cleveland and batted .304 in that time. It was Speaker's idea to insist on his inclusion in the trade for Gardner.

A few days after he became manager, Tris began negotiations for another player who made Cleveland history, Ray (Slim) Caldwell, a right-handed pitcher with a well-earned reputation as a drinker and an all-around headache to managers. Caldwell had pitched nine years for the Yankees, and pitched well, but Miller Huggins, despairing of keeping him sober and fearful of the effect of his dissipation on the habits of the other players, had sent him to Boston in 1919. The Red Sox learned quickly that they had acquired a handful; they gave Caldwell his outright release. Speaker sent for him, handed him a contract and said, "Read it." Caldwell glanced at the salary figures and his face lighted.

"Gimme a pen," he said eagerly, but Speaker demurred.

"I told you to read it. Read it all."

Caldwell read. It was probably the most unusual document baseball has known. It stipulated that Caldwell was to get drunk after each game he pitched and was not to show up at the ball park the next day. On the second day, he was to report to Speaker early and run around the park as many times as the manager ordered. The third day, he was to be available to pitch batting practice. The fourth day, he was to pitch another championship game.

"The contract means what it says, Slim," Speaker assured him. "If you want to sign at those terms, you've got a job. Otherwise, I don't want you."

In the last ten weeks of the 1919 season, Caldwell won seven games for the Indians. Among them was a no-hitter over the Yankees. To say that he became a model of deportment would be to exaggerate, but it was noted early in his career in Cleveland that the contractual obligation to get blotto seemed to have taken much of the fun out of it. At no time was he a serious "handling" problem for Speaker. And he was a 20-game winner in 1920, an ace of the mound staff that included Jim Bagby, Sr., who won 31, and Stan Coveleskie, who contributed 24 victories.

If Tris didn't invent the right-left batting shift, he played it for all it was worth, and perhaps more, in driving the Indians to their first pennant. Against right-handed pitchers he played Wheeler (Doc) Johnston at first base, Elmer Smith in right and Charley Jamieson or Jack Graney in left. When a southpaw was pitching for the opposition, it was George Burns at first, Joe Wood in right and Joe Evans in left. Speaker was the only left-handed hitter who played against left-handed pitchers. He is still of the opinion that southpaws are more difficult than right-handers for nine out of ten batsmen who swing from the first-base side of the plate.

In 1921, H. G. Salsinger wrote in the Detroit *News:* "Should Tris ever hear of a player that can hit left- and right-handed pitchers, he will refuse to sign him, for a bird like that would wreck the Speaker system.

"Speaker is now looking for a second trainer. This guy Percy Smallwood, who is doing the work now, is a right-hander and he does very well with the left-handers on the club, but the right-handed players are suffering and Speaker will have to get a left-handed trainer for them.

Right or left, the 1920 Indians were no team of super-stars. They had three first-rate pitchers in Bagby, Coveleskie and Caldwell and one of the game's best catchers in the sturdy, combative Steve O'Neill. And they had Tris Speaker. The rest were only fair—on paper. But for that one season, they rose to superb heights.

Speaker was an enormously popular leader. Not only did he set an inspiring example by his own performance, but he was proving himself a warm and understanding handler of the varied temperaments, dispositions and talents under his command. There was never any doubt among the players that instructions from him were orders to be obeyed, but he didn't place himself on a pedestal. While the ball game was in progress, he was the boss. When it was over, he was one of the gang. On the road, he roomed with one of the players, usually Wood or Les Nunamaker, another former Boston teammate.

His system passed the one supreme test. It worked.

The Indians broke to the front in late April and, except for two days in May and four in July, stayed there until mid-August. Then tragedy struck. It was on August 16 that Ray Chapman, a brilliant if sometimes erratic shortstop, a strong hitter, a fast and daring baserunner and one of the best bunters the game has ever seen, was struck on the left temple by a ball pitched by the Yankees' Carl Mays in the Polo Grounds. He died early the next morning without regaining consciousness.

Grief-stricken, the Indians seemed to lose interest in the pennant race. Speaker, who was one of Chappie's closest friends, could rally neither himself nor his team. Four days after Chapman's death they suffered a double shutout at the skilled hands of Waite Hoyt and Herb Pennock in Boston and surrendered first place to the White Sox. Tris badgered the front office for help. "Get me someone. Get me anyone who wasn't here when Chappie got it. Get me that big Mails from Portland," he pleaded.

Walter (Duster) Mails was a left-handed pitcher who had failed with

Brooklyn three years before. But he had tremendous natural ability and Speaker hoped he would not only help the three-man pitching staff in the home stretch but perhaps supply the lift that was so badly needed. He did both. The Indians were three and a half games behind the White Sox when he joined the team—and fading fast. A week later, they were back on top. Another fortnight, which took the race to the middle of September, found them a game and a half behind the Yankees. Two days later, they were tied. It was that kind of race.

Mails won seven straight victories without a loss and the final standings showed Cleveland on top, with the White Sox two games behind and the Yankees three.

The city lost its mind. The war over and prosperity in sight, there was nothing more important in the world.

The World Series was anticlimactic. The Indians won the opener in Brooklyn, dropped the next two, but came home to take four straight in the best-of-nine Series. Speaker batted .320 in the seven games. Elmer Smith hit the first grandslam home run in World Series annals. Bill Wambsganss executed an unassisted triple play.

It was the Grey Eagle's first and last championship as a manager. The Indians were generally picked to repeat in 1921, but a series of accidents, culminating in a knee injury that kept Speaker out of the lineup the last three weeks, cost them their chance. They finished second, four and a half games behind the Yankees, who won their first pennant.

In 1922, they fell to fourth and climbed one notch in '23. Then came two successive sixth-place finishes. Despite his advancing age (he was 37 in 1925), Tris showed little sign of slipping. A step slower, perhaps, but still unsurpassed as an outfielder, he was hitting better than ever. His .389 in 1925 was the high mark of his career. But his teammates had grown old around him—and on them it showed.

Still, they had one last try for all the marbles in 1926. In a thrilling stretch run, they came within a game of catching the Yankees but couldn't maintain the pace and fell out of contention in the final two weeks.

Speaker was tired. Too much of a realist not to know that his days in baseball as an active player were numbered, he was looking for a chance to invest his considerable savings in some business venture.

Ty Cobb resigned without explanation as manager of the Tigers on November 2, 1926. Exactly a month later, Speaker quit as manager of the Indians. Coming as it did on the heels of Cobb's resignation, it set tongues wagging. Baseball was still scandal-minded as the result of the World Series sellout by the Black Sox, and the stern figure of Commissioner Landis towered in Chicago as a reminder that the game must be and was well-policed. Rumors that Cobb and Speaker were being forced out of baseball began to circulate.

Shortly after Speaker's resignation, E. S. Barnard, then president of the Cleveland club, received a call from Ban Johnson. The league president said he had information that Cobb, Speaker, Joe Wood and Hubert (Dutch) Leonard, a former pitcher for the Tigers, had bet on a Cleveland-Detroit game in 1919. Barnard questioned Tris, who denied any knowledge of the charge.

"But I want to know about it," he said. "And I'm going to find out about it."

He found out soon enough.

Leonard, not to be confused with the Emil (Dutch) Leonard now with the Chicago Cubs, had written the details of the alleged betting plot to Johnson, enclosing two letters which he, Leonard, had received seven years earlier—one from Wood, one from Cobb. Leonard charged that the four men had "happened to get together under the stands three days before the end of the season." Cleveland had clinched second place and Detroit was fighting the Yankees for third place. It was a chance to pick up some soft money.

The four conspirators agreed, according to Leonard, to put up several hundred dollars each. A clubhouse attendant named Fred West was to have placed the bets, but succeeded in "getting up" only a small fraction of the money. The inference, although it was not so directly charged, was that Speaker was to allow the Tigers to win the game in question. They did win it, 9–5, and Leonard exhibited a letter from Wood by way of substantiation of his story.

"Dear Friend Dutch (it read in part): The only bet West could get up was $600 against $420 (10 to 7). Cobb did not get up a cent. He told us that and I believe him. Could have put up some at 5 to 2 on Detroit but did not as that would make us put up $1,000 to win $400. We won the $420. I gave West $30, leaving $390, or $130 for each of us."

The letter from Cobb to Leonard was more guarded. "Wood and myself," Ty wrote, "are considerably disappointed in our business proposition."

No reference to Speaker's participation appeared in either the Wood letter or the Cobb letter. Landis had only Leonard's unsupported word that the Grey Eagle was in on the plot. In the eyes of the commissioner, Leonard's flat refusal to face the other three weakened the case for the prosecution.

Thus far, Landis' investigation had been conducted in secrecy, but Cobb brought it out in the open when, angered at being detained in Chicago at the commissioner's order while Leonard stalled in California, he called the Chicago newspapers and broke the whole story.

"If what Leonard says is true," he asked, "would we have stopped for a few moments under the stands to arrange so important a matter?"

He charged that the American League had paid Leonard $20,000 for the letters.

On January 17, 1927, Landis handed down his decision: "This is the Cobb-Speaker case. These players have not been, nor are they now, found guilty of fixing a ball game. By no decent system of justice could such a finding be made . . ."

Landis made one stipulation: the two great stars must stay in the American League. Although he did not explain his decree, it was freely guessed that his purpose was two-fold. To allow the players to go to the National League might be interpreted as evidence that the American was convinced of their guilt and no longer wanted them. And it would have the appearance of a victory for Ban Johnson, the commissioner's avowed enemy and no admirer of Cobb.

Speaker went to Washington for the 1927 season, played 141 games in the outfield and at first base and batted .327. The following year, he joined Cobb in Philadelphia, Tris batted only .267. The Grey Eagle was grounded at last.

A year as manager at Newark and a brief whirl at Kansas City convinced him that wasn't his dish. It was the major leagues or nothing. He took on a radio job in Chicago, broadcasting and interpreting baseball. But Cleveland was his home; there were some attractive opportunities there, and he returned. In 1934 he went into the wholesale liquor business with an old Cleveland friend, Dave R. Jones. Later he became the Cleveland representative of a Detroit steel firm, and prospered. But he was never, in his heart, far away from baseball. In 1947, Bill Veeck, then president of the Cleveland club, signed the American League's first Negro player, second-baseman Larry Doby of the Newark Eagles. When it was decided the next Spring that Doby's speed belonged in the outfield, Veeck invited baseball's greatest outfielder to serve as his tutor. Spoke accepted eagerly and that Fall the man from Texas beamed with pride while his pupil starred in center field as the Indians defeated the Boston Braves in the World Series. Ever since, he has been a fixture as a coach in the Indians' spring training camp and at the collective farm-club base in Daytona Beach.

It's like the man said more than 30 years ago: He can't hold still long enough to loaf properly.

WALTER JOHNSON

The Big Train

Sport Magazine   January 1950

Here, long-time Washington, D.C. sports columnist and editor, Shirley Povich, commemorates one of the city's and baseball's most legendary and classy athletes.

By Shirley Povich

Legend couldn't wait on the death of Walter Perry Johnson, as properly it was supposed to do. Even while he lived, he was a fabled figure of the pitching mound, for so fanciful were his feats, so all-fired fast was his fast ball, that only by over-drawing the tales of Johnson's speed could the man be put in proper perspective, even in contemporary times . . .

Ray Chapman was the hitter for the Cleveland Indians on a day in 1915. First one, then another blurred streak of white hissed past Chapman's cocked but motionless bat and pounded into the mitt of catcher Eddie Ainsmith.

"Strike two!" intoned Umpire Billy Evans.

Suddenly, Chapman tossed his bat away and started toward the Cleveland bench. "That's only strike two!" yelled Evans.

Chapman didn't even break stride as he said to Evans over his shoulder, "I know it. You can have the next one. It won't do me any good."

Since that August day in 1907 when the 19-year-old Johnson with the dangling arms and the behind-the-plow gait first walked into the major-league baseball scene, it has been a mark of distinction in Washington to be able to boast, "I saw Johnson pitch his first game." The man who could say that said it proudly, as if he were in on the beginning of time. Honest guys, who wouldn't bandy the truth otherwise, found an irresistible urge to hop on the "I was there" bandwagon. It still is heard and still ranks as the most common lie in Washington, the nation's capital. That was proved a few years ago when the Washington Baseball Club invited all who had seen Johnson pitch his first game for the Senators to sit in a special section. More than 8,000 fans declared themselves eligible, overflowing the reserved seats. Slightly skeptical, I delved into the Washington club's yellowing records for that season of 1907. On the day of Johnson's maiden start, the books showed that exactly 2,841 fans were in the park. However, for all the phonies, there was a wonderful lack of conclusive guilt.

Even the late Ring Lardner succumbed to the furore over Johnson and the speed with which he threw a baseball. In thinly disguised fashion, he hauled Johnson into his script when he wrote "Horseshoes," and quoted his fictional rookie like this: *They can't tell me he throws them balls with his arm. He's got a gun concealed on his person and he shoots 'em up there. I was leading off in Murphy's place, and I just tried to meet the first one and stuck out my bat. When I did, Henry (a John Henry caught for Washington) was throwing the pill back to Johnson. Then I thought maybe if I start swinging now at the second one, I'll hit the third one . . ."*

There he was, a giant of a fellow whose pitching weight was an even 200 pounds, and who towered an inch over six feet. But it was those arms that hung nearly to his knees that gave him the leverage, coordinated with all the wonderfully rhythmic power of his massive frame. If Willie Keeler gave baseball its famous "Hit 'em where they ain't," then Johnson was responsible for an expression equally memorable. It was Ping Bodie who took three Johnson strikes with his bat on his shoulder and returned to the Yankee dugout to moan: "You can't hit what you can't see!"

The reverence in which the Big Train was held was typified one day by Edward T. Folliard, Pulitzer prize winner of the Washington *Post* and historian of virtually all important national and international events of the past 20 years. Speaking before a brilliant assemblage in the National Press Club, Folliard was introduced as a famous war correspondent, an on-the-spot reporter at White House conferences when history was made, and an authority on national affairs. When asked what was his greatest thrill, he said unhesitatingly: "That was the day when I covered Walter Johnson's attempt to throw a silver dollar across the Rappahannock River, as George Washington had done. As a small boy in Washington, I was a Johnson fan. That day, when Johnson threw the dollar across the Rappahannock, I got my greatest thrill. You see, I was the fellow who held Walter Johnson's coat."

Where do you begin to relate what records fell to the fast ball of Johnson? Do you start with those most games won—413 in 21 seasons with the Senators? Or do you like better the fact that he pitched the most games in the American League—803? Maybe it was his 1913 performance of allowing only 1.09 earned runs per game. There's a wide choice of Johnson records. How about 1912, when he won 16 in a row to tie the record? Or those 56 consecutive innings when he didn't allow any kind of run, in 1913?

The man is proud who can boast a single major-league pitching record. Johnson achieved them wholesale. We go on: The most men struck out in the majors, 3,497; the most innings pitched, 5,925; the most games started, 666; the most complete games, 531; the most complete games pitched in the league for seven years in a row, 1910–16 inclusive; the most shutouts in three different seasons, tied for the most in four others; led the league's pitchers in fielding, three times.

He lies now in Rockville, Maryland, not far from the lush green hills of his Germantown farm, the victim of a tumor that struck him down on December 10, 1946.

Ty Cobb, during the last World Series, revealed how only by taking advantage of the nature of the man, could he even get a single off Johnson . . . "and it was useless to try for anything more than a single. You had to poke and try to meet the ball. If you swung, you were dead . . . I had to figure Johnson out. I realized quickly that he wasn't a vicious pitcher, despite all that speed. I saw him wince when he fired one close to somebody's head, and he used to tell me that he was afraid some day that he would kill a man with that fireball. So I used to cheat. I'd crowd that plate so far that I was actually sticking my toes on it when I was facing Johnson. I knew he was timid about hitting a batter, and when he saw me crowding the plate, he'd steer his pitches a little bit wide. Then, with two balls and no strikes, he'd ease up a bit to get it over. That's the Johnson pitch I hit. I was depending on him to be scared of hitting me."

The Washington club stumbled across Johnson 42 seasons back. A self-appointed scout, a fan, bombarded manager Joe Cantillon in 1907 with tall tales of the prowess of a young semi-pro. Cantillon put it down to the over-exuberance of a mere fan and paid little heed to the letters that told of the boy's feats. But still they came, and finally Cantillon succumbed when he read: "This boy throws so fast you can't see 'em . . . and he knows where he is throwing the ball because if he didn't there would be dead bodies strewn all over Idaho . . ."

Cantillon took the long chance and dispatched a crippled catcher, Cliff Blankenship, to Idaho to look Johnson over.

Blankenship's first look at Johnson was an eyefiller. He saw the big country boy lose a ball game, but it was 1–0, and two booted ground balls beat
him in the 12th. At the end of the game, he sought out Johnson to talk
business. To impress the pitcher, he flashed a $100 bill as a cash bonus
for signing and guaranteed him $350 a month for the rest of the season if
he would join the Washington club. He found Johnson eager but at the
same time cautious. How about traveling expenses to Washington? Yep,
said Blankenship, he'd pay that, too. Satisfied on that point, the boy took
the proposition to his Dad and got an okay. Blankenship had Johnson's
contract the next day on a piece of brown wrapping paper, but not without one more formality. He had to guarantee Johnson a return train
ticket if he failed to make good. His Dad had thought of it, Walter
explained.

   Blankenship hadn't acted any too soon. En route to Weiser that very
day was a scout from the Seattle club, owned by D. E. Dugdale, with
emphatic instructions to sign young Johnson and bring him back to Seattle "even if it costs us a $1,000 bonus."

   With Johnson under contract, Blankenship wired Cantillon in New
York: "Signed Johnson today. Fastest pitcher since Amos Rusie." The
dispatch to the Washington *Star* read: "New York, June 29—Manager
Joe Cantillon has added a great baseball phenom to his pitching staff.
The young man's name is Walter Johnson. Johnson pitched 75 innings in
the Idaho State League without allowing a run, and had a wonderful
strikeout record of 166 in 11 games, or more than 15 strikeouts per game.
Blankenship is very enthusiastic, but fails to state whether the great phenom is right or left-handed."

   When Cantillon did unveil Johnson, he picked no soft spot for the youngster. He sent the gangling recruit against the Detroit Tigers, the slug-
gingest team in the league, in the first game of a doubleheader on August
2, 1907. Washington fans already were buzzing at the build-up given the
19-year-old farmboy with the fast ball that sang. The Tigers, too, had
been hearing about Johnson. They watched him warm up, and gasped—
but in bewilderment, not in awe. Why, the kid was throwing side-arm,
almost underhanded. That wasn't what fastballers were made of.

   Then Johnson took the mound and that long right arm began to spurt
white horsehide comets, and now the Tigers *were* impressed. Sam Crawford did tag one pitch for a home run, but Ty Cobb was finding it expedi-
ent to try to bunt his way on base.

   Walter Johnson, in later years, was to lead all the league's pitchers in
fielding skill, but on that day of his major-league debut he was without
fielding grace. Cobb laid one bunt down and beat it out against the crude-

fielding rookie. On another bunt that followed, Cobb scrambled all the way to third. Eventually, he scored, and the Tigers led, 2–1.

Johnson went out in the eighth inning for a pinch-hitter, and the game wound up in a 3–2 defeat for Washington. But the boy was on his way to fame. Cobb recalled, "I knew that day that here was a fellow who couldn't miss being a great pitcher. I asked the Detroit club to buy him, even if they had to offer Washington $25,000. They just stared at me."

Even in defeat, Johnson was tabbed as a sensation. "In two years, he'll be greater than Mathewson," declared Detroit manager Hughey Jennings. For the latter-day baseball historian, who identifies Walter Johnson as the symbol of fastball pitching, there is a shock, however, in the yellowing newspaper files of 1907, which also quote Jennings as saying to Cantillon: "If I were you, Joe, I'd tell that big green kid of yours to quit fooling around with that spit-ball he was trying to use against us. He doesn't need anything but that wonderful speed he showed us. All spit-ballers except Ed Walsh are in-and-outers who throw their arms away." It is the only known reference to Walter Johnson as a spit-baller.

In his second start for the Senators, Johnson was a winner. Significantly, it was written in the morning newspaper that "Johnson's speed was so terrific, several Cleveland players acted as though they took no particular delight in being at the plate." It was the forerunner of later, admitted confessions of fright by men who faced him.

Johnson's third start for the Senators was a defeat—one of the many cruel 1–0 beatings he was to take in the hire of a club that could give him little support either at bat or in the field. He held the Browns to six hits but lost the game when second-baseman George Nill failed to cover second base and Johnson's throw to the bag went into center field. Johnson figured in 59 of those 1–0 pitching gems, and 40 times he was the winner.

Who was this fellow Johnson, anyway? Humboldt, Kansas, claims him, and rightfully, because he was born there on November 6, 1887, to Frank Edwin and Minnie Johnson, farmer folks whose forebears had gone West with the wagon trains from Pennsylvania, and later moved to California.

At 14, young Walter was already man-sized in the pattern of his broad-shouldered father, and baseball talk was first being heard around the Johnson household. Walt was playing with the Oil Field Juniors. He was the catcher. But the kids were talking not so much of his catching as of the bullets he was throwing to the bases when guys were trying to steal.

At Fullerton Union High School in Olinda, young Johnson took one look at the school's pitchers and modestly allowed as how he could do better. He pitched, but the school had no catcher who could hold him. In 1906, he accepted a tryout with the Tacoma, Washington, team of the Northwestern League. The company was too fast for the 16-year-old kid and they cut him loose. But by now, Walt was determined that he could make a living at baseball. An offer came. He would get $75 a month for the combined jobs of pitching for the team and digging post-holes for the Weiser Telephone Company. That's where Cliff Blankenship found him the next June.

In his first five years with the Senators, Johnson was pitching for a ball club that always finished seventh, or worse. Yet in that time he won the admirable total of 80 games. On a week-end in early September, 1908, his second year in the majors, Johnson's fame was solidly launched. He pitched three shutouts against the New York Yankees (then called the Highlanders) in four days!

On September 4, he mowed them down with four hits in a 3–0 shutout. They probably gasped a bit the next day, Saturday, at their 168th Street and Broadway park, when they saw Johnson taking a pre-game warmup with no other Washington pitcher in sight. Sure enough, it was Johnson pitching for the second straight day. The tireless 20-year-old blanked them again, this time with a three-hitter to turn in a 6–0 victory.

The next day was Sunday—no baseball in New York. The Yankees must have been startled, however, to read in the Monday morning papers that manager Cantillon was hinting a third successive start by Johnson. "He's kidding," said the Yankees. Johnson thought so, too.

That Monday program was to be a double-header. Before the first game, Johnson was playing what he presumed to be a game of catch with Gabby Street, the newly acquired catcher of the Senators. Then he was aware that he was the only Washington pitcher warming up. All the others had returned to the dugout. Cantillon was giving him the go-ahead sign. It was all right with Walter. He quickened the pace of his warm-up, and then it happened . . . his third straight shutout of the Yanks. He won it, 4–0. This time, he gave up only two hits.

For that kind of pitching, the Washington club was paying the great Johnson a salary of $2,700 a season!

Washington got its first look at The Big Train as an opening-game pitcher on April 14, 1910. That was to become an historic date, and not only because for the first time a President of the United States threw out the first ball. Johnson created another "first"—the first of the seven shut-outs he was to turn in as a pitcher in 14 opening games. He beat the Athletics and Eddie Plank that day, 3–0. Frank Baker got a hit off Johnson and that was all for the A's.

Sixteen years later, at 39, Walter pitched his last opening game for the Senators. That was on April 13, 1926. He hooked up with Eddie Rommel of the Athletics in a pitching duel that lasted 15 innings. At the finish, it was Johnson the winner over Rommel, 1–0.

But back in 1909, there was the brief suspicion that Johnson, for all his three straight shutouts over the Yankees the season before, was just a flash in the pan. He couldn't win consistently, and was battered for defeats. The same hitters he had terrified were making free with him. In one game, he set a record of forty wild pitches. The great Johnson was an apparent flop. Actually, he was a sick man, dogged all season by a fever that first gripped him in Spring training at Galveston, Texas.

In 1910, though, Johnson was back in form. He exchanged those 25 defeats of the year before for 25 victories and led the league with his 313 strikeouts. He was winning his games for a seventh-place club with a team batting average of .236.

Even before the 1911 season started, Johnson made front-page headlines. The big, amiable fellow who had been paid $4,500 a season for winning those 25 games in 1910, was now a holdout, refusing to report for Spring training at Atlanta. Manager Jimmy McAlee, who had succeeded Cantillon, was frantic. Johnson was demanding the fabulous salary of $9,000 a year. "Just as much as Ty Cobb gets," said The Big Train in a sudden burst of stubbornness and a new evaluation of himself. The frantic McAleer asked the club president, Thomas Noyes, to come down to Atlanta and negotiate with Johnson. Noyes refused and told McAleer to offer him $6,500 a season if he'd sign a three-year contract.

At that news, Johnson bolted camp and declared he would quit the game and join his father at their Coffeyville, Kansas, poultry farm. He did, too. Washington fans fell upon Noyes in furious indignation, accusing him of being a tightwad. Noyes' defense was: "No other American League pitcher is earning as much as the $6,500 offer Johnson is turning down."

Johnson's stay in Coffeyville lasted only 30 hours. Sheepishly, he joined the team in Washington and accepted a contract for $7,000. Two days after the 1911 season opened, he was making new pitching history of the Walter Johnson kind. He struck out four Red Sox in the same inning, yet was scored on! A dropped third strike, a steal of second, and a double by Tris Speaker made this neat trick possible.

Clark Griffith moved in as the Washington manager in 1912, and the effect was almost magical. The Senators bolted out of the second division, won 16 games in a row, threatened to win the pennant, and finished second to the Red Sox to gain the highest position in their history. Johnson won 32 games, lost only 12.

The Big Train was all but invincible. In fact, from July 3 to August 23, he *was* invincible. During that period, he reeled off 16 consecutive victories to break Jack Chesbro's record of 14 in a row. His streak ended in St. Louis, always claimed by Johnson to be his jinx city. Defeat finally came to him as a relief pitcher. He moved in to relieve Tom Hughes in the eighth with the score tied at 2–2, one out, and men on first and second. He fanned Burt Shotton for the second out, but Compton got a hit that brought home the runs that won for the Browns, 4–2.

Washington screamed that Johnson was unfairly charged with the defeat, but American League president Ban Johnson himself made the ruling that Walter was the losing pitcher. National League president John Heydler agreed that in his league, Johnson would not be charged with the loss, which would go to Hughes, but Johnson was adamant.

Johnson threw the only bean-ball pitch of his life in a series against the A's in 1912. It wasn't his own idea. He always carried with him the dread fear that some day one of his pitches might kill a batter, and he winced at the near-hits. But this day he was being goaded by Mike Martin, the Senators' trainer, who challenged Walter to knock down Frank (Home Run) Baker. "That Baker has been ruining us all season," Martin protested. "If you don't knock him down. I'll always think you've got no guts!"

To that, The Big Train succumbed. He steeled himself for it, the next time Baker was up. The wide sweep of the Johnson delivery turned loose a high, hard one, inside, that barely missed Baker's skull and sent him floundering and pale into the dirt. Johnson, white with terror, was the first to reach him.

Recalling that one in later years, Johnson would say, "The moment I threw the pitch, I wished I had it back."

The Johnson control, good from the moment he walked into the majors, and the Johnson fear of hitting a man were the only comforts of the batters who faced him. On the few occasions when he did hit a batter, panic swept the park.

There was the day in Washington when Johnson hit Eddie Collins on the leg with a fast ball. Even getting hit on the leg by The Big Train could be tragic. Collins went down and his teammates raced to him. Johnson was off the mound in a flash to help Collins up. He not only helped Eddie to his feet, but supported him on the way to first base when it was learned that Collins would stay in the game. On first, Collins called time. The leg was still hurting him. He tested it out again in what appeared to be a pitiful limp. From the mound, Johnson watched apologetically. The umpires said, "Play ball!" Johnson sadly returned to his work and on his first, lazy pitch, the joker Collins stole second with ease.

The Big Train's 1913 contribution to Washington was a total of 36 victories, only seven defeats, and an earned run average of 1.09 per game! An even 12 shut-outs! An average of less than one walk per game! A new major-league record of 56 consecutive scoreless innings! The exclamation points fairly leaped out of his performances. The guy was super. Five one-hitters! Different winning streaks of 10, 11 and 14 games in the same season!

Those 56 scoreless innings in a row—they were something. The Yankees scored on him in the first inning on April 10. He blanked them after that and won his game, 2–1. A couple of days later, he whitewashed the Yanks, 4–0, on four hits. Four days after that, he subjected Boston to a two-hit, 6–0 shutout. There was a scoreless one-inning relief shift against Boston before his next start. And then he took the Athletics, 2–0, on four hits. He tacked on a two and two-thirds inning relief job against Boston, and two days later another five-inning shutout effort in relief against the same team. Against Chicago, he turned in a classic 1–0 two-hitter, and needed only one more scoreless inning to surpass Jack Coombs' record of 53 in a row.

The Big Train whistled right past the record with a couple of innings to spare. He did it sensationally, at St. Louis, striking out six of the first nine Browns he faced. And then, in his jinx town, the streak ended when Gus Williams doubled and Derril Pratt singled to get a run home.

For that kind of pitching, the Washington club now was paying Johnson $12,000 a year. But between the 1913–'14 seasons, the nation's capital was suddenly shocked. From Johnson's Winter home, came the flash: Johnson had jumped to the Federal League!

Unbelievably, it was confirmed. Joe Tinker, agent for the new Federal League, had Johnson's signature on a contract that gave his services to the Chicago North Side Club of the new league. Johnson had accepted a $16,000 salary and a $10,000 bonus for signing which had already been paid over. For Griffith, perhaps it was retribution. As an organizer of the American League in 1901, he had pirated players in exactly the same way. But he swung into action quickly.

Griffith demanded that Ben Minor, the new president of the Senators, give him the authority to match the Federal League's offer and reclaim Johnson.

Minor had complicated Griffith's position by denying a salary raise to Johnson. Against Clark's advice, he had written a letter to Johnson refusing to increase his $12,000 salary on the grounds, "You had a poor season in 1914, but we are not cutting your salary." Because Johnson won "only" 28 games, 10 of which were shutouts, they called it a "poor" season. As Griffith rightly guessed, Johnson was hopping mad. He listened to the Feds' offer, and accepted.

Griffith turned to an old friend, Fred Clarke, the former Pittsburgh outfielder, who lived at Independence, Kansas, not far from Coffeyville. He asked Clarke to arrange a meeting for him with Johnson at the

Coates House in Kansas City, on a date agreeable to Walter. Clarke arranged it and they met, but Johnson wouldn't melt. However, Mrs. Johnson was with him and Griffith knew that she preferred to live in Washington. So he asked her to "take a walk for an hour while Walter and I thresh this thing out." When she returned, Johnson was safely back in the fold with the Washington club.

Griffith re-won him with a $16,000 salary that matched the Feds' contract, but in the bargain was his offer to let Johnson keep the $10,000 bonus he had already received and donated to help prop up his brother Earl's failing automobile business in California. Griffith said he would make restitution to Tinker.

But the Washington manager had exceeded his authority with those arrangements. Where was he to get the $10,000 bonus money? Not from Ben Minor, Griffith knew. He had an idea where it would come from. He telephoned Ban Johnson at Chicago, learned that Johnson was vacationing with White Sox owner Charles Comiskey at West Baden, Indiana, and phoned Johnson there. Griffith explained his predicament and asked for $10,000 from the league funds to pay off The Big Train and save baseball in Washington. When Ban Johnson expressed no interest, Griffith railed about "all that money you call the American League's fighting fund. This is the time to spend it!" When Johnson turned him down, Griffith put in another call, for Comiskey.

"You have a problem as well as I," he told Comiskey. The White Sox owner said he didn't understand why he should provide Griff with $10,000 to reclaim a jumping ballplayer.

"Oh, yes you'll understand," said Griffith. "You just bought Eddie Collins, didn't you? And that new Fed club on the North Side will get Walter Johnson and make it tough competition for you, won't it? Well, then, come across with the $10,000 or we'll both sink!"

Comiskey put up the money that saved Johnson for the American League.

Johnson was handsome, too. Sandy hair with a reddish tint bristled generously if somewhat wildly atop his strong-looking face. The eyes were blue, naturally. The jaw a good one, firm and square cut. The nose, a straight one that was to be a model for later-day plastic surgeons. If there was a gimmick to the strength of the Johnson countenance—well, it registered the blush more readily than the smile, it must be said.

Johnson avoided all the ballplayers' after-game rendezvous. "Aw, shucks, I don't like the taste of beer and I don't smoke," he apologized. "Never learned to take a liking to it, I guess." He'd glance at the clubhouse poker games, scratch his head in bewilderment, and drift over to his own locker.

There never was any feeling among his teammates that Johnson was a prude. They put him down for what he was—a country boy. They had an honest admiration for the things he could do on the mound, and they knew why he was saving his money. There were other Johnsons in the West who weren't doing so well, and, besides, Walter sometimes paid more for dogs than they earned in a month.

"We only talked about two things, baseball and hunting," Clyde Milan relates, "most of the years I lived with Walter. He knew I was a little sharper than he was about baseball, and that's when he'd change the subject to dogs and try to get even. Then he bought that Stutz and got the idea that he was Barney Oldfield, too."

Walter Johnson's social life in those early years in Washington was limited to movie-going. He never had a girl—at least, not until 1913. But in 1913, he was suddenly smitten. In the apartment hotel to which he had moved with Milan, he noticed with deepening interest the presence in the lobby and the elevators of a tall, pretty girl whose name he discovered was Miss Roberts. "Mighty purty," Johnson used to say to Milan.

A few weeks later, heaven on earth came to The Big Train. As he warmed up one day near the field boxes in Griffith Stadium, a distinguished-looking gentleman hailed him and extended his hand. "I want to introduce myself," he said. "I'm Congressman Roberts of Nevada, and I have long admired your pitching. This is my daughter, Hazel Lee Roberts." Johnson could only stammer his reply, because the girl was *she!* He tried to strike everybody out, did fan 10, won a three-hitter, and walked back to his hotel with his head swimming.

Naturally, they met again and again. The blonde Miss Roberts, of stately figure, could talk baseball and even hunting with Johnson. They announced their engagement before the year was out and in 1914, Walter Johnson took Hazel Lee Roberts, daughter of Congressman Edward Roberts, as his June bride.

By now, the Big Train was the highest-paid pitcher, by far, in the American League. He could afford the little dream world he long had envisioned—a model country place for himself and his wife, with children and dogs, and some cattle and ducks, too. So he took his bride to the rolling country beyond Bethesda, Maryland, within an hour's drive of the ball park, and there they farmed and began to stock pure-bred Herefords, and began to raise the family that was to total three sons and two daughters.

Meanwhile, Johnson was earning the money the Washington club paid him. Not only was he taking his regular turn and starting games out of turn, but he would come off the bench, cold, without a warmup, if there was a sudden emergency. Like the day in Detroit, in 1915, when Griffith had a one-run lead to protect. Bert Gallia, the starting pitcher, was having a hard time of it with the bases full of Tigers and nobody out. Johnson turned his head toward Griffith on the bench, and got the nod. Taking only the six practice pitches allowed him from the mound, he moved into action. The Tigers sent up three pinch-hitters—Bush, Kavanaugh, and Vitt. They amounted to three strikeouts.

A string of one-hitters came off the pitching arm of Johnson, and there were a flock of two- and three-hitters. Yet the no-hit game always escaped him, until 1920. Paradoxically, it happened in the worst year he had had since hitting his stride with the club. For the first time in his career, Johnson in 1920 suffered a sore arm. He labored to win only eight games that season, was beaten 10 times. Yet, on July 1 at Boston, he achieved his first no hitter.

Johnson arrived in Boston only an hour before game time. He had been detained in Washington by the illness of his five-year-old son, Walter, Jr., and reached the park with little idea he would pitch that day. But Griffith asked him to work and he did. Only one man reached base against him that day—Harry Hooper, whose ground ball was muffed by Bucky Harris, the rookie second-baseman. But it was Harris who atoned for that blot on what would have been a perfect game for Johnson by driving in the winning run with a single in the seventh inning.

The Red Sox went all out to try to spoil Johnson's no-hitter. In the ninth, they sent up pinch-hitters Karr and Eibel. Johnson struck them both out. Hooper represented the last hump, and Johnson knew he was dangerous. For a moment, The Big Train's no-hitter seemed to have exploded. Hooper connected for a fierce smash down the first-base line. But Johnson found a friend then in first-baseman Joe Judge, who snared Hooper's whack on a wicked hop, fell on his face, and threw to Johnson, who had rushed over to cover first. Hooper was out on Walter's bare-hand catch of the ball.

The next morning, the Boston newspapers reported it—somewhat reluctantly, however. The late Paul Shannon, in the Boston *Post,* described the defeat of the Red Sox "on a lucky single by Bucky Harris off the shortstop's glove in the seventh inning." Eventually he got around to mentioning that: "For the Senators, Walter Johnson pitched a no-hitter."

In a clubhouse meeting, Griffith told his ballplayers of the situation and asked them to beat the Yankees and take some of the sting out of it for the Johnson-less crowd.

A rookie pitcher, Al Schacht, volunteered to start the game and take the rap if necessary. Schacht was hooted at every step as he went to the mound. Griffith shrank from sight in the dugout.

Well, it was wonderful. Young Schacht was superb. He didn't give the

Yankees a hit until the fourth inning, when Babe Ruth singled. At the finish, he had a seven-hitter and a 9–3 victory, and the promise of a life-long contract from the grateful Griffith. Griff kept him on the payroll for the next 13 years as pitcher and coach, and holds another job open for Al on the day he asks for it.

In 1924, Walter Johnson was in a World Series! The Senators, under Bucky Harris, had won their first pennant. The Big Train had taken them a long way toward it with his record of 23 wins and only seven defeats. He was voted the American League's Most Valuable Player of 1924.

Sure enough, they chose him to start the opening game against the Giants.

And then there was sadness in Washington and the country over. Johnson was beaten. The Giants licked him. It took 12 innings, in a 4–3 game, but the Big Train was a beaten pitcher in his duel with little Art Nehf, the Giants' left-hander. For five innings, the Senators didn't give Johnson a run. Then, suddenly, they tied at 2–2 in the ninth. Johnson took 'em past the 10th and 11th, but then . . . a walk to Hank Gowdy, a Texas League fly by Nehf, a wild throw by Earl McNeely, singles by Ross Youngs and Bill Terry . . .

Yet, in defeat, Johnson tied a World Series record by striking out 12 men.

At the end of four games, the teams were tied, and now it was John-son's turn again, this time in the Polo Grounds. But he had given too much in that 12-inning opener. A modest total of three strikeouts showed that his fast ball wasn't smoking. Jack Bentley reached him for a home run with Gowdy on base. For eight innings, it was close, with the Giants leading, 3–2. And then they beat him, 6–2. Now, indeed, it was a sad World Series for Johnson, loser of both his starts.

This, then, was probably the last to be seen of Johnson in the Series. But in that sixth one, Tom Zachary's pitching and Bucky Harris' hitting got the Senators home in front, 2–1, and the clubs prepared for the crucial seventh game. Johnson wouldn't start, of course. But in the ninth, the Senators needed somebody of his type. They had just tied the score at 3–3 in the eighth after Fred Marberry was lifted for a pinch-hitter.

Johnson faced the Giants and in a trice was in deep trouble. With one out in the ninth, Frankie Frisch tripled to deep center field. Harris shuf-fled in from second base, talked to Johnson, and they agreed that Ross Youngs should be passed to bring up George Kelly. A long fly now could beat Johnson. There was no long fly. There were three wickedly pitched strikes, and Kelly sat down. Walter had the big second out. He got Emil Meusel for the third one.

In the 11th, he was in trouble again. Heinie Groh led off with a single and Travis Jackson sacrificed a pinch-runner to second. Now it was the dangerous Frisch. Johnson poured it on and fanned Frisch. Now it was Ross Youngs again. They gave him a walk, to bring up Kelly. One strike, two strikes, three strikes . . . and Johnson was safely out of another inning.

More trouble in the 12th. Meusel leads off with a single to right. Hack Wilson up, Johnson strikes him out. The next two, no trouble, and the Senators go into their own 12th. Muddy Ruel leads off with a double. Johnson is safe when Jackson fumbles his grounder, and then . . . the pebble hit! Earl McNeely's grounder bounces over Freddy Lindstrom's head, the Senators win the World Series, and Walter Johnson is the winning pitcher.

Johnson slumped in 1925. He could win "only" 20 games. But he was beaten only seven times and he pitched the Senators to another pennant and into another World Series, against Pittsburgh. He breezed past the Pirates in the opening game, 4–1. Only five hits for the Bucs. Ten of them struck out.

In the fourth game, Johnson took them again, with a six-hit 4–0 shutout, to give the Senators a 3–1 lead in the Series. He was presuming that he wouldn't face the Pirates again. But they beat Stanley Coveleskie in the fifth game and Alex Ferguson in the sixth, and the Series moved into the seventh game.

Of course, it would be Johnson pitching for the Senators now. It came up rain and cold on October 15, 1925, but Judge Landis insisted they go through with the game. The Senators gave Johnson a 4–0 lead in the first inning but he couldn't hold it. He was having a hard time of it, trying to pitch off a mound that was slimy with rain and mud, and the Pirates were swatting him hard. For their own pitchers, the Pirates were providing sawdust on the mound, to give a better footing, but for Johnson there was no such help. A home run by Roger Peckinpaugh in the eighth put Johnson in front again, 7–6.

In the Pirates' own half of the eighth, Johnson was staggering badly. There was wonder why Harris was leaving him in. Peckinpaugh's eighth error of the Series, a new record, put The Big Train in trouble. With the bases loaded, Kiki Cuyler doubled and Johnson was licked, 9–7.

American League president Ban Johnson publicly castigated Harris for not taking Johnson out. The fearless Harris contradicted the executive profanely and told the press, "No man is going to tell me that when I need a pitcher to get us out of a spot, Walter Johnson isn't the man for me. I'll go down the line with him until they carry either of us off the field."

Suddenly, there was evidence in 1926 that The Big Train was fading. He won only 15, lost 16. Then, in Spring training at Tampa in 1927, tragedy struck. Pitching in batting practice, Johnson was struck on the right leg by a line drive off the bat of his roommate, Joe Judge. Johnson's leg was broken. He never pitched again, except with an iron brace on his leg.

He did get into 11 games in 1927, winning five and losing six, but The Big Train was through. He wanted out as a pitcher now, and Griffith arranged for him to take over as manager at Newark in 1928.

Griffith had recommended Johnson to his friend, Newark publisher Paul Block, who owned the team. Block was determined to give Newark at least a semblance of big-league baseball. He actually out-bid major-league clubs for available players and stocked Johnson's team with a flock of former major-leaguers, including Tris Speaker and Bill Lamar of the A's. Newark won no pennant, though it finished in the first division. Johnson's only pitching contribution was a courtesy appearance in which he faced one batter and walked him.

At the end of the 1928 season, the managerial job in Washington opened up for The Big Train. Clark Griffith apparently irked because Bucky Harris had won only two pennants in five years, released him so Harris could accept the manager's post at Detroit.

The Big Train managed the Senators for the next four years. He never finished below fifth place, and in 1930 he took the club into second. In 1931–32, he had third-place teams. But Johnson as a manager was not the supreme idol in Washington that he had been as a pitcher. The fans were restive at his failure to win a pennant. The day came when Walter Johnson actually was booed in Washington.

Most of the fans accepted the belief that The Big Train was too easy-going as a manager, too kindly by nature to crack down on his ballplayers when needed. But the hold-over veterans of the club who had played with Johnson and now were playing under him, were hurt by what they called a change in his nature. As a manager, he lost the stoic patience he always had showed when pitching for a losing club. Toward such old pals as the fading first-baseman, Joe Judge, and the slowing outfielder, Sam Rice, he was even surly.

Griffith, in fact, had to call Johnson on one display of stubbornness. That was in 1930, when Walter insisted that Judge was washed up as a first-baseman and refused to play him in the early games. Johnson insisted that Joe Kuhel, the $65,000 rookie from Kansas City, could out-play Judge.

"Not yet he can't, Walter," said Griffith. "Judge is honest. When he's through, he'll tell us."

At Griffith's insistence, Judge got the chance to play and ran Kuhel

out of the job with his superior performance. Thus convinced, Johnson
sent Kuhel back to Baltimore for more seasoning.

At the end of the 1932 season, his fourth as manager, Johnson was called
into Clark Griffith's office and the club owner talked plainly to his old
friend. "We need a change of fans, Walter," he said. "How are you fixed?
If you don't need the job, let me get a new manager." "It's all right with
me, Griff, in fact I think it's a good idea." And they shook hands. A
week later, Griffith announced Joe Cronin as his new manager.

The Big Train's retirement from baseball lasted only six months after
the 1933 playing season opened. Back to what he thought was full time
with his family, his dogs, and his farm, he received a telegram from
Cleveland. There was no telephone in the Johnson house. He wouldn't
have one. "The durn things are always ringing when I'm busy milking or
doing the other chores," he said.

Out in Cleveland, his old friend Billy Evans, now general manager of
the Indians, wanted Johnson to take over as manager in place of Roger
Peckinpaugh, who was being fired. It was an unhappy experience, a failure worse even than his managerial attempt in Washington despite the
fact that the Indians finished fourth under him in 1933 and third in 1934.
He got the gate, simply and bluntly, in mid-season of 1935.

At Cleveland, Johnson had going for him none of the native affection
which Washington fans had always extended. He was respected initially
as a former great pitcher, but otherwise he got no special treatment from
either the press or the fans, both traditionally pennant-minded in Cleveland. There were rumblings of discontent with Johnson among the Cleveland players even before the 1933 season was completed, and in 1934 the
boiling situation blew wide open with the famed Willie Kamm case.

While the club was in the East, Johnson suddenly announced that he
had suspended and sent home both Kamm and catcher Glenn Myatt for
"the best interest of the team." Kamm, the veteran third-baseman, was
charged by Johnson with interfering with his management of the club.
Kamm was immensely popular with the fans and the press, and Johnson
by this time wasn't.

Team owner Alya Bradley's first reaction was a spineless, weak-kneed
attempt to duck the whole issue. Certainly he wasn't supporting The Big
Train when he announced that, "I'm referring the whole matter to Commissioner Landis." Asked what he would do if Landis should decide that
Kamm was in the right, Bradley announced, "I'd have to dismiss Johnson."

The Big Train was bristling now at Bradley, too. "Even if I'm fired, I'll
insist I'm in the right. Two Cleveland newspapers stirred up all this
trouble. They've always been against me. I suffer a whole lot more than

they do when we lose." It was Johnson's first dealing with an unfavorable press after more than two decades in Washington, where the sports pages treated him as a god.

Very properly, Landis refused to have anything to do with the case and tossed it back into Bradley's lap. Johnson wasn't fired. His suspension of Kamm and Myatt stuck, and Kamm was given a scouting job by Bradley. But Johnson never did charm the Cleveland players, despite a pledge of loyalty that was published in the papers as a paid advertisement by Bradley.

In Cleveland, they were never impressed with the long-acclaimed sweet nature of The Big Train. His critics tabbed him as cold, aloof, and distant with his players, and generously put it down to the fact that he was out of the friendly Washington orbit he knew so well. At Cleveland, Johnson indeed lost much of his friendly nature and adopted a strange, whining tone when he felt he was misused. He was a nagger, claimed first-baseman Harley Boss. "He used to bawl me out for hitting to left field, the only place I could drop any hits safely, and insist that I pull the ball to right. One day, I tripled with the bases full, into left field, and came back to the bench and Johnson was still not satisfied. 'Goodness gracious,' he said, 'when are you ever going to learn to pull a ball to right field?' I wanted to give up."

His Cleveland debacle couldn't eradicate memories of The Big Train as the greatest game-winner the American League ever knew, however, and a year later he got the supreme tribute—election to the Cooperstown Hall of Fame on the first ballot. In gratitude, he turned over to Cooperstown all the prized autographed balls of his collection, the ones signed by the famous men who had been his friends—including Presidents Taft, Wilson, Harding, and Coolidge.

Out of baseball, Johnson regained the gentleness of character that his Washington admirers had known. He was content to farm his Maryland acres, but his neighbors pleaded with him to run for political office. After consistent refusals, he finally consented to nomination for a place on the three-man board of Rockville County Commissioners. In the overwhelmingly Democratic election year of 1938, Johnson was nevertheless elected to the board as the lone Republican member. He had filed his nomination only 10 minutes before the midnight deadline. Party officials were not disturbed when he said, "I'll run, but I won't campaign or make any speeches." They told him, "You don't have to. Everybody knows what Walter Johnson stands for." After his election, when he had to file a report of his campaign expenses, he submitted one item: "Fifty cents—for printed cards."

When Arch McDonald moved up to New York in 1939, to broadcast the Yankees' and Giants' home games after years as the play-by-play radio man in Washington, there was a campaign to bring Johnson back to baseball as a broadcaster. Griffith heartily endorsed it, and made Johnson's selection a condition when he sold the radio rights to a cereal company. Walter held the job for a year, until McDonald's return. He wasn't exciting, but he was adequate. Gladly, he retired once more to his farm, saying, "I think I've had enough of public life."

But others thought otherwise. Enthused by Johnson's success in the county election, Republican officials beseeched him to run for Congress in the Sixth Maryland District in 1940. He refused, then melted at their insistence, after declaring, "I'll run if you can't find anybody else to take it on." He won the nomination but lost the election by a narrow margin to the Democratic candidate, who was strong in the upstate mining counties.

Once before, he had come out of what he thought was his permanent retirement from pitching, to make an historic throw. That was in 1936, when he consented to try to match George Washington's feat of throwing a silver dollar across the Rappahannock River at Fredericksburg, Virginia, scene of Washington's youth. Standing on the river bank, his shoes in the mud, the strangest mound he had ever toed, Johnson wound up and was short with his first heave. He took off his coat, wound up again, and on his second try sent the silver cartwheel sailing to the other bank, 272 feet distant. The complete length of his throw was estimated at 317 feet.

With characteristic modesty, he said, "I guess the river is narrower now than it was in George Washington's time."

The Big Train was not disturbed by the fact that none of his sons followed in his footsteps as a star pitcher. Walter, Jr., and Eddie both pitched for the University of Maryland team, but they generated none of the speed of their pappy. "They're not as big as I am," Johnson noted, "and anyway, I always did understand that ballplayers' sons were long shots to make the grade in the majors. I'm not disappointed."

The only card game he ever learned was casino. He'd have his old pals of the Washington team out some nights to play, and then it was that such as Bucky Harris, Clark Griffith, Joe Judge, and Sam Rice would cut up old touches with The Big Train.

They'd swap stories like the one Joe Judge liked to tell of the night in St. Louis when he was trying to drag Johnson out of the lobby so they could make the movie they'd decided on that night. "How about that, Walter?" Judge would say, and then relate how some old codger detained The Big Train for 20 minutes in earnest conversation. "Finally I got Walter away from the fellow, and then I asked him what in the world he'd been talking about," said Judge. "Walter said 'the fellow wanted to tell me that he was a good friend of my sister in Denver, so I had to listen.' I told Walter I didn't know he had a sister in Denver and he said, 'Well, frankly, I don't.' "

Farmer Johnson loved his acres, 552 of them at his Germantown place. He had no investments besides his farm holdings, but when his place was sold in 1947, it brought $55,000 with an added sum for 90 head of pure-bred cattle.

On the night of September 22, 1946, a crowd of 24,000 fans stood hushed and bare-headed in Griffith Stadium and prayed for a Walter Johnson who was fighting for his life in Georgetown University Hospital, where 16 years before his beloved Hazel had passed away. The Big Train, it was feared, was making his last run.

From President Truman in the White House, and from high personages far and wide, from fans who saw him pitch and from those who knew him only from the records, the condolences poured in to the now fatherless Johnson family. "The President is greatly grieved to hear of the death of one of his athletic heroes," announced White House Secretary Charles Ross. Saddened, 77-year-old Clark Griffith wept openly.

In the ecclesiastical splendor of the Washington Cathedral, the Very Reverend John D. Suter conducted services. The Cathedral's nave, with nearly 1,000 seats, was filled by a crush of those who had come to pay a last tribute to The Big Train.

Today, in the plaza of Griffith Stadium, Walter Johnson fans can still see Walter Johnson, in bronze. In 1947, President Harry Truman made a special pilgrimage to the stadium to unveil the life-like plaque of Johnson in the midst of his rhythmic pitching delivery and proclaim him, "The greatest pitcher, the greatest man in the history of our great game of baseball."

One final anecdote to illustrate the character of the man. Shortly before the outbreak of World War II, when Bob Feller's fast ball was the new rage, I invited Johnson to come into town and take a look at the Cleveland fireballer. Walter was interested. "Never have seen that young feller pitch," he said, "think I'll have a look at him."

Feller was working the next day and I sat with Johnson in a field box. He squinted at Bob for two innings. "Mighty fast," was his only comment for a while. And then, as Feller continued to pour it in, Johnson added, "He's awful fast. He smokes that ball, goodness gracious."

In the fifth inning, I popped the question. "Tell me, Walter, does Feller throw that ball as fast as you did?"

He dropped his head and thoughtfully ran a hand through his hair.

Now the Johnson modesty was colliding full tilt with the honesty of the man. For a moment, it seemed an unfair question. His honesty finally prevailed. The Big Train shook his head. "No," he said.

It hurt to do it, but Walter had to tell the truth.

Dizzy Dean   Photo credit: National Baseball Library/Cooperstown, N.Y.

DIZZY DEAN

The One and Only

Sport Magazine   May 1948

From its inception in 1946, each issue in **Sport** *Magazine has featured an in-depth profile of an athletic superstar. Few subjects could have been more charming than Dizzy Dean, who was on his way as a television broadcaster.*

By Jack Sher

T he day was dry and hot, with just the whisper of a wind stirring the warm air. Big, white clouds moved lazily in the sky, traveling North over the land of Texas. The elements were at peace, but a man-made storm was occurring in a Houston ball park. For on this fine day in 1930 the name and reputation of one of the greatest pitchers of the 20th Century was being born.

The occasion was an exhibition game between the Houston team and the Chicago White Sox. And the arm and antics of the 20-year-old Texas League pitcher were causing wailing and gnashing of teeth in the White Sox dugout.

The pitcher's name, when he went into the game, was Jerome Herman Dean. But, before the contest ended, he was to be given a new first name. He was henceforth to be known as "Dizzy." And the name of Dizzy Dean was to dominate the baseball world for a decade. The chatter and wisecracks he was dishing out were full of brash, confident, homespun humor.

"Well, lookee, now watta we got here? Jes' keep that ol' bat on the shoulder, fellah. I'm a gonna breeze this here one right across the middle. Now don't get the catcher fussed up by swingin' at it. Jes' save yer strength and watch 'er go by!"

Down in the Chicago dugout, manager Owen Bush was more than slightly steamed. His voice floated out to the batter, loudly and derisively.

"What's going on out there! You're supposed to be a major-leaguer! You're lettin' that dizzy kid make a fool outa ya!"

Jerome Herman turned the big grin toward the White Sox dugout. Before facing the batter again, he delivered a few wisecracks to the manager, some derogatory words about the ability of the Chicago hitters.

"Listen to that!" Bush railed, jumping up and down in anger. "Are you guys gonna take that from this dizzy kid?"

It was dizzy, dizzy, dizzy, all afternoon. The adjective was a better description of the batters than of the kid pitcher. They swung and missed until most of them felt as though they had their heads in a revolving door.

A name can be born in a moment. It takes action to make it mean something, to breathe life and color into it. Diz gave it that life. A lesser man might have resented the name "Dizzy," but not a guy like Dean. Even then, this warm, lovable, uneducated (but wise) kid understood that baseball is more than mere automatons who can hit, catch, or pitch. He knew that the game is also the personalities of the men who play it, their diverse backgrounds and peculiarities.

As his onetime brilliant teammate, Pepper Martin, said: "When ol' Diz was in there pitching it was more than just another ball game. It was a regular three-ring circus and everybody was wide awake and enjoying being alive."

Even as Jerome Herman Dean, his big right arm undoubtedly would have made him a great winning pitcher. But as Dizzy Dean, he was more than that. He was a tremendous, exciting personality, a strictly screwy, magnificently American character, an advertisement for baseball, an attraction that drew to the game those hitherto unfortunate people who didn't know a scratch hit from a double steal.

Most pitchers will sit by the hour and tell you the special technique they use in their deliveries. Not Diz. Nobody ever taught Dizzy anything about how to pitch, and it never held any mysteries for him. He believed wholeheartedly, without doubt or jealousy, that he was the most colossal pitcher in the world. And for six years, during the height of his career with the Gas House Gang, he was as good as every boast he ever made.

"They used to talk about that natural rhythm I had and all that," Diz said to me recently, as he sprawled on a golf course in Miami, Florida.

"That ain't no way to tell people how I pitched," he grinned. "Tell 'em that I jest used to rare back and fog 'em in there."

That is as fine a description of the way Dean pitched as any of the millions of words about him now in the musty files. Standing six feet, two and half inches, weighing 175 pounds, with huge, sloping shoulders and tremendous hands, Ol' Diz just took a long, easy stretch and fogged them across the plate. When he settled himself on the mound, it was not only to win a ball game; it was to have a hell of a whale of a good time.

"I never bothered about what those guys could hit and couldn't hit," he laughed. "All I knowed is that they weren't gonna get a holt of that ball Ol' Diz was throwin'."

Boston will never forget that wonderful afternoon when Diz loudly announced to all the Braves that he wasn't going to throw a curve during the entire game. All he was going to need was his fast ball. He didn't unfurl a curve all afternoon, and he shut out the Boston club, 3–0, allowing only three hits.

He sometimes drove a catcher nearly out of his mind by insisting on pitching to a batter's strength. The way Babe Ruth couldn't be bothered "hittin' them singles," Diz never worried about playing it safe. A great pitcher was supposed to strike 'em all out the hard way, and that was what Dean always tried to do.

Frankie Frisch, who was his great, good friend and who suffered and sweated and wept and rejoiced while managing the Cards and Dizzy Dean, finally gave up telling Diz how to pitch to enemy batters. The last time he tried it was on a memorable day in September, 1934, when Diz and Paul were going up against the Dodgers. In the clubhouse, before the game, Frisch started down the Brooklyn lineup, trying to explain to Dizzy how to feed 'em to each hitter. Diz had a snort or a wisecrack for each tip. He finally held up his hand.

"Now, take it easy, Frankie," he said in a friendly way. "I've win 26 games this year and it don't look exactly right for no infielder to be tellin' a star like me how to pitch a game o' ball.

"I doubt if them Brooks gets a hit off'n me or Paul this afternoon."

Diz hiked blissfully to the mound and, with exasperating and effortless motion, held the Dodgers hitless through eight breathless innings. With two out in the eighth, the Brooklyn boys got their only hit in the ball game. Then Paul took over in the next game and, in his usual stoic fashion, pitched a no-hitter.

The record book gives you only a small idea of how great a pitcher he was. Dizzy Dean was "the pitcher for today," not for posterity. "I love to pitch," he said in 1936 when he was marching to the mound more frequently than anyone in the league. "I could go on pitchin' forever." And that is why, when the lights were doused on his pitching career, it was such a cruel, miserable time for him.

In spite of himself, Ol' Diz set some stunning records, regardless of the fact that he seemed to be out on the hump only to enjoy life and the warm sun on his back and the crowds and the good feeling of a called strike. Dean set a modern record for strikeouts when he whiffed 17 Cubs in one game on July 30, 1933. Bob Feller tied Dean's mark in 1936 and broke it in 1938.

Starting in 315 games, Dizzy won 150, lost only 83. During his first six years with the Cards, before he hurt his arm, Diz averaged 22 wins a year. During his best season, 1934, Dean won 30 ball games, lost seven. In '34 and '35, he led the league in games won. His lifetime earned-run average was 3.03 per game. And Diz wouldn't like you to forget that he was also a dangerous long-ball hitter.

"In one of them Worlt Series," he said, "I got two hits in one inning. Only a couple of guys ever got two hits in one inning in a Worlt Series. And no pitcher never done that except me."

Diz is right. He rapped out a double and a single in one inning of the 1934 Series against the Tigers. But what you love about the guy is when he adds: "My brother Paul, he's got a better Worlt Series pitchin' record than me. Paul wins two out of two. Me, I win two and I lose two."

One day in Chicago, with the thermometer registering 100 in the shade, the delightful Dean built a bonfire in front of the dugout and huddled around it wearing a blanket, rising now and then to war-whoop like an Indian. In St. Louis, he announced that he'd show the world how to cook. When curious spectators arrived to watch Diz whip up a fancy omelet, he pegged eggs at them—eggs made of rubber and painted white.

But the innumerable stunts Dizzy staged were not nearly so funny as his natural, everyday actions, his homely, hilarious way of speaking, his glorious and honest bragging. Diz was a comedian in the truest sense of the word, a great showman.

Listen to Dizzy, back in 1934 before the World Series, talking to re-porters: "Ol' Frank is sayin' he don't know who is gonna pitch that first game. But he ain't foolin' me none. I told him this afternoon that there wasn't no use kiddin' hisself. There is only one guy to pitch that first game and that's ol' Diz. I guess Frisch is trying to use what they call this Sikology on ol' Diz, figurin' he don't want me nervous on the eve of battle. He can't fool me none. Ol' Diz never got nervous in his life about no ball game. Who won the pennant? Why, me and Paul. And who's gonna win the Series? Me and Paul. Them Tigers is lucky if they get a good foul off'n us."

Or Diz sounding off about his sudden prosperity, the money that was being showered upon him for endorsing dozens of products that were bearing his celebrated name: "Doggone, but I'm gettin' tuckered out havin' to take in all this money. Ol' Diz is wearin' a regular path to the bank, storin' it up like a squirrel a-hoardin' nuts. I'm gettin' to be a regular business fellah. An' I'm a-gettin' plumb tired of it all. For two cents, I'd chuck the old ball and glove and go fishin' up to Novus Scofus."

It was just Diz talking, loving the sound of his voice, generous, easygoing, collecting his share of yuks, wisely knowing that he reeked with color and was the answer to a sports reporter's prayer. "Boy, I sure poured it on them Pirates yesterday. Ol' Diz has sure got it. 'Course, stacked up agin my brother Paul, I'm just a great big semi-pro."

It is a struggle to keep from comparing Diz to Babe Ruth. There is a similarity in their poverty-stricken background, their belief in themselves, their raw, natural humor, their love of people, their availability to the public on all occasions, their generosity, their love of kids.

One day in St. Louis, Dizzy visited a hospital ward filled with sick and crippled children. He sat around for hours telling them about baseball and the great games he had pitched. One of the kids mentioned that he thought Bill Terry of the Giants was just about the greatest hitter in the world.

"Say," Diz beamed, "that Bill can hit the ball, but he ain't no match for the Diz. Tell you what, you listen to that game we're a-playin' with the Giants this afternoon. I'm a-gonna fill up the bases and when Ol' Bill comes up there, I'm gonna strike him out, one, two, three."

In the ninth inning, with the Cards leading, 3–2, Diz obligingly stacked the bases to get at Terry. The Giant came to bat and struck out on three pitched balls! After the game, Diz complained to the catcher that "them kids sure put me in a tough spot, picking a good hitter like that Terry. But I sure fooled him. He never knowed Ol' Diz was gonna throw that third one right down the middle."

Nothing hurt Dizzy more than the suggestion that he was a braggart or a windbag, or that he occasionally strayed from the truth. Words like "truth" are vague, at best, linked only to the morals of our time, and to Diz the truth was anything that people wanted to hear.

He was once approached by an advertising man who offered him a hundred bucks to make a five-minute radio transcription about his baseball career. Diz readily accepted. Ballplayers and friends sat openmouthed when they heard Dizzy, who had gone only to the second grade in school, blandly telling the public, "I mastered the art of pitchin' while I was attendin' Oklahoma State Teacher's College."

When the boys in the clubhouse asked Diz where he got off telling such a whopper, Diz grinned and told them that he figured that the advertising people who gave him the hundred dollars deserved some new and fresh information about him for that kind of money.

Manager Bill Terry, who was always being surprised by Dean, was astounded one day to discover Dizzy leaning against the wall in the Giant dressing room at the Polo Grounds. It was just a few minutes before the game, and Terry was going over the St. Louis lineup.

"You'll have to get out of here, Diz," Terry said. "We're going over the St. Louis hitters."

"Go right ahead, Bill," Diz said. "You can't learn me nothin' about them fellahs. I know all their weaknesses."

In doing people favors, in bending over backwards to please all those who thought Diz was a great guy, the madcap Dean sometimes got them into trouble. Three New York sportswriters were hauled on the carpet one day by their editors, demanding to know why each of the three writers had Dizzy born in a different town on a different day of the year.

Diz explained it this way: "Well, I liked all three of them boys. They was always nice to ol' Diz when it come to givin' him a good write-up. I figured I'd give each of them a scoop, an' that's why I mentioned these three different places. What was all the fussin' about, anyway? Ain't one place as good as another?"

The pitcher the world was to know as Dizzy Dean was born in Lucas, Arkansas, on January 16, 1911, the third son of destitute, cotton-picking sharecroppers. His work-worn mother, with love and high hope, named her son Jay Hanna, after a Wall Street financier, Jay Gould, and a celebrated publisher, Mark Hanna.

At the age of six or seven, when he was not even high enough to see over a stalk of cotton, one of Jay's friends, a boy his own age, took sick and died. One of the first to visit the grief-stricken father was young Jay Dean. He struggled for a way to console the man. Finally he told him that he thought so much of his friend who had died that he would take the boy's name for his own. And that is how he became known as Jerome Herman Dean.

During the years Diz was at his height as a hurler, he seldom spoke of his childhood other than in a joking manner. He gave the public an impression of a happy-go-lucky, uneducated boy for whom the world had always been a choice oyster. He joked about his lack of schooling, his days in the cotton fields. Only those very close to him knew the intimate details of the rough and pathetic life that preceded his career in baseball.

He was born on a rickety, wooden bed in a clapboard shack that stood on worked-over cotton soil, a patch of Arkansas ground that his father did not own and would never earn enough to own. The wife of Albert

Monroe Dean bore five children. Diz never saw his oldest sister, Sara May. She died at the age of four months. His oldest brother, Charlie, died when he was nine years old. Diz's mother died when the boy was three. Elmer was then five and Paul was two years old.

"I don't remember much about my mother," Diz said, "except sometimes I can remember how she looked. She died of tuberculosis. Sara May? Well, I don't know what took her away. I know my brother Charlie died 'cause he wasn't able to get proper food and medicine. If we had them things, maybe my mother wouldn't have died either."

Albert Dean was a migratory worker, moving his family from one patch of land to another, from state to state, Arkansas, Oklahoma, Texas, following the crop. It was sunup to sundown work, children doing the work of grown men to add to the meager, below-subsistence wages.

"My Dad did the best he could," Diz said. "I never knowed a man who had it tougher. He was a regular pal to us kids and he hadda be a mother, too."

When Diz was six years old, alongside his brother Paul, who was four, they were planting in the fields with a team of mules. At the age of 10, when most kids are in the fifth grade learning geography, Diz was learning his lessons first hand, riding across Oklahoma in an old jalopy.

"When I was 10 years old," he said, not without pride, "I could do a man's work. I could pick me four to five hundred pounds o' cotton a day. I'd get up at five in the mornin', set to milkin', eat me some sowbelly and black-eyed peas, an' go into the field. We was gettin' 25 cent to 50 cent a hundred for cotton in them days.

It is not true, as has sometimes been jokingly printed (some joke!) that the Dean boy did not have a pair of shoes until he went into the Army. "We, Paul and Elmer and me, had one pair of shoes each," Diz said. "They was our Winter shoes, and we took 'em off in the Summer to save the leather. That didn't hurt us none. It was warm in the Summer. What sometimes hurt us was the way Dad looked when the food was skimpy. We knowed how hard he worked and there never seemed to be enough."

Diz will tell you now that his biggest thrill, next to some of the ball games he has pitched, was seeing a field of cotton all picked, knowing that he had taken part in the labor that would bring money to the family. He also will tell you that there is no bond closer than that of a working family, those who toil together. That wonderful affection that Diz and Paul have always felt for each other, the loyalty and pride in each other's achievements, began long before either of them took to the big-league mounds and became famous through the strength of their right arms.

Diz felt the same way about his older brother Elmer. It was always a sort of sad thing to him that Elmer could never make the grade in the big leagues. Even today, Diz will loyally and stoutly maintain that Elmer was as good a ballplayer as Paul and himself.

"Gol darnit," Diz said, "the trouble was that Elmer hadda work too hard and he never got no chance to show what he could do until it was too late. Why, that boy was a great catcher an' infielder. He could whip that ol' ball around like any Dean. He just got his chance too late, that's all, when he was too old."

Even at the height of their success, the Dean boys were always in there pitching for Elmer. On that fine day in Brooklyn, when Paul and Diz trounced the Dodgers, 1–0 and 3–1, they got in a lick about Elmer.

"Hey," manager Casey Stengel wailed at the end of the second game, "are there any more at home like you two?"

"You betcha life!" Diz sounded off. "There's my brother Elmer. Casey, you ought to go down there and sign him right up. He's as good as we two ever was. He'd be a-playin' for the Cards right now," Diz grinned, "but that Frisch has got his hands full o' Deans right now, more'n he kin handle."

Stengel was so impressed that he looked into the matter. He discovered that Elmer was a ballplayer, but that the astute Rickey hadn't overlooked any bets. Branch had listened to the pep talks of Paul and Diz and had given Elmer a tryout with the Cardinals. The oldest of the Dean boys had not been good enough for big-league competition. Not wanting to be separated from his brothers, Elmer had taken a job as a peanut vendor in the St. Louis ball park.

There is an oft-told story about Elmer that must be repeated in any chronicle of the Dean family.

"It was back there about '24 or '25," Diz began, "and we was travelin' around from field to field huntin' for work. Dad an' Paul and me was ridin' in one car and Ol' Elmer, he was ridin' in a car behind us with some friends of ours. Well, we crossed some railroad tracks jest as an ol' freight is comin'. This cotton-pickin' feller drivin' the car Elmer is in, he's held up by the train. We was supposed to all meet in Dallas that night. We wait an' we wait, but they don't show up. Well, now, we had to hustle us up some work before we go to starvin', so we drive someplace else and get us a job."

Diz paused and shook his heavy head. "Gol' darn if we don't lose Elmer for four years! We sure missed 'im, but Dad ain't worried much 'cause Elmer is a grown man an' can take care of himself. But it's kinda sorry without him. Elmer, he finally reads in a newspaper about me pitchin' a ball game in Houston and he hot-foots it to see me and we are all together again ever since."

Al Dean couldn't buy his kids gloves and balls and bats, so he made them. He fashioned a bat out of hickory wood, padded worn-out work gloves into fielders' mitts. "He could make the best darn baseball you ever seen," Diz related. "He could make a baseball outa almost anything, jest scraps of stuff, like an ol' shoe tongue, a hunk of innertube for the insides, a piece of sock, and mebbe some twine.

"I guess I always wanted to be a pitcher," Diz went on. "I never knowed much about this pro ball and gettin' paid for playing and all that until I was about 14. I never saw a big-league game until I played in one, but I heard one onc't. It was on the radio, one of them crystal sets. One of the neighbors built hisself one and he lemme lissen to a ball game. I'll never forget it. The Senators are playin' the Pirates and ol' Walter Johnson was sure slammin' em in there that day. I was sure excited about it."

Diz joined the Army when he was 16, got in through the help of his two step-brothers, Claude and Herman. Diz was big and strong and when he said he was 18 nobody doubted him. Besides, the 12th Field Artillery needed a pitcher.

"I was all right so long as I was wearin' that baseball uniform the Army give me," Diz said. "It was the first baseball uniform I ever wore and I was mighty proud of it. But I had a sorry time in them fatigue clothes and that khaki. Ol' Diz jest wasn't cut out to be no soldier."

Diz served three years and nine months of a four-year hitch. With only three months to go, Jerome got a week's leave and journeyed to see his father, who was working in a cotton field near San Antonio, Texas. His Dad had had a good year and had saved almost $600, more than he had ever been able to get together in his whole life.

"Well, son," Albert Dean said, "by the look of your face that Army life ain't agreeing with you."

"Dad," Diz said, "it sure would make me happy to get outa there."

"How much do you reckon it would take?" his father asked.

"A lotta money," Diz said, "I figure about one hunnert and twenty bucks."

The elder Dean dug down into his pocket and came up with the money, instructing his son to go back to the Army and buy his way out.

The year was 1929 and Jerome Herman Dean was 19 years old when he joined his Dad again in San Antonio, Texas. He took a job with the San Antonio Public Service, working as an assistant to a man who read gas meters. "I used to follow that fella around jest to keep him company and carry his tools. But I guess my main job was to pitch ball for that Public Service Company team."

The loud thump of Dean's fast ball hitting the PS catcher's glove attracted the attention of a St. Louis Cardinal scout, Don Curtis. He watched Diz pitch one ball game and signed him then and there. Diz was shipped to St. Joseph in the Western League, won his first game, 4–3, started a triple play.

While winning 17 games and losing only eight, the Dean kid borrowed cars from the hero-worshipping citizens and, driving pellmell through the streets, wound up in the cubbyhole provided by the Chief of Police. He registered and paid bills at three sleeping places, the YMCA, the St. Francis Hotel, and the Hotel Robidoux, explaining that he wanted to be handy to a bed whenever he felt like hitting the sack. Oliver French, the club's business manager, was still trying to straighten out Dizzy's bills when the startling young fireballer was transferred to Houston in the Texas League.

Diz made his debut in Houston by pitching a 12–1 victory. The next day, the story all over town was about how Jerome Herman Dean had apologized for his performance to Fred Ankenman, who owned the Houston ball club. "That sure was a sorry game I pitched yesterday, Mr. Ankenman," Diz said. "Can you imagine me allowin' them fellahs to get a run off'n me? It ain't gonna happen again."

The St. Louis Cards brought him up at the tail-end of the 1930 season.

The Gas House Gang loved Diz before he ever pitched a ball game for them. He was their kind of ballplayer, loud, fun-loving, supremely confident. But Gabby Street, then the Card manager, a rather dour, skeptical, ex-Army sergeant, never did take to Dean's ways very much. With a deep desire to tone Diz down, he picked the roughest opponent he could for the young rookie, sending him in on a September day in 1930 to tame the hard-hitting Pirates.

In the first inning, the Pittsburgh club pasted Diz for two hits. When he trooped back to the bench, Gabby Street presented him with a smirking face. That didn't sit very well with ol' Diz, who marched back out and from that inning on pitched almost perfect ball, allowing the Pirates only one more hit and winning the game.

In 1931, Diz turned up for Spring training in Bradenton, Florida, as big as life and as full of the old breeze as a sideshow barker. Life was a glorious, free 'n' easy thing now, and Ol' Diz didn't mind telling all and sundry folk that he was goin' to stand the National League on its ear.

When Diz grew a little lax about reporting to practice on time, Street would let go a vituperative barrage that reminded Diz of his Army days. It was touch and go all the time, with Diz threatening every other day to take mind and body back to Houston where he was appreciated.

Diz made his first appearance of the 1931 Spring training campaign as a relief pitcher. With the Cards leading the world champion Athletics by a narrow 5–4, in an exhibition game, and with the A's staging a rally, Gabby crooked a finger at Diz. The pitcher got off the bench and, as he passed Street on his way to the mound, he said, "Don't worry none, Gab. These guys couldn't hit me with a handful o' birdshot."

The first Philly batter that Diz faced rapped a screaming double to left field. Diz grinned. Then he turned around and grinned again, so the bleacher fans could see it, too. And then that great, wonderful, goofy character struck out the next three batters. Street could hardly be held when Ol' Diz filled the bases the next inning, then fanned the next two men and retired the third on an easy infield pop fly to win the ball game.

The home fans didn't get a glimpse of dynamite Dean's delivery in 1931. Just as the season got under way, Diz was shipped back to Houston. At the time, the sportswriters' version of Dizzy's dismissal was that the pitcher was sent down to save Street from the nut house. It was also rumored that the way Diz was handling his financial affairs was causing the strict, cautious Branch Rickey some sleepless nights. It is true that the slip of paper called a "check" was a new and wonderfully magic thing to the once poverty-stricken Diz. When the pieces of paper wound up in El Brancho's office, the Deacon was fit to be tied.

It was during this time that Rickey, through the club secretary, Clarence Lloyd, put Diz on the famous "Dollar-A Day" allowance. That was just what Diz received, one dollar a day. The single piece of greenery was dished out to him every morning and was generally spent by eleven o'clock.

"You could never say Ol' Branch was free with a dollar," Diz grinned, "but he did try to get me to save my money." Diz suddenly began to laugh. "Boy, oh boy! I remember one day I was a-standin' in the clubhouse yellin' and rootin' around about club owner Ol' Breadon and how he was starvin' me. I was sayin' that this Breadon is the tightest ol' coot what ever lived, and a-callin' him names, when somebody taps me on the shoulder. I never seen this Breadon until then and there he was as big as life an' he says to me, 'just what is the trouble, Dean?' Well, I was in it then, so I says that this here Breadon is a mean old so-and-so who should be givin' me two dollars a day instead of one. He says to me, 'Come up to my office, Dean.' "

Diz adjourned to the privacy of Sam Breadon's office and the ballplayers who were in the clubhouse that day will never forget the triumphant look on Dizzy's face when he came back into the room a half-hour or so later.

"What happened, Diz?" Andy High asked.

"I got the two bucks!" Dean said, hoisting the money aloft.

Diz went out with his two bucks to paint the town red. Not long after that he was sent back to the Texas League.

Diz did not return to Houston chastened in spirit. He went back in triumph and won 26 games for Houston that year, and lost only 10.

Talking about his return trip ticket to the minors, Diz blamed nobody. "They didn't think they needed me," he said. "They had a great ball club in '31, and plenty of pitchers. I was a big draw in Houston and could do more good there. But when they called me back in 1932, as I knowed they would, they had sold most of their good players. They was tied for sixth with the Giants in '32, but just the same I win 18 ball games.

"Just after I get to Houston," Diz said, "I go into Paul's Shoe Store where my step-brother's wife is working. I set my eyes on this girl behind the hosiery counter and I ask my brother who is that pretty black-haired girl? His wife introduces her to me and I ast her for a date, and one week from that day we get married, and we been together ever since and we always will be.

"Gol' darn," Diz grinned, "that was some courtin'! I was broke, as usual, and I just had to make an impression on Pat. Jest before our first date I go to a car dealer in town and I tell him my troubles. He says, "Don't you worry none, Diz. You just take this brand new automobile here—it was a Hupmobile—and you can pay me on time." Boy, I sure thought that would make a hit with her! I drive up as smart and sassy as ever and I say, 'Lookee here, this is what I'm buying you for a wedding present.' You know what she done? She just give me a look and she says, 'Diz, you drive that automobile right back to where you got it. It's high time you plan on savin' your money for the future and you can't afford this car.'

Diz took the car back. A few nights later, in a borrowed car, somewhat less flashy, he turned up for another date. "I never did no drinkin'," Diz said, "but I bought me a bottle this night, figuring I'd do a little showin' off. Well, we are drivin' along and I take out this bottle and start to take a drink. Pat just snatches it outa my hands and tosses it out the window, and she says, 'Baseball players shouldn't drink.' And, gol' darn, anyone will tell you that Ol' Diz never took a drink from that day until he hurt his arm back there in 1937."

The future Mrs. Dean was actually making more money than Diz was when they got married a week from the day they met. Diz confesses to borrowing two dollars to pay for the marriage license. In more ways than one, it was the wisest investment he has ever made. "Diz always made me feel as though he needed me. Diz has always leaned over backwards to give me credit for helping him, but don't forget you can't help a person who doesn't want to be helped. Diz always wanted help and advice.

We've always gotten along beautifully. We're sort of like ham and eggs, Diz and I."

Even under Pat's watchful eye, Dizzy's irrepressible, showy spirit could not be curbed. He missed trains, drew fines, made outlandish statements to the press and, by the way, in 1933 he also won 20 ball games for the Cards. There were numerous squabbles over money, which is not hard to understand when you consider that the magnificently generous Breadon was paying the National League's most colorful attraction $3,000 per year.

There was that beautiful incident that took place in the dining-room and kitchen of the swank Bellevue-Stratford Hotel in Philadelphia.

Just as the dinner hour was getting under way, in stormed Diz, Pepper, and Heine Schuble, decked out in greasy workmen's clothes, looking like a combination of railroad brakemen and members of the painter's union. They proceeded to renovate the dining room, pounding and hammering and swinging ladders around.

"The next night we was back," Diz recalled, laughter rocking his huge frame. "Ol' Branch is sittin' there at a table with a fancy salad in front of him. Pepper and me go past the table an' we pound it with our fists and the salad jest up and flies all over the Deacon's lap. Then we hi-tail it out. 'Who was them fellows?' Branch yells at the headwaiter. 'That's yer ball club,' the headwaiter tells him. 'I'm modified,' Ol' Branch says. 'They've ruint me!' "

It is doubtful whether the impeccable grammarian, Branch Rickey, used exactly that language, but he was indeed mortified. On other occasions, when Dizzy's tremendous imagination and colorful stunts earned him the kind of publicity that money can't buy, the remonstrances and high-sounding moral statements of the Deacon seemed just a little on the phony side.

As one Cardinal ballplayer, who is still playing ball and shall remain nameless, said: "Branch and Breadon used to roll their eyes and shake their fingers and tell newspapermen how unmanageable Diz was. But at private luncheons, and among their friends, they were always telling funny stories about Ol' Diz, helping to make him a wacky figure."

The Cardinal owners also had Dizzy Dean to thank for bringing them another great pitcher in his brother Paul. Diz talked it up about Paul and was mostly responsible for bringing his brother into the big league.

"Just after I broke into the majors," Diz said, "Paul and Dad was pickin' cotton down in El Campo, Texas. I take a scout with me and we go to see 'em. Do you know where Paul signed his Cardinal contract? He signed right down there in the middle of a cotton field at El Campo."

"Paul and me are the best pitchers in the National League, and between us we'll win 45 games," Diz was not bragging, he was just stating it straight from the heart when he said at the start of the 1934 season. By the middle of August, they had won 37 games. When the Dean boys hung up their gloves that year, they had a total of 49 victories between them, 30 for Diz, 19 for the kid brother, including four crucial World Series wins!

There was that day in Chicago when the boys were feeling rather sad because of their lowly salaries and, between them, had dropped a double header to the Cubs, 2–1 and 1–0. When Frisch counted noses on the train that night, Paul and Diz were not in the line-up. They were relaxing at a party on the outskirts of Chicago.

Before going AWOL, the Deans had staged a show in the Cards' dressing room. Surrounded by reporters, they posed for pictures, tearing up their uniforms to the accompaniment of Diz's dialogue about how Breadon and Rickey were under-paying him and his brother, Paul. Frisch fined the boys $100 apiece while Rickey and Breadon clucked their tongues. The Deans went to see Judge Landis, who upheld the fine and told the boys to behave.

"We went on strike again a little later," Diz said. "Why, between us, we was only gettin' $10,500 a year salary. Can you imagine, Paul is winnin' all those ball games and he is being paid only $3,000 per year. All I got to tell you is that Frankie got us together with Ol' Branch, and Paul gets hisself a $2,500 raise."

You won't find a ballplayer in either league who will tell you that Diz and Paul weren't worth twice what they were being paid. At the close of the 1934 season, when the Deans had pitched the Cards to the world championship, the St. Louis front office magnanimously offered each of them a $500 bonus.

"Paul was plumb disgusted," Diz grinned. "He wasn't gonna take the money. 'Take it, Paul, I tells him, that's all you're gonna get.'"

In '32 and '33, Diz was paid $3,000 per season. In '34, when he won 30 games, he was upped to $7,500. In 1935, he got a raise to $18,500, and he was paid $27,500 in 1936 and 1937. The total sum in salary the Card management paid him in six years is only slightly more than Bob Feller now gets for one season with the Indians.

"I just want to say that they sure worked me in 1934. Why, I worked in 50 ball games, and at the end of the season Ol' Diz was down to 161 pounds."

In fairness to the St. Louis club, it must be admitted that Diz seldom railed against pitching a game of baseball. He believed that he could pitch and win a ball game every day in the year. But it would seem to any objective observer that a wiser management would have had a little more mercy on the Great Man's arm and spirit.

"I guess the trouble with me," Diz said, "was that I jest loved to throw that ball. Why, I would get out there an' pitch battin' practice an' then go in there an' pitch a gol' darn ball game. I never paid much attention to the batters I was pitchin' to, except them Waner boys, Paul and Lloyd. Them two Pirates was always the toughest on Ol' Diz. An' them Cubs, as a team, were always rough. They're the only club in the National League who beat me more games than I beat them."

Few pitchers grieved and moaned about losing as sincerely as Dizzy; none has ever been so elated over a win. He seldom blamed others when he lost, the sole exception being the Cardinal catcher, Virgil Davis. Diz never liked to pitch to Davis. Their battles reached a climax one day in Cincy when Davis, according to Diz, failed to try for an easy foul fly right in front of the plate. Diz lost a 3–2 heartbreaker.

A few days later in the clubhouse, Diz announced that he was not going to pitch to Davis. Trainer Pop Haines brought this news to Frankie Frisch. The little manager threw his hands into the air.

"What is that boy trying to do to me?" Frankie wailed. "You go back and tell him he's *got* to pitch!"

Pop Haines returned to Diz, saying, "Son, I've been around this game for a good many years. You take my advice and don't get Frankie all rared up. Go out and pitch to Davis."

"Nope," Diz said stubbornly. "I made up my mind. You tell Ol' Frankie that Diz will pitch to anybody's mother-in-law, but he ain't a-gonna pitch to Davis."

Frisch finally gave in and put catcher Bill Delancy behind the plate. Delancy hit a homer in the eighth inning to win the ball game, 1–0. He caught most of Dean's games after that.

It wasn't until 1934 that Albert Monroe Dean, who gave baseball two great pitchers, saw his first big-league ball game. "I always figured," Diz said, "that Dad didn't want to see me in action up there, until Paul was workin' alongside me. You know, he always thought that Ol' Paul was a better pitcher than me. Paul being the baby of the family, it was only natural for him to have them sentiments."

Diz and Paul sent their father the money to make a plane trip from Houston, where he was working, to St. Louis to see the 1934 World Series games between the Cardinals and the Tigers. "Dad took a bus," Diz grinned, "because he said it was cheaper."

The father watched his two sons win the first two games against the Tigers. After the second game, he joined them in the dressing room, clapped them both on the back, and said, "I don't think I'll go on to

Detroit with you. You two boys got them under control an' I'd better get on back to work."

In 1935 and 1936, Albert Dean's boys still "had 'em under control." In those two years, Diz racked up 52 wins and Paul hurled 24 victories. Paul won only five games in '36, but it looked as though Diz's talk and his performances would actually go on forever.

The axe fell on July 7, 1937, in Griffith Stadium in the city of Washington. The Great Man, Dizzy Dean, took the mound to pitch for the All-Star team of the National League against the American League.

Diz was in his glory when that ball game started. His big grin was never more in evidence as he stood up there on the mound a-foggin' them in. Until the third inning it was a close game, the sort of give-and-take competition Ol' Diz loved. With two out in the third inning, Earl Averill came to the plate. He connected with one of Dizzy's fast balls and sent a sizzling line drive straight at the mound. It struck Diz in the left foot. He went down, got up again, his face twisted with pain.

Diz stayed in the game. He didn't know it then, but the ball had broken his big toe. In pain, trying to keep his speed, Diz wrenched his arm on a follow-through motion. That one throw, after all of the years of heaving a baseball over cotton-field land and the smooth dirt of National League ball parks, was the throw that ruined one of the greatest pitching arms of our time.

But you couldn't keep Diz down. Without proper rest or care, with his foot still bothering him, Diz stuck out the year with the Cards and trotted dutifully to the mound every time he was summoned. But he was through, irrevocably through. He dropped from 24 wins in 1936 to 13 victories in 1937.

"I know that one pitch was what did it," Dean said. "I was kiddin' myself in there after that. I didn't want to believe I was through. Maybe a rest, layin' off pitchin' might have helped. I dunno. Maybe not."

After he injured his arm, the Cards didn't keep Diz with them for very long. At the start of the 1938 season, they sold him to owner Phil Wrigley of the Chicago Cubs. Breadon got $185,000 in cash, an outfielder, and two pitchers—one of them Curt Davis, who won 20 games for the Cardinals.

"I never worked for a finer man than Mr. Wrigley," Diz said. "Breadon and Rickey knew I wasn't in shape when they sold me to the Cubs. That didn't seem to matter to Mr. Wrigley. He told me, 'Diz, we're just glad to have you with us.' And he paid me as much money in three years as the Cards did in seven."

Wrigley sent Diz to Johns Hopkins and the Mayo Clinic. The doctors told Dean that he was suffering from an inflammatory condition of the deltoid muscle (near the shoulder) a stretched and inflamed muscle in the back, and a subdeltoid bursitis aggravated by a spreading sinus condition. They told Diz that he was through as a pitcher. Diz refused to quit.

How could he quit, reading what Wrigley had told newspapermen: "I am satisfied that we have purchased the game's greatest playing attraction, on or off the field. We got Dizzy's spirit, courage, and enthusiasm, in addition to his arm."

So Dizzy insisted on staying in there and pitching. He won seven games and lost only one for the Cubs in 1938. But here the records are no indication of the way he was pitching. He started many games for Charlie Grimm, games he could not finish because of the pain in his shoulder.

The Cubs won the National League pennant in 1938, the first year Diz was with them. The Cubs played the Yankees for the world championship and that series brought about the most tragic moment in Dizzy Dean's career.

For eight excruciating innings, Dizzy Dean stayed on the mound throwing them in there. With his arm aching and his speed gone, the matchless Dean held down the big bats of the Yankees. With two away in the eighth, with the Cubs leading 3–2, with only four more possible batters to face, it looked as though Diz would do the impossible, win a last World Series game and go out in a blaze of glory.

There was a Yankee on first base. Frankie Crosetti came to the plate.

"Geeze," Diz said, his face suddenly sad, "a-comin' up was somethin' that was going to cause me the lowest moment in my life. I knowed my arm was gone. I couldn't break a pane of glass. But Crosetti never was a powerful hitter, so I figured I had a chance."

Crosetti hit Dizzy's first ball over the right-field fence. It sent the Yanks ahead, 4–3, and broke up the ball game. As Frankie trotted toward first base, Diz stood on the mound a beaten, tragic, hopeless, and utterly pathetic figure. But, as Crosetti rounded second, some of that wonderful, indomitable Dean spirit came back. He squared his shoulders and cupped his hands in the direction of the runner.

"Frank," Diz yelled. "I wish I could call back one year. You wouldn't get a loud foul off'n me!"

And, without breaking his stride, Crosetti called back, "Diz, you're sure right!"

"That was the longest, most terrible ball game I've ever watched," Dizzy Dean's wife said. "That was the high and the low, watching Diz in there for eight innings with nothing but a glove and a prayer. I could see the pain on Diz's face as he threw each ball. I knew, after that game, that he was through. It was a terrible thing to know."

Diz stayed with the Cubs through 1939. He won only six games and lost four. But the Chicago fans loved him as much, if not more, than he had been idolized by the St. Louis rooters when he had been at the height of his glory. "They loved Diz not for what he did," Mrs. Dean said quietly, "but for what he tried so hard to do and couldn't."

One night in 1935, Diz attended a barbecue given by the president of the Falstaff Brewing Company of St. Louis. At the affair, Diz got to talking to a young man who was suffering from infantile paralysis. The pitcher asked him how he managed to get around.

"Friends come with me," the young man said. "They drive my car and help in and out of places."

"Tell you what," Diz said instantly. "We ain't playin' a game tomorrow. Suppose I make the rounds with you. I kin drive and help you out some."

The next afternoon, and on several free afternoons after that, Diz turned up to help out. They became fast friends, then Diz went to the Cubs and didn't see the young man for several years. One day in 1941, the president of the Falstaff Brewing Company was meeting with the board to discuss the possibility of hiring someone to broadcast the St. Louis ball games. His son, the young man who had infantile paralysis, suddenly spoke up and said, "Dad, what about Diz? I think he'd be great."

And that was how Dizzy Dean became a sportscaster in St. Louis.

Ten years after he was picked as the best pitcher and most valuable player of the year, Diz was given an award as the best baseball announcer on the air.

Becoming an announcer didn't change the Dean personality in the slightest. He brought to the mike all the color, humor, high spirits, and unpredictable type of performance that he once exhibited on the diamond. His unorthodox vocal delivery, his free and easy manner, his deep love and knowledge of baseball, and the way he manhandles the King's English has earned him fanatical followers.

Sitting alongside Johnny O'Hara, who once broadcast all of Dean's doings on the mound, the irrepressible Dean delights his listeners with the casual ungrammatical, folksy Americana that once used to send players, fans, and managers into such appreciative and hysterical laughter.

Diz is a very bright guy and he could, if he wanted to strain and sound unnatural, tell the people about a ball game in pretty fair English. But Diz feels that people want to know what is happening in a game, that this is much more important than an announcer struggling for just the correct, descriptive word.

And let me ask you, what describes a ballplayer's action better than Diz saying, as he often has, "He slud into third base and he was throwed out." Or, "That was a foul ball, folks, an' the players has returned to their respectable bases."

When it comes to telling you why he speaks the way he does, Diz likes to quote a hero of his, the late Will Rogers. "Will onc't said, 'A lot of a people who don't say ain't—ain't eatin'," Diz grinned. "I'm gonna keep on sayin' ain't an' keep on eatin'."

At the microphone, Diz is in that ball game heart and soul, with all the fire and fun, the love and enthusiasm that he brought to pitching. He hates to see the home team lose, and he is not above participating in the game whenever he sees an opportunity. This activity has often caused deep chagrin among players on the opposing team.

One day in St. Louis, with the visiting team up, Diz looked the situation over and caught the opposition signs. He got excited and nervous because it seemed to him that the Browns were sound asleep. He leaned out over the rail of the broadcasting booth and, in a voice that could be heard all over the park, yelled: "Wake up out there, fellahs! Watch this guy! The ol' hit and run is on."

Diz may stumble over the big words, but his picturesque language creates the sort of images that all baseball fans enjoy. A runner at first base is "out by a heifer step." A star like Ted Williams is described as "Loose-goose Williams." And when the game begins to drag, Diz talks to the people about his ranch in Texas, inviting them all down, describing it as, "A Texas penthouse, an' you know what that is, folks. That's a hogpen with Venetian blinds."

The Great Man sometimes admits to making a *faux pas* on the air. During the war, there was a security order issued to all announcers, warning them not to mention anything about the weather conditions during, before or after a game.

"We get out to the park one day," Diz laughed, "an' it was rainin' like there was a hole in the sky. While we was waitin' for it to clear, O'Hara goes on and talks 'til he is plumb wore out. The he turns it over to me and I go to talkin'. I let the cat outa the bag that day. I just couldn't help it. I said, 'Folks, we can't tell you why this game is being held up, but if you'll jest stick yer necks outa the window, you'll find out.'

By 1943, Diz had created a vast radio audience, particularly among the younger element of St. Louis. Then trouble began to plague him in the form of the St. Louis school teachers. These hard-working exponents of high-falutin' language became appalled by the manner in which many of their students began to express themselves.

The teachers traced this deplorable (to them) use of English to one Jerome Herman Dean, a sports announcer who, in their opinion, was having "a simply atrocious effect in the matter of influencing the speech of our children." The teachers banded together and made a determined effort to have Dizzy Dean removed from the air.

The moppets who listened to Dean, who loved and idolized him, were terrified by the thought of never being able to hear again the voice of this great-hearted, baseball-wise gent who had been teaching them so many fascinating things about our national game.

It went all the way up to the Mayor's office.

Then Diz took the matter in his own large hands.

He went on the air one afternoon, his voice choking with emotion, and addressed the teachers of the city of St. Louis.

"All I kin say," Diz began, "is that I believe in education. I wisht that I hadda been able to get an education. But my mother died when I was three years old, an' I hadda go chop and pick cotton to make enough money fer black-eyed peas and sourbelly. I hadda work to make enough to eat on. I woulda gone to school if I had been able."

Diz's simple speech hit the St. Louis schoolmarms where they lived. All that week, letters poured in to Dizzy, letters from teachers apologizing for the attitude they had taken, sympathizing, stating that their complaint had been withdrawn and that they would do all they could to atone for the injustice they had done to him.

"It was agreed," Diz sighed, happily, "that the teachers would learn them kids English, an' I would learn 'em baseball."

But Diz, in spite of his success at the mike, is still a pitcher first and a sports announcer second. Half the population of St. Louis lays claim to the fact that they have played in a ball game in which Ol' Diz was the pitcher. It is almost true.

Whenever Dizzy can get away from his current job, he journeys around the country playing in exhibition games, hard and soft ball. He plays upon invitation, or just because he "happens to be around" where a game of baseball is being played and the greatest pitcher in the world is needed.

"Doggone," Diz said, "Pat and I will be drivin' along and I'll see a ball game and I jest have to stop the car and go to pitchin'. I jest can't seem to pass a ball game without gettin' into it."

Patricia, the pitcher's wife, will back up this statement 100 percent. The Deans live in the suburbs of St. Louis and all the kids for blocks around know the house where Dizzy Dean lives. "Along about five in the evening," Mrs. Dean said, "they ring the doorbell and ask me if Diz can come out and play ball with them. I've never known him to refuse."

Grover Cleveland Alexander Photo credit: National Baseball Library/Cooperstown, N.Y.,

GROVER CLEVELAND ALEXANDER

The Ups and Downs of Old Pete

Sport Magazine   April 1950

Written just a few months before Grover Cleveland Alexander's death, this poignant story was Jack Sher's tribute to a long-time friend. A few years later, with this article and others as a basis, a film biography was made of Alexander, titled "The Winning Team," and starring Ronald Reagan.

By Jack Sher

Maybe there's a fancy way of telling it, playing it for tears, or drama, or laughs, but the truth is such a bitter and beautiful thing that it seems a shame to trick it up. Anyway, life played enough tricks on Pete. His fate took so many unexpected twists and turns that unless you stick to the facts it comes out maudlin or shabby—or worse.

When Pete was born, his folks tacked a long handle on him—Grover Cleveland Alexander. One day in Texas, shortly after he went up to the big leagues, he set out with a couple of baseball cronies to do a little hunting and drinking, a pair of pastimes he loved almost as much as pitching. Riding on the back of a buckboard, filled with liquid cheer, he suddenly toppled off and landed flat on his face in a large pool of alkali and mud. When they finally got him back on the wagon, one of the ballplayers began to laugh at the splattered face, saying, "Well, if you ain't ol' Alkali Pete himself!"

The name stuck. All his life he kept falling in the mud and getting up.

Grover Cleveland Alexander, was one of the greatest pitchers the National League ever had, or, for that matter, ever will have. His records stretch further than that long right arm of his, which flung those sweeping side-arm curves for 20 years in the major leagues. Only Cy Young and Walter Johnson won more ball games than Grover Cleveland Alexander's 373. And Pete tops every pitcher, except Walter Johnson, in shutouts. He hurled 90 of them.

Back in the 1916 season, Alexander pitched 16 shutouts, which is still the major-league record for one year's work. The year before that, in '15, he chalked up four *one-hit* shutouts, another major-league record. His earned-run average that season was 1.22 per game. He won 31 games that year, 33 in 1916, 30 in 1917. And Pete also holds the NL record for number of years leading the league in games won—and earned-run average.

Well, Alex started out strong back there in 1911. His first year up, he won 28 games. No rookie had done this before, or has done it since. Most of his 20 years on the mound were spent with second-division clubs, in-and-outers. Pep Lee, a former big-leaguer and a friend of Alexander's, likes to tell how kids would run up to Pete before a game and ask him what the score was going to be.

"Gonna be a tie game, nothin' to nothin'," Pete would grin. "We don't figure to get any runs, but I don't aim to give any, neither."

When Alexander left the Phillies and went to the Cubs, he was well past his prime as a pitcher. But his eight-year stay in Chicago averages out to about 18 wins a season, which would satisfy most stars of today. At the age of 33, in 1920, he won 27 games for the Cubs. Six years later, at thirty-nine, he pitched the St. Louis Cards to a pennant and then, almost single-handed, beat the Yanks in the World Series! When he was 40 years old, in 1927, he won 21 games for the Redbirds!

Old Pete was always slow getting to the mound. But once he climbed up on that heap of dirt, he fired the ball across with so much stuff and accuracy that he could pitch a double-header in the time it takes most hurlers to go nine innings.

One of Alex's shutouts was clocked at 58 minutes. It was the second game of a doubleheader. The Phillies were playing the St. Louis Cards. Pete had won the first tiff.

"We need this one," Pat Moran, Philly manager said, "but get it over fast, Pete. We've only got little better'n an hour to catch that train."

They made the train.

Walter Johnson, a farmboy like Alex, needed only one word every time anyone would ask him who was the greatest pitcher in the major leagues. He would answer "Pete."

Down through baseball history, great and near-great pitchers have hurled no-hit games. Alexander never did. Dozens of times, coming into the seventh, eighth, even the ninth frame, he'd have a no-hitter in his hip pocket, only to have it spoiled by a dinky bingle off the bat of a man he had struck out innumerable times. But Pete had enough records. His philosophy out there on any hot day was to get a man out easy, without back-breaking effort. He once threw only 12 pitches in four complete innings. Few batters ever worked Alex for more than two balls; he would rather see one of his offerings clouted out of the park than allow a man a free ride to first base.

There are endless stories about the big Nebraskan's amazing control. Once, during Spring training Bill Killefer, his old battery-mate, stood behind the plate with a tomato-can. Alex wound up and tossed one at the opening. It plopped in as clean as a whistle. Killefer changed the position of the can and Pete bullseyed another. He kept it up, without missing once, for 15 minutes.

The sight of Alexander strolling to the mound to start a World Series fracas always made the game's greatest slugger, the Babe, wince. Ruth could never fathom old Pete's deceptive curves.

Old ballplayers will tell you that Pete was a real nice guy, too. He wasn't one for counting his money. There was always a stack of it on his dresser in the hotel room for anybody who cared to pick up a 10 or 20 and pay him back when they got around to it.

Of course, he could afford to be a soft touch then. Why, the Cubs paid him as high as $8,000 a year, even throwing in a $1,000 bonus at the end of the season, if he won more than 30 games! Of course, the Phillies' management was sort of tight with Pete. They paid him $250 a month that first year he won 28 games for them, and those years he won 30 or more games they never could see their way clear to paying him much more than that. Now the Cardinals were downright generous. They paid him an all-time top salary (for Pete) of $17,000 a year in 1927, and all they probably expected him to do was win another pennant and World Series. Pete let them down. He couldn't push up more than 21 victories that year.

Pete had some mighty important friends in those days. Why, there was Governor Tener of Pennsylvania, General Pershing, Mayor Jimmy Walker, John Barrymore, people like that, always coming around to talk with Old Pete about baseball. Hundreds of them. Bill Jeffers, the president of the Union Pacific Railroad, and John Heydler, president of the National League, used to play a lot of golf with Pete.

A couple of days after Pete had finished that last World Series game in 1926, Sam Breadon called up Pete's wife, Aimee, to tell her that they wanted him right away at an important banquet in honor of the world champion Cardinals. Aimee found Pete at the Governor's Mansion, explaining to Governor Reid of Missouri the pitches he had used to strike out Tony Lazzeri.

"The Governor got real mad when I wanted to take Alex away," Aimee Alexander related. "You see, everybody loved him, all sorts of people."

That's the truth. They did. Even strangers felt a sort of a glow when Pete strolled by in those days and somebody would point and say, "That's him, that's Alexander, the pitcher that beat the Yanks."

But speaking of strangers, one stumbled across Pete not long ago. It was the day before Christmas, at two o'clock in the morning, and this fellow was taking a short cut home, his steps leading him through an alley behind a small hotel located near Hollywood Boulevard in the movie capital. A few feet in front of him, a coatless figure lay crumpled on the cracked and dirty pavement. . . .

The stranger approached the body cautiously and bent down. Then he rolled it over to have a look at the face. It was battered, stubborn. One ear was completely missing. Blood trickled down from a gash just above it, split open by the fall.

It was old Pete's face, of course.

When the ambulance arrived, there seemed to be little of the breath of life left in Pete's huge body. He was taken to an emergency hospital for treatment, then transferred to the county hospital, the Los Angeles General. There was no money in his pockets, but his identity was established by a battered Social Security card and, curiously enough, two valuable rings. Etched in the gold band of one of the rings were the following words: *St. Louis Cardinals World Champions,* 1926.

This reporter had a head full of questions when he went down to the county hospital shortly afterward with his ex-wife Aimee Alexander. We found Pete in a room with three other men patients, who looked maybe a little worse than the ballplayer. They were old, beaten, with hopelessness and death in their faces.

Pete was sitting up on his bed, staring at the floor, when we came into the room. Aimee crossed to him and he took both her hands.

"I want to get out of here," he said.

"I'm trying to find a place for you to live, Alec," Aimee said.

"I can't hear what you're saying," Pete said. "I don't hear a thing now."

Before the fall, he had only partial hearing in one ear. Now he is totally deaf.

As we stood there, Aimee Alexander wrote notes on pieces of paper, which she would pass to Grover Cleveland Alexander. I have some of those scribbled notes on my desk before me now.

"We have to find a place for you to live where you won't have to cross too many streets," she wrote.

"I just want to go home," Pete said, reading the note.

"You must be patient, Alec," Aimee wrote.

"Please get me out of here, Aimee," he said.

She wrote, "When I get you a place, do you think you'll need someone to take care of you?"

"No," Alec answered. "No. I can take care of myself."

Aimee wrote, "You know you can't go galloping over streets and into traffic when you can't hear."

"Where are my rings?" Pete asked. "I want my rings."

"They're keeping them for you, Alec," Aimee wrote. "They're safe."

On the rough wooden table beside the bed was a box with three baseballs in it. A fan of long ago, had sent them to him to be autographed. There was also a telegram, which read, "Pete, you were in tighter pinches. Get out of this one." It was signed, Cozy Dolan, Croydon Hotel, New York City. There was a letter with a small check from a well-known, retired major-league umpire. And a letter with a check for $5 from a childhood friend who hadn't seen Pete in 40 years.

When visiting hours were over, when it came time for us to go, Pete took Aimee's hand again.

"Cheer up," she said. "Come on, smile, Alec."

He couldn't hear her. He began to cry, softly. . . .

"If you write about him," Aimee said, "tell what really happened. Nobody ever has."

Well, it's going to be rough going. Pete's life was like that. He kept falling down and getting up again. And when you know the whole story, you'll know that he deserved better than a county hospital when he got to the end of the road.

The road began on February 26, 1887, on a farm near St. Paul, Nebraska. Grover Cleveland Alexander was born into a family of 13 children, 12 boys and one girl. His father was a farmer and the finest hunter in the community. Dode, as Alec was then called, did his first hunting with stones and rocks.

"He was always throwing at something," his mother once said. "When

I wanted a chicken or a turkey killed, Dode would go out and bring it down with a rock, hitting it on the run."

Whenever he could, young Alexander would slip into town and get into a ball game. He pitched in pickup games on the schoolyard lot, using that awkward, funny, side-arm delivery that knocked down chickens on the run. None of the kids in the small Nebraska town could seem to get a piece of that ball which Dode whipped at them.

When he was 19, Alec took a job as a lineman for a telephone company. The linemen had a ball team and Alec pitched for them. His first time out, the big farm boy beat a team of "paid players" in Central City, Nebraska. He whipped them four games in a row. The telephone team didn't play often enough to suit Alexander, so he picked up with scrub teams. One day, when a game went into extra innings, Alec showed up late for work with the line gang. The foreman fired him.

"You won't be any good to anybody until you get this ballplayin' out of your blood," the foreman said.

Alec never did.

The manager of the Central City team hired Alex at $50 a month. When the season ended in Central City, Alexander drifted to a County Fair at Burwell, Nebraska, to pitch two games against a crack semi-pro team from Illinois. He won both games and a shortstop named Miller, playing for the rival team, carried the news back to the manager of a professional team in Galesburg, Illinois.

On January 12, 1909, Grover Cleveland Alexander signed his first contract as a professional ballplayer with Galesburg in the Class D Three-Eye League. His salary was $100 a month. He won 15 games for Galesburg before he got slapped into the dirt, hit so hard it almost closed his career forever.

It was mid-season, during a hard-fought game. Alex, who wasn't much of a hitter, loped down to first on a scratch single. On the hit and run, he started for second in that comical, awkward way he always ran. The Galesburg batter hit a ground ball to the shortstop, who flipped it to the second-baseman for a force-out. The second-baseman wheeled and fired the ball toward first in an attempted double play. Alex came charging on, the ball struck him full on the side of the head. He lay in the dirt, out cold, not a muscle moving.

The big kid pitcher was unconscious for 56 hours. When Alex came back into the world, when he was able to sit up in the hospital bed, he saw two of everything. He was told by the doctors, honestly if cruelly, that he might suffer from double vision for the rest of his life.

When they let him out of the hospital, Alex stubbornly insisted on getting back into uniform. Day after day, he tried to pitch. But he kept seeing two batters, two catchers. Finally, without revealing his ailment,

Galesburg sold Alexander to the Indianapolis ball club, managed by Charlie Carr.

Scared, heartsick, still seeing double, young Alexander reported to Indianapolis. He distinguished himself at the first practice by breaking three of Charlie Carr's ribs with the first ball he pitched. Carr sent him home.

Day after day, Pete would go into town, hunt up someone to catch for him, and keep on throwing at the two figures. He kept it up all through the long Winter.

"I knew I was through, but I couldn't stop throwin'," he once said. "If I stopped, I knew I'd go all to pieces."

Alex couldn't believe it when the Indianapolis management notified him the following Spring that he had been traded to Syracuse in the New York State League. Carr, who wanted a favor from the Syracuse manager, gave Alexander to that ball club for exactly nothing!

"This Alexander is wild as hell," Carr told the Syracuse pilot, "but he's got plenty of speed."

And so Syracuse got, for free, the greatest control pitcher of all time.

Two or three days before Alex left to report to the Eastern ball club, his vision returned to normal, miraculously. He was pitching to a friend in a schoolyard in St. Paul, Nebraska. As he wound up, two catcher's mitts danced before his eyes and then, as the ball cracked into the receiver's glove, everything suddenly became one, clear and whole.

Into Syracuse like a windstorm came the tall Nebraskan with the freckled face, the shock of sandy hair, and the peculiar side-arm delivery. Straight from the farm, from hopelessness and despair, came the young pitcher who was to be called Alex the Great, who was to set mound records that would never be matched.

Maybe he was greater in later years, but the Syracuse Stars thought that Grover Cleveland Alexander, pitching for them in 1910, was something of a miracle—and, in a way, he was. Almost half of the games he won, 29 in all, were shutouts.

The claw of a major-league club reached out and the 22-year-old hurler from nowhere was purchased by owner Horace Fogel of the Philadelphia Phillies. Alexander was bought for the incredible sum of $500. He was promised $250 on the line every month, providing he made good.

"It seemed like a stack of money," Alex told a reporter in later years, "so I tried extra hard."

The big Nebraska rookie shuffled out to a big-league mound for the first time in a pre-season, intra-city game against the world champion Philadelphia Athletics.

"You'll pitch the first five innings," manager Pat Moran said to Alexander. "They'll be murder, but you'll learn something."

The spectators who sat in Baker Bowl that afternoon, the players on both benches, and the umpires saw the beginning of a career that was to become a legend. With barely a pause for breath between pitches, the long, young arm of Grover Cleveland Alexander swept the A's down like a scythe. Not a run crossed the plate, not a man got a hit, nor did he give up a walk.

The rookie pitcher, with only one full season in the minors behind him, went on to win 28 games that year. Up went his first record, in a high, clean place, never to be touched. All those subsequent falls in the mud could never erase that. And late in the season, with the victories piled up behind him, Alexander faced the immortal Cy Young in what was undoubtedly the greatest pitchers' duel of the century.

It was Denton True Young's last game. He had won 511 ball games, the record book as the all-time high. He still had the skill, the heart, all the ingredients that comprise greatness in a pitcher. Hurling for the Boston Nationals that day, the gallant Cy used every pitch he had learned in 22 years of baseball—sweeping curves, drops, the deceptive spitball. Inning after inning, the game wore on, neither side able to dent the matchless hurling of the fat, ancient veteran or the young rookie. Cy gave out in the 12th, the Phils pushed across one run, Alex held fast, and the game was his.

Young was 44 years old when he pitched that last game. It must have been a tough one for old Cy to lose. But he lost it to a man who could carry the torch—the best pitcher in the National League then and 20 years later.

Alex pitched easy that day. He always did. He'll tell you that his string of victories was won, not with sweat and speed, but with ease and cunning. He gives a great deal of credit for his method and his staying power to that first manager of his, the wily old catcher, Pat Moran.

"You got eight men to help you," Pat would pound at his young rookie. "Never forget that. Don't be trying to strike 'em all out. Use the men behind you. *Be smart, save that arm!*"

Alex listened. He held back his fast one. He did pretty well. In his first seven years in the majors, he won 190 ball games, an average of about 27 a year!

Pete loved to help young pitchers. As late as 1939, Pete was still trying to get in a word on how a ball game should be pitched. In an article in *Liberty,* he wrote, "Every kid pitcher wants to set a batter's shirt on fire with every pitch, just to make an impression. They do just that on the sandlots, in the minors. And, having landed with a big-league team, keep right on doing it in an effort to prove they are worth more than they are being paid.

"They throw away their arms before they are mature," Pete fumed. "They want to flash into baseball's Hall of Fame by pitching a no-hit game. Each and every one of them tries to throw that ball past the batter, using everything but his head on every pitch. Well, I got myself into the Hall of Fame without a no-hitter.

Only one hitter ever bothered Pete. Ironically, it was the man who made possible Alexander's greatest day in baseball; the man who reached down and helped Alec to his feet during one of those tumbles into the mud; the game's top right-hand slugger—Rogers Hornsby.

The first time Alexander faced Rogers, he sent him down swinging on four pitched balls. Rog's next time up, he went out on a measly pop fly. The third trip up, Pete took pity on the fledgling. Alexander and Bill Killefer held a brief confab halfway between the plate and mound.

"We got these Cards in our hip pockets," Alex yawned. "This kid needs a break. Tell him I'm gonna throw one right in there for him, about waist high across the middle."

Killefer returned to his position behind the batter, passed on the news, and held out his big mitt. The ball never reached it. Hornsby slashed it against the left-field wall for a double. And from that day on, he hit Pete as though he owned him.

What the battery of Mathewson and Bresnahan had been in the early 1900's, the duo of Alexander and Killefer became in the years 1912 to 1920. Killefer weighed 200 pounds and was a big, burly catcher with a deadly arm, the smartest judge of pitchers in the league.

Old ballplayers will tell you that Alexander and Killefer would often work an entire game without exchanging signals. Bill would tell Alex before a game, "You just throw 'em and I'll catch 'em and we'll get outa the park early today."

Both men were quiet, cool, seemingly nerveless. One day in Pittsburgh, as Honus Wagner tells it, Alex had a two-run lead over the Pirates going into the eighth inning. Then two errors and a single filled the bases. Alex got Miller on a pop fly and struck out Clarke. Honus waddled up to the plate.

Killefer stepped in front of the dish and walked a few feet toward Alexander. The big pitcher's grin reached almost to Wagner's bat.

"What's the trouble, Bill?" Alex asked, casually.

"Got to strike this bird out," Bill said, conversationally.

"Well, I don't figure it would help none to walk him," Alexander said in that slow, dry way he had of speaking.

Honus ends the yarn with a wry grin, saying, "Pete threw three to me and I missed 'em all."

Casey Stengel was playing the outfield for Brooklyn on that historic Labor Day in 1917 when Alex slapped down the Brooks twice in one afternoon. He shut them out, 5–0, in the opener, beating the renowned Rube Marquard. As though the first nine had been a bullpen warmup, Pete climbed up on the hill and pitched nine more innings that same afternoon, whipping Brooklyn again, 9–3.

It marked the second year that Alex the Great had pushed a mediocre Philadelphia team to within a breath of the pennant but he wound up his seven-year stretch with the Phils.

These were the important offseason headlines in 1917:

"Alexander and Killefer Sold To Cubs for $50,000."

"Alexander Likely to Be Drafted."

"Alexander Demands $10,000 Bonus From Phillies."

William F. Baker, the owner of the Phils, didn't tell Alexander in advance that he was selling him to the Cubs. Alex, hurt and angry, read it in his hometown paper, in St. Paul, Nebraska, during the Winter of 1917–'18. Pete knew he was going to war. The pittance he had made with the Philadelphia ball club had not left him enough to take care of his mother while he would be away.

While he was home, the ballplayer continued a courtship that had begun at a dance a few years before. The girl was Aimee Arrants, from a nearby town, a small, lively young woman with titian hair and bright blue eyes.

She was the only one who could handle him, ever. She was the only person who understood why a hero of millions, a great, courageous figure, could fall so often and so far.

Pete wanted $10,000 to sign with the Chicago team—enough to take care of his mother, his family, and the girl he planned to marry while he would be away at war.

Alexander and Wrigley talked it over on a Pasadena golf course early in the Spring of 1918. Wrigley, a generous man with ballplayers, offered to send Aimee $500 every other month for three years. If Alexander stayed in the service longer than that, Wrigley said he would give Alec's wife $10,000 and take care of her until the ballplayer returned.

Alexander put out his hand. "I'll report when you send for me," he said, "and thanks."

There was never a written contract. Wrigley stuck to his bargain.

Alex and Aimee were married at Camp Funston, Kansas, just three weeks before he sailed for France. He was 31 years old, in perfect health, extremely happy, confident that he had years of great baseball and good living ahead of him.

The Chicago papers headlined: *"Alex On His Way Home," "Alexan-*

der Returns From France!" Huge crowds flowed into the LaSalle Street Station to greet him, to carry him on their shoulders to the street. Alex the Great was home from the wars, the Cubs were mighty and would prevail. But it wasn't the same Grover Cleveland Alexander.

In France, Pete had been up in the lines as an artillery sergeant with the 342nd Artillery Battalion of the famed 89th Infantry Division. The constant roar of the guns had made him deaf in one ear, and the war had done something else to him, which his wife was to find out about, terrifyingly, within a few weeks.

It happened suddenly, in the middle of the night, in their hotel room in Chicago. Aimee was awakened by Alex clutching her arm, groaning, twisting, turning. He was having an attack of epilepsy. The disease was to stay with him all the rest of his life, strike him when he least expected it. It was to haunt him, torture him, make him drink himself into a stupor time and time again.

"Sometimes the fit would strike him while he was out on the mound," Aimee Alexander said. "He always carried a bottle of spirits of ammonia with him. They would have to carry him off the field. Some thought he was drunk. They would take him into the locker room, Alec would whiff the ammonia, fight to get control of himself, and then go right back out and pitch again."

It happened many times. And for years, nobody but Aimee and a few doctors knew about it. It might have been the result of getting struck in the head that first year as a professional ballplayer with Galesburg. But the war had certainly aggravated it.

"We were never certain when they were going to happen," Aimee went on. "Sometimes he'd get three or four in one month. Then he'd go months without anything happening. I remember once in Pittsburgh," she said, "I saw Alec signal the umpire suddenly and call time. I knew what was happening. He went into the dressing room for about 15 minutes, came out again, and pitched the entire game. That takes a great deal of courage. They always left him so weak and, well, sort of hopeless."

Old Pete got drunk a lot. There wasn't any question about that. He started drinking heavily right after the war and he kept it up.

"Alex always thought he could pitch better with a hangover," Aimee smiled, "and maybe he could, at that. I did my best to keep him straight. When he was with me, he was all right. But then he'd wander off. Even so, he did pretty well as a pitcher, didn't he? I don't see any reason to hide the fact that he drank—everyone knows it."

No, there's nothing to hide. He was a decent guy, generous, sweet, loved by the men who played the game with him. He drank like a fool.

He'd fall into the mud. They'd help him home late at night. And the next day he'd be out on the mound, trying to win.

In 1925, when Pete was 38, George Gibson called on him to hurl an intracity game with the White Sox. The game went 19 innings. When the umps called it on account of darkness, Alex was still out on the hill firing away, sort of tired, but holding up his end of a 2–2 score.

It had been a tough year on Pete, not a very satisfying one. He had broken his wrist at the start of the season. The Cubs had wound up in the cellar and the best the old-timer had been able to do for them in the way of wins was 15 games.

He kept his troubles to himself. He asked no favors. He walked with fear tugging at him all the time. But his wry sense of humor would peek out at the most unexpected times, when the trouble was heaviest, when a game had to be won, or else.

"During the Winter of 1925–'26, Alex went to a sanitarium in Dwight, Illinois, to cure himself of drinking," Aimee revealed. "I didn't ask him to. Nobody did. He loved baseball so much, and he felt that he was giving it a bad name drinking the way he did, so he made up his mind, alone, to do something about it. He stayed there for months and he was well when he came home. He looked better than he ever had. And then," tears coming into her eyes, she added, "well, trouble just seemed to be waiting for him, always."

During Spring training at Catalina that year, Pete broke his ankle. While he was laid up in the hospital, everyone on the ball team came to see him but his manager, Joe McCarthy.

Day after day, Alexander kept hoping McCarthy would stop by and see him. Pete began to brood about it. Maybe they didn't think he mattered to the team anymore? He wasn't through—he was only 39—why, old Cy Young was a hard man to whip at 42 and 43 years of age, and he figured to outlast Cy.

When he could hobble around on crutches, McCarthy ordered Alexander to make the trip every day from Catalina to Wrigley Field in Los Angeles for exhibition games. It was a long, painful trip. In all his years in baseball, nobody had ever disliked him or treated him roughly.

Early in June, his ankle in good shape again, Pete went on the first road trip with the Cubs. But he still couldn't seem to get along with McCarthy. When it came Pete's turn to get out there on the mound, Mac would tell him how he wanted the game pitched, how to serve them up to each batter. Nobody had ever told Pete how to pitch a game before.

Some of the exchanges between old Pete and the then-young McCarthy were amusing. Like the day in Pittsburgh, when McCarthy called a meeting before the game to discuss strategy to be used against the Pirates. One of the Buc players had been the property of the Cubs at the start of the season, and had then been traded to the Pirates. He was the man McCarthy was discussing.

"We'll change our signs whenever he gets on second base," McCarthy ordered.

Alexander looked up suddenly and drawled, "If there was any chance of that guy ever getting to second base, we wouldn't have sold him, would we?"

The final blow-up came in Philadelphia, in that City of Brotherly Love where Grover Cleveland Alexander had made all those enduring records. Joe McCarthy gave him his walking papers.

Old Pete was down in the mud again.

"It was probably one of the lowest moments in his life," Aimee Alexander said. "He thought he was through in baseball forever. Whenever he'd try to speak, tears would come into his eyes."

In St. Louis, during the time Pete was on his back in bed in Chicago, Bill Killefer, was talking things over with Rogers Hornsby, manager of the red-hot St. Louis Cards.

"They say Pete is through," Killefer said. "He's not, Rog. As long as he can stand on his feet, he's still the pitcher I'd want out there if we were in a rough spot."

The stolid faced Hornsby nodded. "Call him and tell him we can use him," Rog said.

The following Sunday, the loudspeaker in Sportsman's Park in St. Louis blared the information that the battery for the Cardinals that afternoon would be "O'Farrell and Alexander." The team the Cards opposed? Joe McCarthy's Chicago Cubs.

Mac won't forget that day. The seemingly tireless, ancient right-hander with the weird side-arm delivery never pitched a better game of baseball in his life. Down the Cubs went, as Old Pete got each hitter out of the way on three, four, usually not more than six pitched balls. The final score was St. Louis 3, Chicago 2.

McCarthy was still sitting forlornly on the bench when Grover Cleveland Alexander passed him on the way to his new clubhouse. Pete looked him right in the eye, smiled, tipped that too-small cap that always perched so precariously on his head, and walked on.

Perhaps no incident in baseball has been written and rewritten so many times as that seventh inning in the seventh and final game of the 1926 World Series when Grover Cleveland Alexander saved the day for the Cardinals.

But what few have told about are those first Series games. The Redbird team went into the World Series a 15–1 underdog! And why not? It was facing the most powerful Yankee club in history, armed with such great hurlers as Pennock, Hoyt, Shocker, Ruether, and Shawkey. And the Yanks had pretty fair country hitters, too—broad-beamed Gehrig, the Babe, Push-'em-up Tony Lazzeri, Meusel, and Combs, to name a few.

The Cards started Wee Willie Sherdel, a great portside hurler, in the opener in Yankee Stadium. Herb Pennock pitched for the Yanks. Everything went according to schedule. The Yankee pitcher bottled up the Cards, allowed them but three hits, and won his game, 2–1.

The sportswriters, the baseball authorities, the fans, must have thought that young Rogers Hornsby's mind had jumped the track when he announced the morning of the second game that Old Pete was going to pitch it. They were still thinking along those same lines when the Yanks exploded for a pair of runs in the second inning. But Alex had a sort of mean grin on his face when he walked out on the mound to start the third inning. Earle Combs opened up with a single, but from that moment on, not a New Yorker reached first base.

The Cards got to Shocker for six runs and old Pete had another ball game in his hip pocket.

"Well," the sportswriters pecked out on their typewriters that night, "Old Pete had one great ball game left in that arm and he pitched it today."

After the game, Aimee, who had been sitting in the stands, asked Pete how he felt.

"Fine," he smiled. "May win another for Hornsby. You know, I sure like that young fellow. He don't tell me nothin', except to go in there and throw 'em the way I see fit."

In St. Louis, behind the superb throwing of Jess Haines, the keyed-up Cards slapped the Yanks down in the third game. But the big Yankee bats began blasting in the fourth game and whacked four Cardinal hurlers out of the box, tying up the Series. They took the fifth game, too. It was Sherdel against Pennock again, one of those brilliant ding-dong pitchers' duels, and hard-luck Willie lost it in the 10th inning, 3–2. Now the Yanks were one game ahead and the Series moved back to the Stadium.

The sixth game, the Yankee fans sat open-mouthed as old Grover Cleveland Alexander ambled out on to the mound. Crowding 40 years of age, deaf in one ear, maybe a little worried about one of those "spells" hitting him suddenlike. Pete stayed out there the full nine innings and won his ball game. He was in trouble a couple of times, but he just couldn't see his way clear to allowing the New York Yankees more than two runs. Pete's win tied up the series.

"Well, it was a pretty fair ball game at that," Alexander said. "I could sort of use a nap."

"And maybe a nip?" Hornsby said, his eyes twinkling.

"I don't know about that," Pete said, "but I'll see you tomorrow."

Hornsby began looking for him, as every sports fan knows, in the fatal seventh inning when the Cards were leading, 3–2, and the bases were loaded. Jess Haines had a blister on his finger and couldn't continue. Hornsby called the bullpen and the man on the phone turned to Old Pete, sitting idly on the bench. Was he asleep, drunk, hungover? What's the difference? He was still the greatest pitcher in the baseball business.

Pete stirred, stretched, got to his feet. Hornsby told me, several years ago in Chicago, that his pitcher wasn't drunk when he met him along the base-line. Hornsby probably would have pitched him drunk or sober, because he could depend on Old Pete.

It was quite a situation, at that. Combs, Meusel, and Gehrig filling up all three bases. The deadly, young Tony Lazzeri at the plate. Two out, a World Series title at stake, the Cards just one slim run ahead. You can always repeat what Old Pete said that day.

"There just don't seem to be no place to put Lazzeri. Guess I'll have to get him out."

And down Tony went on four pitched balls.

Alex stayed in there for the eighth and ninth innings, and was pretty well warmed up by the time O'Farrell threw Ruth out trying to steal second, thereby giving the Cardinals the world championship for 1926.

They offered Pete the world on a silver platter after that Series. Vaudeville engagements, endorsements, business opportunities. He could have exploited them for thousands and thousands of dollars, enough to keep himself in the chips for the rest of his life. But he didn't take them. He figured he'd wait a bit. He figured there were still quite a few more years he could make a decent enough living throwing a baseball.

While the city of St. Louis went around for weeks shouting his name, Pete snuck away to do a little hunting and drinking. The world was a pretty good old place after all, and he had a contract for $17,000 in his pocket calling for his services in 1927.

The Cardinal management traded Hornsby late in 1926, and when Rog left, some of Alex's heart went with him. Alexander, at 40 years of age, won 21 games for the Cards. They finished in second place.

In 1928, the fits that had been striking him on and off through the years became more frequent. The Cards were in a hot race for the National League flag one day late in September. They needed a ball game. So Pete was on the mound, throwing them up there at the Cubs. He seemed to be going easy. He was ahead. Suddenly he crumpled, slid face down on the dirt.

They carried him into the dressing room and worked over him until he finally came around. Manager Bill McKechnie bent over him, patted him on the shoulder.

"Take it easy, Pete," he said.

"Sure I am," Alexander said, sitting up. "Just a little dizzy spell. Let me finish this one, Bill."

The pleading in Pete's eyes was too much for the manager. Alexander went back into the ball game and won it. The game got the Cards rolling again. They breezed through to the pennant. Pete won 16 games that year.

But he fell down quite a few more times that year, too. Took those headers into the mud. In 1929, the Cardinals let him go. He had won nine games and lost eight when they turned him out to pasture with a "thank-you-very-much, Pete, but you're getting a little too hard to handle." Aimee divorced him that year. He was drinking too much and he had no regard for money. To keep herself going, she got a job in Cincinnati and tried to keep tabs on Pete.

In 1930, the Philadelphia Phillies signed again the greatest pitcher that club had ever had, or ever would have. Pete slogged through Spring training. He kept falling down and getting up, trying hard but never quite making it back into form.

Pete lost three games for the Phils. He didn't have it. He gave up a couple of walks early in one game, and that wasn't like old Pete. It must have just about killed him to see those players trotting down to first on a free pass at the hand of Grover Cleveland Alexander.

The Phils turned him loose, too.

Dallas, in the minors, squeezed out room on the bench for him. He stayed a few months, won a game, lost a few, then drifted out of sight.

Nobody knows much about what happened to Pete between the years 1931 and 1933. Those were pretty tough years for everyone. We had breadlines, WPA, NRA, and the Blue Eagle went up in store windows. Pete just drifted around. He stayed for a while with his sister in St. Paul, Nebraska, talked about their childhood, about the kids in the family he hadn't seen in years, some of whom he had helped through school during those days when the salary checks came in regular. And then he drifted on.

In 1934, the House of David baseball team signed a new pitcher, an old-timer named Grover Cleveland Alexander. They figured that people might pay hard cash to watch Pete toss a few innings now and then. He looked all of his 47 years of age, but he could still loop them up to the plate and damn if he still couldn't fool some of the boys with that soft, tricky curve ball.

The manager of the House of David called Aimee. He told her they had signed Grover and that he had heard she was the only one who could handle him. Then Pete got on the phone and asked her would she please come back to him again. Aimee came back. And married him again.

Pete stayed with the team for three years. He went into a flock of ball games as a relief hurler. Amazingly, he always seemed to have it when the club was in a tight spot when they were up against a scrappy bunch of youngsters in some hinky dink of a town.

But he kept on drinking. Aimee had to leave him for the second time. He was 50 years old when he pitched his last ball game. He drifted on, dead broke and not walking too steadily.

In 1938, they elected Grover Cleveland Alexander to the Hall of Fame. Wynn Clark, head of the Ballplayers' Association on the West Coast, tells me that they gave Pete a job as a guard at Cooperstown along about then, but that he couldn't seem to hold on to it.

The National League coughed up $50 a month for Pete's sister in St. Paul, so she could take care of him. He didn't stay there too long. Sort of kept on the move, proud and stubborn and mighty certain that he'd get along and be able to take care of himself for quite a spell longer.

Johnny Conners, a featherweight fighter, found Pete broke and wandering around the streets in Springfield, Illinois, one night. Johnny had a beer parlor and he gave Alexander a job as a sort of host.

Shortly after that, there were several articles in the New York papers about Pete. They told about how Grover Cleveland Alexander, one of the greatest pitchers the National League ever had, a 373-game winner, was now on exhibit at Hubert's Museum, a honky-tonky on 42nd Street between Seventh and Eighth Avenues. Hundreds of people flocked in daily to have a look at the old ballplayer, talking away up there on a platform, sandwiched in between a snake charmer and the penny slot machines, the nickel games, the freak shows, and the shooting gallery.

If the sob stories stung a little, Pete shook them off, the way you shake off a catcher's signal that you know won't send a man down swinging. The job in the flea circus paid $100 a week. Every half hour or so, Pete would come out of a cubbyhole, climb to the platform, and talk about baseball. The highlight of Alexander's spiel, of course, was the 1926 World Series. Hour after hour, day after day, he would tell about the dramatic moment when he struck out Tony Lazzeri.

He told the reporters that it wasn't a bad setup, as jobs go. He liked the lively, interested questions that the sport fans, young and old, tossed at him. He packed a lot of drama and humor into the stories he told. He was the best show on the street.

Pete stayed at Hubert's Museum for several years. The second world war came along and he got a job, for a while, as a guard in a gun factory.

And he worked for a short time in a Washington hotel. Then he drifted back to St. Louis, the home of his past glories and his great days. There, he lectured for school kids about baseball and gave them instructions on sandlots.

Aimee, who had been in touch with him from time to time, lost track of him. She began to worry about him. She was in Los Angeles and she got someone to promise him a job. Then she began the search to find him. It went on for months. Nobody had the slightest idea of what had happened to Grover Cleveland Alexander.

Where was Old Pete? How was he making out? Nobody knew. In desperation, she wrote to Bill Stern, the sportscaster, asking him to ask the question on the air—the $64 question—where are you, Pete?

Stern did ask the question and, through the broadcast, they found Grover Cleveland Alexander. He was tucked away in a veterans' hospital in the Bronx, about to undergo an operation made necessary by an old war wound. Aimee stayed with him until he got better. She arranged to get him back to California. She found him a room in a small hotel near her and talked the National League into giving him a pension of $100 per month.

Pete took to waiting out his life in the hotel room. When the loneliness of the room got too much for him, he would amble over to a nearby bar, take a few drinks, watch the television, look at the faces of people, hoping that maybe the subject of baseball would come up and he might be able to say a few words that would mean something.

From time to time, Aimee would try to talk Pete into going to the home for old soldiers in Sawtelle. But Grover Cleveland Alexander has always been a pretty stubborn man. He couldn't see his way clear to accepting what he felt, in his peculiar way, was charity. There's a home for old ballplayers in Schenectady, New York, but Pete didn't cotton much to that.

"I don't belong to the organization that's behind it," he would say, shaking his head, "and I don't think I know any of the fellows there."

Now and then, something good would happen to him. Not long ago, the Oakland Oaks, were holding an exhibition practice for some Los Angeles school kids. Charlie Dressen called Pete and asked him if he would like to come out to the game.

"It would be sort of nice if you could throw some for the kids," Charlie said. "I'll send along a catcher."

Dressen couldn't make the exhibition, but he sent Cookie Lavagetto, who was accompanied by a tall, broad-shouldered, young ballplayer.

"Is this the fellow who's gonna catch me?" Pete asked.

"No, this one's a pitcher," Cookie said. "Charlie figures that as long as you promised to throw some, this fellow could watch you and learn a few things."

So Alex threw some. Then he watched the young pitcher toss some. Then old Pete talked to him about what makes a good pitcher, the sort of control it takes to stay up there year after year in the big time, how to protect your arm so you'll last a long, long time in the hot sun of the good life of baseball. For that afternoon, life seemed to be brighter for old Pete.

Then he went home, alone, to his small hotel room.

Baseball is still Alex's whole life, and he'd give the shirt off his back to get into it again—in almost any capacity. It would give him something to live for. Aimee told me that Happy Chandler once wrote to Alex and said he would try to find a spot for him. When Aimee wrote back, in 1946, and asked if anything could be done, the commissioner answered:

"Your letter of 14 December has been read with sympathetic interest. I am today writing to Mr. Win Clark, Secretary of the Association of Professional Ball Players of America, 524 S. Spring Street, Los Angeles, California, asking him whether there is not some way that the Association can be of some financial assistance. I have not been successful in finding any sort of employment.

So Pete went on sitting in his room, living on the National League pension and whatever other irregular sums he could pick up from time to time.

Last Christmas time, Pete must have been feeling sort of low. He was never the sort of man who could live contentedly and serenely on past memories, on days of glory, on days when they carried him from the field on their shoulders. Old Pete was always the sort of guy who lived in the present, who played the game for today and let tomorrow take care of itself. Maybe that was why you could always depend on Old Pete to get you out of a pinch—because he always faced each moment as it came along and gave it all he had.

Well, he was probably trying very hard to stay on his feet during those terrible moments he was attempting to find his way home on the night before Christmas last year. He couldn't quite make it, and his big, tired body took one more fall. The stranger came along and rolled him over and, there was just another old man down, out cold, badly hurt, and lying in an alley.

How was he to know it was Pete?

They didn't know it at the hospital, either. Not until a young intern stripped off those rings and saw that inscription—*St. Louis Cardinals, World Champions, 1926.*

So it was the county hospital for Pete. Maybe some guys get rich on baseball, but Pete never did. Aimee Alexander says that all his life, he just took what they gave him and let it go at that.

Anyway, he got out of the hospital again in January. Not that he had much to go home to. But Aimee got him a small apartment to live in, and Alex guessed he'd be all right.

It's a good thing Pete has his memories. These days, what with one thing and another, he doesn't have much else to show for his 20 years on the big-league hill.

There's another way of looking at it though. Old Pete may be stone broke, but all the money in the world won't buy you 373 major-league victories. He's got them, forever.

PART TWO

TED WILLIAMS

Hub Fans Bid Kid Adieu

The renowned novelist and Red Sox fan, John Updike here examines "the tissue thin difference between a thing done well and a thing done ill": Ted William's final home game.

By John Updike

Fenway Park, in Boston, is a lyric little bandbox of a ball park. Everything is painted green and seems in curiously sharp focus, like the inside of an old-fashioned peeping-type Easter egg. It was built in 1912 and rebuilt in 1934, and offers, as do most Boston artifacts, a compromise between Man's Euclidean determinations and Nature's beguiling irregularities. Its right field is one of the deepest in the American League, while its left field is the shortest; the high left-field wall, 315 feet from home plate along the foul line, virtually thrusts its surface at right-handed hitters. On the afternoon of Wednesday, September 28, as I took a seat behind third base, a uniformed groundkeeper was treading the top of this wall, picking batting-practice home runs out of the screen, like a mushroom gatherer seen in Wordsworthian perspective on the verge of a cliff. The day was overcast, chill and uninspirational. The Boston team was the worst in 27 seasons. A jangling medley of incompetent youth and aging competence, the Red Sox were finishing in seventh place only because the Kansas City Athletics had locked them out of the cellar. They were scheduled to play the Baltimore Orioles, a much nimbler blend of May and December, who had been dumped from pennant contention a week before by the insatiable Yankees. I, and 10,453 others, had shown up primarily because this was the Red Sox's last home game of the season, and therefore the last time in all eternity that their regular left fielder, known to the headlines as TED, KID, SPLINTER, THUMPER, TW, and, most cloyingly, MISTER WONDERFUL, would play in Boston. "WHAT WILL WE DO WITHOUT TED? HUB FANS ASK" ran the headline on a newspaper being read by a bulb-nosed cigar smoker a few rows away. Williams's retirement had been announced, doubted (he had been threatening retirement for years), confirmed by Tom Yawkey, the Red Sox owner, and at last widely accepted as the sad but probable truth. He was 42 and had redeemed his abysmal season of 1959 with a—considering his advanced age—fine one. He had been giving away his gloves and bats and had grudgingly consented to a sentimental ceremony today. This was not necessarily his last game; the Red Sox were scheduled to travel to New York and wind up the season with three games there.

I arrived early. The Orioles were hitting fungoes on the field. The day before, they had spitefully smothered the Red Sox, 17–4, and neither their faces nor their drab gray visiting-team uniforms seemed very gracious. I wondered who had invited them to the party. Between our heads and the lowering clouds a frenzied organ was thundering through, with an appositeness perhaps accidental, "You *maaaade* me love you, I didn't wanna do it, I didn't wanna do it. . . ."

The affair between Boston and Ted Williams has been no mere summer romance; it has been a marriage, composed of spats, mutual disappointments and, toward the end, a mellowing hoard of shared memories. It falls into three stages, which may be termed Youth, Maturity, and Age; or Thesis, Antithesis, and Synthesis; or Jason, Achilles, and Nestor.

First, there was the by now legendary epoch when the young bridegroom came out of the West, announced, "All I want out of life is that when I walk down the street folks will say, 'There goes the greatest hitter who ever lived.' " The dowagers of local journalism attempted to give elementary deportment lessons to this child who spake as a god, and to their horror were themselves rebuked. Thus began the long exchange of backbiting, bat-flipping, booing and spitting that has distinguished Williams's public relations. The spitting incidents of 1957 and 1958 and the similar dockside courtesies that Williams has now and then extended to the grandstand should be judged against this background: The left-field stands at Fenway for 20 years have held a large number of customers who have bought their way in primarily for the privilege of showering abuse on Williams. Greatness necessarily attracts debunkers, but in Williams's case the hostility has been systematic and unappeasable. His basic offense against the fans has been to wish that they weren't there. Seeking a perfectionist's vacuum, he has quixotically desired to sever the game from the ground of paid spectatorship and publicity that supports it. Hence his refusal to tip his cap to the crowd or turn the other cheek to newsmen. It has been a costly theory—it has probably cost him, among other evidences of good will, two Most Valuable Player awards, which are voted by reporters—but he has held to it from his rookie year on. While his critics, oral and literary, remained beyond the reach of his discipline, the opposing pitchers were accessible, and he spanked them to the tune of .406 in 1941. He slumped to .356 in 1942 and went off to war.

In 1946 Williams returned from three years as a marine pilot to the second of his baseball avatars, that of Achilles, the hero of incomparable prowess and beauty who nevertheless was to be found sulking in his tent while the Trojans (mostly Yankees) fought through to the ships. Yawkey, a timber and mining maharajah, had surrounded his central jewel with many gems of slightly lesser water, such as Bobby Doerr, Dom DiMaggio, Rudy York, Birdie Tebbetts and Johnny Pesky. Throughout the late '40s, the Red Sox were the best paper team in baseball, yet they had little three-dimensional to show for it, and if this was a tragedy, Williams was Hamlet. A succinct review of the indictment—and a fair sample of appreciative sports-page prose—appeared the very day of Williams's valedictory, in a column by Huck Finnegan in the Boston *American* (no sentimentalist, Huck):

> Williams's career, in contrast [to Babe Ruth's], has been a series of failures except for his averages. He flopped in the only World Series he ever played in (1946) when he batted only .200. He flopped in the playoff game with Cleveland in 1948. He flopped in the final game of the 1949 season with the pennant hinging on the outcome (Yanks 5, Sox 3). He flopped in 1950 when he returned to the lineup after a two-month absence and ruined the morale of a club that seemed pennant-bound under Steve O'Neill. It has always been Williams's records first, the team second, and the Sox non-winning record is proof enough of that.

There are answers to all this, of course. The fatal weakness of the great Sox slugging teams was not-quite-good-enough pitching rather than Williams's failure to hit a home run every time he came to bat. Again, Williams's depressing effect on his teammates has never been proved. Despite ample coaching to the contrary, most insisted that they *liked* him. He has been generous with advice to any player who asked for it. In an increasingly combative baseball atmosphere, he continued to duck beanballs docilely. With umpires he was gracious to a fault. This courtesy itself annoyed his critics, whom there was no pleasing. And against the ten crucial games (the seven World Series games with the St. Louis Cardinals, the 1948 playoff with the Cleveland Indians, and the two-game series with the Yankees at the end of the 1949 season, winning either one of which would have given the Red Sox the pennant) that make up the Achilles heel of Williams's record, a mass of statistics can be set showing that day in and day out he was no slouch in the clutch. The correspondence columns of the Boston papers now and then suffer a sharp flurry of arithmetic on this score; indeed, for Williams to have distributed all his hits so they did nobody else any good would constitute a feat of placement unparalleled in the annals of selfishness.

Whatever residue of truth remains of the Finnegan charge those of us who love Williams must transmute as best we can, in our own personal crucibles. My personal memories of Williams begin when I was a boy in Pennsylvania, with two last-place teams in Philadelphia to keep me company. For me, "W'ms, lf" was a figment of the box scores who always seemed to be going 3-for-5. He radiated, from afar, the hard blue glow of high purpose. I remember listening over the radio to the All-Star Game of 1946, in which Williams hit two singles and two home runs, the second one off a Rip Sewell "blooper" pitch; it was like hitting a balloon out of the park. I remember watching one of his home runs from the bleachers of Shibe Park; it went over the first baseman's head and rose meticulously along a straight line and was still rising when it cleared the fence. The trajectory seemed qualitatively different from anything anyone else might hit. For me, Williams is the classic ballplayer of the game on a hot August weekday, before a small crowd, when the only thing at stake is the tissue-thin difference between a thing done well and a thing done ill. Baseball is a game of the long season, of relentless and gradual averaging-out. Irrelevance—since the reference point of most individual games is remote and statistical—always threatens its interest, which can be maintained not by the occasional heroics that sportswriters feed upon but by players who always *care;* who care, that is to say, about themselves and their art. Insofar as the clutch hitter is not a sportswriter's myth, he is a vulgarity, like a writer who writes only for money. It may be that, compared to managers' dreams such as Joe DiMaggio and the always helpful Stan Musial, Williams is an icy star. But of all team sports, baseball, with its graceful intermittences of action, its immense and tranquil field sparsely settled with poised men in white, its dispassionate mathematics, seems to me best suited to accommodate, and be ornamented by, a loner. It is an essentially lonely game. No other player visible to my generation has concentrated within himself so much of the sport's poignance, has so assiduously refined his natural skills, has so constantly brought to the plate that intensity of competence that crowds the throat with joy.

By the time I went to college, near Boston, the lesser stars Yawkey had assembled around Williams had faded, and his craftsmanship, his rigorous pride, had become itself a kind of heroism. This brittle and temperamental player developed an unexpected quality of persistence. He was always coming back—back from Korea, back from a broken collarbone, a shattered elbow, a bruised heel, back from drastic bouts of flu and ptomaine poisoning. Hardly a season went by without some enfeebling mishap, yet he always came back, and always looked like himself. The delicate mechanism of timing and power seemed locked, shockproof, in some case outside his body. In addition to injuries, there were a heavily publicized divorce, and the usual storms with the press, and the Williams Shift—the maneuver, custom-built by Lou Boudreau, of the Cleveland Indians, whereby three infielders were concentrated on the right side of the infield, where a left-handed pull hitter like Williams generally hits the ball. Williams could easily have learned to punch singles through the vacancy on his left and fattened his average hugely. This was what Ty Cobb, the Einstein of average, told him to do. But the game had changed since Cobb; Williams believed that his value to the club and to the game was as a slugger, so he went on pulling the ball, trying to blast it through three men, and paid the price of perhaps 15 points of lifetime average. Like Ruth before him, he bought the occasional home run at the cost of many directed singles—a calculated sacrifice certainly not, in the case of a hitter as average-minded as Williams, entirely selfish.

After a prime so harassed and hobbled, Williams was granted by the relenting fates a golden twilight. He became at the end of his career perhaps the best *old* hitter of the century. The dividing line came between the 1956 and the 1957 seasons. In September of the first year, he and Mickey Mantle were contending for the batting championship. Both were hitting around .350, and there was no one else near them. The season ended with a three-game series between the Yankees and the Sox, and, living in New York then, I went up to the Stadium. Williams was slightly shy of the 400 at-bats needed to qualify; the fear was expressed that the Yankee pitchers would walk him to protect Mantle. Instead, they pitched to him—a wise decision. He looked terrible at the plate, tired and discouraged and unconvincing. He never looked very good to me in the Stadium. (Last week, in *Life*, Williams, a sportswriter himself now, wrote gloomily of the stadium, "There's the bigness of it. There are those high stands and all those people smoking—and, of course, the shadows. . . . It takes at least one Series to get accustomed to the stadium and even then you're not sure.") The final outcome in 1956 was Mantle .353, Williams .345.

The next year, I moved from New York to New England, and it made all the difference. For in September of 1957, in the same situation, the story was reversed. Mantle finally hit .365; it was the best season of his career. But Williams, though sick and old, had run away from him. A bout of flu had laid him low in September. He emerged from his cave in the Hotel Somerset haggard but irresistible; he hit four successive pinch-hit home runs. "I feel terrible," he confessed, "but every time I take a swing at the ball it goes out of the park." He ended the season with 38 home runs and an average of .388, the highest in either league since his own .406, and, coming from a decrepit man of 39, an even more supernal figure. With eight or so of the "leg hits" that a younger man would have beaten out, it would have been .400. And the next year, Williams, who in 1949 and 1953 had lost batting championships by decimal whiskers to George Kell and Mickey Vernon, sneaked in behind his teammate Pete Runnels and filched his sixth title, a bargain at .328.

In 1959, it seemed all over. The dinosaur thrashed around in the .200 swamp for the first half of the season, and was even benched ("rested," manager Mike Higgins tactfully said). Old foes like the late Bill Cunningham began to offer batting tips. Cunningham thought Williams was jiggling his elbows; in truth, Williams's neck was so stiff he could hardly turn his head to look at the pitcher. When he swung, it looked like a Calder mobile with one thread cut; it reminded you that since 1953 Williams's shoulders had been wired together. A solicitous pall settled over the sports pages. In the two decades since Williams had come to Boston, his status had imperceptibly shifted from that of a naughty prodigy to that of a municipal monument. As his shadow in the record books lengthened, the Red Sox teams around him declined, and the entire American League seemed to be losing life and color to the National. The inconsistency of the new superstars—Mantle, Colavito, and Kaline—served to make Williams appear all the more singular. And off the field, his private philanthropy—in particular, his zealous chairmanship of the Jimmy Fund, a charity for children with cancer—gave him a civic presence somewhat like that of Richard Cardinal Cushing. In religion, Williams appears to be a humanist, and a selective one at that, but he and the cardinal, when their good works intersect and they appear in the public eye together, make a handsome and heartening pair.

Humiliated by his '59 season, Williams determined, once more, to come back. I, as a specimen Williams partisan, was both glad and fearful. All baseball fans believe in miracles; the question is, how *many* do you believe in? He looked like a ghost in spring training. Manager Jurges warned us ahead of time that if Williams didn't come through he would be benched, just like anybody else. As it turned out, it was Jurges who was benched. Williams entered the 1960 season needing eight home runs to have a lifetime total of 500; after one time at bat in Washington, he needed seven. For a stretch, he was hitting a home run every second game that he played. He passed Lou Gehrig's lifetime total, then the number 500, then Mel Ott's total, and finished with 521, 13 behind Jimmy Foxx, who alone stands between Williams and Babe Ruth's unapproachable 714. The summer was a statistician's picnic. His 2000th walk came and went, his 1800th run batted in, his 16th All-Star Game. At one point, he hit a home run off a pitcher, Don Lee, off whose father, Thornton Lee, he had hit a home run a generation before. The only comparable season for a 42-year-old man was Ty Cobb's in 1928. Cobb batted .323 and hit one homer. Williams batted .316 but hit 29 homers.

In sum, though generally conceded to be the greatest hitter of his era, he did not establish himself as "the greatest hitter who ever lived." Cobb, for average, and Ruth, for power, remain supreme. Cobb, Rogers Hornsby, Joe Jackson and Lefty O'Doul, among players since 1900, have higher lifetime averages than Williams's .344. Unlike Foxx, Gehrig, Hack Wilson, Hank Greenberg, and Ralph Kiner, Williams never came close to matching Babe Ruth's season home-run total of 60. In the list of major-league batting records, not one is held by Williams. He is second in walks drawn, third in home runs, fifth in lifetime averages, sixth in runs batted in, eighth in runs scored and in total bases, 14th in doubles and 13th in hits. But if we allow him merely average seasons for the four-plus seasons he lost to two wars, and add another season for the months he lost to injuries, we get a man who in all the power totals would be second, and not a very distant second, to Ruth. And if we further allow that these years would have been not merely average but prime years, if we allow for all the months when Williams was playing in sub-par condition, if we permit his early and later years in baseball to be some sort of index of what the middle years could have been, if we give him a right field fence that is not, like Fenway's, one of the most distant in the league, and if—the least excusable "if"—we imagine him condescending to outsmart the Williams Shift, we can defensibly assemble, like a colossus induced from the sizable fragments that do remain, a statistical figure not incommensurate with his grandiose ambition. From the statistics that are on the books, a good case can be made that in the *combination* of power and average Williams is first; nobody else ranks so high in both categories. Finally, there is the witness of the eyes; men whose memories go back to Shoeless Joe Jackson—another unlucky natural—rank him and Williams together as the best-looking hitters they have seen. It was for our last look that 10,000 of us had come.

Two girls, one of them with pert buckteeth and eyes as black as vest buttons, the other with white skin and flesh-colored hair, like an under-developed photograph of a redhead, came and sat on my right. On my other side was one of those frowning, chestless young-old men who can frequently be seen, often wearing sailor hats, attending ballgames alone. He did not once open his program but instead tapped it, rolled up, on his knee as he gave the game his disconsolate attention. A young lady, with freckles and a depressed, dainty nose that by an optical illusion seemed to thrust her lips forward for a kiss, sauntered down into the box seats and with striking aplomb took a seat right behind the roof of the Oriole dugout. She wore a blue coat with a Northeastern University emblem sewed to it. The girls beside me took it into their heads that this was Williams's daughter. She looked too old to me, and why would she be sitting behind the visitors' dugout? On the other hand, from the way she sat there, staring at the sky and French-inhaling, she clearly was *some-body*. Other fans came and eclipsed her from view. The crowd looked less like a weekday ball-park crowd than like the folks you might find in Yellowstone National Park, or emerging from automobiles at the top of scenic Mount Mansfield. There were a lot of competitively well-dressed couples of tourist age, and not a few babes in arms. A row of five seats in front of me was abruptly filled with a woman and four children, the youngest of them two years old, if that. Someday, presumably, he could tell his grandchildren that he saw Williams play. Along with these tots and second-honeymooners, there were Harvard freshmen, giving off that peculiar nervous glow created when a quantity of insouciance is saturated with insecurity; thick-necked army officers with brass on their shoulders and lead in their voices; pepperings of priests; perfumed bouquets of Roxbury Fabian fans; shiny salesmen from Albany and Fall River; and those gray, hoarse men—taxi drivers, slaughterers, and bartenders—who will continue to click through the turnstiles long after everyone else has deserted to television and tramporamas. Behind me, two young male voices blossomed, cracking a joke about God's five proofs that Thomas Aquinas exists—typical Boston College levity.

The batting cage was trundled away. The Orioles fluttered to the sidelines. Diagonally across the field, by the Red Sox dugout, a cluster of men in overcoats were festering like maggots. I could see a splinter of white uniform, and Williams's head, held at a self-deprecating and evasive tilt. Williams's conversational stance is that of a six-foot-three-inch man under a six-foot ceiling. He moved away to the patter of flash bulbs, and began playing catch with a young Negro outfielder named Willie Tasby. His arm, never very powerful, had grown lax with the years, and his throwing motion was a kind of muscular drawl. To catch the ball, he flicked his glove onto his left shoulder (he batted left but threw right, as every schoolboy ought to know) and let the ball plop into it comically. This catch session with Tasby was the only time all afternoon I saw him grin.

A tight little flock of human sparrows who, from the lambent and pampered pink of their faces, could only have been Boston politicians moved toward the plate. The loudspeakers mammothly coughed as someone huffed on the microphone. The ceremonies began. Curt Gowdy, the Red Sox radio and television announcer, who sounds like everybody's brother-in-law, delivered a brief sermon, taking the two words "pride" and "champion" as his text. It began, "Twenty-one years ago, a skinny kid from San Diego, California . . ." and ended, "I don't think we'll ever see another like him." Robert Tibolt, chairman of the board of the Greater Boston Chamber of Commerce, presented Williams with a big Paul Revere silver bowl. Harry Carlson, a member of the sports committee of the Boston Chamber, gave him a plaque, whose inscription he did not read in its entirety, out of deference to Williams's distaste for this sort of fuss. Mayor Collins presented the Jimmy Fund with a thousand-dollar check.

Then the occasion himself stooped to the microphone, and his voice sounded, after the others, very Californian; it seemed to be coming, excellently amplified, from a great distance, adolescently young and as smooth as a butternut. His thanks for the gifts had not died from our ears before he glided, as if helplessly, into "In spite of all the terrible things that have been said about me by the maestros of the keyboard up there. . . ." He glanced up at the press rows suspended above home plate. (All the Boston reporters, incidentally, reported the phrase as "knights of the keyboard," but I heard it as "maestros" and prefer it that way.) The crowd tittered, appalled. A frightful vision flashed upon me, of the press gallery pelting Williams with erasers, of Williams clambering up the foul screen to slug journalists, of a riot, of Mayor Collins being crushed. ". . . And they *were* terrible things," Williams insisted, with level melancholy, into the mike. "I'd like to forget them, but I can't." He paused, swallowed his memories, and went on, "I want to say that my years in Boston have been the greatest thing in my life." The crowd, like an immense sail going limp in a change of wind, sighed with relief. Taking all the parts himself, Williams then acted out a vivacious little morality drama in which an imaginary tempter came to him at the beginning of his career and said, "Ted, you can play anywhere you like." Leaping nimbly into the role of his younger self (who in biographical actuality had yearned to be a Yankee), Williams gallantly chose Boston over all the other cities, and told us that Tom Yawkey was the greatest owner in baseball and we were the greatest fans. We applauded ourselves heartily. The umpire came out and dusted the plate. The voice of doom announced over the loudspeakers that after Williams's retirement his uniform number, 9, would be permanently retired—the first time the Red

Sox had so honored a player. We cheered. The national anthem was played. We cheered. The game began.

Williams was third in the batting order, so he came up in the bottom of the first inning, and Steve Barber, a young pitcher who was not yet born when Williams began playing for the Red Sox, offered him four pitches, at all of which he disdained to swing, since none of them were within the strike zone. This demonstrated simultaneously that Williams's eyes were razor-sharp and that Barber's control wasn't. Shortly, the bases were full, with Williams on second. "Oh, I hope he gets held up at third! That would be wonderful," the girl beside me moaned, and, sure enough, the man at bat walked and Williams was delivered into our foreground. He struck the pose of Donatello's David, the third-base bag being Goliath's head. Fiddling with his cap, swapping small talk with the Oriole third baseman (who seemed delighted to have him drop in), swinging his arms with a sort of prancing nervousness, he looked fine—flexible, hard and not unbecomingly substantial through the middle. The long neck, the small head, the knickers whose cuffs were worn down near his ankles—all these points, often observed by caricaturists, were visible in the flesh.

One of the collegiate voices behind me said, "He looks old, doesn't he, old; big deep wrinkles in his face. . . ."

"Yeah," the other voice said, "but he looks like an old hawk, doesn't he?"

With each pitch, Williams danced down the base line, waving his arms and stirring dust, ponderous but menacing, like an attacking goose. It occurred to about a dozen humorists at once to shout, "Steal home! Go, go!" Williams's speed afoot was never legendary. Lu Clinton, a young Sox outfielder, hit a fairly deep fly to center field. Williams tagged up and ran home. As he slid across the plate, the ball, thrown with unusual heft by Jackie Brandt, the Oriole center fielder, hit him on the back.

"Boy, he was really loafing, wasn't he?" one of the boys behind me said.

"It's cold," the other explained. "He doesn't play well when it's cold. He likes heat. He's a hedonist."

The run that Williams scored was the second and last of the inning. Gus Triandos, of the Orioles, quickly evened the score by plunking a home run over the handy left-field wall. Williams, who had had this wall at his back for 20 years, played the ball flawlessly. He didn't budge. He just stood there, in the center of the little patch of grass that his patient footsteps had worn brown, and, limp with lack of interest, watched the ball pass overhead. It was not a very interesting game. Mike Higgins, the Red Sox manager, with nothing to lose, had restricted his major-league players to the left-field line—along with Williams, Frank Malzone, a first-rate third baseman, played the game—and had peopled the rest of the terrain with unpredictable youngsters fresh, or not so fresh, off the farms. Other than Williams's recurrent appearances at the plate, the *maladresse* of the Sox infield was the sole focus of suspense; the second baseman turned every grounder into a juggling act, while the shortstop did a breathtaking impersonation of an open window. With this sort of assistance, the Orioles wheedled their way into a 4–2 lead. They had early replaced Barber with another young pitcher, Jack Fisher. Fortunately (as it turned out), Fisher is no cutie; he is willing to burn the ball through the strike zone, and inning after inning this tactic punctured Higgins's string of test balloons.

Whenever Williams appeared at the plate—pounding the dirt from his cleats, gouging a pit in the batter's box with his left foot, wringing resin out of the bat handle with his vehement grip, switching the stick at the pitcher with an electric ferocity—it was like having a familiar Leonardo appear in a shuffle of *Saturday Evening Post* covers. This man, you realized—and here, perhaps, was the difference, greater than the difference in gifts—really intended to hit the ball. In the third inning, he hoisted a high fly to deep center. In the fifth, we thought he had it; he smacked the ball hard and high into the heart of his power zone, but the deep right field in Fenway and the heavy air and a casual east wind defeated him. The ball died. Al Pilarcik leaned his back against the big "380" painted on the right-field wall and caught it. On another day, in another park, it would have been gone. (After the game, Williams said, "I didn't think I could hit one any harder than that. The conditions weren't good.")

The afternoon grew so glowering that in the sixth inning the arc lights were turned on—always a wan sight in the daytime, like the burning headlights of a funeral procession. Aided by the gloom, Fisher was slicing through the Sox rookies, and Williams did not come to bat in the seventh. He was second up in the eighth. This was almost certainly his last time to come to the plate in Fenway Park, and instead of merely cheering, as we had at his three previous appearances, we stood, all of us —stood and applauded. Have you ever heard applause in a ball park? Just applause—no calling, no whistling, just an ocean of handclaps, minute after minute, burst after burst, crowding and running together in continuous succession like the pushes of surf at the edge of the sand. It was a somber and considered tumult. There was not a boo in it. It seemed to renew itself out of a shifting set of memories as the kid, the marine, the veteran of feuds and failures and injuries, the friend of children, and the enduring old pro evolved down the bright tunnel of 21 summers toward this moment. At last, the umpire signaled for Fisher to pitch; with the other players, he had been frozen in position. Only Williams had moved during the ovation, switching his bat impatiently, ignoring everything except his cherished task. Fisher wound up, and the applause sank into a hush.

Understand that we were a crowd of rational people. We knew that a home run cannot be produced at will; the right pitch must be perfectly met and luck must ride with the ball. Three innings before, we had seen a brave effort fail. The air was soggy; the season was exhausted. Nevertheless, there will always lurk, around a corner in a pocket of our knowledge of the odds, an indefensible hope, and this was one of the times, which you now and then find in sports, when a density of expectation hangs in the air and plucks an event out of the future.

Fisher, after his unsettling wait, was wide with the first pitch. He put the second one over, and Williams swung mightily and missed. The crowd grunted, seeing that classic swing, so long and smooth and quick, exposed, naked in its failure. Fisher threw the third time. Williams swung again, and there it was. The ball climbed on a diagonal line into the vast volume of air over center field. From my angle, behind third base, the ball seemed less an object in flight than the tip of a towering, motionless construct, like the Eiffel Tower or the Tappan Zee Bridge. It was in the books while it was still in the sky. Brandt ran back to the deepest corner of the outfield grass; the ball descended beyond his reach and struck in the crotch where the bullpen met the wall, bounced chunkily, and, as far as I could see, vanished.

Like a feather caught in a vortex, Williams ran around the square of bases at the center of our beseeching screaming. He ran as he always ran out home runs—hurriedly, unsmilingly, head down, as if our praise were a storm of rain to get out of. He didn't tip his cap. Though we thumped, wept and chanted, "We want Ted," for minutes after he hid in the dugout, he did not come back. Our noise for some seconds passed beyond excitement into a kind of immense open anguish, a wailing, a cry to be saved. But immortality is nontransferable. The papers said that the other players, and even the umpires on the field, begged him to come out and acknowledge us in some way, but he never had and did not now. Gods do not answer letters.

Every true story has an anticlimax. The men on the field refused to disappear, as would have seemed decent, in the smoke of Williams's miracle. Fisher continued to pitch, and escaped further harm. At the end of the inning, Higgins sent Williams out to his left-field position, then instantly replaced him with Carrol Hardy, so we had a long last look at Williams as he ran out there and then back, his uniform jogging, his eyes steadfast on the ground. It was nice, and we were grateful, but it left a funny taste.

One of the scholasticists behind me said, "Let's go. We've seen everything. I don't want to spoil it." This seemed a sound aesthetic decision. Williams's last word had been so exquisitely chosen, such a perfect fusion of expectation, intention, and execution, that already it felt a little unreal in my head, and I wanted to get out before the castle collapsed. But the game, though played by clumsy midgets under the feeble glow of the arc lights, began to tug at my attention, and I loitered in the runway until it was over. Williams's homer had, quite incidentally, made the score 4–3. In the bottom of the ninth inning, with one out, Marlin Coughtry, the second-base juggler, singled. Vic Wertz, pinch-hitting, doubled off the left-field wall, Coughtry advancing to third. Pumpsie Green walked to load the bases. Willie Tasby hit a double-play ball to the third baseman, but in making the pivot throw Billy Klaus, an ex-Red Sox infielder, reverted to form and threw the ball past the first baseman and into the Red Sox dugout. The Sox won, 5–4. On the car radio as I drove home I heard that Williams had decided not to accompany the team to New York. So he knew how to do even that, the hardest thing. Quit.

Jackie Robinson   Photo credit: Associated Press

JACKIE ROBINSON

The Emancipation of Jackie Robinson

Sport Magazine   October 1951

Some of **Sport***'s best "Specials" found players at the cross-roads of their careers—either on the way up or down. Here Milton Gross spots Jackie Robinson at a personal, as well as professional, moment of triumph.*

By Milton Gross

Jack Roosevelt Robinson of the Brooklyn Dodgers made his precedent-shattering invasion of organized baseball wearing an armor of humility. It was, for him, an unnatural garment that chafed continually and on certain occasions dug ruthlessly into both his flesh and his spirit. Hiding his true combativeness behind the armor carefully selected for him by Branch Rickey, allowed to vent his boundless competitive instincts only with his bat, glove and flying feet, Jackie was the unresponsive target for barbs of humiliation that no man but Robinson could fully appreciate.

The humility he practiced so conscientiously—rigidly might be an even better word—did not come naturally. No meek and humble man could possibly play baseball with the fire and dash Robinson exhibits. But there was reserve in Jackie, far more reserve than any white ballplayer ever had shown. He had to have it. But it has been five years since Jackie broke into the National League, years chock full of astonishing feats, of endless honors, and each year the great second-baseman of the Dodgers has been inclined to placate fewer and fewer people.

Jackie has thrown off the shackles gradually but purposefully. In 1949 he was forced by Commissioner A. B. Chandler to tender an apology to umpire Cal Hubbard during the World Series. In 1950, he took the brakes off his feud with Leo Durocher. He accused certain National League umpires of having formed a heckling cabal against him. This past spring in an exhibition game at Asheville, North Carolina, he stood on the diamond chin to chin and argued heatedly with umpire Frank Dascoli for several minutes.

He resented bean balls being thrown at his head and the heads of his teammates in their interboro scraps with the Giants. In one game, he laid down a bunt to force pitcher Sal Maglie to field the ball on the first-base line where he could bump him.

"I did it deliberately," Jackie admitted, "to force the league to step in and stop this beanballing before somebody gets hurt. I'll take the fine, the suspension or anything else that goes with it, but his throwing at a man's head has got to be stopped."

"Last Sunday," Robinson said, "Larry Jansen hit me with a pitch. The mark's still there. Maglie had already thrown one too close to me. I made up my mind to do something to protect myself and the other fellows. I set out to create enough of a disturbance to bring this thing to a head."

That night, watching the game from her usual seat at Ebbets Field, Jackie's charming wife, Rachel, was particularly aware of the tension. As she has from the very beginning, she kept her ears attuned to the comments about her husband. A man seated near her said, as Jackie bumped Maglie, "There's a guy getting big-headed." It is a comment that has been made many times within recent months in one way or another as Robinson has demonstrated that he recognizes no longer any limitations upon him which do not circumscribe other players.

Once, the Phillies turned their dugout into a vile cesspool, denouncing him in what passes for "jockeying." They carried black cats on the field and shouted, "Hey, Jackie, here's one of your relatives."

Some of Robinson's teammates came to him and said, "You can't give it back to them, but we'll do it for you." Robby answered, "No, I can take it as long as they can give it. If I've got what it takes to be a big-leaguer, I'll make the grade on my own."

There was a manager in the International League, when Jackie was at Montreal, who admitted, "We have tried everything against him. We have thrown at him, knocked him down, called him names, but we just can't get a rise out of him."

But those days are gone. Never again will Jackie wear the armor of humility. Has Robinson merely passed from stage to natural stage in the evolution of his great experiment in baseball?

Bench-jockeying is a part of baseball and the man who gives it expects to get it back. But at the start, Jackie could not give, only receive. In tight flag races, in slumps, in spurts, on bad plays and close decisions by umpires, in the thousand little disturbing moments that mark the 154 games of every baseball season, there are times a man must let off steam or burst. But for Robinson there was no safety valve, no outlet.

Within him welled a resentment at being stifled, bound by restrictive do's and don'ts that chafed not only physically, but threatened his own mental stability.

Perhaps the first to know about it was Mel Jones, Jackie's general manager at Montreal. Once, Robinson came into his office and said, "Nobody knows what I am going through this season."

"He couldn't eat," Mrs. Robinson said, "and at night he'd toss constantly in his sleep. Finally, I insisted that Jack consult a doctor, who warned him if he didn't stay away from the ball park he would surely suffer a nervous breakdown. But Jack wouldn't give it up. In two days, he was back, playing as well as he ever did before and carrying the same problems around within him."

There have been stages in Jackie's life as he advanced from being a hungry little boy in a fatherless family of five children to the dominating personality he is today. There was the kid who sold papers, did odd jobs, searched for lost golf balls and junk and peddled them in and around Pasadena, California, to bring money into the house and help put food on the table.

There was the young college student pushing a broom to stay in school, while he also played football, baseball, basketball and starred for the track team. There was the Army lieutenant, in uniform as millions of other Americans were, railroaded into a court martial, charged with serious military infractions because he refused to abide by Jim Crow laws while riding a bus on an Army reservation in the South.

A point in each stage must be examined before the full significance of what Mrs. Robinson had said can be realized. For only by examining the boy and the circumstances under which he lived can one come to know the man.

Jackie's grandmother was a Georgia slave and his mother was a half-cropper on a big plantation. As she later was to tell her five children and a cousin who came to live with them after their father deserted them, "It was all right. If you tend to your own business, nobody bothers you."

But Jackie never got to know about that. When he was barely over a year old, Mallie Robinson moved her family to Pasadena, California. A woman who would work, doing domestic chores for others, could raise a family there. They were the only Negroes on their street, but the Robinsons got along. He played with white boys, Japanese and Mexicans and even a little white girl, who, at ten, was Jackie's own age when they had their first argument.

The two kids had the same chore. Each morning, they were assigned to sweep the sidewalk in front of the house in which they lived. Jackie doesn't remember who started the name-calling, but as all kids do he said, "You're a this," and she accepted the challenge by shouting, "You're a that." It was strictly kid stuff, the kind of spats that are all but forgotten ten minutes later. But when the girl shouted, "You little black nigger," Robinson grabbed a stone and threw it at her. The girl, in tears, called for her father, and as he came from his house, she shouted what had happened. The adult called Jackie the same name and tossed a stone at him.

Tears streaming down his face, Jackie threw some debris at the father. It started a rock fight which lasted well over an hour. The neighbors, locked behind their doors, watched the pitched battle. Mallie Robinson tried to stop it, but each time she would open her door, a stone would force her to bang it shut. Jackie's brothers, Edgar, Frank and Mack, loved it. They formed an ammunition train for their youngest brother, running from tree to tree carrying armfuls of stones.

The shame of the spectacle finally forced the man's wife to dare the barrage and drag her husband off the street and into their home.

In Muir Tech, Jackie scaled only 143 pounds, but light as he was, he could not be convinced to stay away from varsity tryouts. He made the football team, as well as basketball, baseball and track, but his first public notice came on the gridiron. Pasadena Junior College wanted him, and after two years there, it was the big time with Robinson running beside Kenny Washington at UCLA.

In the years to come, Rickey and his "bird dogs" narrowed their search for the Negro player they sought. They dipped deeply into Jackie's athletic record, of course, but they went beyond Jackie's 12-yard ball-carrying average in 1939.

He learned, for example, that in high school and college, Robinson had not been the kind other students, players, officials and coaches embraced and took to their bosoms. They cheered his performances on the athletic field if they were on his side, but most of them disliked him. The sum-up was that as an athlete Jackie had been "over-assertive."

As Rickey searched in the remote corners of Jackie's personal life, he came across one interlude which should have made it crystal clear that Robby was not the kind of man who would knuckle under to intolerance.

In April, 1942, Robinson entered the Army as a cavalry private. By 1943, he had won a commission. An old football injury had left bone chips in one ankle, however, and Army medics soon discovered these and placed him on limited service. One night, Robby decided to visit the officers' club. To reach the club from the hospital was several miles from Waco to the post, a change of busses and another ride on Army property. When Jackie reached his destination he learned the friends he wished to see were out on maneuvers.

Jackie started back to the hospital almost immediately, accompanied by the wife of one of his fellow officers. She was a light-skinned Negro, whose fair color was emphasized by Jackie's dark skin. As the pair took seats midway in the bus, other occupants stared at the two. But Jackie didn't notice. He was exasperated by the Army's indecision over his status and was explaining it to his companion.

In the midst of his explanation, Jackie became aware that his companion was no longer listening. She was looking to the front of the bus and as Robinson followed her gaze he heard, for the first time, the bus driver shouting at him.

"You hear me?" he called. "I said go back and sit in the rear of this bus."

The driver rose from his seat and snarled, "Get in the back where you belong or there'll be trouble."

The driver must have known there was no segregation on the post. Jackie restrained his companion as she started to rise. "I'm not moving any place," he answered. "You better drive this bus and leave me alone."

He couldn't cow the lieutenant, the driver knew. He turned to his seat, but still he did not throw the vehicle into gear.

"When this bus gets to the front gate you better be in the rear or there's going to be trouble," he warned.

Robinson was resolute. "The directive said there's no segregation. Now just drive this bus and let me alone."

The bus moved toward the gate. When it got there, the driver jumped off before his passengers. As Robinson and his companion stepped down, the driver was there. He thrust a finger at Jackie. "This is the nigger's been giving me a hard time," he said, talking to a dispatcher.

Jackie wanted no trouble. He had broken no rules. He led the girl across the street where the bus to Waco would come in. As they waited, a jeep stopped at the curb. An M.P. sergeant said to Jackie, "Excuse me, sir, but the bus driver and dispatcher have complained to me there's been some trouble.

"Would it be all right with you to come over to the Provost Marshal and get this thing cleared up? I've got to carry it through because of the complaint." Jackie entered the M.P. jeep and told his companion it shouldn't take long for the matter to be straightened out. She wanted to come with him, but he assured her he would not need her testimony.

As Robinson recalls the incident now, there is understandable bitterness in his recollection and voice. To this day, he has never taken a drink of whiskey, but before that day was over, Jackie was charged with drunkenness, conduct unbecoming an officer, willful disobedience of an order and disrespect to a commanding officer.

His fellow Negro officers at Camp Hood were dismayed by what had happened. They protested the action and appealed for assistance to the National Association for the Advancement of Colored People. Jackie was forced to stand a court martial and was completely exonerated. The restrictions which were placed upon him when he started made for an unnatural baseball life, which would have been strange enough as it was because of the color of his skin. A complete code of conduct was foreordained for Robinson before he ever stepped on a field. Wherever he was due to appear as baseball's pioneering Negro, Rickey sent his advance man.

Committees were set up through churches and social organizations and civic leaders were formed into "how to handle Robinson" clubs. Each prepared its own list of do's and don'ts for Jackie. His deportment received more attention before he ever swung a bat or fielded a ball than is lavished on Princess Elizabeth.

He could not endorse breakfast foods or lend his name to magazine articles or newspaper stories, which go to swell a player's income and reputation. He came to the ball park secretly and left the same way. Adulation had to be avoided as much as criticism from the stands and the fans. It was feared Jackie would represent a symbol more than a ballplayer attempting to make good.

How long could a man be expected to take this? Indefinitely, if what was once said by Rickey can be accepted as the real meaning of his plans. It was a bitter, wintry night on February 5, 1947. Robinson had made good at Montreal the season before. The fact was indicated by the announcement that the Dodgers had shifted their base of spring training operations from Florida, where they were threatened with locked ball parks because of Robinson, to Havana and Panama. Herbert T. Miller, executive secretary of the Carlton YMCA had assembled 30 distinguished Brooklyn Negroes as Rickey's guests at a dinner. They expected that Branch would announce Robinson's historic promotion to the Dodgers.

The only white people in the room, as Rickey rose to speak, were Judge Edward Lazansky, Rickey's friend, and a stenographer, who had been brought along to inscribe the minutes of the meeting.

"You good people who have come here on a bitter night such as this," he said slowly and with great pause, "sort of embarrass me. The pleasant smiles on your faces are not entirely due to the fine chicken dinner. Well, I'm not going to tell you what you expect, what you want to hear."

With these words the atmosphere of the room changed suddenly. There was a tenseness, a chill, as though a cold draft of wind had somehow come through the windows into the warm room. "I was told by someone close to me that I couldn't tell you what I wanted to say. That I didn't have the courage to give it and that you people won't be able to take it.

"Well, I don't believe that," Rickey said. "I think all of us here tonight have courage enough to give or take anything. I have a ballplayer named Jackie Robinson. He is on the Montreal team. He may stay there. He may be brought up to Brooklyn. I don't know at this point exactly when or if at all. But I want to say that if it happens, if Jackie Robinson does come up to the Dodgers as a major-leaguer, the biggest threat to his success—the one enemy most likely to ruin that success—is the Negro people themselves."

Rickey had anticipated the effect of his words on his audience. Through the room there were exclamations of shock, amazement, even anger. "I mean it and I'll repeat it as cruelly as I can, to make you all realize and appreciate the weight of responsibility that is not only on me and my associates but on Negroes everywhere. Every step of racial progress you have made has been won by suffering and often bloodshed. This step is being taken for you by a single person whose wounds you cannot see or share.

"And yet, on the day that Robinson enters the big league, if he does, every one of you will go out and form parades and welcoming committees. You'll hold Jackie Robinson Days and Jackie Robinson Nights. For let me tell you this:" Rickey shouted, his voice brimming with the full measure of emotion within him. "If any individual group or segment of Negro society uses the advancement of Jackie Robinson in baseball as a symbol of a social 'ism' or schism, I will curse the day I ever signed him to a contract, and I will personally see that baseball is never so abused and misrepresented again."

As a result of this extraordinary meeting and speech, further committees were formed dedicated to one purpose: "Don't spoil Jackie's chances."

On the whole, it was an admirable campaign. Yet it stifled unnaturally the enthusiasm of the millions who saw in self-identification with Robinson their own step toward 100 per cent citizenship.

Rickey's detractors still say that when he opened the door for Negroes in baseball, his eye was on the ticket gate rather than on any humanitarian possibilities. Rickey himself has insisted, and those who were close to him all during the period leading up to the great experiment agree, that the motivating force behind the challenging action was pennants for the Dodgers.

This may be correct, but surely of considerably more enduring significance were the sociological aspects of Robinson's pioneering.

The objective bystander inside and outside Wrigley Field, Chicago, for example, is struck by the full meaning of Jackie Robinson for his people. They regard him with nothing less than adoration, which, in its strictest sense, is a word that can be applied only to the deity. It is a recognition of things as they are—of what Robinson has come to mean to the Negro people.

Every Dodger is a hero of sorts, of course, for any who come in contact with Robinson have assumed, in the mind of his worshippers, certain of Jackie's attributes. Roy Campanella and Don Newcombe, Jackie's Negro teammates, come in for their share of attention, naturally, but the true adoration is reserved for Robinson. There is an ecstasy that borders on religious relief as the crowd sees Jackie and crushes itself into an immobile mass on either side of him.

They call his name in a way no other player's name is called. They plead to shake his hand or ask for his autograph. They touch his clothes as he walks by, unhurrying, pleasant, friendly, cooperative, because Jackie has never once lost sight of what the game has meant to him and what he has meant, means now, and will always mean to his people.

Despite his pioneering, Robinson never wanted a role of reformer. All he ever asked, once he had proved himself to Rickey, who believed in him from the beginning, was to be accepted as a player among other players. He began his career in organized baseball under a manager reared in the anti-Negro tradition of Mississippi and was faced in his first season with the Dodgers with threat of two strikes against him, both literally and figuratively.

Robinson may never have heard what Clay Hopper, his Montreal manager, said about him, but Jackie surely knew how the pilot felt. During his first spring training at Daytona Beach in 1946, Robinson was splendid in the field and Rickey, who sat next to Hopper, raved about Robinson's performances. Robby ranged far toward second base, scooped a hard-hit ground ball from the dirt, wheeled and threw to first base for a spectacular out.

"No other human being could have made that play," Rickey exclaimed to Hopper.

The Mississippi man, who had remained completely uncommunicative in the previous days which must have constituted the most tumultuous period of his life, turned to Rickey. "Mr. Rickey," he said, "do you really think he *is* a human being?"

Before Robinson and Hopper parted company as Jackie moved up to the Dodgers, the man from Mississippi came to Rickey and said: "You don't have to worry about that boy. He's the greatest competitor I ever saw. And what's more, he's a gentleman."

This was what Rickey wanted to hear, but it took more than Hopper's okay to convince some of the men with whom and against whom Jackie was destined to play in 1947.

The Dodgers had definite weaknesses at first base and third base. Robby's arm was not fit for the long throw from third. The shift of Robinson to the position at which he had never played before seemed indicated. Rickey also had in mind the series of exhibition games between the Dodgers and Royals in which he felt sure Robinson would impress himself on the minds of the Brooklyn players as the man who could help them win the flag. There was even a dramatic meeting planned at which Durocher was to shout he didn't care about the color of a man's skin. He wanted Robinson advanced from Montreal to Brooklyn because he was the kind of player who could do a winning job. He would point to Robby's great performances in the intra-organization exhibitions as proof that Robby belonged. He would demand Robinson.

The first step in this complicated plan was put into effect while the Dodgers were off for three weeks of side trips to Venezuela and Panama. Left behind was the Montreal club, with Robby ostensibly still a third-baseman. One morning, Mel Jones, the Royals' general manager, handed Robinson a first-baseman's glove.

"What's this all about?" Jackie asked.

"It's Mr. Rickey's idea," Jones explained. "He wants to give you a chance to make his club. He thinks you can learn to play first base in no time."

Robinson was definitely against the switch. He had been a shortstop with the Kansas City Monarchs and had spent a full year mastering second base. Now he was being asked to break in at a new position.

Hopper, the Montreal manager, was equally enraged. He was beginning to get the idea that Rickey was using Montreal merely as the proving ground for Robinson.

At first, the plan seemed to be proceeding in the fashion Rickey had hoped. Branch soon learned that all was not well. The grapevine reported a petition was being prepared. Harold Parrott, the Dodgers' traveling secretary, was the first member of the front-office staff to learn of the underground dissension, although not to this day has anybody uncovered the initiator of the revolt.

One evening, Parrott and pitcher Kirby Higbe of Columbia, South Carolina, were testing the strength of some local beer and their stomachs.

After several of the brews, Higbe suddenly said to Parrott. "I just won't do it. The old man's been fair to Ol' Hig and I ain't going to join any petitition to keep anybody off this club."

Harold didn't push Higbe for further information. He rushed to Rickey with this information.

Most of the players backed down when Rickey confronted them with the knowledge of their plot. Two men, reared in the tradition of the South, gradually emerged as particularly obstinate. Bobby Bragan, and Dixie Walker, who, in his years of playing with Brooklyn had become the most popular performer at Ebbets Field.

Rickey's interview with Bragan was heated, but Bobby, a third-string catcher, remained firm in his conviction against Robinson.

"Would you like your contract transferred to another club?" Rickey asked.

"Yes, sir, I would," Bragan said. "But I don't want to be made the goat of a mess I didn't create."

"Then I may accommodate you, sir!" Rickey replied. "Good night."

On March 26, 1947, Rickey received a letter from Walker, which Dixie later sought to have returned to him. In it, Walker spoke feelingly of his years in Brooklyn but said it would be best for all concerned if a trade to another team could be arranged for him. Branch quickly attempted to effect such a deal.

"Pittsburgh agrees to accept Walker for $40,000 cash, Gionfriddo and Kalin," Roy Hamey, general manager of Pittsburgh, wrote in agreement.

But the deal did not go through when Rickey asked for Wally Westlake in Frank Kalin's place, and would have been satisfied to accept a rookie named Ralph Kiner who had hit .247 for the Pirates in 1946. It's to Hamey's credit he spurned this suggestion.

So it was that Bragan and Walker played through a season with Robinson. The trouble they had anticipated from within did not arise, but as Jackie's teammates, they had front row seats in observing how he reacted to the hostility from the opposition, if not from his own teammates.

When the season was over, Bragan came to Rickey and said while his attitude toward Negroes in general had not changed, he felt it only fair to say he had begun to like Robinson and playing on the same team with him. When a managerial opening developed at Fort Worth, Rickey gave the job to Bragan. Walker, of course, was eventually sent to Pittsburgh, but not until he had spurned an offer from Rickey to manage the Dodgers' St. Paul farm.

In their one season together on the team, Robinson and Dixie were particularly circumspect in their relations with each other. Robby knew and appreciated the torment that the season must have been for Dixie and when it was done and Robinson was asked about their relationship, he said: "I think Dixie had accepted me on the ball club so far as the playing end of it went. Socially, no," Jackie estimated. "But that was perfectly all right with me. I understood and it wasn't embarrasing except once or twice when he hit a home run while I was on base.

"Normally, you wait at the plate to shake hands with the man who hits the home run. With Dixie, I wasn't sure what he expected me to do but I thought it would be the smart thing to get out of there. I would just go to the dugout without waiting for him to reach the plate."

In this case difficulty was avoided by walking around the corner, so to speak. But there were others that would have to be met bluntly, with a head-on attack, if necessary.

Jackie took a letter from his pocket. "This came in the mail for me today. It may be nothing but a crank. It may be serious."

The contents of the letter was, indeed, reason to act because it was the first of many such threatening notes Jackie was to receive. Even to this day, when Negroes are secure in the big league and Robinson has proved he is the kind of a player any club would hasten to obtain, Jackie still receives such letters. "Anybody who was going to shoot me wouldn't be advertising about it in a letter," he says today.

But back in 1947 no one could be sure. The letter, threatening physical harm to Jackie and his family, was turned over to New York's police commissioner. The authorities learned the name signed to it was fictitious and so was the address.

Hardly had this crisis been discovered when one arose which had reperoussions all through the nation. Stanley Woodward, sports editor of the New York *Herald Tribune,* uncovered a plan by the St. Louis Cardinals to strike in protest against Robinson on May 16. To this day, Jackie himself expresses uncertainty that any strike was contemplated. Yet despite denials by the Cardinal players, president Sam Breadon, their owner, as well as Branch Rickey and Ford Frick, president of the National League, admitted that such a movement had gained headway in the Red Bird locker room. Quick action had rendered it stillborn.

Frick sent an ultimatum to the Cardinals. In it he said, "If you do this, you will be suspended from the league. You will find that the friends you have in the press box will not support you, that you will be outcasts. I do not care if half the league strikes. Those who do will encounter quick retribution."

There was no strike and as the season progressed the opposition, which had contended that the idea of playing a Negro in the majors could not possibly work and would only breed trouble, noted soon enough that

Robinson's presence on the diamond was good for baseball instead of being bad for it.

Not since the heyday of Babe Ruth had a player come along to have so profound an effect on baseball. The player helped make the game more exciting and helped the Dodgers win pennants. The side show was beneficial to the boxoffice.

Robinson was a pioneer, but identification in the role of a reformer was something he never sought and did not relish when it came to him. But he felt that hectic night at Ebbets Field last April that he had to see it through even at the risk of his reputation, his body, his wealth and against the advice of his wife. Such was the explanation he made to me when he told why he had decided to make himself the avenging aggressor for the beanballing feud which had become the motif of the Dodger-Giant series.

I told Jackie that Maglie had denied throwing at him.

"Every time something happens, I pick up a paper and read I'm at fault. After the bunt, I came back to the plate and picked up my bat and Westrum said, 'Sal wasn't throwing at you. You've been wearing us out. He was just brushing you back.'

"That's too fine a difference for me," Robinson said. "This morning I read where Durocher said it was a bush-league trick. If I'm bush, Durocher made me that way. He taught it to me. Right here in this clubhouse, he used to tell us every day, 'If they throw one at your head, don't say anything. Push one down and run right up his neck.'

Following the game that night, Jackie and Mrs. Robinson drove back to their Long Island home and Jackie explained his point of view to her. She, in turn, talked of the larger picture. "I've been trying to make Jack see it from the fans' point of view. They don't appreciate that he's willing to run the risk of injury to stop what he believes is wrong. To them it appeared he was maliciously trying to injure Maglie. How can they know what is in his mind.

"Maybe today Jack feels differently about what happened," she said. "I think I understand his problem better than most. When he's at bat, he doesn't have much time to stop and think. Maybe a few hours later, he thinks and does differently."

The fact is Jackie today feels under no restraint whatsoever. Perhaps even less than any other player because, in effect, he has accomplished more. Jackie doesn't mind explosive quotes. He despises Durocher and he says so. He thought he was ticketed for trade before the start of this season and he felt free to tell me about it.

"You really dislike Leo, don't you?"

It was the first time Robinson smiled. "I say the hell with that . . . Yes, I dislike him. He feels the same way about me. He doesn't keep it a secret. Neither do I. That makes us even."

Even . . . it's the way Jackie wants it and has it now. Starting from scratch with all the rest and letting the best get there first. Once this season Russ Meyer of the Phils had the Dodgers beaten. Jackie's voice joined the others in riding the hot-tempered pitcher.

Finally, in a late inning, Robby got on base. He drove Meyer crazy with his antics, stealing second and going to third on an error. He came dashing for the plate and Meyer was there with the ball to meet him, but Jackie charged him, knocking it from the pitcher's glove to score.

Russ went livid with anger. Philly manager Eddie Sawyer, took him from the game. Sitting on the bench, Meyer shouted across the field to Jackie. The television cameras, trained on the dugouts, picked up Russ' arm-waving and shouting and finally his unmistakable challenge for Robby to meet him and fight under the stands in the alleyway that connects the rival dugouts.

Meyer rushed down the steps to the battleground. Jackie dashed after him and both dugouts emptied into the narrow passageway. The umpires came off the field and fortunately put an end to the business before a blow could be struck, but it is significant that Jackie felt free to take up the challenge and that his teammates raced behind him to back him up.

This is the unencumbered Robinson and his relation with his teammates. The only difference between Jackie and the others is that he, and Don Newcombe and Roy Campanella cannot stay in the same hotel in St. Louis because of the city's segregation customs.

Where he once could not make endorsements, Jackie now considers there are no strings upon him in the matter of cashing in off the field on his talent on the field. If he wants to make a public appearance, for free or for money, he does so without first taking the matter to the Brooklyn higher-ups.

On the field his bat speaks louder than the others and in the clubhouse there is no deference in his voice and his actions because of his delicate position. Not physically, morally or spiritually does Robby consider himself delicate any longer. He proved to Rickey he could take it. He kept his mouth shut and his emotions bottled for a reasonable period of time, but that time has come to an end. And there's none who cares to challenge him or has a right to say he is wrong.

Joe DiMaggio

Photo credit: Associated Press

JOE DiMAGGIO

The Silent Season of a Hero

Esquire Magazine   July 1966

"Joe," said Marilyn Monroe, just back from Korea, "you never heard such cheering." "Yes I have," Joe DiMaggio answered.

By Gay Talese

"I would like to take the great DiMaggio fishing," the old man said. "They say his father was a fisherman. Maybe he was as poor as we are and would understand."

—Ernest Hemingway, *The Old Man and the Sea*

It was not quite spring, the silent season before the search for salmon, and the old fishermen of San Francisco were either painting their boats or repairing their nets along the pier or sitting in the sun talking quietly among themselves, watching the tourists come and go, and smiling, now, as a pretty girl paused to take their picture. She was about twenty-five, healthy and blue-eyed and wearing a red turtle-neck sweater, and she had long, flowing blonde hair that she brushed back a few times before clicking her camera. The fishermen, looking at her, made admiring comments but she did not understand because they spoke a Sicilian dialect; nor did she notice the tall grey-haired man in a dark suit who stood watching her from behind a big bay window on the second floor of DiMaggio's Restaurant that overlooks the pier.

He watched until she left, lost in the crowd of newly arrived tourists that had just come down the hill by cable car. Then he sat down again at the table in the restaurant, finishing his tea and lighting another cigarette, his fifth in the last half hour. It was eleven-thirty in the morning. None of the other tables was occupied, and the only sounds came from the bar where a liquor salesman was laughing at something the headwaiter had said. But then the salesman, his briefcase under his arm, headed for the door, stopping briefly to peek into the dining room and call out, "See you later, Joe." Joe DiMaggio turned and waved at the salesman. Then the room was quiet again.

At fifty-one, DiMaggio was a most distinguished-looking man, aging as gracefully as he had played on the ball field, impeccable in his tailoring, his nails manicured, his six-foot two-inch body seeming as lean and capable as when he posed for the portrait that hangs in the restaurant and shows him in Yankee Stadium swinging from the heels at a pitch thrown twenty years ago. His grey hair was thinning at the crown, but just barely, and his face was lined in the right places, and his expression, once as sad and haunted as a matador's, was more in repose these days, though, as now, tension had returned and he chain-smoked and occasionally paced the floor and looked out the window at the people below. In the crowd was a man he did not wish to see.

The man had met DiMaggio in New York. This week he had come to San Francisco and had telephoned several times but none of the calls had been returned because DiMaggio suspected that the man, who had said he was doing research on some vague sociological project, really wanted to delve into DiMaggio's private life and that of DiMaggio's former wife, Marilyn Monroe. DiMaggio would never tolerate this. The memory of her death is still very painful to him, and yet, because he keeps it to himself, some people are not sensitive to it. One night in a supper club a woman who had been drinking approached his table, and when he did not ask her to join him, she snapped:

"All right, I guess I'm *not* Marilyn Monroe."

He ignored her remark, but when she repeated it, he replied, barely controlling his anger, "No—I wish you were, but you're not."

The tone of his voice softened her, and she asked, "Am I saying something wrong?"

"You already have," he said. "Now will you please leave me alone?"

His friends on the wharf, understanding him as they do, are very careful when discussing him with strangers, knowing that should they inadvertently betray a confidence he will not denounce them but rather will never speak to them again; this comes from a sense of propriety not inconsistent in the man who also, after Marilyn Monroe's death, directed that fresh flowers be placed on her grave "forever."

Some of the older fishermen who have known DiMaggio all his life remember him as a small boy who helped clean his father's boat, and as a young man who sneaked away and used a broken oar as a bat on the sandlots nearby. His father, a small mustachioed man known as Zio Pepe, would become infuriated and call him *lagnuso,* lazy, *meschino,* good-for-nothing, but in 1936 Zio Pepe was among those who cheered when Joe DiMaggio returned to San Francisco after his first season with the New York Yankees and was carried along the wharf on the shoulders of the fishermen.

The fishermen also remember how, after his retirement in 1951, DiMaggio brought his second wife, Marilyn, to live near the wharf, and sometimes they would be seen early in the morning fishing off DiMaggio's boat, the *Yankee Clipper,* now docked quietly in the marina, and in the evening they would be sitting and talking on the pier. They had arguments, too, the fishermen knew, and one night Marilyn was seen running hysterically, crying as she ran, along the road away from the pier, with Joe following. But the fishermen pretended they did not see this; it was none of their affair. They knew that Joe wanted her to stay in San Francisco and avoid the sharks in Hollywood, but she was confused and torn then—"She was a child," they said—and even today DiMaggio loathes Los Angeles and many of the people in it. He no longer speaks to his onetime friend, Frank Sinatra, who had befriended Marilyn in her final years, and he also is cool to Dean Martin and Peter Lawford and Lawford's former wife, Pat, who once gave a party at which she introduced Marilyn Monroe to Robert Kennedy, and the two of them danced often that night, Joe heard, and he did not take it well. He was very possessive of her that year, his close friends say, because Marilyn and he had planned to remarry; but before they could she was dead, and DiMaggio banned the Lawfords and Sinatra and many Hollywood people from her funeral. When Marilyn Monroe's attorney complained that DiMaggio was keeping her friends away, DiMaggio answered coldly, "If it weren't for those friends persuading her to stay in Hollywood she would still be alive."

Joe DiMaggio now spends most of the year in San Francisco, and each day tourists, noticing the name on the restaurant, ask the men on the wharf if they ever see him. Oh yes, the men say, they see him nearly every day; they have not seen him yet this morning, they add, but he should be arriving shortly. So the tourists continue to walk along the piers past the crab vendors, under the circling sea gulls, past the fish 'n' chip stands, sometimes stopping to watch a large vessel steaming toward the Golden Gate Bridge which, to their dismay, is painted red. Then they visit the Wax Museum, where there is a life-size figure of DiMaggio in uniform, and walk across the street and spend a quarter to peer through the silver telescopes focused on the island of Alcatraz, which is no longer a Federal prison. Then they return to ask the men if DiMaggio has been seen. Not yet, the men say, although they notice his blue Impala parked in the lot next to the restaurant. Sometimes tourists will walk into the restaurant and have lunch and will see him sitting calmly in a corner signing autographs and being extremely gracious with everyone. At other times, as on this particular morning when the man from New York chose to visit, DiMaggio was tense and suspicious.

When the man entered the restaurant from the side steps leading to the dining room he saw DiMaggio standing near the window talking with an elderly maître d' named Charles Friscia. Not wanting to walk in and risk intrusion, the man asked one of DiMaggio's nephews to inform Joe of his presence. When DiMaggio got the message he quickly turned and left Friscia and disappeared through an exit leading down to the kitchen.

Astonished and confused, the visitor stood in the hall. A moment later Friscia appeared and the man asked, "Did Joe leave?"

"Joe who?" Friscia replied.

"Joe DiMaggio!"

"Haven't seen him," Friscia said.

"You haven't *seen* him! He was standing right next to you a second ago!"

"It wasn't me," Friscia said.

"You were standing next to him. I saw you. In the dining room."

"You must be mistaken," Friscia said, softly, seriously. "It wasn't me."

"You *must* be kidding," the man said, angrily, turning and leaving the restaurant. Before he could get to his car, however, DiMaggio's nephew came running after him and said, "Joe wants to see you."

He returned expecting to see DiMaggio waiting for him. Instead he was handed a telephone. The voice was powerful and deep and so tense that the quick sentences ran together.

"You are invading my rights, I did not ask you to come, I assume you have a lawyer, you must have a lawyer, get your lawyer!"

"I came as a friend," the man interrupted.

"That's beside the point," DiMaggio said. "I have my privacy, I do not want it violated, you'd better get a lawyer. . . ." Then, pausing, DiMaggio asked, "Is my nephew there?"

He was not.

"Then wait where you are."

A moment later DiMaggio appeared, tall and red-faced, erect and beautifully dressed in his dark suit and white shirt with the grey silk tie and the gleaming silver cuff links. He moved with big steps toward the man and handed him an airmail envelope, unopened, that the man had written from New York.

"Here," DiMaggio said. "This is yours."

Then DiMaggio sat down at a small table. He said nothing, just lit a cigarette and waited, legs crossed, his head held high and back so as to reveal the intricate construction of his nose, a fine sharp tip above the big nostrils and tiny bones built out from the bridge, a great nose.

"Look," DiMaggio said, more calmly. "I do not interfere with other people's lives. And I do not expect them to interfere with mine. There are things about my life, personal things, that I refuse to talk about. And even if you asked my brothers they would be unable to tell you about them because they do not know. There are things about me, so many things, that they simply do not know. . . ."

"I don't want to cause trouble," the man said. "I think you're a great man, and. . . ."

"I'm not great," DiMaggio cut in. "I'm not great," he repeated, softly. "I'm just a man trying to get along."

Then DiMaggio, as if realizing that he was intruding upon his own privacy, abruptly stood up. He looked at his watch.

"I'm late," he said, very formal again. "I'm ten minutes late. *You're* making me late."

The man left the restaurant. He crossed the street and wandered over to the pier, briefly watching the fishermen hauling their nets and talking in the sun, seeming very calm and contented. Then, after he had turned and was headed back toward the parking lot, a blue Impala stopped in front of him and Joe DiMaggio leaned out the window and asked, "Do you have a car?" His voice was very gentle.

"Yes," the man said.

"Oh," DiMaggio said. "I would have given you a ride."

Joe DiMaggio was not born in San Francisco but in Martinez, a small fishing village twenty-five miles northeast of the Golden Gate. Zio Pepe had settled there after leaving Isola delle Femmine, an islet off Palermo where the DiMaggios had been fishermen for generations. But in 1915, hearing of the luckier waters off San Francisco's wharf, Zio Pepe left Martinez, packing his boat with furniture and family, including Joe who was one year old.

San Francisco was placid and picturesque when the DiMaggios arrived, but there was a competitive undercurrent and struggle for power along the pier. At dawn the boats would sail out to where the bay meets the ocean and the sea is rough, and later the men would race back with their hauls, hoping to beat their fellow fishermen to shore and sell it while they could. Twenty or thirty boats would sometimes be trying to gain the channel shoreward at the same time, and a fisherman had to know every rock in the water, and later know every bargaining trick along the shore, because the dealers and restaurateurs would play one fisherman off against the other, keeping the prices down. Later the fishermen became wiser and organized, predetermining the maximum amount each fisherman would catch, but there were always some men who, like the fish, never learned, and so heads would sometimes be broken, nets slashed, gasoline poured onto their fish, flowers of warning placed outside their doors.

But these days were ending when Zio Pepe arrived and he expected his five sons to succeed him as fishermen, and the first two, Tom and Michael, did; but a third, Vincent, wanted to sing. He sang with such magnificent power as a young man that he came to the attention of the great banker, A. P. Giannini, and there were plans to send him to Italy for tutoring and the opera. But there was hesitation around the DiMaggio household and Vince never went; instead he played ball with the San Francisco Seals and sportswriters misspelled his name.

It was DeMaggio until Joe, at Vince's recommendation, joined the team and became a sensation, being followed later by the youngest brother, Dominic, who was also outstanding. All three later played in the big leagues and some writers like to say that Joe was the best hitter, Dom the best fielder, Vince the best singer, and Casey Stengel once said: "Vince is the only player I ever saw who could strike out three times in one game and not be embarrassed. He'd walk into the clubhouse whistling. Everybody would be feeling sorry for him, but Vince always thought he was doing good."

After he retired from baseball Vince became a bartender, then a milkman, now a carpenter. He lives forty miles north of San Francisco in a house he partly built, has been happily married for thirty-four years, has four grandchildren, has in the closet one of Joe's tailor-made suits that he has never had altered to fit, and when people ask if he envies Joe he always says, "No, maybe Joe would like to have what I have. He won't admit it, but he just might like to have what I have." The brother Vince most admired was Michael, "a big earthy man, a dreamer, a fisherman who wanted things but didn't want to take from Joe, or to work in the restaurant. He wanted a bigger boat, but wanted to earn it on his own. He never got it." In 1953, at the age of forty-four, Michael fell from his boat and drowned.

Since Zio Pepe's death at seventy-seven in 1949, Tom at sixty-two the oldest brother—two of his four sisters are older—has become nominal head of the family and manages the restaurant that was opened in 1937 as Joe DiMaggio's Grotto. Later Joe sold out his share and now Tom is the co-owner of it with Dominic. Of all the brothers, Dominic, who was known as the "Little Professor" when he played with the Boston Red Sox, is the most successful in business. He lives in a fashionable Boston suburb with his wife and three children and is president of a firm that manufactures fiber cushion materials and grossed more than $3,500,000 last year.

Joe DiMaggio lives with his widowed sister, Marie, in a tan stone house on a quiet residential street not far from Fisherman's Wharf. He bought the house almost thirty years ago for his parents, and after their death he lived there with Marilyn Monroe; now it is cared for by Marie, a slim and handsome dark-eyed woman who has an apartment on the second floor, Joe on the third. There are some baseball trophies and plaques in the small room off DiMaggio's bedroom, and on his dresser are photographs of Marilyn Monroe, and in the living room downstairs is a small painting of her that DiMaggio likes very much: it reveals only her face and shoulders and she is wearing a very wide-brimmed sun hat, and there is a soft sweet smile on her lips, an innocent curiosity about her that is the way he saw her and the way he wanted her to be seen by others—a simple girl, "a warm bighearted girl," he once described her, "that everybody took advantage of."

The publicity photographs emphasizing her sex appeal often offended him, and a memorable moment for Billy Wilder, who directed her in *The Seven Year Itch,* occurred when he spotted DiMaggio in a large crowd of people gathered on Lexington Avenue in New York to watch a scene in which Marilyn, standing over a subway grating to cool herself, had her skirts blown high by a sudden wind below. "What the hell is going on here?" DiMaggio was overheard to have said in the crowd, and Wilder recalled, "I shall never forget the look of death on Joe's face."

He was then thirty-nine, she was twenty-seven. They had been married in January of that year, 1954, despite disharmony in temperament and time: he was tired of publicity, she was thriving on it; he was intolerant of tardiness, she was always late. During their honeymoon in Tokyo an American general had introduced himself and asked if, as a patriotic gesture, she would visit the troops in Korea. She looked at Joe. "It's your honeymoon," he said, shrugging, "go ahead if you want to."

She appeared on ten occasions before 100,000 servicemen, and when she returned she said, "It was so wonderful, Joe. You never heard such cheering."

"Yes I have," he said.

Across from her portrait in the living room, on a coffee table in front of a sofa, is a sterling-silver humidor that was presented to him by his Yankee teammates at a time when he was the most talked-about man in America, and when Les Brown's band had recorded a hit that was heard day and night on the radio:

> . . . *From Coast to Coast, that's all you hear*
> *Of Joe the One-Man Show*

He's glorified the horsehide sphere,
Jolting Joe DiMaggio . . .
Joe . . . Joe . . . DiMaggio . . . we
want you on our side. . . .

The year was 1941, and it began for DiMaggio in the middle of May after the Yankees had lost four games in a row, seven of their last nine, and were in fourth place, five-and-a-half games behind the leading Cleveland Indians. On May 15th, DiMaggio hit only a first-inning single in a game that New York lost to Chicago, 13–1; he was barely hitting .300, and had greatly disappointed the crowds that had seen him finish with a .352 average the year before and .381 in 1939.

He got a hit in the next game, and the next, and the next. On May 24th, with the Yankees losing 6–5 to Boston, DiMaggio came up with runners on second and third and singled them home, winning the game, extending his streak to ten games. But it went largely unnoticed. Even DiMaggio was not conscious of it until it had reached twenty-nine games in mid-June. Then the newspapers began to dramatize it, the public became aroused, they sent him good-luck charms of every description, and DiMaggio kept hitting, and radio announcers would interrupt programs to announce the news, and then the song again: *"Joe . . . Joe . . . DiMaggio . . . we want you on our side . . .*

Sometimes DiMaggio would be hitless his first three times up, the tension would build, it would appear that the game would end without his getting another chance—but he always would, and then he would hit the ball against the left-field wall, or through the pitcher's legs, or between two leaping infielders. In the forty-first game, the first of a doubleheader in Washington, DiMaggio tied an American League record that George Sisler had set in 1922. But before the second game began a spectator sneaked onto the field and into the Yankees' dugout and stole DiMaggio's favorite bat. In the second game, using another of his bats, DiMaggio lined out twice and flied out. But in the seventh inning, borrowing one of his old bats that a teammate was using, he singled and broke Sisler's record, and he was only three games away from surpassing the major-league record of forty-four set in 1897 by Willie Keeler while playing for Baltimore when it was a National League franchise.

An appeal for the missing bat was made through the newspapers. A man from Newark admitted the crime and returned it with regrets. And on July 2, at Yankee Stadium, DiMaggio hit a home run into the left-field stands. The record was broken.

He also got hits in the next eleven games, but on July 17th in Cleveland, at a night game attended by 67,468, he failed against two pitchers, Al Smith and Jim Bagby, Jr., although Cleveland's hero was really its third baseman, Ken Keltner, who in the first inning lunged to his right to

make a spectacular backhanded stop of a drive and, from the foul line
behind third base, he threw DiMaggio out. DiMaggio received a walk in
the fourth inning. But in the seventh he again hit a hard shot at Keltner,
who again stopped it and threw him out. DiMaggio hit sharply toward
the shortstop in the eighth inning, the ball taking a bad hop, but Lou
Boudreau speared it off his shoulder and threw to the second baseman to
start a double play and DiMaggio's streak was stopped at fifty-six games.
But the New York Yankees were on their way to winning the pennant by
seventeen games, and the World Series too, and so in August, in a hotel
suite in Washington, the players threw a surprise party for DiMaggio and
toasted him with champagne and presented him with this Tiffany silver
humidor that is now in San Francisco in his living room. . . .

Marie was in the kitchen making toast and tea when DiMaggio came
down for breakfast; his grey hair was uncombed but, since he wears it
short, it was not untidy. He said good-morning to Marie, sat down and
yawned. He lit a cigarette. He wore a blue wool bathrobe over his paja-
mas. It was eight a.m. He had many things to do today and he seemed
cheerful. He had a conference with the president of Continental Television, Inc., a large retail chain in California of which he is a partner and
vice-president; later he had a golf date, and then a big banquet to attend,
and, if that did not go on too long and he were not too tired afterward, he
might have a date.

Picking up the morning paper, not rushing to the sports page, DiMaggio read the front-page news, the people-problems of '66: Kwame
Nkrumah was overthrown in Ghana, students were burning their draft
cards (DiMaggio shook his head), the flu epidemic was spreading
through the whole state of California. Then he flipped inside through the
gossip columns, thankful they did not have him in there today—they had
printed an item about his dating "an electrifying airline hostess" not long
ago, and they also spotted him at dinner with Dori Lane, "the frantic
frugger" in Whisky à Go Go's glass cage—and then he turned to the
sports page and read a story about how the injured Mickey Mantle may
never regain his form.

It had all happened so quickly, the passing of Mantle, or so it seemed;
he had succeeded DiMaggio as DiMaggio had succeeded Ruth, but now
there was no great young power hitter coming up and the Yankee management, almost desperate, had talked Mantle out of retirement and on
September 18, 1965, they gave him a "day" in New York during which
he received several thousand dollars' worth of gifts—an automobile, two
quarter horses, free vacation trips to Rome, Nassau, Puerto Rico—and
DiMaggio had flown to New York to make the introduction before
50,000: it had been a dramatic day, an almost holy day for the believers

who had jammed the grandstands early to witness the canonization of a new stadium saint. Cardinal Spellman was on the committee, President Johnson sent a telegram, the day was officially proclaimed by the Mayor of New York, an orchestra assembled in center field in front of the trinity of monuments to Ruth, Gehrig, Huggins; and high in the grandstands, billowing in the breeze of early autumn, were white banners that read: "Don't Quit Mick," "We Love the Mick."

The banners had been held by hundreds of young boys whose dreams had been fulfilled so often by Mantle, but also seated in the grandstands were older men, paunchy and balding, in whose middle-aged minds DiMaggio was still vivid and invincible, and some of them remembered how one month before, during a pregame exhibition at Old-timers' Day in Yankee Stadium, DiMaggio had hit a pitch into the left-field seats, and suddenly thousands of people had jumped wildly to their feet, joyously screaming—the great DiMaggio had returned, they were young again, it was yesterday.

But on this sunny September day at the Stadium, the feast day of Mickey Mantle, DiMaggio was not wearing No. 5 on his back nor a black cap to cover his greying hair; he was wearing a black suit and white shirt and blue tie, and he stood in one corner of the Yankees' dugout waiting to be introduced by Red Barber, who was standing near home plate behind a silver microphone. In the outfield Guy Lombardo's Royal Canadians were playing soothing soft music; and moving slowly back and forth over the sprawling green grass between the left-field bullpen and the infield were two carts driven by groundskeepers and containing dozens and dozens of large gifts for Mantle—a six-foot, one-hundred-pound Hebrew National salami, a Winchester rifle, a mink coat for Mrs. Mantle, a set of Wilson golf clubs, a Mercury 95-horsepower outboard motor, a Necchi portable, a year's supply of Chunky Candy. DiMaggio smoked a cigarette, but cupped it in his hands as if not wanting to be caught in the act by teen-aged boys near enough to peek down into the dugout. Then, edging forward a step, DiMaggio poked his head out and looked up. He could see nothing above except the packed towering green grandstands that seemed a mile high and moving, and he could see no clouds or blue sky, only a sky of faces. Then the announcer called out his name—"Joe DiMaggio!"—and suddenly there was a blast of cheering that grew louder and louder, echoing and reechoing within the big steel canyon, and DiMaggio stomped out his cigarette and climbed up the dugout steps and onto the soft green grass, the noise resounding in his ears, he could almost feel the breeze, the breath of 50,000 lungs upon him, 100,000 eyes watching his every move and for the briefest instant as he walked he closed his eyes.

Then in his path he saw Mickey Mantle's mother, a smiling elderly woman wearing an orchid, and he gently reached out for her elbow, holding it as he led her toward the microphone next to the other dignitaries lined up on the infield. Then he stood, very erect and without expression, as the cheers softened and the Stadium settled down.

Mantle was still in the dugout, in uniform, standing with one leg on the top step, and lined on both sides of him were the other Yankees who, when the ceremony was over, would play the Detroit Tigers. Then into the dugout, smiling, came Senator Robert Kennedy, accompanied by two tall curly-haired young assistants with blue eyes, Fordham freckles. Jim Farley was the first on the field to notice the Senator, and Farley muttered, loud enough for others to hear, "Who the hell invited *him?*"

Toots Shor and some of the other committeemen standing near Farley looked into the dugout, and so did DiMaggio, his glance seeming cold, but he remaining silent. Kennedy walked up and down within the dugout shaking hands with the Yankees, but he did not walk onto the field.

"Senator," said the Yankees' manager, Johnny Keane, "why don't you sit down?" Kennedy quickly shook his head, smiled. He remained standing, and then one Yankee came over and asked about getting relatives out of Cuba, and Kennedy called over one of his aides to take down the details in a notebook.

On the infield the ceremony went on, Mantle's gifts continued to pile up—a Mobilette motor bike, a Sooner Schooner wagon barbecue, a year's supply of Chock Full O'Nuts coffee, a year's supply of Topps Chewing Gum—and the Yankee players watched, and Maris seemed glum.

"Hey, Rog," yelled a man with a tape recorder, Murray Olderman, "I want to do a thirty-second tape with you."

Maris swore angrily, shook his head.

"It'll only take a second," Olderman said.

"Why don't you ask Richardson? He's a better talker than me."

"Yes, but the fact that it comes from you. . . ."

Maris swore again. But finally he went over and said in an interview that Mantle was the finest player of his era, a great competitor, a great hitter.

Fifteen minutes later, standing behind the microphone at home plate, DiMaggio was telling the crowd, "I'm proud to introduce the man who succeeded me in center field in 1951," and from every corner of the Stadium the cheering, whistling, clapping came down. Mantle stepped forward. He stood with his wife and children, posed for the photographers kneeling in front. Then he thanked the crowd in a short speech, and, turning, shook hands with the dignitaries standing nearby. Among them now was Senator Kennedy, who had been spotted in the dugout five minutes before by Red Barber, and been called out and introduced. Kennedy posed with Mantle for a photographer, then shook hands with the

Mantle children, and with Toots Shor and James Farley and others. DiMaggio saw him coming down the line and at the last second he backed away, casually, hardly anybody noticing it, and Kennedy seemed not to notice it either, just swept past shaking more hands. . . .

Finishing his tea, putting aside the newspaper, DiMaggio went upstairs to dress, and soon he was waving good-bye to Marie and driving toward his business appointment in downtown San Francisco with his partners in the retail television business. DiMaggio, while not a millionaire, has invested wisely and has always had, since his retirement from baseball, executive positions with big companies that have paid him well. He also was among the organizers of the Fisherman's National Bank of San Francisco last year, and, though it never came about, he demonstrated an acuteness that impressed those businessmen who had thought of him only in terms of baseball. He has had offers to manage big-league baseball teams but always has rejected them, saying, "I have enough trouble taking care of my own problems without taking on the responsibilities of twenty-five ballplayers."

So his only contact with baseball these days, excluding public appearances, is his unsalaried job as a batting coach each spring in Florida with the New York Yankees, a trip he would make once again on the following Sunday, three days away, if he could accomplish what for him is always the dreaded responsibility of packing, a task made no easier by the fact that he lately has fallen into the habit of keeping his clothes in two places —some hang in his closet at home, some hang in the back room of a saloon called Reno's.

Reno's is a dimly-lit bar in the center of San Francisco. A portrait of DiMaggio swinging a bat hangs on the wall, in addition to portraits of other star athletes, and the clientele consists mainly of the sporting crowd and newspapermen, people who know DiMaggio quite well and around whom he speaks freely on a number of subjects and relaxes as he can in few other places. The owner of the bar is Reno Barsocchini, a broad-shouldered and handsome man of fifty-one with greying wavy hair who began as a fiddler in Dago Mary's tavern thirty-five years ago. He later became a bartender there and elsewhere, including DiMaggio's Restaurant, and now he is probably DiMaggio's closest friend. He was the best man at the DiMaggio-Monroe wedding in 1954, and when they separated nine months later in Los Angeles, Reno rushed down to help DiMaggio with the packing and drive him back to San Francisco. Reno will never forget the day.

Hundreds of people were gathered around the Beverly Hills home that DiMaggio and Marilyn had rented, and photographers were perched in the trees watching the windows, and others stood on the lawn and behind the rose bushes waiting to snap pictures of anybody who walked out of the house. The newspapers that day played all the puns—"Joe Fanned on Jealousy"; "Marilyn and Joe—Out at Home"—and the Hollywood columnists, to whom DiMaggio was never an idol, never a gracious host, recounted instances of incompatibility, and Oscar Levant said it all proved that no man could be a success in two national pastimes. When Reno Barsocchini arrived he had to push his way through the mob, then bang on the door for several minutes before being admitted. Marilyn Monroe was upstairs in bed, Joe DiMaggio was downstairs with his suitcases, tense and pale, his eyes bloodshot.

Reno took the suitcases and golf clubs out to DiMaggio's car, and then DiMaggio came out of the house, the reporters moving toward him, the lights flashing.

"Where are you going?" they yelled.

"I'm driving to San Francisco," he said, walking quickly.

"Is that going to be your home?"

"That *is* my home and always has been."

"Are you coming back?"

DiMaggio turned for a moment, looking up at the house.

"No," he said, "I'll never be back."

Reno Barsocchini, except for a brief falling out over something he will not discuss, has been DiMaggio's trusted companion ever since, joining him whenever he can on the golf course or on the town, otherwise waiting for him in the bar with other middle-aged men. They may wait for hours sometimes, waiting and knowing that when he arrives he may wish to be alone; but it does not seem to matter, they are endlessly awed by him, moved by the mystique, he is a kind of male Garbo. They know that he can be warm and loyal if they are sensitive to his wishes, but they must never be late for an appointment to meet him. One man, unable to find a parking place, arrived a half-hour late once and DiMaggio did not talk to him again for three months. They know, too, when dining at night with DiMaggio, that he generally prefers male companions and occasionally one or two young women, but never wives; wives gossip, wives complain, wives are trouble, and men wishing to remain close to DiMaggio must keep their wives at home.

When DiMaggio strolls into Reno's bar the men wave and call out his name, and Reno Barsocchini smiles and announces, "Here's the Clipper!", the "Yankee Clipper" being a nickname from his baseball days.

"Hey, Clipper, Clipper," Reno had said two nights before, "where you been, Clipper? . . . Clipper, how 'bout a belt?"

DiMaggio refused the offer of a drink, ordering instead a pot of tea, which he prefers to all other beverages except before a date, when he will switch to vodka.

"Hey, Joe," a sportswriter asked, a man researching a magazine piece on golf, "why is it that a golfer, when he starts getting older, loses his putting touch first? Like Snead and Hogan, they can still hit a ball well off the tee, but on the greens they lose the strokes. . . ."

"It's the pressure of age," DiMaggio said, turning around on his bar stool. "With age you get jittery. It's true of golfers, it's true of any man when he gets into his fifties. He doesn't take chances like he used to. The younger golfer, on the greens, he'll stroke his putts better. The older man, he becomes hesitant. A little uncertain. Shaky. When it comes to taking chances the younger man, even when driving a car, will take chances that the older man won't."

"Speaking of chances," another man said, one of the group that had gathered around DiMaggio, "did you see that guy on crutches in here last night?"

"Yeah, had his leg in a cast," a third said. "Skiing."

"I would never ski," DiMaggio said. "Men who ski must be doing it to impress a broad. You see these men, some of them forty, fifty, getting onto skis. And later you see them all bandaged up, broken legs. . . ."

"But skiing's a very sexy sport, Joe. All the clothes, the tight pants, the fireplace in the ski lodge, the bear rug—Christ, nobody goes to ski. They just go out there to get it cold so they can warm it up. . . ."

"Maybe you're right," DiMaggio said. "I might be persuaded."

"Want a belt, Clipper?" Reno asked.

DiMaggio thought for a second, then said, "All right—first belt tonight."

Now it was noon, a warm sunny day. DiMaggio's business meeting with the television retailers had gone well; he had made a strong appeal to George Shahood, president of Continental Television, Inc., which has eight retail outlets in Northern California, to cut prices on color television sets and increase the sales volume, and Shahood had conceded it was worth a try. Then DiMaggio called Reno's bar to see if there were any messages, and now he was in Lefty O'Doul's car being driven along Fisherman's Wharf toward the Golden Gate Bridge en route to a golf course thirty miles upstate. Lefty O'Doul was one of the great hitters in the National League in the early Thirties, and later he managed the San Francisco Seals when DiMaggio was the shining star. Though O'Doul is now sixty-nine, eighteen years older than DiMaggio, he nevertheless possesses great energy and spirit, is a hard-drinking, boisterous man with a big belly and roving eye; and when DiMaggio, as they drove along the highway toward the golf club, noticed a lovely blonde at the wheel of a car nearby and exclaimed, "Look at *that* tomato!", O'Doul's head suddenly spun around, he took his eyes off the road, and yelled, "Where,

where?" O'Doul's golf game is less than what it was—he used to have a two-handicap—but he still shoots in the 80's, as does DiMaggio.

DiMaggio's drives range between 250 and 280 yards when he doesn't sky them, and his putting is good, but he is distracted by a bad back that both pains him and hinders the fullness of his swing. On the first hole, waiting to tee off, DiMaggio sat back watching a foursome of college boys ahead swinging with such freedom. "Oh," he said with a sigh, "to have *their* backs."

DiMaggio and O'Doul were accompanied around the golf course by Ernie Nevers, the former football star, and two brothers who are in the hotel and movie-distribution business. They moved quickly up and down the green hills in electric golf carts, and DiMaggio's game was exceptionally good for the first nine holes. But then he seemed distracted, perhaps tired, perhaps even reacting to a conversation of a few minutes before. One of the movie men was praising the film *Boeing, Boeing,* starring Tony Curtis and Jerry Lewis, and the man asked DiMaggio if he had seen it.

"No," DiMaggio said. Then he added, swiftly, "I haven't seen a film in eight years."

DiMaggio hooked a few shots, was in the woods. He took a No. 9 iron and tried to chip out. But O'Doul interrupted DiMaggio's concentration to remind him to keep the face of the club closed. DiMaggio hit the ball. It caromed off the side of his club, went skipping like a rabbit through the high grass down toward a pond. DiMaggio rarely displays any emotion on a golf course, but now, without saying a word, he took his No. 9 iron and flung it into the air. The club landed in a tree and stayed up there.

"Well," O'Doul said, casually, "there goes *that* set of clubs."

DiMaggio walked to the tree. Fortunately the club had slipped to the lower branch and DiMaggio could stretch up on the cart and get it back.

"Every time I get advice," DiMaggio muttered to himself, shaking his head slowly and walking toward the pond, "I shank it."

Later, showered and dressed, DiMaggio and the others drove to a banquet about ten miles from the golf course. Somebody had said it was going to be an elegant dinner, but when they arrived they could see it was more like a county fair; farmers were gathered outside a big barnlike building, a candidate for sheriff was distributing leaflets at the front door, and a chorus of homely ladies were inside singing *You Are My Sunshine.*

"How did we get sucked into this?" DiMaggio asked, talking out of the side of his mouth, as they approached the building.

"O'Doul," one of the men said. "It's his fault. Damned O'Doul can't turn *anything* down."

"Go to hell," O'Doul said.

Soon DiMaggio and O'Doul and Ernie Nevers were surrounded by the crowd, and the woman who had been leading the chorus came rushing over and said, "Oh, Mr. DiMaggio, it certainly is a pleasure having you."

"It's a pleasure being here, ma'am," he said, forcing a smile.

"It's too bad you didn't arrive a moment sooner, you'd have heard our singing."

"Oh, I heard it," he said, "and I enjoyed it very much."

"Good, good," she said. "And how are your brothers Dom and Vic?"

"Fine. Dom lives near Boston. Vince is in Pittsburgh."

"Why, *hello* there, Joe," interrupted a man with wine on his breath, patting DiMaggio on the back, feeling his arm. "Who's gonna take it this year, Joe?"

"Well, I have no idea," DiMaggio said.

"What about the Giants?"

"Your guess is as good as mine."

"Well, you can't count the Dodgers out," the man said.

"You sure can't," DiMaggio said.

"Not with all that pitching."

"Pitching is certainly important," DiMaggio said.

Everywhere he goes the questions seem the same, as if he has some special vision into the future of new heroes, and everywhere he goes, too, older men grab his hand and feel his arm and predict that he could still go out there and hit one, and the smile on DiMaggio's face is genuine. He tries hard to remain as he was—he diets, he takes steam baths, he is careful; and flabby men in the locker rooms of golf clubs sometimes steal peeks at him when he steps out of the shower, observing the tight muscles across his chest, the flat stomach, the long sinewy legs. He has a young man's body, very pale and little hair; his face is dark and lined, however, parched by the sun of several seasons. Still he is always an impressive figure at banquets such as this—an *immortal,* sportswriters called him, and that is how they have written about him and others like him, rarely suggesting that such heroes might ever be prone to the ills of mortal men, carousing, drinking, scheming; to suggest this would destroy the myth, would disillusion small boys, would infuriate rich men who own ball clubs and to whom baseball is a business dedicated to profit and in pursuit of which they trade mediocre players' flesh as casually as boys trade players' pictures on bubble-gum cards. And so the baseball hero must always act the part, must preserve the myth, and none does it better than DiMaggio, none is more patient when drunken old men grab an arm and ask, "Who's gonna take it this year, Joe?"

Two hours later, dinner and the speeches over, DiMaggio is slumped in O'Doul's car headed back to San Francisco. He edged himself up, however, when O'Doul pulled into a gas station in which a pretty red-haired girl sat on a stool, legs crossed, filing her fingernails. She was about twenty-two, wore a tight black skirt and tighter white blouse.

"Look at *that*," DiMaggio said.

"Yeah," O'Doul said.

O'Doul turned away when a young man approached, opened the gas tank, began wiping the windshield. The young man wore a greasy white uniform on the front of which was printed the name "Burt." DiMaggio kept looking at the girl, but she was not distracted from her fingernails. Then he looked at Burt, who did not recognize him. When the tank was full, O'Doul paid and drove off. Burt returned to his girl; DiMaggio slumped down in the front seat and did not open his eyes again until they'd arrived in San Francisco.

"Let's go see Reno," DiMaggio said.

"No, I gotta go see my old lady," O'Doul said. So he dropped DiMaggio off in front of the bar, and a moment later Reno's voice was announcing in the smoky room, "Hey, here's the Clipper!" The men waved and offered to buy him a drink. DiMaggio ordered a vodka and sat for an hour at the bar talking to a half dozen men around him. Then a blonde girl who had been with friends at the other end of the bar came over, and somebody introduced her to DiMaggio. He bought her a drink, offered her a cigarette. Then he struck a match and held it. His hand was unsteady.

"Is that me that's shaking?" he asked.

"It must be," said the blonde. "I'm calm."

Two nights later, having collected his clothes out of Reno's back room, DiMaggio boarded a jet; he slept crossways on three seats, then came down the steps as the sun began to rise in Miami. He claimed his luggage and golf clubs, put them into the trunk of a waiting automobile, and less than an hour later he was being driven into Fort Lauderdale, past palm-lined streets, toward the Yankee Clipper Hotel.

"All my life it seems I've been on the road traveling," he said, squinting through the windshield into the sun. "I never get a sense of being in any one place."

Arriving at the Yankee Clipper Hotel, DiMaggio checked into the largest suite. People rushed through the lobby to shake hands with him, to ask for his autograph, to say, "Joe, you look great." And early the next morning, and for the next thirty mornings, DiMaggio arrived punctually at the baseball park and wore his uniform with the famous No. 5, and the tourists seated in the sunny grandstands clapped when he first appeared on the field each time, and then they watched with nostalgia as he picked up a bat and played "pepper" with the younger Yankees, some of whom were not even born when, twenty-five years ago this summer, he hit in fifty-six straight games and became the most celebrated man in America.

But the younger spectators in the Fort Lauderdale park, and the sportswriters, too, were more interested in Mantle and Maris, and nearly every day there were news dispatches reporting how Mantle and Maris felt, what they did, what they said, even though they said and did very little except walk around the field frowning when photographers asked for another picture and when sportswriters asked how they felt.

After seven days of this, the big day arrived—Mantle and Maris would swing a bat—and a dozen sportswriters were gathered around the big batting cage that was situated beyond the left-field fence; it was completely enclosed in wire, meaning that no baseball could travel more than thirty or forty feet before being trapped in rope; still Mantle and Maris would be swinging, and this, in spring, makes news.

Mantle stepped in first. He wore black gloves to help prevent blisters. He hit right-handed against the pitching of a coach named Vern Benson, and soon Mantle was swinging hard, smashing line drives against the nets, going *ahhh ahhh* as he followed through with his mouth open.

Then Mantle, not wanting to overdo it on his first day, dropped his bat in the dirt and walked out of the batting cage. Roger Maris stepped in. He picked up Mantle's bat.

"This damn thing must be thirty-eight ounces," Maris said. He threw the bat down into the dirt, left the cage and walked toward the dugout on the other side of the field to get a lighter bat.

DiMaggio stood among the sportswriters behind the cage, then turned when Vern Benson, inside the cage, yelled, "Joe, wanna hit some?"

"No chance," DiMaggio said.

"Com'on, Joe," Benson said.

The reporters waited silently. Then DiMaggio walked slowly into the cage and picked up Mantle's bat. He took his position at the plate but obviously it was not the classic DiMaggio stance; he was holding the bat about two inches from the knob, his feet were not so far apart, and, when DiMaggio took a cut at Benson's first pitch, fouling it, there was none of that ferocious follow through, the blurred bat did not come whipping all the way around, the No. 5 was not stretched full across his broad back.

DiMaggio fouled Benson's second pitch, then he connected solidly with the third, the fourth, the fifth. He was just meeting the ball easily, however, not smashing it, and Benson called out, "I didn't know you were a choke hitter, Joe."

"I am now," DiMaggio said, getting ready for another pitch.

He hit three more squarely enough, and then he swung again and there was a hollow sound.

"Ohhh," DiMaggio yelled, dropping his bat, his fingers stung, "I was waiting for that one." He left the batting cage rubbing his hands together. The reporters watched him. Nobody said anything. Then DiMaggio said to one of them, not in anger nor in sadness, but merely as a simply stated fact, "There was a time when you couldn't get me out of there."

Satchel Paige

SATCHEL PAIGE

The Fabulous Satchel Paige

Collier's   1953

Written originally for Collier's *and anthologized on several occasions, this visit with the game's greatest showman, and perhaps its greatest pitcher, is too good not to be presented again.*

By Richard Donovan

Mr. Satchel Paige, the lank and languid patriarch, raconteur and relief pitching star of the St. Louis Browns, fairly vibrated with dignity and satisfaction as he strolled around the St. Louis railroad station one recent evening. To begin with, his physical tone was splendid—no stomach gas, store teeth resting easy, plenty of whip in his pitching arm. More important, he was in a powerful moral position.

Because of an error in reading his watch, Mr. Paige had arrived almost an hour early for the train that was to take the Browns to Chicago for a series of games with the White Sox. Never before in nearly thirty years of baseball had Paige, called by many the greatest pitcher who ever lived, been early for a train or anything else. It gave him an uneasy, but exceedingly righteous, feeling.

As he strolled past the baggage stand, a police officer tapped his shoulder. "What's your name?" he asked, dispensing with preliminaries.

"Leroy Paige," said Paige, surprised.

"How old are you?"

Satchel pondered; it was a question he had heard many times before.

"Well, now," he said guardedly, "people says different things. I'd judge between thirty and seventy."

"Is that so?" said the policeman, his eyes narrowing. "Just get into town?"

"Oh, I'm in and out, in and out."

"What're you out of lately?" asked the officer.

"California," said Paige, referring to his recent participation in the Browns' spring training.

"And what were you doing in California?"

"Playing," sighed Paige.

The officer was reaching for his handcuffs when Browns catcher Les Moss arrived on the scene. "What's he done?" asked Moss.

"We're looking for a murder suspect," the officer replied triumphantly, "and I think we've got him."

"How old is this suspect?"

"Twenty-two," said the cop.

Moss grinned, and Paige swelled visibly. "Twenty-two!" the pitcher exulted. "You hear that?"

Lately, however, it has been noticed that Paige's delight at being mistaken for a youth by the officer has vied with uneasiness at not being recognized by the man. "He probably thought I was passed on," he has been heard to grumble. Even more aggravating are those who stubbornly accuse him of impersonating himself.

Paige recently was asked to make a round of bars in Harlem with two reporters who introduced him to patrons and recorded their reactions. Twelve of the twenty-three people approached told him to his face that he was too young to be the original Satchel.

That is an exasperating situation for Paige, who, before the 1953 season was a week old, had helped save three games for the Browns and who last year was probably the most valuable relief hurler in the American League (12 wins, 10 games saved, 10 losses), earned-run average, 3.07— good enough to lead the Browns' regulars.

Rising six feet three and a quarter inches on semi-invisible legs, with scarcely 180 pounds strung between foot and crown, he sometimes seems more shadow than substance. His face mystifies many fans who peer at it to discover the secrets of time. Head on, it seems to belong to a cheerful man about thirty. From another angle, it looks melancholy and old, as though Paige had walked too long in a world made up exclusively of pickpockets. From a third angle, it seems a frontispiece for the great book of experience, with expressions of wisdom, restrained violence, cunning and easy humor crossing it in slow succession.

"We seen some sights, it and I," says Paige of his face.

Inside Paige, conditions are even more confusing. He faces batters, crowds, TV cameras or whatever, with the regal calm of a Watusi chieftain; yet his nervous stomach shows signs of long and severe emotional tension. He is a congenital AWOL, missing appointments, practice and, on a couple of occasions, games without much excuse ("My feet told me it was gonna rain," he explained after failing to show for a Red Sox game). He is one of the last surviving totally unregimented souls. Contracts box him in; off-field demands on his time make him jumpy; long stays in one place give him nervous stomach.

Although records of his career are lost, forgotten or twisted by generations of sports writers, it is reasonably certain that he pitched twenty-two years of organized sand-lot, semipro or Negro League ball (about one and a half lifetimes for the average pitcher) before he ever ascended to the majors, and he has been in that high company almost five years. Although he may be the oldest man on record to perform regularly in the big leagues, last year he was invited to play in the All-Star game. Year upon year, he has pitched summer (over most of the United States and Canada) and winter (in California and Central and South America), and has pulled in more customers than Babe Ruth.

It seems certain that Paige has worked a record total of at least 2,500 ball games in his life, often pitching 125 games a year, frequently working five to seven days a week without rest. He has won around 2,000 of those games, it is estimated, including some 250 shutouts and 45 no-hitters. In one month in 1935, he pitched 29 days in a row against smart hitters with but one loss; in four winter seasons (1932 to 1936), often playing against the best of the Negro leaguers and various off-season combinations of major-league all-stars, he lost but four games.

For some twenty years Paige was booked as a solo star, wearing a uniform with "Satchel" across the shirt, and playing with any team that could dig up $500 to $2,000 for three innings of his work. He was advertised as "Satchel Paige, World's Greatest Pitcher, Guaranteed to Strike Out the First Nine Men." Either he performed as advertised or he took side streets back to his hotel.

The Browns, who now have the legend as well as the man under contract, and Paige's presence often tends to make opposing teams gun for early scores. Whenever the Yankees start to take the Browns too lightly, for example, Yankee manager Casey Stengel begins to pace up and down in front of the bench, intoning: "Get the runs now! Father Time is coming!"

Once last season, Walt Dropo, Detroit's giant first baseman, swung embarrassingly wide of two Paige pitches, lost his head and loudly accused him of showboating. For reply, Paige threw a vicious fast ball.

Dropo swung so hard that he whirled around, ending in an odd, stooped position with the seat of his pants pointing toward the stands.

"My, my," clucked Paige, reproachfully. "Talk about showboatin'."

The anxious desire of most hitters, old and new, to drive him from the mound is regarded by Paige with fatherly amusement.

"Bangin' around the way I was, playing for guarantees on one team after another that I never heard of, in towns I never seen before, with players I didn't know and never saw again, I got lonesome," says Paige. "People didn't come to see the ball game. They came to see me strike out everybody, all the time. Occasionally I didn't."

One such breakdown took place in Union Springs, Alabama, one steaming Sunday in 1939. Paige had ridden all night in a bus, and had holed up at a hotel for a few hours' sleep before game time. He overslept, but it made little difference since the game was a social occasion and it was considered gross to arrive much before the third inning.

When Paige appeared, red-eyed and dragged out, in the middle of the fourth, the folks were just settling themselves, waving to friends, talking, sweating, looking everywhere but at the field.

"Then," says Paige, "I went in and it got quiet."

He retired the first five men in order. Then, with the nonchalance of a seasoned barnstormer, he turned and waved the outfielders off the field. The crowd rose with a roar.

"I laughed to see it," Paige says. "I was still laughing when a little, no-account-looking fella come up, took that big, greasy swing and put my fast ball where my left fielder formerly was."

Paige sighed heavily at the memory. "The polices escorted me from the place as the little man crossed home," he said. "Without my guarantee."

Country boys were not the only ones seized with intimations of immortality after hitting Paige. In 1935, Joe DiMaggio, who was to go up to the Yankees the next year, got a single off Satchel and immediately lost all doubts about how he would fare in the majors.

Paige has forgotten this game, along with a couple of thousand others, but Oakland, California sports writers have not. At the time, DiMaggio was playing around the Bay Area with an off-season team of major-league all-stars. Yankee scouts, who wished to see how their new find reacted to serious fire, finally got hold of Paige, who was taking the sun in Los Angeles. Paige was willing, after hearing about the guarantee, and started north with his team, composed entirely of Ebel Brooks, catcher for the New York Black Yankees of the Negro National League.

In Oakland, Paige found three local semipro players, filled out the roster with high-school boys and gazed solemnly at the terrifying line-up of major-league talent. Then he proceeded with the business of the day, which was to fan fifteen, allow three hits in ten innings and lose the game, two to one, when his youths, possibly rendered hysterical by the reputation of the opposition, threw to the winds the three balls that came their way. With a man on third in the tenth inning, DiMaggio, who had struck out twice and fouled out once in his previous official times at bat, finally hit a hopper which Paige lost in the shadows of dusk. One ex-Yankee scout remembers sending a telegram east: DIMAGGIO ALL WE HOPED HE'D BE. HIT SATCH ONE FOR FOUR.

Paige, whose memories of names, dates and faces tend to blend in the haze of time, is always interested to learn of such past feats from archivists in the various towns he visits. But he is essentially a forward-looking man, besides being a seasoned raconteur, sage, wit and student of the human race.

As a guest of the Second International Gerontological Congress, held in St. Louis in 1951, Paige was almost as interested in the gerontologists as they were in him. The doctors had gathered to report on their studies of the effects of age upon the human body. "They heard there was a man ninety years old playing major-league baseball in the United States," says Paige, "so, naturally, we had to meet."

The doctors interested Paige because he had the impression that only one of them spoke English. "They was all from Venice [Vienna]," he explains. Everything about Paige interested the doctors—his legs, which resemble golf-club shafts, his great feet, his stringy chest and neck muscles. When they got to his right arm, there was acclaim and astonishment.

"Most of you could be between thirty-five and fifty-five," translated the English-speaking doctor, tensely, "but your arm—" the doctor hesitated—"your arm doesn't seem to be a day over nineteen."

"I just explained to the gentlemen," Paige says, "that the bones running up from my wrist, the fibius, which is the upper bone, and the tiberon, which is the lower bone, was bent out, making more room for my throwing muscles to move around in there. I attributed most of my long life, and so on and so forth, to them two bones. The gentlemen was amazed to hear about that."

The doctors did not examine Paige's head, which is a pity, for there is enough in it to go around the average infield. He is a mountain of information on hunting dogs, expensive cars, jazz, Central American dictators, quartet singing, cameras, Kansas City real estate, Missouri River catfish, Indian maidens, stomach powders, mules and other matters. Whenever the Browns gather in a railroad club car, Paige is generally in the middle, spreading light on such matters as the futility of spring training under men like Rogers (Rajah) Hornsby, the Browns' manager the first part of last season.

"With Mr. Hawnsby, it's all runnin'," Paige told some listeners recently. "Now, I don't generally run at all, except for the showers, because of the harmful effects. I believe in training by rising gently up and down from the bench. But old Mahjong had me flyin' around, shakin' my legs and carryin' on until I very near passed. Now, what did all that do for my arm?"

Despite his sharp observance of many things, Paige's coaches complain that he does not look closely enough at the faces of the men batting against him. According to St. Louis sports announcer Bud Blattner, for example, switch-hitter Mickey Mantle hit a left-hand home run off Paige his first time up in one Yankee-Browns contest last year, then changed over and batted right-handed from there on. All the rest of the game, Paige kept asking: "Where is that boy done me the injury?"

Chicago first baseman Ferris Fain has an explanation for the confusion Mantle created. "Paige always seems to be looking at my knees. I think he recognizes batters by their stance."

Besides his difficulty in identifying his opponents, Paige is said to suffer from a couple of delusions—that he is swift on the base paths and that he is a powerful hitter. Paige runs like an unjointed turkey, except when covering a bunt. (When last checked, his major-league fielding average was 1.000.) As for his hits, he bunches them. He got five hits in 1952, three fifths of them in one 17-inning game against the Senators. Paige came on in the eleventh with the score 2-2 and, besides holding Washington hitless for five and two-thirds innings, got three singles, the last of which drove Joe DeMaestri home with the winning run. In gratitude and astonishment, owner Bill Veeck bought him a new suit.

Paige's uncertainty about names, while confusing to his audiences, rarely bothers him; he invents reasonable approximations of the original handles: Mark Griffin (Clark Griffith, owner of the Senators) Bob Rapid (Feller) and ol' Homer Bean (Dizzy Dean) Grover (Big Train) Cleveland (a composite of Grover Cleveland Alexander and Walter Johnson) Tom Lemons (Cleveland's Bob Lemon) The Actor (ex-Brownie Gene Bearden of Chicago, who has been in two movies).

Hitters loom larger in Paige's mind, naturally. Josh Gibson, late home-run king of the Negro leagues, is the best batsman he ever faced, he says, with Detroit's Charley Gehringer next, and Larry Doby, Cleveland's stylish and cultivated outfielder, third. DiMaggio, with whom Paige never had much trouble, is also well remembered, probably as a social gesture. So is Boston's Ted Williams, now of the U.S. Marines.

Now that Paige is getting on toward evening, reporters are constantly prying into him for treasures of the past.

"Who's gonna straighten out 2,500 ball games in my head?" he inquired indignantly a few weeks ago. "How many cow pastures you played on, Satchel? How many bus rides you took? Why is your feet flat? Who was it offered you $50 to pitch a triple-header that time?" Satchel screwed up his face, which indicated that the concentration was giving him indigestion. "Man," he said, "the past is a long and twisty road."

Leroy Robert Paige started down the road from a small frame house in the Negro section of Mobile, Alabama. His father was a gardener. His mother, Tula Paige, who is now eighty-three said he was the sixth of eight children. She put his birth year at 1903.

"What mama knows when her little child was bawn?" Paige said patiently when he got this news. "My draft card says 1906. I say 1908. Take your pick."

Food and living room were permanent problems for the family, but for Leroy, who was almost six feet tall at age twelve, the big problems apparently lay on the outside. One problem—where to find money to buy baseball equipment—he solved by becoming a redcap at a Mobile railroad station. After a couple of days' labor, he rigged a "totin' device" of sticks and ropes on which he could hang as many as ten bags for one trip. Staggering along one day, looking like a tree of satchels, he caught the name he has carried down the road.

The predatory warfare between Mobile's boy gangs was a much bigger problem for Paige. Several times he was beaten; just as often, he participated in the gang-beating of others. He rarely went to school. Reasoning that continuous battle against odds was the staff of life, he turned sniper, breaking windows and lumping heads with deadly, accurate rocks from his hand. Finally, a juvenile judge sentenced him to the Alabama Reform School for Boys, at Mount Meigs. He was approximately twelve when he went in, sixteen when he got out.

"One thing they told me in the refawm school," Paige says, "they told me that all that wild-a'-loose feelin' I put in rock throwin', I ought to put in throwin' baseballs."

Paige was six feet three inches tall and weighed 140 pounds when he rejoined society; he was reedy, solemn and taciturn but highly expressive on the mound. Most afternoons he spent in sand-lot games, one of which happened to be witnessed by a Pullman porter from Chattanooga. This man spoke to Alex Herman, owner of the Chattanooga Black Lookouts, and forthwith Mr. Herman appeared. Mrs. Paige, refused to let Satchel go until Herman promised to watch him like a father and send his $50-a-month salary home. Full of reform-school warnings and memories at seventeen Satchel took the next train into the outer world.

When he appeared on the Lookouts' field for the first time, the legend-to-be was an arresting sight. His uniform flapped about him, his neck, arms and legs indicated severe emaciation, spikes had to be nailed to his street shoes until some size-12, triple-A baseball shoes could be found.

The first man to face him in a practice session held his bat in one hand, for charity's sake.

Then Satchel threw his fast ball.

That evening, as the newly established most valuable player on the Lookouts, he was invited to dinner by several veterans.

By the time he was twenty-one, Satchel Paige was a seasoned traveler and an apprentice philosopher, to say the least. He had run through two roadsters. He had sat in with Louis Armstrong and his band; he had had ham and whisky with ol' Jelly Roll Morton at a wake in Memphis; he had gone across the river from New Orleans to have his palm read by the seers of Algiers, who found a short life line; he had been a running story in the Negro press, and from Savannah to Abilene and Mobile to St. Joe, he had heard of dozens of young ladies he had never seen who were letting it be known that they might shortly become Mrs. Paige.

"It was an education," Paige recalls now. "I was tired all the time."

As he put on a little more meat, Paige's fast ball got faster. This phenomenon has been explained by Biz Mackey, a memorable catcher for the Baltimore Elite Giants, of the late Negro National League.

"A lot of pitchers have a fast ball," says Mackey, "but a very, very few —Feller, Grove, Johnson, a couple of others besides Satchel—have had that little extra juice that makes the difference between the good and the great man. When it's that fast, it will hop a little at the end of the line. Beyond that, it tends to disappear."

Word of such disappearances got around the Negro leagues quickly, it seems, for competition for Satchel's services was intense. Since clubs issued loosely worded agreements in lieu of contracts, players could switch to the highest bidder.

Paige, a man of sound fiscal policies except in the savings department, jumped often, playing for such teams as the Birmingham Black Barons, the Nashville Elite Giants and the New Orleans Black Pelicans. But always he had in mind the goal of most Negro players of the time, Gus Greenlee's Pittsburgh Crawfords, a team that at one time might have won pennants in either major league. In 1930, Satchel received an off-hand note: "The Crawfords might possibly be interested in having you pitch for them next season." Paige replied: "I might possibly be interested in pitching for the Crawfords sometime."

With the Crawfords, Satchel's pitching bag grew. He threw overhand, sidearm and underhand; he served up the "two-hump blooper," a queer-acting slow ball; "the barber," an upshoot that grazed the batter's chin; "Little Tom," a medium fast ball; "Long Tom," *the* fast ball, and the "hesitation pitch," a bewildering delivery in which Paige stops in mid-throw before following through.

Toward the end of the 1931 season, he got a pleasing offer from a Señor Linares, owner of the Santa Clara, Cuba club, to play winter ball.

As a pitcher in the United States, Paige had been expected to win most of the time, but it was also realized that he might lose someday. In Cuba, this realization never came to the fans. When he got behind in a game, a terrible hush settled over the low, rudely constructed stands; if he got further behind, he could see the sun glinting on machetes all around him. While Satchel toiled, his teammates would hop around, chattering in Spanish.

"Speak English, brothers!" Paige would cry helplessly. "I is with you!"

After twenty-four straight wins for the Santa Clara club, Paige finally did lose.

"I didn't wait," he says. "I started yellin' Polices! Polices! and then I begin flyin' around the infield with the fans flyin' behind. They caught up with me at second base but the polices was a couple of jumps in the lead and we stood 'em off. They wrote me up in the paper the next day," Paige said sourly. "Said I throwed the game."

2

An air of uneasiness hung over the home stadium of the last-place St. Louis Browns one day last August. Over six innings, the Browns had compiled a 2-0 edge over the league-leading Yankees. But now, with two out in the last of the seventh, pitcher Gene Bearden was beginning to wobble. One Yankee run scored. Then, Bearden loaded the bases.

Browns' shortstop-manager, Marty Marion, glanced guiltily at his relief pitchers warming up in the bull pen. Then, stifling an impulse to call for volunteers, he made what seemed to be the only possible decision. He nominated Leroy (Satchel) Paige to douse the fire.

Mr. Paige, began his usual interminable stroll toward the mound.

In his thirty-or-so years in professional baseball, he had been in worse spots.

Humming a little tune, Paige took his regular half-dozen warmup pitches on the mound, sighted on pinch hitter Irv Noren, and fed him a fast curve. He smiled pleasantly as Marion gathered in a short pop-up, retiring the side.

Later, still humming contentedly, Mr. Paige did away with Phil Rizzuto, Joe Collins and Hank Bauer in the eighth, and Yogi Berra, Gil McDougald and Gene Woodling in the ninth, to save the game.

Now, as always, Satchel is so certain of his powers, both physical and mental, that sometimes he makes himself uneasy.

In the shower room after a recent game, several players were tossing a slippery cake of soap at a wall dish, trying without success to make it stick there. Paige entered, picked up the soap casually, and tossed it. It stuck. There was a general raising of eyebrows, none higher than Satchel's. He tossed another bar, even more slippery. It stuck, too.

"Boys," he said, "there is apparently things that even I don't know I can do."

Paige's powers have raised him to a patriarchal position among the Browns. Such recognition is not easily won, but when a man can explain to a club car full of ballplayers not only what the hull and superstructure of Noah's ark were made of, but the composition of its doors and hinges as well, respect must be paid where it is due.

Paige's observations on love are naturally sought by other Browns players. For a man who has made lifelong researches into the subject, it turned out that he had a rather low opinion of it.

"Love," said Paige, "is a proposition I wouldn't advise you to mess with, as regards the general run of women. You restrict yourself to one or two lady friends and you're gonna be all right. But you expand to include the field and you're bound to get cut up. Myself," he added dismally, "I'm a passel of scars."

When Paige made this retreat across the wilds of Cuba, he was the summer property of one of the most formidable teams then in existence, the all-Negro Pittsburgh Crawfords. The late Gus Greenlee, owner of the Crawfords, had been vaguely aware of Paige from the year 1923, when Paige's two pitches, hard and harder, had begun to terrorize semipro teams in his home town of Mobile. Greenlee had followed Paige's career from the time he joined the Chattanooga Black Lookouts in 1926 through various subsequent jumps to other teams in the Negro Southern Association. By 1930, when Greenlee offered Paige $200 a month to join the Crawfords, Satchel was winning up to 60 games a year, striking out from 10 to 18 men in every game.

In three years at Pittsburgh, he won an estimated 105 games while losing 37.

Paige's battery mate on the Crawfords was the late Josh Gibson, the *aficionado's* choice for the long-ball hitter of all time. Paige has the greatest reverence for Gibson, and it shocks him to run into people who have not heard of the great man.

Not long ago, a sassy young reporter, fuddled with the doings of the Musials, the Mantles and so on, tried Paige severely by yawning while he was recounting some of Gibson's prodigies. To fix him, Paige recalled one game.

"We was playin' the Homestead Grays in the city of Pitchburgh," he said quietly. "Josh comes up in the last of the ninth with a man on and us a run behind. Well, he hit one. The Grays waited around and waited around, but finally the empire rules it ain't comin' down. So we win.

"The next day," Paige went on, eyeing the youth coldly, "we was disputin' the Grays in Philadelphia when here come a ball outta the sky right in the glove of the Grays' center fielder. The empire made the only possible call.

" 'You're out, boy!' he says to Josh. 'Yesterday, in Pitchburgh.' "

Paige was quite a sight around Pittsburgh at this time—six foot three and a quarter inches tall, slow-moving, meatless and loose-limbed, with a wide-roving eye. The calm, dry, sadly comic air, the sly humor and itchy foot, the unwillingness to be pinned down by statistics, appointments or contracts were all there in embryo. So was the now famous Paige self-confidence.

Satchel thought—and still thinks—of himself as a great hitter and base runner. Perhaps the best measurement of his current capacity at the plate, however, is his last season's batting record—five hits in thirty-nine tries. As to his speed, there is much debate among observers. Some question that he could beat Casey Stengel to first base. Others note that he moves quickly enough afield to have handled all chances in his first four years in the majors without a single error.

"In my opinion," says White Sox manager Paul Richards, a Paige fan, "he could play short-stop."

The fact is, he has, in his time, been an infielder and a pretty good one. Catcher Roy Campanella of the Brooklyn Dodgers tells of playing against Paige in Puerto Rico during the winter of 1939–'40. "In Sunday double-headers," says Campanella, "Satch would pitch the first game and strike out maybe seventeen batters, and then play first base in the second game. Did all right, too."

Although there may have been some basis for Paige's belief while at Pittsburgh that he could run and hit with the best of them, there was less justification for another view he held at the time—that he was a danger-ous man in the ring. When Gus Greenlee had Paige under contract he was also managing the light heavy-weight champion of the world, John Henry Lewis. Watching Lewis work out, Paige became overpowered with manly urges and challenged him.

Greenlee visited the gym one day and was horrified to see his two most expensive commodities in the ring, the one weaving and laughing, the other stilting fiercely about in many-colored shorts like an enraged fla-mingo. Before Greenlee could get to them, Paige managed to hit Lewis on top of the head, whereupon Lewis feinted, stood off and rapped the pitcher on the chin. Some time later, while Lewis, Greenlee and the trainers worked feverishly with ammonia and massage, Paige opened his eyes.

"I stang him," he was saying happily. "Git me a shot at Joe Louis."

It was the opinion of most of the local young ladies at the time that

Satchel was just too ornery to settle down. Miss Janet Howard, a bright and resourceful waitress at Gus Greenlee's Crawford Grill, thought otherwise, however.

"From the minute she first set a plate of asparagus down in front of me," Satch Paige recalls, "I began to feel paralyzed."

Marriage to Janet brought responsibilities undreamed of by Paige. He had saved no money at all. When he had to bring his salary home, only to find it wasn't enough, and when Greenlee balked at giving him a raise, he began looking around. One offer of $250 a month came in, but it made Paige uncomfortable.

"It was from a car dealer named Neil Churchill away out in a place called Bismarck, North Dakota," Paige recalls. "Churchill had a semipro team of mostly white boys, but he needed pitchin' so he calls Abe Saperstein, who owns the Harlem Globetrotters, and asks who he should get. Abe says me. Well, now," said Paige, "I wasn't exactly sure that North Dakota belonged to Sam (the U.S.A.) at the time, and I didn't want to go. But Janet says jump, so we jumped."

In Bismarck, a city that contained few Negroes, Paige and his wife looked fruitlessly for housing and finally settled in a boxcar. Still broke, Satchel rustled up early meals with a shotgun in the surrounding jackrabbit country.

At the time, 1934, Paige was just rounding into his prime, which is to say that he was probably the greatest pitcher then alive. When some of the other Bismarck players seemed inclined to doubt the Paige prowess, he quickly set them right. He placed a small matchbox on an upright stick beside home plate and knocked it off with thirteen of twenty pitches from the mound. That established the control. Then he pitched a fast ball which took a nasty hop near the plate, skipping off the catcher's mitt to graze his temple. The catcher called for a chest protector and mask. He needed them, for he was unable to hold the next eight pitches out of ten. That established the speed. (Satch's present receiver, the Browns' Clint Courtney, reported nine years later that Paige's fast ball was still hard to follow. "It has a hop on the end," complained Courtney, "and it keeps ticking off the top of my mitt.")

For a couple of years, the Bismarck team had been humiliated regularly by the neighboring Jamestown Red Sox. In his first game against Jamestown, Paige allowed no runs and fanned fifteen, using only Little Tom, his medium fast ball, and leaving Long Tom, his real fast ball, for future use. Paige beat Jamestown four more times that season, in addition to winning 37 other games for Bismarck. Jamestown beat Bismarck once.

The one Jamestown victory came about in a strange way. During the season, Paige had occasionally electrified the prairie fans by signaling his outfield to walk off the field, thus leaving himself with nothing but an infield for defense. The signal was easy to see. Paige stood on the mound, wiping his brow elaborately with his pitching hand.

On the night of the final game against Jamestown, Paige was off form. The opposition batters hit everything—floaters, curves, the "two-hump blooper," the chin-grazing "barber pitch," the "hesitation pitch" and even Long Tom. Luckily, Bismarck was also hitting, so Paige was able to keep a shaky lead as the score mounted.

In the last of the ninth, with the score 15 to 14 in Bismarck's favor and Jamestown's murderers' row coming up, Paige began to perspire freely. Curves got the first man. The second man singled and Paige's blood pressure rose. Long Tom dispatched the third batter, but as the cleanup man walked to the plate, Paige was seized by a premonition of evil. He mopped his brow nervously.

Paige is still outraged by the memory of that night game.

"While my outfield was strollin' off the field behind my back," he says, "I fed the cleanup man a little outcurve which I intended him to hit on the fly to right field. He did. It was some time," says Paige grumpily, "before I again visited the city of Bismarck." (Actually, he rejoined the team the next summer.)

In the autumn of 1934, Paige and his wife headed for Denver, where he had been invited to pitch for the House of David in the *Denver Post* semipro tournament. The House had a talented organization, but what impressed Paige most was the amazing growth of whiskers on all the players. Although he won his first three tournament games for the House without facial hair, he complained bitterly. Finally, his teammates presented him with a lengthy false beard of reddish hue.

Thoroughly pleased, Paige wore the red whiskers in his final appearance. While he was winding up to deliver a hesitation pitch in the fourth inning, however, the beard became entwined with his pitching arm and was torn from his jaws with the delivery.

Finding himself denuded again, Paige became so unsettled that he very nearly lost the game. He squeaked through, however, and the House went on to win the tournament.

"It was the tamperin' with nature that rattled me," Satchel says.

In California that winter, Paige commanded the Satchel Paige All-Stars, an impressive pickup team of Negro-league players. This team included catcher Josh Gibson, third baseman Judy (Sweet Juice) Johnson, the catlike Harry Williams at second base, and Cool Papa Bell, whose speed and daring in the outfield and on the bases may have surpassed that of Willie Mays. In three previous years wintering on the West Coast, the Paige Stars, with or without the members named, had won some 128 games—at least 40 of them against teams of major-league all-stars—while losing 23.

The games against big-leaguers were of tremendous importance to Paige and the others. They knew, the sports writers knew, and many of the fans knew that many of the Negro stars were better ballplayers than some of the high-salaried, internationally famous men they faced. He felt that someday the color line would be broken. But his great fear, he says, was that he would be too old, his prime wasted in cow pastures, when the great day came.

The bigger the major-league stars, the more Paige bore down. According to accounts passed down by witnesses, he struck out Rogers Hornsby five times in one game, Charley Gehringer three times in another, Jimmy Foxx three times in a third. In 1934 in Hollywood, in a game, which lasted 13 innings, Paige was opposed by Dizzy Dean. Dean was superlative, holding the Paige Stars to one run and fanning 15. But Paige shut out the Dean Stars and fanned 17. After the game, Dean informed the press that Paige was the best pitcher in the business.

In the summer of 1935, Paige rejoined Bismarck while his wife stayed in Pittsburgh. The team's problem that year was to find competition. Of the 102 games played, it lost five. In midseason, Paige pitched 29 days in a row with one loss; his total for the summer was 43 wins and two losses. As Bismarck's renown grew, the inevitable team of major-league all-stars appeared, this one boasting Earl Averill, Heinie Manush and Jimmy Foxx, among others. Bismarck beat the big-leaguers 7-4 at Grand Forks, North Dakota, 10-1 at Valley City and 16-2 at Bismarck before they could get out of the bush country.

Among the customers who sat fascinated by the sight of Paige at his peak were many Sioux Indians from nearby reservations. They named him the Long Rifle.

"One day," Paige recalls, "this Dorothy Deer invited me out in the hills to meet her papa who raised rattlesnakes in a deep pit in back of his hut. I looked at the snakes and said good-by. Before leavin', however, I ask the old man if he'd ever been bit, and he said lots of times, but he had an ointment that took out the harm. When he gave me a great big jug of it, I ask him if the ointment might be good for rubbin' my arm. He said he wouldn't advise it."

After heeding the warning for a couple of days, Paige finally dabbed a finger into the snake oil and cautiously rubbed a few drops on his tired biceps. Forthwith, he declares, energies and sensations of a kind he had never known vibrated from shoulder to fingers.

"My mistake was I didn't dilute it," Paige says reflectively. "Man, it's a wonder my arm didn't fly outta the room."

For many years since then, ballplayers in hundreds of locker rooms, including those of the Cleveland Indians and the St. Louis Browns, have speculated endlessly about the ingredients of the secret preparation which the Long Rifle uses to revitalize his arm. Some say it's kerosene and olive oil and some say it's wolfbane and wild cherry stems. Paige doesn't say. He just calls it Deer oil.

The 1935 Bismarck team was invited to play in the national semipro tournament at Wichita, Kansas. En route, in McPherson, Kansas, they encountered a problem. Local citizens, apparently rendered unsteady by a winning team of their own, openly referred to the Bismarcks as hayshakers.

A six-inning challenge game was promptly arranged and the Bismarcks took an early two-run lead. In the final inning, the disgruntled McPherson fans began to hoot at Paige.

That was a mistake. Paige fanned the first man. Then, repeating his Jamestown gesture, he called in his outfield and struck out the next man. Then, he called in his infield. With nobody representing Bismarck but Paige and catcher Quincy Troupe, he struck out the third man. He used nine fast balls in all.

Bismarck won the Wichita tournament in seven games, and barnstormed west for new fields to conquer. In Denver, Paige confronted the House of David, which he had pitched to victory in the *Post* tournament the year before. The beards still fascinated him. One unusually lush growth so attracted him, indeed, that he fired a pitch into it, thus raising a technical baseball point so fine that no one has yet been able to settle it.

The argument took place in the seventh inning. Paige had two strikes on the owner of the great beard when he was seized by an overpowering desire to part the man's whiskers with a Long Tom. When he did, the umpire promptly ruled that the man had been hit by a pitched ball and waved him on to first.

According to an impartial witness, Paige then raised an arm to halt the game. Striding up to the struck man, he asked permission to exhibit his beard to the umpire.

"Empire," said Paige, combing the luxuriant growth with long fingers, "if you will kindly observe here, you will see that these whiskers can't rightly be called no part of a man. They is air."

The umpire, seeing the logic, began to hem and haw. After about five minutes, however, he got mad and returned to his former ground. Paige was defeated, but the crowd was with him and the question is still considered wide open.

After his second appearance in Denver, Paige's fame as a pitching phenomenon began to spread across the nation, and beyond. One Denver wire-service story, translated into Spanish, reached the eyes of Dr. José Enrique Aybar, dean of the University of Santo Domingo, deputy of the

Dominican Republic's national congress. Some days before, Dr. Aybar had been given $30,000 by President Rafael L. Trujillo, absolute dictator of the country and by all odds the fiercest strong man in Central America, and told to go out and get a ball club. An election was coming up and Trujillo's opponent was showing surprising strength—due almost entirely to the fact that he had imported ballplayers who were beating everything in sight and thus ballyhooing his name.

After reading the stuff on Paige, Dr. Aybar got in touch with him at once, asking him to round up as many American Negro players as he could find and fly to Ciudad Trujillo, the capital. Thinking he'd like to spend a restful winter in the tropics, Paige recruited Josh Gibson, Cool Papa Bell, Harry Williams and some others and took off.

At Ciudad Trujillo, Paige and his teammates were met by barefoot soldiers with ammunition belts over their chests and long, bayoneted rifles in their hands. The soldiers convoyed the players to a hotel and took up posts outside their rooms. Thereafter, every place Paige and his friends went, the soldiers went with them. When Paige met Dr. Aybar, the doctor explained that the situation was very serious and that Trujillo's team must win an upcoming series of seven games against the Estrellas de Oriente, the opponent's team, at whatever cost.

When the day of the great series arrived, the city was decorated with flags and the streets were jammed with people. Gaiety and laughter, machetes and shooting irons were everywhere. At the ball park, the heavily armed followers of Trujillo bulked threateningly along the third-base line; and the heavily armed followers of Trujillo's opponent bulked just as threateningly along the first-base line.

"I knew then that whichever way the series went, I lost," says Paige.

The series went as badly as possible. With the strain giving Paige nervous stomach, the Trujillo forces dropped two straight. The reaction from the president's office was very bad. Then they lost one more, and all Dr. Aybar could do was wring his hands when Paige asked how his chances were for getting back to the States. In desperation, Paige and his mates played as never before, taking the next three in a row while tension mounted throughout the country. On the last day, with the score in games three and three, Paige might have been excused had he been unable to walk to the mound. Instead, he strode out confidently, his stomach gas all gone.

"I had it fixed with Mr. Trujillo's polices," Paige says. "If we win, their whole army is gonna run out and escort us from the place. If we lose . . ." Paige hesitated. "If we lose, there is nothin' to do but consider myself and my boys as passed over Jordan."

Communities he had never heard of suddenly wanted to see him pitch. Offers ranging from $100 to $500 for three innings' work began to come in. Paige began traveling around the country solo, making guest appearances with one club after another, week after week. With every appearance, the pressure mounted, his fame grew and his nervous stomach got worse. He was billed as "Satchel Paige, the World's Greatest Pitcher, Guaranteed to Strike Out the First Nine Men!" The trick word was "guaranteed." Crowds jammed ball parks to see him win—all the time. He was not supposed to lose any more than Bojangles Robinson was supposed to fall down while executing a buck-and-wing.

In Venezuela at the height of this clamor, Paige pitched two innings of a three-inning guest shot without incident, which is to say he struck everybody out. In the third inning, throwing a routine sidearm fast ball, however, he felt a small, sharp pain in his pitching shoulder.

That evening he caught a plane for his next guest appearance in Mexico City. With the first ball he pitched in that rarefied atmosphere, his shoulder joint snapped audibly and he sat down on the mound, in the midst of a rising storm of catcalls, bewildered by the pain.

Back in Kansas City, unable to lift his right arm, Paige thought he had better see a doctor. The examination took only a couple of minutes.

"Satchel," said the doctor, briskly, "you're through."

3

Mr. Leroy (Satchel) Paige, the tall, urbane and seemingly imperishable relief-pitching star of the St. Louis Browns, cast a startled glance at Joe DiMaggio during an all-star charity game in Hollywood a while ago. Before his eyes, the thirty-seven-year-old Clipper, who had come out of retirement to make one last appearance at bat, took a couple of swings in an elderly fashion, then popped out feebly to short. The sight absolutely dismayed Mr. Paige.

Back in 1926, when Paige was pitching for the Chattanooga Black Lookouts, in the Negro Southern Association, DiMaggio was a San Francisco schoolboy of eleven. In 1935, when Paige was a 10-year semi-pro veteran and already a legend in the land, DiMaggio was still a year away from the Yankees. Thirteen years later, when Paige was just breaking into the majors as a Cleveland rookie, sports writers were calling DiMaggio the Yankees' grand old man. Now, when Paige was being hailed as one of the best relief prospects in baseball, DiMaggio was bowing out of the game.

With time jumping around like that, no wonder Paige was confused.

Mr. Paige, whose own age is believed to fall somewhere between forty-five and fifty-three, is unalterably opposed to time. As soon as he learns the hitting weaknesses of one generation of sluggers, for example, time does away with them. Time also makes off with pitchers—a circumstance

Paige feels is not only an inexcusable affront to his profession, but harmful to society in general.

"All this comin' and goin'," he says indignantly. "Rookies flyin' up the road and old-timers flyin' down, and nobody in between but me and ol' John Mize, standin' pat, watchin' 'em go by.

"And I ain't even sure about ol' John," says Paige. "Maybe he's flyin' on, too. If he is," Paige adds, accusingly, "I can always watch 'em go by myself. Time ain't gonna mess with me!"

Paige is too busy with the here and now to consider such questions. Age or no age, he is the Browns' highest-paid player, at $25,000 a year. To hold this exalted status, he is obliged to keep pace with the other Browns, some of whom were born after he started pitching for pay.

The sight of Paige keeping pace can be deceptive, of course. Before games, when other players are prancing around, swinging four bats, doing knee-bends and so on, Paige may be seen reclining gracefully in his canopied contour chair by the Browns' bull pen, throwing gently to a catcher, counting the house or possibly playing "skidoodle."

"Skidoodle is a game I invented some years ago to exercise without doin' myself permanent harm," Paige says. "I throw the ball on one bounce to another man, he bounces it back at me. We jangle around. Nobody falls down exhausted."

Paige has conditioned himself so long and so well that on a hot day he can warm up his celebrated right arm with five or six pitches. Par for most pitchers is about fifteen minutes of steady throwing.

Paige's battery mate, Courtney, gives three reasons why the elderly pitcher is a present danger instead of a disturbing memory to hitters. "You hear about pinpoint control," Courtney says, "but Paige is the only man I've ever seen who really has it. He threw me six strikes out of ten pitches over a chewing-gum wrapper one time. Also," says Courtney, "his fast ball still burns my mitt when he lets it go, which is whenever he needs it. Finally, he just thinks faster than most hitters. Satchel is a very smart man."

What Paige thinks about various hitters can usually be heard by fans some distance from the Browns' bull pen during games. Sitting in his chair, Paige keeps a running commentary going, most of it seemingly for his own benefit.

"Don't ever feed that man low outside," he cautioned himself recently, as Mantle came to bat. "He will harm you." Ferris Fain, the 1952 American League batting champion, once caused Paige to cry a rhymed warning to the man pitching to him. "Throw it high, the skin will fly," hollered Paige. When Larry Doby of the Indians is up, Paige usually suggests using "the barber." The barber is Paige's name for a high, inside pitch that shaves the batter's chin.

The Browns' management feels squeamish about cramping him with rules. He does not have to stay in hotels with the team on road trips if he wishes to stay with friends, as he does in about half the towns the Browns play. He is presumed to have outlived most of the ballplayer vices and so escapes spiritual lectures. All he is expected to do, besides win, is to appear on time for trains, practice or games.

"I'm Satchel," he sometimes explains simply, when people try to fit him into various molds. "I do as I do."

Doing as he does, Paige communicates his personality to whole ball parks full of fans with theatrical ease.

Even opposing fans are for Paige. In Boston last year, for example, he went in to put down a Red Sox uprising and was promptly shelled for an unbelievable six runs before he could get the side out. Throughout this disaster, the Red Sox stands sat in stony, embarrassed silence. When he finally wobbled off the diamond, the cheers could be heard in Cambridge. Paige has never been booed in the majors.

Because he has pitched so long, and has disappeared so many times into backwoods baseball in this and other countries, many fans have lost track of Paige and have come to the conclusion that he is deceased. During spring training this year, he says, he was riding in a Los Angeles cab when he noticed the driver scrutinizing him in the rear-vision mirror. Finally the driver shook his head and exclaimed: "No, it ain't possible. He's passed."

"Who's passed?" Paige inquired guardedly.

The driver explained that for a minute he could have sworn his passenger was a famous, long-gone pitcher named Satchel Paige.

"I knew Ol' Satch well," the driver sighed. "Even though I was only a little child of eight when he was in his prime."

"When was that?" asked Ol' Satch, gloomily.

"About 1913," said the driver.

Paige's mother, Mrs. Tula Paige, who is eighty-three and has never seen Satchel play, also has certain delusions about him. She thinks of him as a child who has wandered into a shiftless, sinful life. For thirty years, she has remained inexorably opposed to his playing baseball, writing him regular instructions about attending Mass and avoiding gambling, late hours, wild women and other evils.

Paige has grown so used to autograph hunters among his stateside fans that he often fails to observe them closely. In Phoenix last spring, a slight, partially bald, agitated-looking man came bounding into the Browns' dressing room after an exhibition game. Paige was reclining in a whirl bath at the time, but he borrowed a pen from the man and signed his program obligingly. When the man suddenly began firing ad-lib witticisms, however, twitching his eyebrows and sidling around bent-kneed,

Paige, who is the official humorist on the Browns, began to regard him so coolly that he finally crept away.

"Who was that character?" Paige asked.

"Groucho Marx."

Paige, who mourns this unfortunate meeting, blames it almost entirely on the fact that Marx was not wearing his stage eyebrows at the time, not on his own failure to scrutinize Marx properly.

On train trips, Paige almost inevitably appears at the center of a large and enthusiastic delegation. Friendly and relaxed, he nevertheless maintains a certain reserve toward his admirers, as befits a man who has been one of the authentic folk heroes of America's Negroes, not to mention thousands of others, for many years.

When Paige takes to the road, he usually carries one enormous bag containing four conservative suits, several pairs of shoes, bottles of pills, ointments and philters to combat anticipated ailments, and a great miscellany of other items. One of the twenty cameras he owns inevitably dangles from a shoulder strap. Redcaps compete desperately to carry his luggage.

"All right, brothers," Paige exclaims, waving and grinning broadly as he passes. "Let us ramble."

Paige's home activity tends to dampen the natural ebullience of the many relatives and friends always to be found in the household, several of them on a semipermanent basis. But it has little effect on Mrs. Paige, who has a strong character, or on his four children: Pamella, five; Caroline, two and a half; Linda, one and a half; and Leroy, Jr., six months. Mrs. Paige, who first caught her husband's eye as a clerk in a Kansas City camera store when he wandered in to buy film six years ago, keeps him on rather short tether, which he seems to find agreeable, since he grumbles about it all the time.

Outside his home life, no field of conversational inquiry is too remote for Paige to venture into. If other players have problems with love, finances, batting averages, falling hair or whatever, Paige may be counted on for remedies. Occasionally, of course, he comes upon something that ruffles his composure.

In the club car of a Chicago-bound train this year, some players presented Paige a book called *How to Pitch,* by Cleveland's wealthy squire, Bob Feller, Paige's junior by perhaps fifteen years. Retiring to a window seat with this volume, Paige, who has beaten Feller a staggering number of times in exhibition games, at once began snorting and shifting about.

"Here, now!" he exclaimed, starting up in astonishment at one point. "Is that how you do it?"

A few pages later, he leaped up and began to execute one of the illustrated techniques. But he couldn't seem to get the hang of it.

"That's a good book," he informed one of his teammates later. "Only thing is, if I start pitchin' the correct way now, I'll probably break my arm. I just about broke it once," he said, darkly, "and I can't risk it again."

When Paige just about broke his arm, he was in Mexico City, in 1938, at the peak of his fame and pitching power. Throwing a simple sidearm curve one day, he snapped his arm so badly that he couldn't lift it. Back in Kansas City, the doctor who examined him said flatly that he was through.

No news could have been more inconceivable to Paige. His arm had lifted him from poverty and childhood delinquency in Mobile. It had survived Canadian cold, 117-degree desert heat, thousands of all-night bus rides and greasy hamburger joints and cheap boarding-houses. It had stood up to every trial to which Paige could subject it, including four Negro World Series and East-West all-star games before crowds of 50,000 and up. Had it been of a different hue, major-league club owners might have paid up to $150,000 cash for it at 1938 prices.

All this notwithstanding, Satch Paige couldn't lift it. Within a month, the only job he could get was a coach for the Kansas City Monarchs. For the next year, he traveled with the Monarchs' second team, growing more and more obscure and irascible. "Man," Paige says, "it was a long year."

It was an interminable year, hard on the young players trying to expand under the brooding shadow of the former "greatest pitcher in the world," and impossible for Paige, who seemed to grow taller, thinner and grimmer-looking every day. By 1940, when he was thirty-four, or thereabouts, and hadn't pitched for fourteen months, Paige was ready to quit.

Then, just before a Monarchs game one afternoon, someone overthrew first in a pre-game warmup and Paige ambled over, picked up the ball and threw it back to the pitcher. It was the most unobtrusive of acts, but just about every player on the field seemed to see it and to stop stock-still.

Walking thoughtfully toward the dugout, Paige picked up a glove and called for a ball. Without a word, the Monarchs' catcher left the plate and stationed himself about pitching distance from Paige. Then Paige began to throw, easily at first, then harder and harder. Nobody moved, the stands were silent, the game waiting. Then, abruptly, he stopped, and gazed around at all the eyes upon him.

"Well," he said, "I'm back."

The news traveled fast. Semipro club owners flocked around with contracts as soon as they heard, and the fans began to roar. Life once again became a pleasure for Paige. He traveled far and wide, showing new generations of hitters a whole new assortment of curves, floaters and so on, to go with his fast ball, which he now used only in the pinches. His income as a solo performer ranged up to $35,000 a year.

"It was all so nice," Paige recalls, "that I almost forgot time was passin' and I hadn't begun to do what I'd always wanted."

What Paige had always wanted was to play for a major-league club. By 1946, when every hot stove buzzed with rumors that the big-league color line was about to be broken, Paige lived at a high pitch of excitement.

"Maybe I was too eager," Paige says. "But then I figured that with all those writin' men sayin' I'm due for the Hall of Fame and all that ruckus —well, I figured I'd be the first one under the wire."

When Jackie Robinson became the first one, Paige went on pitching for semipro teams without comment. When Larry Doby and others followed Robinson, Paige spoke less and less.

"When 1948 come around," Paige says, "and I still got my nose to the window, I realized what the club owners was thinkin'. They was thinkin' that when I was with Chattanooga, Larry Doby wasn't bawn."

However, Bill Veeck, then owner of the Cleveland Indians, was not thinking just that way.

"Abe Saperstein, who owns the Harlem Globetrotters basketball team, and who always seems to turn up when Satch needs him, had been after me for a long time to sign him up," Veeck says. "But Lou Boudreau, who was managing Cleveland, was desperate for relief men so he put on a catcher's mitt at the stadium one day and says to Satch: 'All right, here's the plate. See if you can get it up here.' Well," Veeck says, "Lee-roy threw fifty pitches. Forty-six of them were strikes. That was that."

If the Indians management was convinced, some sports writers were not. J. G. Taylor Spink, publisher of the influential St. Louis *Sporting News,* let go as follows:

"Many well-wishers of baseball emphatically fail to see eye to eye with the signing of Satchel Paige, superannuated Negro pitcher. . . . To bring in a pitching rookie of Paige's age . . . is to demean the standards of baseball in the big circuits."

"I demeaned the big circuits considerable that year," Paige says. "I win six an' lose one."

The night that Paige walked out of a quarter century of circus baseball into the rarefied atmosphere of the big leagues, some 20,000 fans at Cleveland Stadium rose for ten minutes of unbroken roaring. Paige obliged by blanking the Browns for two innings in relief.

By the end of the season, Paige, besides his six-and-one record, had an earned-run average of 2.47, had struck out 45, made no errors afield and got himself two hits. Sports writers were so amazed that several of them voted to name him Rookie of the Year.

"I declined the position," Paige says. "I wasn't sure which year the gentlemen had in mind."

The climax was reached on August 20th, when Paige started against eighth-place Chicago at Cleveland, and the all-time record night crowd of 78,382 paid to see him win.

Toward the end of the 1948 season, to Paige's vast surprise, certain creaks in his physical mechanism had begun to appear. "Ol' No. 1," which is what Paige calls his back muscles and diaphragm, remained in good shape. So did "Ol' No. 2," his pitching arm. But he was having a time with his nervous stomach. His flat feet hurt and the emaciated calves attached to them seemed weighted with stone. On top of all this, the dentist had a message for him.

"The dentist says to me that all my teeth will have to come out," Paige recalls, with horror. "I says, doctor, I will not abide with store teeth, and he says, then you will not abide."

He was full of miseries when he reported to the Indians in Arizona for the 1949 season. However, in mid-season, when the hot weather began, he felt better and began to expand and advise the young pitchers in the devious ways of the game.

During one grindingly tight game with Boston, Paige was advising Mike Garcia, a young Cleveland pitcher of great promise. It was the last of the eighth, Cleveland led by one run, the Red Sox were up with nobody out and Garcia was squirming with nervousness in the Indian bull pen. He had just been told that he might have to go in for relief.

"Boy," said Paige, lounging back on the bullpen bench and exuding vast confidence, "I wouldn't worry about them Red Sox. There ain't a hitter among 'em."

As Paige spoke, a pinch hitter singled sharply, and lead-off man Dom DiMaggio came to bat. "Now, this fella," Paige drawled, "there is a mess." DiMaggio singled to center and Johnny Pesky came up.

"Pesky!" Paige snorted, disdainfully. "Why they say that man can hit, I don't know. You just feed him in close on his knees . . ."

Pesky hit the first pitch for a single, loading the bases. While the dreaded Ted Williams strode to the plate, Paige clapped the quaking Garcia on the shoulder and declared jovially: "Now we're gonna be all right."

As Satchel made this announcement, manager Lou Boudreau beckoned to the bull pen—not for Garcia, but for Paige. There was a moment of deep silence in the dugout. Then, as though in a trance, Paige rose from the bench.

"Son," he said, huskily, concluding his message to Garcia, "just remember, when you're disputin' the Red Sox, put your trust in the power of prayer."

Prayer got Paige out of the hole with the loss of but one run.

In 1950, he started back over the old itinerant trail, pitching any-and everywhere, and nearly doubling the $20,000 a year he had made in the majors. When the Giants and Braves offered him contracts in the pennant drive, Paige had to turn them down. "I couldn't afford to lose money pitchin' for nobody but Bill Veeck," he says. "With Burrhead, I didn't feel it so much."

When Veeck bought control of the St. Louis Browns in mid-1951, one of his first acts was to sign Paige.

"Lee-roy was a must," says Veeck. "Everybody kept telling me he was through, but that was understandable. They thought he was only human."

When the juices of spring began to rise in Mr. Paige in early 1952, he set out for the Browns' training camp at Burbank, California. The California weather filled him with such energies that he could hardly wait for the season to begin.

When it did begin, however, the other Browns were also so steamed up that they were astonished to find themselves in first place.

"I was just a bull-pen pitcher," Paige recalls, with dismay. "Every man we put in the first four games went the route. The buck fever was among us."

By June, it seemed to Paige that he was pitching every other day. The fast-slipping Browns would get a slim lead, watch it begin to vanish and call loudly for Paige. If the opposition had managed to tie the score before Paige went in, games would go on endlessly, because Paige would yield no runs and his teammates could never get any when they were most needed.

By July 4th, Paige had appeared in 25 games. He had pitched 10 innings of an 18-inning game at Washington, holding the Senators to a 5-5 tie until the game was called at 1:00 A.M. Against the Indians, he had gone 11 innings of an incredible 19-inning game, finally losing it when he and the fans could hardly keep their eyes open. Time and again, he had gone in to protect one-run leads for the Browns and retired the best hitters of the American League. Watching him do just that to the Yankees one night, Casey Stengel, manager of both the Bombers and the 1952 American League All-Star team, picked Paige as one of his pitchers for the July dream game.

"That took care of the third one of my big ambitions," Paige says. "Before I'd hardly got started in my career, I'd played for a big-league club, pitched in a World Series" (two thirds of an inning with Cleveland in 1948) "and made the All-Star team. That did my stomach gas a lot of good."

The rest of the season did his digestion little good, however. As the Browns went down and down to seventh place, Paige rose more and more often to pitch. By season's end, he had worked a staggering total of 46 games, struck out 91, and won 12 games, lost 10 and saved 10.

"When the shootin' finally stopped," says Paige, "I found out I was tired. I figured a few hot baths and a few days layin' around the house would take care of that, and it did, as far as my frame was concerned. But I had another kind of tired. I was kinda tired of baseball."

This new fatigue took a long time to show up. Most of the winter, Paige took it easy around his house, doing a little carpentry and plumbing here and there, thinking he ought to fix up the back yard, and worrying about his 35 per cent income tax. Time and inaction were great problems. Winter, itself, was a problem. Satchel hated the cold—it had always driven him to the tropics in other years. In winter, time seemed to drag, leaving nothing to do but shoot some pool, or do a little after-dinner speaking around Kansas City, or answer his fan mail, or hunt, or regard the television, which wasn't much good for his pitching eye.

By early February of this year, the new fatigue really began to work on Paige. He descended the long staircase, scattering relatives and friends right and left with a cold eye. He got out his Spanish guitar and sang gloomy tunes up in his room.

Then, one gray day, things came to a head. The first thought Paige had on awakening was of a talk he was supposed to give at a luncheon in his honor that noon. The thought wearied and depressed him. He put it out of his mind until midday, when some civic leaders called for him in a limousine. On the way downtown, he sat silent and somber. At a loss to explain Paige's mood, the leaders talked around it, finally inquiring, heartily, what he intended to say at the banquet.

Paige took his time answering. He roused himself slowly from a slouched position. He stared at the gentlemen.

"I'm gonna say that they got the wrong man for this speech," he said finally. "I'm gonna say I'm through with baseball! Worn out runnin' around! Sick and tired!"

That stopped all conversation. Many blocks farther on, the limousine approached a vacant lot where some piping, stick-legged boys were rushing the season with a pickup ball game. Paige began to stir restlessly at the sight. He looked away but his eyes seemed to be drawn back. He coughed nervously. When the limousine was passing the lot, Paige suddenly sat up and ordered the driver to stop. Despite the heated protests of the civic gentlemen, he got out.

"You run on along to the lunch," he said. "I'll just set here a while."

After the lunch, says one witness, the gentlemen satisfied their curiosity by driving back past the lot. They arrived in the middle of a hot ball game. The battery was Paige, six feet three and a quarter inches tall, weight 180, age indefinite, pitching; Slattery, four feet two inches tall, weight 85, age nine, catching. The up team, the Jackson Street White Sox, was hitting Satchel Paige unmercifully. Also, the umpire, Yogi Olzewschki, wasn't giving him the corners.

PART THREE

John McGraw   Photo credit: National Baseball Library/Cooperstown, N.Y.

JOHN McGRAW

The Little Napoleon

Sport Magazine   January 1949

Watching the modern game develop—night baseball, platooning, expansion—Jack Sher takes a few moments to look back on the career and personality of the first "modern day" manager.

By Jack Sher

When he came to the New York Giants as a player-manager in 1902, Johnny McGraw was a slim, runty, big-jawed, truculent, obstinate, and ambitious young man. The day was July 9, and the ball club was in the cellar.

On June 3, 1932, John Joseph McGraw left the Giants just as he had found them—in last place. He was then almost 60 years old, a corpulent, three-chinned, cantankerous, sick old man who, during 30 turbulent years, had proven beyond all doubt that he was one of the greatest managers the game of baseball has ever known.

The name "Giants" would mean little today if it hadn't been for McGraw. For 30 years, McGraw's preposterous personality and baseball genius were more dazzling than the deeds of his greatest stars, from Christy Mathewson to Mel Ott. There were reasons for calling him the "Little Napoleon." No manager ever dominated the diamond in a more complete and dictatorial fashion.

"With my team, I'm an absolute czar," McGraw snapped in 1914. "I order plays and they obey. If they don't, I fine them."

Snarling and screaming, driving his players, brawling with umpires, insulting rival managers and clubowners, using his fists as well as the most brilliant brain in baseball, McGraw smashed his way to 10 National League pennants and three world championships. He flaunted his victories before rival clubs and fans. He took his defeats with all the graciousness of an enraged bulldog, rising to awesome heights of foaming fury.

"McGraw was sometimes a terrible sight on that bench when we were losing," said Travis Jackson, former Giant coach and the last of McGraw's great shortstops. "His neck would swell up and his face would turn purple."

One day in 1928, McGraw, Jackson, and several other players were leaving Wrigley Field, Chicago, after dropping a close one to their hated rivals, the Cubs. The stormy manager was in one of his more furious moods, enraged by the decision of an umpire. He was absolutely blind with anger, as Jackson described it, and walked directly in the path of a taxicab. He was knocked flat. The players and a cop picked McGraw up. His face was contorted with pain.

"Do you want to prefer charges?" the officer asked.

"Hell, no!" McGraw yelled. "It was my fault!"

Still fuming, Mac went on to Pittsburgh for a series with the Pirates. Not until he returned to New York, several days later, did he discover that his leg was broken!

John J. (Muggsy) McGraw was not the stuff of which fiction-book heroes are made. He was too wholly human, irascible, and changeable in character. And yet, no man gave more to baseball. McGraw was a pioneer, an innovator, an exciting, creative ballplayer and manager. He gave us the hit-and-run play that revolutionized baseball. He developed the use of the bunt to its now important status. He was the first manager to hire a ballplayer for the sole duty of being a pinch-hitter.

The stunts McGraw pulled drove opposing players and managers to distraction. No modern manager, not even Leo Durocher, would dare take the chances John J. McGraw took to win ball games.

"We were playing St. Louis one day," he would relate, "and we were five runs behind in the ninth inning. With nobody out, we got two men on base. The next batter hit a long single, which would have scored Murray from second base. As Murray rounded third and started for home, I waved him back. Now why did I do that?" McGraw would pause dramatically. "I'll tell you why. Because I wanted those bases loaded. I knew what effect that would have on the pitcher."

That day, as it was most of the time, the McGraw strategy was right on the beam. Three shouting, dancing, gesticulating Giant base-runners caused the Cardinal hurler to blow sky high and the Giants romped away with the ball game.

In his own peculiar way, McGraw had a tremendous love for his ball-players. He paid them high salaries. He was the first manager to shepherd them into the best hotels in town, insisting in the early rowdy days of baseball that his "Giants" were gentlemen when not on a ball field. He hovered over his charges in watchdog fashion, behaving toward some like a boy-scout leader, towards others like a tough Army top-kick.

"I know every man under me," he would state. "I get under his skin. Then I cater to him with roughness or kindness as the case demands."

Christy Mathewson, credited McGraw with winning pennants almost single-handedly. "Every play in the 1904 season was directed from the bench," Matty once wrote. "He took a group of young and inexperienced players and master-minded them into champions."

For a manager to direct a team from the bench was an unheard-of procedure in those days. McGraw played third base for the Giants during his first year as manager, but during a crisis in a game he'd leave the field and guide the team from the bench by signals. Fans and players on the other team rode him viciously for leaving the diamond, hooted that he was yellow and a quitter. "John J. McGraw never knew the meaning of the word fear," Mathewson explained long afterwards. "He knew he could pull the team through from the bench, concentrate better, see more of what was going on. And he missed nothing."

McGraw had an absolute contempt for most ballplayers as thinkers. Christy Mathewson was one of the few he allowed to make his own decisions. The magnificent Matty never let him down, piling victory upon victory. The big right arm, rising and falling in the World Series of 1905, pitched three shutouts against the A's to hang up a record that still stands. But again, it was McGraw who deserves credit for giving baseball one of its finest moundsmen. When the young manager took over the Giants, Christy Mathewson was playing first base. McGraw saw Matty throw a couple of balls, hustled him to the mound, and kept him there.

Mathewson, a lifelong friend of McGraw's, was one of the few Giant players who escaped the blood-curdling tirades Mac would often unleash. Catcher Hank Gowdy has vivid memories of those after-game sessions in the old, wooden locker room at the Polo Grounds.

"I called for the wrong pitch in a 1924 World Series game against the Senators in Washington," Hank grinned. "That's a day I'll never forget. After the game, Mr. McGraw gave it to me in the locker room. I've never been chewed out like that in my life. He got me so upset that the second he finished, I scrambled into my clothes and ran straight for the train that was taking us back to New York. I was so riled and confused that I clean forgot that my wife was at the ball game. It wasn't until I got to the train that I remembered I was supposed to meet her in the stands after the game!"

Yet Gowdy will tell you no manager in baseball ever did so many kind and gracious things for old ballplayers as John J. McGraw. "He gave them money. He got them good jobs. He did hundreds of decent and wonderful things for players which the public knew nothing about."

There was a saying in the old days, "If you have a bad actor, trade him to McGraw." The Giant authoritarian had a reputation for straightening out the rambunctious young rowdies other managers found too difficult to handle. One of the classic non-conformists was "Bugs" Raymond, whom Ring Lardner immortalized in fiction.

Bugs, when right, was one of the most terrific twirlers of his time, tossing a spitball that was almost impossible to hit. Mr. Raymond was also equally adept at tossing drinks down his tonsils, eating tons of indigestible food, indulging in madcap stunts, and becoming the life of several parties during the course of one evening. McGraw signed him up in 1909 and Bugs, inspired by Mac's advice and impressed by his threats, promised to reform.

From Spring training at Marlin, Texas, to the Polo Grounds in New York, Bugs led McGraw a merry chase. The reporters had a field day scribbling about the capers of their beloved hero.

"Worrying over Bugs Raymond took five years off my life," John J. wrote near the close of his career. "I clung to Raymond simply because I felt there was a chance he might come to know himself. I blame the newspapers for his downfall. They called him 'Bugs.' They faked up stories about him. They exploited his bad habits until, in his weak, childish way, he thought every lark was an achievement that was making a hero out of him."

Depriving Bugs of money and forbidding Giant players to lend him any was useless. Raymond could always think up some hilarious ruse that would let him continue his night-time adventuring. McGraw even hired a detective to shadow the slap-happy spitballer. The Giant manager kept Bugs on the club until it was hopeless. The end came one day at the Polo Grounds and it was one of the funniest incidents in baseball history.

Rube Marquard, who was pitching, began to weaken and McGraw sent Raymond to the bullpen to warm up. The Giant bullpen, in the old Polo Grounds, was behind the bleachers. Bugs sauntered out of sight. The next inning, the opposing team began to lambast Marquard. McGraw sent the batboy after Raymond. A few minutes later, the boy came back alone.

"I can't find him," he said. "He's nowhere in sight."

The batboy was sent out again, this time accompanied by a player.

They found Bugs in a saloon on Eighth Avenue across from the ball park, happily downing his third slug of rye. He had traded the shiny new baseball McGraw had given him to the bartender for the drinks. McGraw, sent him to the mound. Bugs wound up, unsteadily, and threw the first ball over the catcher's head, allowing a run to score.

The enraged McGraw chased Bugs out of the Polo Grounds. "You blinkety-blankety, no good bum!" he screamed. "I never want to see you around here again!" Bugs never returned.

Over 200 major-leaguers learned the science of baseball from this determined genius. At one time, almost half the managers in the two major leagues were products of McGraw's skillful tutelage—men like Billy Southworth, Art Fletcher, Casey Stengel, Freddie Fitzsimmons, Bill McKechnie, Frankie Frisch, and Bill Terry, to name just a few.

McGraw used drastic and often cruel methods to change them from average performers to stars. The way he taught Josh Devore to hit left-handed pitchers was a brilliant bit of psychology. Devore, who could belt right-handers with the greatest of ease, was scared witless every time he faced a port-side hurler. One day, Josh was about to go to bat against a speedy St. Louis southpaw. "Josh," McGraw barked. "You go up there and let him hit you."

"I don't know about that," Devore said, fearfully.

"If you don't," McGraw said, firmly, "it'll cost you ten dollars."

The manager knew Devore was very close with a buck. Josh edged to the plate and looked back at the flint-eyed McGraw pleadingly. Then he took a deep breath and shoved his hip out in front of the pitcher's fast one. The ball struck him and he trotted down to first, grinning from ear to ear. When he finally got back to the bench, he was still smiling. "Say, Mac," he said, "that fellow couldn't break a pane of glass. It sure gets me sore to think I was afraid of him!"

And from that day on, Devore was murderous against left-handed pitching.

McGraw expected his ballplayers to obey him blindly and accept his harsh discipline without complaint. Most of them did. In 1915, he slapped a $25 fine on Sammy Strang for hitting a home run!

"Go up there and lay down a bunt," he ordered Strang.

With two men on base and nobody down, Sammy measured the first ball pitched and hoisted it over the left-field wall.

"I told you to bunt," McGraw growled.

"It was right in there, Mac," Strang said. "It floated up there so pretty I just hadda take a poke at it."

"You did, huh?" McGraw said, hotly. "Well, I hope it was worth it, because it's gonna cost you 25 bucks!"

Such stern measures brought on the ire of many fans and caused the sportswriters of the time to belabor the Giant overseer in print. They seldom did it in person. There was always the danger that McGraw might force them to swallow some teeth. Few dared argue with him about baseball.

"He believed he knew more about the game than any man alive," an ex-Giant told me. "And he did. Whenever you hear talk about one of today's managers being great, someone will always compare him with McGraw. But nobody comes close to him."

It annoyed McGraw that baseball was not always considered the most important thing in American life, on a par with the scientific discoveries that were changing our nation and the policies that were being formed in the White House. To him, baseball was a momentous, serious, day-to-day struggle to which he brought all his emotion and an ever-working, inventive brain.

McGraw divided the job of being a manager into three parts—winning games, handling players, and building a team. He often said, "Winning games is the easiest of the three." And he'd sometimes add, "And when it comes to winning, I'd rather have luck than brains."

Such a phrase would never serve as an epitaph for this man McGraw, because it was the gray matter tucked under his skull that brought the Giants so many years of glory. It was McGraw who first introduced the tactic of playing for the "big inning." He'd size up his opponents' weaknesses as the game progressed. Then he'd come down on them suddenly, splitting their defense wide open. He called this his "stage of the game" method and he could be either patient or daring as he waited for the moment when the Giants could strike in a burst of fury.

Rival players often swore that McGraw knew more about their foibles and weak points than he did about even his own players. The ace Cardinal pitcher, Harry Sallee, gave the Giants many innings of misery until Mac's keen eye ferreted out the southpaw's one weakness.

"I want every man to bunt and keep on bunting," McGraw told his team before the game started. "Poke 'em right near Sallee."

The Giants thought their manager's mind had jumped the track, but they followed his orders. The New Yorkers scored 13 runs in the first inning!

When Babe Adams first broke into the majors, he was considered invincible. McGraw's men licked him the first time he took the mound against them. "Wait him out," he told his players. "Wait him out every time." The Giants waited. They worked Adams almost to exhaustion, fouling off the good ones, making him heave a minimum of four or five balls to each batter. The score was tied in the 13th inning, when the alert McGraw saw Adams drop his arm to his side in disgust and weariness.

"Now, hit away," the Giant manager ordered his batters.

The Giants did, and they broke up the ball game.

One of McGraw's most frequent boasts was that he had no stars on his ball club. What the Giant boss meant was that he never catered to the star system, but strove to develop all-around, team-performers. He wanted men who could do anything he demanded in any given situation, as opposed to a star who might be a crowd-pleasing, home-run belter.

Giant batters were drilled in hitting behind the runner to any field. In the middle of a game, the entire team might suddenly be ordered to switch from trying to knock the cover off the ball to bunting. The Giants and their rivals were always kept on edge in a McGraw ball game.

It is doubtful if such colorful, unpredictable, and show-stealing players as the immortal Babe Ruth or today's temperamental Ted Williams would have lasted very long under McGraw. It was McGraw's careful, brilliant analysis of the Ruth personality that caused Babe's downfall in the 1922 World Series.

The Great Mac had a reason for going after the Babe. Ruth inadvertently caused one of McGraw's predictions to backfire. At the close of the 1918 season, in a magazine interview, McGraw stated somewhat bombastically, "Me and Wee Willie Keeler drove the big men out of baseball. Our hit-and-run technique made the game flashier and faster and you've seen the last of the home-run kings, which is a good thing for baseball."

That was the Giants' "Miracle Manager" speaking, the man whose past predictions had made him seem infallible. In 1919, as an outfielder in 130 games, the Babe smashed 29 homers, an unbelievable feat that fans considered would never again be equalled.

By 1922, when the Giants faced the Yanks in the World Series, Ruth's sensational whacks had proved McGraw very much in error. Until Ruth, McGraw had undoubtedly been the most exciting figure in baseball, the most controversial, the man who had changed the game most. To McGraw, at that time, Ruth was something of a freak and an upstart.

The Series dawned with the Yanks heavily favored. But the Pasha of the Polo Grounds had a plan. He knew the Babe expected to be treated with great respect, even awe, by the Giant pitchers and players. Ruth was riding high. He felt sure that McGraw's moundsmen wouldn't dare feed him anything but bad balls and walks.

As the King of Swat minced to the plate for the first time in that Series, McGraw rose from the bench and bellowed at his pitcher, Art Nehf.

"Lay it over for him, Art!" the Giant manager yelled in a voice that could be heard in the bleachers. "Cut the plate for him! This big ox can't hit!"

Ruth looked toward the Giant bench in amazement. Coming from the greatest manager in baseball, this was a terrible insult. Art Nehf tossed him a slow curve that spliced the dish. The over-anxious Bam almost broke his back trying to hit it out of the park. He missed it by a foot.

McGraw grew more sarcastic. "Tell him where you're going to throw the next one, Art!" he jeered. "Then put it right there! He'll never see it!"

Nehf, following McGraw's instructions, informed Ruth that he was going to toss another one right over the same spot. He did and the fuming Ruth swung and missed. On the third pitch, Ruth struck out and returned to the dugout enormously disgusted.

The gleeful McGraw kept up the humiliating, abusive tirades against Ruth all through the Series, and Babe got only two hits in 17 times at bat for his lowest World Series average on record, .118. Many years later, the Bambino revealed that McGraw's taunts had gotten under his skin and were chiefly responsible for his failure to connect in Ruthian style.

It is also an amazing fact that McGraw called every single pitch his hurlers threw in that World Series!

When McGraw came to the Giants, Fred Clarke, the sparkling player-manager of the pile-driving Pirates was the most pesky of the lot. Clarke, to use a ring expression, was a "cutie"—one who could concoct tricky devices to pull his team out of a hole. The managerial duels between Clarke and McGraw were always spiked with thrills, heightened by the fact that McGraw was hated in Pittsburgh by the fans and was also carrying on a no-holds-barred feud with Barney Dreyfuss, the Pirate owner.

In a game in 1909, the Giants jumped on the Bucs in the first inning and were connecting with everything the Pirate pitcher tossed their way. Clarke was in a spot. He couldn't take his hurler out of the box immediately, because he had failed to warm up a relief pitcher. Clarke, playing center field, suddenly held up his hand and yelled to the umpire that his shoelace had come untied. The ump called time and it took Clarke 15 minutes to tie that shoe lace. As Fred was fussing, a Pirate relief pitcher was hurriedly warming up.

The game finally got under way again, the Giant hitting was stemmed, and the Pirates tied it up in the seventh inning. Pittsburgh got two men on base and Clarke came to bat. McGraw held up the game this time, waving left-fielder Harry McCormick in from deep in the garden to a position not far behind the third-baseman. The fans hooted at McGraw. It seemed like a fantastic spot for McCormick to be standing. But a moment later, Fred Clarke hit a screaming line drive over the third-baseman's head and McCormick made a shoestring catch to save the ball game.

When McGraw couldn't win games and pennants by brain power alone, he did it by sheer force of will power combined with recklessness. Few stories of managerial genius equal that of McGraw's 1921 pennant drive. In early September, the Giants were trailing the league-leading Pirates by seven and a half games. The Pirates breezed into New York confident that the NL flag would soon fly over Forbes Field.

Before the double-header for that day started, McGraw called his Giants into session and threw the book at them. At first, he just got mad, burning mad, and the words bounced off the rafters and filled up the room and ate into the hearts of the players like lye. He called them yellow quitters and worse; he lashed them with profanity; he degraded and humiliated them; he told them they deserved their lickings and said he hoped they'd get worse.

And then, when they were cringing and beaten, he suddenly stopped His voice became quiet and clear. There was sadness in his tone as he recalled Giant history of the past, 20 years of it, as he told them of victories won against terrible odds, of the pride and dignity of men who refused to be beaten.

The Giants he finally unleashed on the Pirates went on the field as though possessed. They pounced on Pittsburgh and won the first game. They started the second game in the same fashion, but by the last of the seventh the stunned Pirates had recovered and unleashed their terrific power to go ahead by one run. The Giants loaded the bases in the last of the eighth and George Kelly came to bat. Babe Adams, hurling for the Bucs, tried to fool Kelly on curves and got behind three balls and no strikes. One more ball would force in the tying run. McGraw signaled Kelly to hit the next pitch!

"What!" exclaimed Casey Stengel, who was sitting beside McGraw on the bench. "What the hell!"

"Shut up!" McGraw growled.

Kelly stepped out of the box and glanced at the dugout again, as though he hadn't seen the sign or couldn't believe it.

McGraw gave him the "hit" sign again. Kelly dug in. Adams threw a fast ball right down the middle. Kelly swung away and parked it into the stands for a grand-slam homer. Everyone went wild. McGraw, cold as ice, turned to Stengel and said, "I knew Adams would throw it in there. And I know what Kelly can do with a fast ball down the alley. I don't only want to win this game. I want to crush these guys."

The Giants swept that series and went on to take the pennant.

After that magnificent sweep of the doubleheader, McGraw looked the players over carefully, and snarled, "You fellows have a chance yet, if my brain holds out!"

McGraw knew that the only way to keep his Giants storming ahead was to dig the spurs into them and never let up.

All his life, McGraw firmly believed he never asked any ballplayer to do what he couldn't have done in the prime of his playing days. It often annoyed or saddened him when he discovered that young ballplayers he liked were not acquainted with the fact that their fat-encased manager had once been trim Johnny McGraw, a great ballplayer.

Frank Graham, in his superlative book, "McGraw Of The Giants," tells of the day Mac ordered a young outfielder named Red Murray to hit behind the runner going down to second. Murray hit into a double play. McGraw jumped him when he came back to the bench.

"I told you to hit to right field!"

"On an outside pitch?" Murray snorted. "I suppose you could have done it!"

"There never was a pitcher who could keep me from hitting behind the runner!" McGraw flared.

For once, McGraw did not go on raving and ranting. His eyes were sad as he turned to Christy Mathewson, sitting beside him. "You know, Matty," he said, "I really believe Murray doesn't know I ever played ball."

Johnny McGraw was a ballplayer, all right. In the 1890's, when the fans rode to the parks in horse-drawn buses, the McGraw kid was one of the most talked-about players of the day. He was a speedy, scrappy dynamo, the Eddie Stanky of his time. Johnny McGraw, standing five feet, six and a half inches, weighing 121 pounds, was the terror of the old American Association and, later on, the National League. From 1891 to 1899, he was the brain and sparkplug of the championship Baltimore Orioles, considered by some to be the greatest ball club of all time.

"When I played the game," McGraw once remarked proudly, "a ball park was a rough, uncultivated lot, a grandstand was a jumble of rickety slats, and a club pay-roll looked like the wage list of a logging camp."

It was a long-ago and far-away time. At 17, years before the Spanish-American War, the itinerant young ballplayer, John McGraw, was playing exhibition games in Havana, Cuba.

John J. McGraw, the son of a farmhand and section-gang worker, was born in Truxton, about 18 miles South of Syracuse, New York, in 1873, the year Ulysses S. Grant began his second term as President of the United States. John was the oldest of four children. Their mother died when he was 12 and the family broke up, the father pushing the kids off on various relatives. He got his son John a job as a candy butcher on the old Elmira, Cortland, and Northern Railroad.

As a boy, McGraw was fresh and argumentative, often annoying passengers with his didactic opinions about baseball. One of these rhubarbs was over whether or not a baseball could be made to curve in flight. At the next stop, the 15-year-old McGraw got off the train to prove his point. He put stakes in the ground 20 feet apart.

"I'll start the ball from the left side of the stake at my end," he explained, "make it pass to the right of the middle stake and it will be caught on the left side of the stake at the other end."

He did, and collected a share of the bets made.

Whenever Johnny could sneak away from his train job, he played ball with a school team in Truxton. He had dreams of becoming a great pitcher. His father often whaled the daylights out of his son when he caught him neglecting his job to play ball.

It is fascinating, in a psychiatric sense, that the two most stormy, pugnacious, successful figures in baseball history, Ty Cobb and John J. McGraw, both defied their fathers to become ballplayers. But how could the poor, work-ridden McGraw senior know that the boy he lectured and thrashed would some day, because of this game of baseball, meet and talk to the King of England, travel the whole world, make and lose fortunes, become a fabulous, international figure?

McGraw's father was responsible for forcing Johnny to teach himself to "place hit" a baseball. A left-handed hitter, Johnny naturally drove the ball to the right. A school house stood at the end of the lot in right field and young McGraw broke more than one window in it, for which his Dad had to pay.

"Experimenting and practicing," he later said, "I found that by changing the position of my feet and by using a chop swing, I could poke the ball into left field, fooling the other team and saving myself a whaling. Learning that as a kid," he would add, "was responsible for my batting record in the major leagues."

At 16, McGraw joined the Truxton Grays, a semi-pro hometown team. He went from there to East Homer, then to the Olean club in the Iron and Oil League, where he was turned into a third-baseman. He was to stay in that spot and shortstop. McGraw then began skipping to many teams, going on exhibition tours, always on the lookout for a way to better himself.

By 1891, when he was not quite 19, the fire-eating ballplayer had gained such a reputation that 29 ball clubs were after his services. He took an offer from the Cedar Rapids club in Iowa at $125 per month. It created quite a furor among other owners of ball teams, because McGraw had made tentative deals with all of them. The owner of one club had the law out looking for McGraw, threatening to drag him into court for his failure to keep a promise that he would play for them.

This threatened law suit was the first of a pattern. Mac was to see the inside of many courtrooms as the years rolled on.

Strangely enough, McGraw seemed to feel more guilt about his conduct as an adolescent than he did as an adult. As a man, he never apologized for his escapades, but he seemed to feel that he shouldn't be held responsible for the scrapes he got into as a youth and the promises he broke in order to get ahead as a ballplayer.

"I was really just a small boy a long way from home," he once told a reporter. "I didn't know exactly what to do. I had no older man to advise me. As long as I had to decide these things all alone, I did the best I could."

McGraw's best was always pretty wonderful for McGraw. He knew how to threaten and bargain. And you have to admire the way he was as a youngster, with guts, a good brain, and the ability to use both.

There was a sentimental streak as wide as a base-path in McGraw, too. He loved those old ball clubs for which he had played. The Polo Grounds was always well stocked with old players who held down minor jobs as gate-keepers and groundsmen simply because they once played with McGraw. Sight unseen, he once signed a pitcher named Otis Crandall because the youngster hailed from Cedar Rapids, Iowa, the last minor-league club for which McGraw played. McGraw's sentimentality paid off on that deal. Crandall developed into a classy hurler.

Manager Billie Barnie and the Orioles were shocked and tickled at the sight of the skinny kid with fierce, dark, deep-set eyes who turned up late in the season of 1891. Barnie had signed him on a tout from Bill Gleason, famed shortstop of the St. Louis Browns.

"Gleason tells me you think you're about as good as they come," Manager Barnie said. "How can a shrimp like you play ball?"

"Let me in there," McGraw sparked. "I'm tougher than I look."

That first day, Johnny McGraw took a seat on the end of the bench. A large, playful character sitting next to him gave the young Irishman the hip, knocking him off the bench into the dirt. McGraw flew at him, screaming like a maniac, his fists beating a tattoo against the big player's face. It took several Orioles to tear him loose from their battered teammate. After that, they left him alone.

The Orioles were not a very sharp ball club when McGraw joined them. It wasn't until the following year, when Ned Hanlon became manager and the Baltimore franchise was incorporated into the National League, that they began to catch fire. McGraw's two closest friends on that Oriole team were Wilbert Robinson and Hughie Jennings. All three later became managers.

In his good-natured, frolicsome way, Jennings was as ambitious and eager to get ahead in life as Johnny McGraw. They roomed together, talked and studied baseball, got out early in the mornings and practiced hitting and fielding before the other players reported to the field. They even decided they needed to be educated, that it would help them in baseball and in the world outside the game.

McGraw made up his mind to take courses at St. Bonaventure College, St. Bonaventure, N. Y., between baseball seasons. Jennings fell in with the idea. But their salaries then were only $1,400 a year, not nearly enough to keep them going and pay for tuition. Johnny dreamed up the idea of teaching baseball at the school in return for their tuition. Their offer was accepted and today there is a McGraw-Jennings Field at St. Bonaventure, in honor of two ballplayers who wanted to learn and grow.

Jennings was one of the few personalities able to remain a lifelong friend of McGraw's. John McGraw was responsible for most of the breaks in other friendships.

McGraw played third base on the championship 1894 Oriole team. Jennings was at short, Brouthers at first, Reitz at second. In the outfield were Steve Brodie, Joe Kelly, and that other "shrimp" who reached Baseball's Hall of Fame in Cooperstown, Wee Willie Keeler. Behind the plate was the massive Wilbert Robinson, who was later to manage the Dodgers for so many years and feud so bitterly with his old friend, McGraw. The pitchers were headed by the immortal Fred Clarkson, McMahon, Esper, and Pond.

The feats of these Orioles have become legend. Their skill, their flaming courage, their team spirit has never been surpassed. McGraw always held them up as the team that did the most to revolutionize baseball. It was a team of youth, speed, quick thinking, and guts.

At New Orleans, in '94, McGraw worked out the "inside plays" that brought the Orioles three straight championships. Before Johnny McGraw, the bunt was used merely as a sacrifice to advance a runner. McGraw taught the Orioles how to use the bunt as a "surprise" that would land them safely on first. With the "hit 'em where they ain't" genius, Wee Willie Keeler, he devised the now standard hit-and-run play.

McGraw was the lead-off man and Keeler followed him. A man reaching first, playing the "old style," would either wait for a hit, try to steal, or hope to advance on a sacrifice. McGraw and Keeler changed all that. Mac would start down as if to steal, feinting the infielder toward second, and Keeler would hit through the hole that had been vacated. If the ball was so bad that Keeler couldn't hit it, McGraw would still keep going. If Keeler hit safely, McGraw would wind up on third.

It is not generally known, but Johnny McGraw was one of the fastest runners in baseball. He stole as many as 77 bases in one season with the Orioles. Between his stealing, the surprise bunts, the hit-and-run, and the spark of the team, the Orioles completely befuddled the "old-fashioned" players of the other teams in the league.

"It's just a bunch of trick stuff those kids pull," said John Montgomery Ward, then manager of the Giants. "It's just tricks and luck and they won't last."

Ward changed his mind late in the season when the hit-and-run Orioles took 24 out of 25 games, winning 18 straight!

In those days, the game had only one umpire. The way McGraw took advantage of that fact earned him the reputation of creating the multiple ump system. Sometimes, in a crisis, with the umpire following the flight of the ball, McGraw would ignore second base and cut directly from first to third.

McGraw had a pocketful of tricks. With a runner on third, ready to take off for home the moment a fly ball was caught, McGraw would surreptitiously hook his finger in the player's belt. He would hold on just long enough to insure the runner being caught at the plate. A Louisville player once fixed McGraw by loosening his belt. He then romped for home, leaving the enraged third-baseman holding a strap in his hands.

During McGraw's first year at Baltimore, he was nicknamed "Muggsy." He deserved the tag but he also despised it. It was given to him by a newspaperman who implied that Johnny McGraw, the wasp of the Orioles, was related to a Baltimore ward-heeler known as Muggsy McGraw. The politico was an uncouth, rough-and-ready, somewhat shady character. The ballplayer, who was then attending college in his off-time and striving to become a gentleman off the field, hated being linked to the ward-heeler.

Always after that, whenever anyone wanted to taunt John McGraw, the name "Muggsy" was trotted out and put to use. At the sound of it, McGraw would immediately assume the role of a "mug," flying into a fierce rage.

Not even Branch Rickey could carry on so many feuds at one time as John J. McGraw. How he managed to stay in baseball, with so many powerful sport figures out to get him, is something of a miracle. McGraw did not limit his antagonisms to rival clubowners and managers, but carried on word-and-fist battles with players, umpires, fans, celebrities in other fields, unknowns, and big shots.

The quarrel with Ban Johnson, American League president, was one of the most enduring and bitter. In 1900, when Baltimore was dropped from the National League, McGraw was sold to St. Louis. He was offered the highest salary then paid to a major-league player, $9,500. He accepted it only on condition that he could become a free agent at the end of the season. There was a terrific war then in progress between the newly formed American League, headed by Ban Johnson, and the old, established National League.

In 1901, Johnson talked McGraw into taking over as the manager of the Baltimore Orioles, which had been picked up by the American League.

"I couldn't get along with Johnson," was McGraw's version. "I wanted a successful team and all Johnson thought about was making the American League pay off. He made unfair and harsh rulings against me and my players. He suspended me frequently. I knew he was angling for a club in New York and would drop us from the league like a hot potato the first chance he got."

At the start of the 1902 season, McGraw beat Johnson to the punch by getting an unconditional release from the stockholders of the Baltimore Orioles. On July 7, 1902, the baseball world was stunned to hear that he had accepted an offer to manage the New York Giants. Ban's bull-like bellows of rage echoed up and down both leagues. He accused McGraw of running out on the Baltimore club, of betraying a promise to stay in the American League, of being a crook and an ingrate.

And so, under a storm cloud of insults and protests, the 29-year-old McGraw arrived at the Polo Grounds. His salary for that year was to be $11,000 and he had stubbornly stipulated that he was to have absolute, unchallenged control of the Giants.

The new manager began tangling with the boss from the moment his hat was on the rack. He picked up the Giant roster and crossed out nine names.

"We get rid of these fellows," he said.

"No, you don't," Freedman came back. "They cost me a lot of money."

"They won't play on my ball club," McGraw snapped. "And I want you to get me Billy Gilbert, Sam Mertes, George Davis."

"Not Davis!" Freedman shouted. "I have no use for him!"

"He's a great ballplayer!" McGraw yelled back, drowning out the owner's protests. "You're going to get him for me and pay him $6,500 a year."

Nobody ever did stop him. McGraw brought Iron Man Joe McGinnity, Roger Bresnahan, Dan McGann, and Jack Cronin from the Orioles. He signed four or five other players he liked and began to build his Giants. He took them from the cellar in 1902 to second place in 1903. In 1904, he brought the Giants their first pennant.

Behind the sound and fury that came from the Giant bench, the abominable outbursts of temper, there was a planning and strategy that was ice-cold and beautiful.

"The only popularity I know," he once remarked, "is to win."

He carried the entire responsibility for the team on his broadening shoulders. His outward behavior was wild and boyish, but his decisions about his ball team were mature. He hired men he despised because he thought they had what it took to be a Giant. No matter how deep an affection McGraw had for a player, if he didn't measure up, the manager released him quickly.

John T. Brush, who is credited with organizing the American-National League World Series, bought the Giants in 1903. He was a hearty, outspoken man, and he and McGraw hit it off immediately. He gave the young manager *carte blanche* and McGraw made him barrels of money. The Giants became the biggest draw in the league and the world champions in 1905.

The wham-bang style of those early-day Giants, their cocky, aggressive manners on the diamond, brought the wrath of fans in rival towns down around their ears. McGraw instigated this and loved it. He was wise enough to realize that hate is as strong an attraction as love.

Cops were called in Cincinnati, Pittsburgh, and Chicago to keep the Giants from being mobbed on their way to the ball park. McGraw would cart his players to the park, not in an ordinary bus, but in gilded carriages with banners proclaiming them World Champions. They were belted with eggs and stale fruit, assaulted and defiled, but the fans followed them right through the gate.

In 1906, a string of injuries robbed the Giants of the pennant. The following year, McGraw again shocked the wise birds of baseball by releasing over half the team. Established stars were traded for young, untried players.

"McGraw is plumb crazy," a sportswriter remarked when he learned of the deal. "He's so swell-headed he thinks he doesn't need players to win. He thinks all he has to have is McGraw."

"Maybe so," another scribe answered, "There are always nine McGraws on the field and one on the bench. But it wouldn't surprise me if the Giants grabbed another pennant pretty soon."

They almost did in 1908. In late September, they were hurtling down the stretch in a tie with the Cubs of Tinker to Evers to Chance fame.

It was the last half of the ninth at the Polo Grounds, with the score tied. Harry McCormick was on third and Fred Merkle was on first. Al Bridwell came to bat with the pennant at stake. He drove the first pitch to center field for a base hit. McCormick came home with the "winning run." Merkle stopped between first and second and ran for the clubhouse.

The fans poured out on to the field. Many of the Giant and Chicago players ran for the clubhouse. Johnny Evers, standing on second, kept screaming for the ball. It was finally relayed to him. He touched the bag and claimed that Merkle should be declared out, making the third out and nullifying the run. The umpires refused to make a decision until the next day, when they called the game a tie.

At the end of the season, the Cubs and Giants were still all even. They played out the "Merkle game" and, with Christy Mathewson pitching, the Giants lost the game and the pennant. There are hundreds of versions of this game and that famed "bonehead play" but the interesting thing is the reaction of John Joseph McGraw. The Giant fans were yelling for Merkle's scalp. They wanted him chastised. Some felt he should be given the gate.

"I don't blame Merkle," McGraw said at the close of the season. "He did what he had seen older ballplayers do many times. He's a fine player and he's going to be even better next year. I intend not only to keep him, but give him a raise."

And that is what McGraw did. If he had made the same error in judgment himself, he probably would have jumped off the nearest bridge. Like a good general, John McGraw could always forgive and forget an error his players made as long as it did not involve disobeying an order. He showed the same tolerance toward Fred Snodgrass, who muffed an easy fly ball against the Red Sox, costing the Giants the World Series in 1912. He also boosted Snodgrass' salary the following year.

The Giants won the pennant for three straight years, starting in 1911. Starting in 1921, the players from the Polo Grounds won four straight, which wasn't equalled until McCarthy's Yanks went on a rampage. And McGraw never had a "Murderer's Row" to run up his scores.

McGraw's 1911 team has been called the speediest baseball club in history. The Giants swiped so many bases, ran the paths in such wild, sliding, ripping style, that they literally tore their uniforms to rags. McGraw gleefully wired to New York for more uniforms.

"The Giants aren't out to win the pennant," Bozeman Bulger reported from Chicago. "They are out to steal it. Josh Devore slid into second with such ferocity today that his pants were completely ripped off, leaving only a few rags hanging to a belt. He had to be escorted from the field half-naked."

The Giants rolled on, quarrelsome, boastful, and unbeatable. The newspapers and fans had, by this time, made McGraw a national figure, holding him up as a mixture of genius and ogre. He was a familiar figure along Broadway and at the race-track, a swaggering, party-loving man with a talent for trouble. He had been married, the year he came to the Giants, to Mary Blanche Sindall, the socially prominent daughter of a Baltimore contractor. It remained a happy marriage.

In 1912, although his Giants lost the World Series, John Joseph

McGraw was the big man of baseball. He decided to cash in on his fame by going on a vaudeville tour for $3,000 per week. He opened at Hammerstein's Theater in New York and went on to the Palace in Chicago. He strutted across the country, happy behind the footlights, enjoying the "act" of building up McGraw. The following year, with still another pennant in his pocket, he and Charles Comiskey set off on a world tour with the Giants and White Sox.

At the close of the World Series that year, when the A's again ripped the Giants and took the world championship, a long smoldering quarrel between McGraw and his old Oriole pal, Wilbert Robinson, broke into the open. Robby, who had been a fine Giant pitching coach, quit McGraw and went across the river to Brooklyn. The hatred between the two men became as intense as their friendship had once been.

McGraw came back from his first world tour riding the crest of the wave. He was getting beefy now, a puffy, wide-chested, broad-seated man with a bulbous nose. He had spread the word about baseball to Egypt, France, the Philippines. He had met and chatted with the King of England. He was now a figure of importance, sought after, quoted, denounced, and praised.

But even the mighty can stumble. The high-handed, despotic, generous, brilliant "Little Napoleon" cursed and drove and pleaded with his 1914 Giants as they fought for still another National League flag. But the inspired Boston Braves were too much.

Still heralded as the greatest manager in baseball, McGraw fumed on the bench through 1915 and into 1916. The latter year, he rose to unequalled heights of leadership and then fell into the dust of despair. In early September, worked into a frenzy by McGraw and aided by the dazzling pitching of Ferdie Schupp, Perritt, Benton, and Sallee, the Giants won 26 games in a row! The Giant infield, composed of Buck Herzog, Art Fletcher, Walter Holke, and Henry Zimmerman, played matchless baseball.

But, by the close of the season, the Giants had been nosed out of the race. During a game against Brooklyn, led by Wilbert Robinson, McGraw left the bench in disgust. He implied to the sportswriters that his players had thrown the game.

It was an unjust accusation.

Rumors flew around town that McGraw was through, that he could no longer control himself or his team. Perhaps, in McGraw's eyes, the Giants were letting him down. They were not Orioles—they were human. As Robby's team was licking the Giants that day, perhaps McGraw was thinking of his playing days with Baltimore, of old Robby grinding a smashed finger into the dust to stop the bleeding and finishing the game behind the plate.

But John McGraw was a country mile from writing finis to his career. In 1917, he signed a contract for $40,000 a year and a share of the profits. It was to be a five-year deal. A newspaper account of the day said. "He has grown gray and tolerant—or at least *more* tolerant."

He came out for the 1917 season like a lion released from a cage. He stewed up a huge cauldron of fuss and trouble and smashed through to still another National League pennant. He had, although few would have believed it at the start of the season, 15 more years ahead of him as a big-league manager. At 44 years old, he was considered one of the "old men" of baseball.

The furious little manager began the season by putting the biff and bam on umpire Bill Byron after a game in Cincinnati. The fight began on a runway that led to the clubhouse. Cops and players finally interceded and pulled the still flailing McGraw away from Byron. A few days later, John K. Tener, then President of the National League, slapped a $500 fine and a 16-day suspension on McGraw.

In an interview with Sid Mercer, a veteran New York sportswriter and then a friend of his, McGraw went on the warpath. He accused Tener of showing favoritism. He heaped abuse on the umpires of the National League and the way Tener handled them.

Sid, a good newspaper man, was also a fair one. He gave McGraw every chance to cool off and back down from his statements. He even showed McGraw the story he had written and offered to kill it. McGraw not only okayed it, but insisted that it be given to all the other reporters.

When the story broke all over the country, McGraw was called to account for his actions. The manager finally signed a statement to Tener that accused the baseball writers of "inventing" the words he had spoken. In short, he called them all liars.

The mess dragged on. The reporters didn't take the rap casually. They demanded an investigation to prove that McGraw had lied. It was finally held, with Tener appointing a lawyer to conduct the hearings and to submit his findings in the case. Mercer, reluctantly, but with his own honor at stake, went on the stand. Mac squirmed and angrily tried to make out a case for himself. When Tener got the report he was certain it was McGraw who had lied and he tagged him with still another fine, a cool $1,000.

McGraw lost many good friends among the baseball writers, including Sid Mercer, who never spoke to him after that and quit covering the Giants.

If the affair bothered McGraw—and it must have cut very deeply—he didn't show it. He went right on snapping and raving. He charged ahead in the race for the National League pennant. He won the flag with practically the same team he had walked away from in disgust that day a year before in Brooklyn. The World Series that year went to six games and the Giants were beaten by the White Sox because of another of those last inning "bonehead plays." This time the hapless culprit was Heinie Zimmerman. With nobody covering home plate, Heinie was forced to chase Eddie Collins of the Sox across the dish with the winning run.

Again, McGraw did not take out his rage on the player. He vented his fury on the White Sox and manager Clarence Rowland, swearing at Rowland and refusing to shake hands with him after the final game. In defeat, John McGraw was seldom an example for the youth of the country. He was a colossal sorehead as a loser, a rotten sportsman. The best you can say is that McGraw always expressed his feelings fully, honestly, and profanely.

The lavish, generous parties McGraw tossed when he won are still remembered as keenly as his behavior when he lost. It is not difficult to understand why McGraw reacted so violently whenever his ball club was beaten. It was not the Giants who had been defeated—it was McGraw. The rage he took out on his rivals was actually directed at himself.

For three years, from 1918 through 1920, under the shadow of World War I, the Giants finished in second place. In 1919, he became a part owner of the ball club along with Charles Stoneham and Francis X. McQuade. That same year, indulging his passion for horse racing, he bought an interest in a racetrack in Havana. In 1920, his large, belligerent face was plastered all over the newspapers as he was dragged into court for using his fists too freely in the Lambs Club and in front of his home.

William Boyd, a prominent actor of the time, was one of John's opponents in the Lambs Club slugfest. They began swinging at each other when Boyd objected to McGraw's swearing in front of some scrubwomen who happened to be nearby. Later that night, McGraw got into another brawl with John C. Slavin, a musical-comedy star. The fight took place in front of McGraw's apartment house and Slavin wound up in a hospital.

The members of the Lambs Club expelled McGraw from the club. The District Attorney swung into action and McGraw was tried in a district court and acquitted. In the meantime, he had beaten the daylights out of still another actor who had visited him to talk about what had happened at the Lambs Club!

The doughty manager opened the 1921 season by brawling with Clark Griffith and his ancient enemy, Ban Johnson. He had hired his old pal, Hughie Jennings, as head coach. Together, they planned to make life miserable for the other clubs in the league. They did just that. For four glorious, exciting, tumultuous years the Giants trampled on their enemies with great abandon, winning four pennants and two world championships. The beefy, glowing, 48-year-old managerial wonder romped and raved like a kid as his team pushed the hated Yankees into the dust two years in a row to become world champions.

The years from 1921 to 1924 in baseball belong to McGraw. He had the time of his life, celebrating his victories like a maharaja. There were parties, wild and wonderful, in the old Waldorf Hotel—champagne, speeches, back-slapping, and rejoicing. The McGraws took trips abroad and the fine, riotous life was continued in London and Paris. McGraw was as high and happy in victory as he was mean and miserable in defeat.

The second world tour with the White Sox, at the close of the 1924 season, was a washout financially. But McGraw and his gang had a rollicking good time.

One of the more amusing of these incidents happened during an exhibition game outside London. A husky Giant batter belted a ball far over the head of a White Sox centerfielder. A member of the English nobility, sitting with McGraw, tapped the manager on the shoulder and said "Ah, I say, too bad, too bad!"

"What do you mean, too bad?" McGraw demanded.

"Out of bounds, dear fellow, out of bounds!" the Englishman clucked.

Always after these tours of triumph or maybe because of them, evil days would fall on McGraw. He got sick at the start of the 1925 season. The Giants began to roll downhill. The Pirates walloped them late in the season to clinch the pennant. The only bright spot that year was the appearance of a husky youngster from Louisiana, a gawky kid carrying a paper-backed suitcase. "Mr. McGraw," the boy said, shaking in the presence of the great manager, "I'm Melvin Ott."

In a sudden unpredictable move which was so typical of McGraw, the manager gave the boy a uniform and made him a Giant. It was Ott who was to become the last of McGraw's great stars, to worship him as few men ever have, and continue to keep the name of McGraw an alive and shining thing long after McGraw passed from the baseball scene. The year McGraw gained this new, young, adoring friend, he lost an old one. Christy Mathewson died. A part of McGraw went with his first star and great pitcher. He had loved Matty very much and it was a loss from which he never really recovered.

Into the ears of Mel Ott, McGraw poured all the wisdom he had gained down through the years. The growth of Ott as a slugger and outfielder was a monument to the genius of John McGraw.

"He helped everyone," Ott said. "Even those he disliked. He was a fine, decent man and the greatest thing that ever happened to me was knowing him. He was also the greatest manager baseball has ever known. Nobody could inspire players as he could, give them such a will to win."

It is somewhat sad that Mel Ott, Bill Terry, Carl Hubbell, the last of the long string of great ballplayers, developed by McGraw, never saw him at his height, during the glory of his pennant-winning streaks. In 1926, the first full year that Ott wore a Giant uniform, the Giants sunk to fifth place. It was the first time in a decade they had failed to finish in the first division.

The year was marred by Frankie Frisch taking off in mid-season brought on by the constant, merciless riding of McGraw. As captain of the team for two seasons, Frisch had borne the brunt of McGraw's cruel tongue-lashings as the Giants slipped down the ladder of the league. Frisch, who was far from being a thin-skinned player, took it until it became unbearable and then packed his grips one night in St. Louis and left in a huff for New York.

McGraw traded Frisch and pitcher Jimmy Ring for the renowned Rogers Hornsby who was to act as a combination player, captain, and assistant manager. That didn't work out, either. Nothing Rog did seemed to please McGraw, who left him in charge of the team late in the season. It was the first time McGraw had turned over his Giants to anyone. It was the beginning of the end. The old firehorse had a few more spurts of fury left in him, but he was rapidly running down, dogged by ill health, inner-club wrangling and rhubarbs with the National League's president, John Heydler.

In 1928, McGraw shook himself like a punchy fighter, cleared his head. He pushed them in with all the shrewd managerial tricks of old. He pushed them out again by flying into such uncontrollable temper tantrums that the players became rattled, frightened, and booted ball games. The Giants finished in second place, two games behind the Cards, after a row in late September in which McGraw accused umpire Bill Klem and Heydler of robbing them of the pennant.

The Giants finished third in 1929 and 1930, and fought gamely to overtake the Cardinals again in 1931. They were hopelessly out-classed and McGraw suffered through moods of helpless rage and frustration and melancholy. But he went right on throwing his weight around, bullying umpires, shouting at his old nemesis, Bill Klem, as though it were 1907 again and he still had enough strength in his body to flatten The Old Arbitrator with one blow.

At 59, John McGraw was sick in body and mind, but he was still raring and furious. He was kicked off the field in St. Louis one afternoon after threatening to annihilate an umpire. Heydler wearily fined him $150.

McGraw lay in wait for Heydler outside the ball park the next day and, in front of an amazed crowd of fans and players and reporters, screamed insults at the bewildered, embarrassed president of the league. His wrath became so terrifying that those gathered feared he would have a stroke. He even wheeled on the crowd and cursed them furiously for listening!

How many gathered there that day realized that McGraw was reviling himself? His team had lost, the fluttering pennant had eluded him, and he knew he was too old and tired and used-up ever to be able to hit the glory trail of a comeback again.

He didn't even enter the ball park that day late in 1931. He went back to his hotel, sat alone in his room, a sick, weary man, heavy head hanging to one side, alone and pitiful like some great, mortally wounded animal.

Matty was gone. So was Ross Youngs and Kid Gleason and Joe Kelly and Ned Hanlon. Who was around who had seen the Orioles of 1894? Who remembered the Giants of 1905 and the way Johnny McGraw, their slim, young, furious manager had been then? Did they remember who had given baseball the hit-and-run, the pinch-hitter? They never wrote about that any more. . . .

He was The Old Man. He could no longer handle his players. He could now inspire only fear or humor. Some of them even dared talk back to him.

He made his last fighting appearance in 1933 as the manager of the National League All-Star team, opposing Manager Connie Mack of the American League. Babe Ruth, one of the "big men" John McGraw once said he had driven out of baseball, broke up the ball game with a home run. McGraw shook hands with Connie Mack after the game. He had, in the very end, learned how to lose graciously. But it wasn't a Giant team he was master-minding that day.

From high in the stands in Washington, he watched the Giants, under his protege, Bill Terry, sweep the Senators off their feet in the 1933 World Series.

Years like that one might have dragged on, but the end came quickly and kindly. Just 19 months after John J. McGraw had resigned as manager of the New York Giants, on February 25, 1934, he died in a hospital in New Rochelle, New York.

There is no simple way to sum up the career of a man like John J. McGraw, the fabulous, furious leader of the New York Giants, the pioneer and genius in the field of managing baseball players. He was too big and important to the game of baseball to attempt to eulogize by tossing off a final, pat phrase.

One day in the early 1900's, a ballplayer who had left the Giants was standing in a hotel lobby cussing out McGraw in language of the sort the "Little Napoleon" had undoubtedly once curled around his ears. The player poured it on, to the delight of the reporters who had gathered.

"Say,——" one of the newspapermen finally said, "you know, since you left the Giants, McGraw always speaks very highly of you."

The ballplayer stopped raving. He rubbed his chin. "He does?" he said. Then he grinned. "Well, let me also tell you this. I'd really rather play ball for that no good blankety-blank so-and-so than any manager that ever lived!"

LEO DUROCHER

Always on the Spot

Sport Magazine   April 1947

*"As the result of the accumulation of unpleasant inci-
dents," baseball commissioner Happy Chandler suspended
Leo Durocher for the 1947 season. In this 1947* **Sport**
profile, you can see it coming.

By Tom Meany

Thalmann, Georgia, is a whistle stop so tiny that its name is spelled
incorrectly on some of the maps. Its population is listed as 100,
but that must include the scrub cattle and the razorback hogs as
well as the human beings. The only reason that Thalmann is even a
whistle stop is because one of the directors of the Seaboard Railway
found it convenient to have the through trains stop there so he and his
Wall Street chums could visit the nearby Georgia coastal resorts of Sea
Island and St. Simon's.

There weren't any bankers or brokers waiting to board the Orange
Blossom Special when it groaned to a protesting stop there one brisk
February night in 1928. There was only Uncle Wilbert Robinson, the
Falstaffian genius of the Brooklyn Dodgers, and a pair of baseball writers
—Garry Schumacher and myself. We were headed for Clearwater, Flor-
ida, and the start of Spring training.

As soon as the porter hustled our luggage aboard, he informed us in
hushed tones that Babe Ruth was in the car ahead, bound for the Yankee
training camp at St. Petersburg.

We found Ruth in a poker game, nickel and a dime, with Eddie Bennett, the hunchback mascot of the Yankees, Pee Wee Dougherty, the clubhouse kid, and a fourth, a young man in his mid-20's, chunky, well put together, and obviously a ballplayer.

Babe dealt Garry and me into the game and performed the introductions in Ruthian fashion:

"And what's your name again, keed?"

"Durocher," replied the stranger. "Leo Durocher."

That was the first time I ever saw Durocher, but I've seen a great deal of him in the subsequent 19 years.

Somehow it was prophetic that the first glimpse of Durocher was in a card game. Here he was, bound for his first major-league training camp, sitting in at a card game with the greatest figure baseball had ever known, as cool, as at home, as though he had been a Yankee all his life.

Durocher looked the part of smart money even then. Ruth was in an eye-arresting dressing gown of blue, trimmed with burnt-orange. Leo sported a smart business sack suit, before the first hand was over, he was calling Schumacher and me by our first names, telling us when to bet, who raised, whose deal it was, and so on.

In the course of the conversation, we asked him about Howie Freigau, an infielder Brooklyn had drafted from Toledo. A good hitter, who had been inclined to heftiness. We wondered if he had put on any weight in the American Association. We figured Leo, fresh from St. Paul—and I do mean fresh—would have all the answers.

"Howie's in great shape," answered Durocher without an instant's hesitation. "He should help your club a lot."

For the record, when Schumacher and I caught up with Freigau at Clearwater the next day, he was round as a barrel and at least 20 pounds overweight. He was released by the Dodgers.

Now that I know Durocher better, I can see that his information wasn't intended to be misleading. He knew Freigau wasn't in shape, knew that we'd know it as soon as we saw him, so he let it go at that. The problem was Freigau's, not his.

Since that night, I've seen Durocher in many places—in the Stork Club, in a World Series, in a tent some 700 yards from the front lines at Loiano, Italy; in other card games in widely separated places, and in the defendant's box before a Grand Jury. I've seen him on the spot many a time—but I've never yet failed to see him get off the spot.

In a way, Durocher is on the spot all over again in 1947. Last year he took a club that wasn't supposed to have much of a chance and brought it to a dead heat with the Cardinals for the National League pennant. This year, Leo is expected to do at least as well because of improved material, and there is only one answer to doing at least as well as a dead heat.

Time was when the good burghers of Brooklyn were content with a team which could make threatening gestures toward the first division and beat the hated Giants on occasion. First Larry MacPhail, then Branch Rickey changed all that. They built up an elaborate farm system which funnelled strong talent into Ebbets Field. Brooklyn waited 21 years— from 1920 to 1941—for its last pennant, but now they're impatient after a six-year drought.

Durocher's extra-curricular activities do not sit so well with the powers that be, either. Commissioner Albert B. Chandler had him on the carpet last Winter in reference to his friendship with George Raft, the movie actor who compiled an amazing string of passes in a famous dice-game at Leo's mid-Manhattan apartment and the strait-laced Rickey was undoubtedly upset at the rapid succession of highly ornamental young ladies who made use of Leo's private box at Ebbets Field.

Durocher's various involvements in connection with his marriage to Miss Laraine Day would be considered for a musical comedy. The first intimation anybody in the East had of a romance was when Hollywood columns coupled their names after the season closed. Then The Lip flew East to sign a new contract and flew back immediately to be greeted at the Burbank airport by Miss Day.

Within a week, the major- and minor-league officials assembled in Los Angeles for their annual winter pow-wow found themselves crowded from the front pages when J. Ray Hendricks, Miss Day's husband, named Durocher as corespondent in a suit that was subsequently withdrawn.

The day after the charges by Hendricks, the tangled romance of Durocher became further involved with the arrival in Hollywood of Edna Ryan, who had been in Durocher's company ever since the Spring of 1945. Edna was on the Coast for a movie try-out. When asked about The Lip, she implied that they had come to a parting of the ways long before Miss Day appeared on the scene.

So much should have been enough, but not for Durocher. Miss Day was granted an interlocutory decree of divorce by Superior Court Judge Dockweiler on January 20. The following day Laraine and Leo flew to El Paso, drove over to Juarez, Mexico, obtained a Mexican divorce, recrossed the Rio Grande, and were married in El Paso, Texas. Under the terms whereby Miss Day had received her California divorce, she was supposed to have waited a year before getting married again.

That Judge Dockweiler was put out by this is to put it mildly. There were rumors that Miss Day would be open to charges of bigamy if she and Durocher lived together as man and wife in California, and that Leo might be cited for contempt of court.

Durocher talked to Judge Dockweiler in tones, and terms, far more dulcet than those he usually employs with umpires.

A transcript of the hearing on January 22 reveals that Durocher literally threw himself on the mercy of the court.

"I know that Mrs. Durocher and I could be tremendously happy if just given the opportunity by yourself. You have the power, judge, to really make us happy and spare us much fright. We did an impulsive thing. It was wrong. We just ask for mercy. We took a chance."

The publicity attendant on Durocher's third matrimonial venture resulted in a story that Commissioner Chandler was considering the suspension of the Brooklyn manager. This was promptly denied by Happy. Yet only two days later, at a Dodger press conference, Branch Rickey, in answer to an abstract question, declared that, in his opinion, the private life of a ballplayer was very much the concern of the Commissioner.

Previously, an assault charge brought against Durocher by John Christian, a fan considered extremely loud-mouthed even in Flatbush, was a source of embarrassment to Rickey, even though Leo was adjudged not guilty by a jury of his peers. Rickey is as publicity-conscious as any executive in baseball, but when his manager is on the front pages, Branch would prefer to have the subject-matter baseball, rather than felony charges, divorce actions, or dice games. And you can hardly blame him.

In fact, the relationship between Rickey and Durocher is strange indeed. Although Leo is publicly on record as saying "Mr. Rickey has been like a father to me," there must have been times when Branch would have liked to exercise the paternal prerogative of the woodshed.

Rickey is an intense moralist, almost Puritanical. He has rehabilitated many a baseball character. Among his most notable reformations are Gabby Street and Billy Southworth, to the point where both won pennants and notable World Series victories for the Cardinals—Gabby over the mighty Athletics in 1931, Southworth over the all-conquering Yankees in 1942.

That Rickey was a tower of strength to Durocher in those uncertain days when Leo was being shuttled from the Yankees to Cincinnati to the Cardinals, there is no doubt. It was Branch who helped straighten out his tangled personal affairs in 1934 when, at the height of a torrid pennant race, Leo married Miss Grace Dozier, a prop to him in his troubled moments ever since, even though they were divorced after nine years.

On the other hand, however, there is substantial ground for believing that Rickey would have been just as well pleased if he could have named his own manager for 1943, instead of proceeding with the holdover Durocher, inherited from MacPhail.

There is a story, with a stronger background than the average rumor, that Rickey had been tipped off by a member of Durocher's draft board that Leo would be tapped for induction by Selective Service in January, 1943. The Mahatma temporized, an art in which he is highly skilled, and declared there were other things which took precedence over the selection of a manager for 1943.

Durocher was called for a physical examination in January of 1943. The belief was that Branch, new to Brooklyn, and not sure of the grip Durocher had on the fans, was going to let the draft board make his decision for him. If Leo was drafted, as Rickey had every reason to believe he would be, Branch could go ahead and name his own manager, without being accused by the public of tossing Durocher down the chute.

Whatever Rickey's plans for a 1943 Dodger manager, if any, they went out the window when Durocher was discovered to have a punctured eardrum and was classified 4-F. Durocher was given his release near the end of the 1943 season and remained a free agent for some weeks, to be hired again by Rickey, but this time, presumably on Rickey's own terms.

Durocher had his one bad season as a manager in 1944. He had a pitiful ball club that year, and it played pitiful ball. The Dodgers finished seventh, 42 games behind the pennant-winning Cardinals. If Rickey had chosen to get rid of Durocher then, there could have been little complaint. Yet luck rode with Leo once again. He was selected to go overseas with a USO baseball unit and Rickey hardly could fire a manager who had volunteered to fly an ocean to help entertain the troops. Rickey signed him to a new contract to manage in 1945. Since then, Leo has never looked back.

There have been so many rumors about bonus clauses in Durocher's contracts with Rickey that it is difficult to determine how much he makes now, or what he made in the past. When it was reported that The Lip, through bonuses, was drawing $65,000 for managing the Dodgers, the story was neither affirmed nor denied. It pleased Durocher's vanity to be considered the highest-paid in the game and the Mahatma, no doubt, was flattered by rumors crediting him with being so open-handed an employer.

The flurry of publicity which accompanied the transfer of Charley Dressen's allegiance and coaching talents from the Dodgers to the Yankees focused the spotlight on Durocher's assistants.

As a sign-snatcher, Chuck is one of the best in the business and he was a perfect foil for Durocher. It was Dressen who paid attention to details, leaving Durocher free to plan the grand, over-all strategy. Chuck complemented Leo much as Art Fletcher did Joe McCarthy in the days when the Yankees were winning pennants with monotonous regularity.

There wasn't so much publicity given to the resignation of Johnny (Red) Corriden from the Dodger coaching staff and his subsequent signing, some six weeks later, by the Yankees. But, Johnny, too, was an important member of the Brooklyn brain trust.

The value of Dressen and Corriden to Durocher, important as it undoubtedly was, will be exaggerated in this coming season if the Dodgers fail to get away well. Wise guys will tell you they knew all along that the coaches were the real brains behind Durocher. This simply isn't so. Leo leaned on them, to be sure, but there is pretty strong evidence to indicate that The Lip is a sound manager.

As a manager, Durocher has one great gift of leadership. He never second-guesses the lieutenant when things go wrong. Confident that he won't be blamed if his suggestion goes wrong, such a coach is twice as valuable as the coach who keeps his mouth shut to avoid trouble.

Durocher leaves nothing to be desired as a tactician. There is no manager in baseball today as resourceful as The Lip. He has lifted the squeeze play from obscurity and made it standard operating procedure for Brooklyn. The solo theft of home, an almost forgotten play, was revived by Pete Reiser last year under the guidance of Durocher. Pete stole home seven times.

One complaint voiced in some quarters against Durocher last year, was that he changed pitchers too often. That the Dodgers wore out a path from bullpen to pitcher's mound there is no doubt, but that was the kind of pitching staff the Dodgers had.

The key to all managerial success is knowing when to remove a pitcher. The late Walter Johnson once told me that it was leaving a pitcher in to face one more batter that kept him from being a winning manager.

"They'd ask me to let 'em pitch to just one more batter," explained Walter, "and having been a pitcher myself, I sympathized with them."

One of Joe McCarthy's outstanding traits was that he could make up his mind just when a pitcher had reached the end of his string. McCarthy, incidentally, never held any conference with a pitcher he was about to lift. Joe would send out Art Fletcher to the mound and the pitcher's stint would be over.

If Durocher has a flaw in his managerial make-up, it is that he frequently loses patience with his younger players. Leo, who was always quick to grasp things himself as a player, can work himself into a lather over a rookie who is slow on the uptake.

On the railroad platform in Cincinnati one night, Durocher was asked if he planned any line-up changes. Leo started to answer the question in a normal tone of voice, but in no time at all he was shouting stridently. He berated young Howie Schultz, among others, and many of those who are familiar with the Dodgers believe the tirade shattered the confidence of Schultz, standing within earshot of the outburst.

Durocher's riding of Luis Olmo robbed that player of much of his effectiveness and could have been one of the motives which prompted him to jump to the Mexican League last year. Bill Hart, a Southern League infielder, was another who faltered under the Durocher tongue-lashings.

Although Durocher is admittedly a successful manager, he is the only manager who had his own players strike against him. In 1943, Leo told Tim Cohane, then a baseball writer, that Bobo Newsom had been suspended because he criticized the catching strategy of Bob Bragan.

When the ballplayers came to the park next day, they staged a protest meeting in the clubhouse at Ebbets Field. Headed by Arky Vaughan and Dixie Walker, they demanded that Durocher tell the truth, which was that Newsom had been suspended because of a verbal run-in with Leo.

The Dodgers, after much persuasion, took the field that day and scored more than 20 runs, but Vaughan was not in uniform. Next morning there were only two stories on the front page of the conservative New York *Times*. One told the story of the Dodger rebellion; the other carried the news that the Allies had landed in Sicily.

Caught, Durocher took the easy way out. He denied he had told Cohane that Newsom had been suspended for criticizing Bragan. In an unprecedented move, Cohane then went before the Dodger players in the clubhouse and told the squad exactly what Durocher said.

With Leo sitting quietly by, in itself a minor miracle, Cohane questioned Newsom and the other players. Durocher admitted that what Cohane had printed had been what he told him, but that it was not the real reason for the suspension of Newsom. Like so many other jams in which The Lip has been involved, this one, too, blew over, but Bobo went to the Browns on waivers within a few days.

I doubt if I ever saw Leo actually worried, unless it was when he was standing trial last Summer on the charge of assaulting a fan. This was rather a complex case, in which Durocher pled not guilty, but in which it was brought out that he had paid the plaintiff $6200 before the case came to trial to forestall any civil action. It didn't take the jury long to acquit Leo and I'll bet he hasn't given the case another thought since.

Durocher has such supreme self-confidence that he can't imagine others not sharing his own opinion of himself. An evidence of Leo's imperturbability regarding the opinions of others came to light in the Summer of 1942. Stanley Frank, then a New York sportswriter, wrote a fiction piece for the *Saturday Evening Post* in which there were two rather thinly-disguised characters, one of whom was recognizable as Babe Ruth, the other as Durocher. Leo was portrayed unflatteringly as a bully, a braggart, and a sneak thief.

Leo never noticed the magazines, or if he did, he didn't get the significance. When he went to the first-base coaching box, and the Giant bench began riding him and asking if he had read the *Post*, Durocher seemed genuinely surprised. He asked his own players, "What the hell post are those guys talking about?"

Durocher did read the story later and his reactions were understandable. He merely remarked that he would belt the bowl off Frank the next time he caught up with him. And then trample him with his spikes. The paths of Durocher and Frank, either through accident or design, didn't cross for nearly three years. When they at last met, there was no action.

When Durocher told people he was going to take Frank apart at the first opportunity, he wasn't merely running off at the mouth. Leo has never had any hesitation about tackling anybody. When he came up with the Yankees as a rookie, he told off Ty Cobb the first time he saw him. In 1939, he pitched into big and burly Zeke Bonura at the Polo Grounds. When Van Mungo got into his famous jam in Havana in 1941, Durocher faced him alone in the clubhouse. Doc Wilson, the Dodger trainer, was there with a firm grip on an ice-pick. But Leo shooed him out and met Van's challenge alone.

Durocher proved his moral courage after he was waived from the Yankees to Cincinnati. He had run up some bills around New York and Commissioner Landis ordered them paid out of his Cincinnati salary before it was handed over to Leo. The Yanks, when Durocher left them, had been World's Champions, whereas the Reds were tail-enders, operating on a short bankroll. He could have become a baseball bum, drifting along with the tide, but he wanted dough, and the only means he had of obtaining any were with his baseball talents. Therefore he continued to bear down with the Reds and was quickly recognized as the best shortstop in the National League, perhaps in baseball.

Early in his fourth season with the Reds, who were heading for the cellar again, Durocher was taken by the Cardinals in a trade for Paul Derringer. By the next season Leo was in the thick of a pennant fight again, the sparkplug of the never-to-be-forgotten Gas House Gang.

It is doubtful if any ballplayer, before or since, was in his element as much as Durocher was with the Cardinals. The Gas House Gang were his kind of guys, from Pepper Martin, who drove a midget racing car for relaxation, to Dizzy Dean.

The Gas House Gang won only one pennant, 1934, and won that on the last day of the season, but they were so spectacular that they are rated, by players and fans alike far higher than teams which won two or three pennants in a row.

Durocher loves to tell a story of the seventh game of the 1934 World Series when the Cards took the title by scoring an 11-0 shutout over the Tigers, Dizzy, of course, pitching. Although big Hank Greenberg was the batting star for the Tigers, Diz had him on the hip that day, fanning him three times.

Dean pitched high and inside to Greenberg, getting the ball close to his letters and above his wrists. After Diz had fanned Hank twice in this way he decided to switch tactics.

"I was watching from short to catch the signs from our catcher, Bill Delancy, so I would know which way to lean when the ball was pitched," related Leo. "I saw Diz shake off Bill a couple of times and then beckon him out to the mound. I knew what was coming. Dean, with our big lead, was going to experiment.

"Frankie Frisch, our manager, came over from second base to the mound and I moved in from short to be in on the conference.

"Dean turned to Frisch and, as innocent as a child, said, 'Where did you say this guy Greenberg's strength was, Frankie?'

"Frisch almost exploded. Here we were a couple of innings away from the pot of gold and Dean was starting to clown around.

" 'You know well enough where his strength is,' roared Frisch. 'You've been doing all right with him. Just don't pitch him high and outside where he can get the fat part of his bat against the ball.'

" 'I don't think he can hit me high and outside,' said Dean slyly.

"Frisch threw up his hands in disgust and went back to his position. Diz pitched high and outside, and Greenberg almost took his cap off with a line single to center. Dean turned to Frisch and winked. 'You're right,' he said, 'that's where his strength is.'

"When Greenberg came up for the last time, Dean pitched according to instructions and struck him out for the third time."

Leo also owes a great deal to Larry MacPhail, who gave him his first managerial chance. The Dodgers had been in the first division twice in eight years before The Lip took over. Since then they've been out of the first division once in eight years.

Listening to a few of the stories being retold about The Lip and his first boss, you get the impression that MacPhail fired Durocher every hour, on the hour.

MacPhail for his part, denies that he ever fired Durocher, but I know that Larry did bounce Leo once, back in 1939, before The Lip ever reached the Clearwater training camp. Durocher had taken the battery men to Hot Springs for a preliminary boiling out. There he got embroiled with a caddy who had tried to swipe one of his golf clubs. He also managed to win a large cash prize at a bingo game.

MacPhail left instructions for Andy High, a scout, to be put in charge of the squad and for Leo to return to New York. In the morning, the Lip was prepared to plead his case, but by then Larry was off on another tack entirely.

One story about MacPhail firing Leo is that Durocher was given the air the very night he guided the Dodgers to their first pennant in 21 years. The Dodgers clinched the pennant in Boston and there were some 50,000 screaming Brooklynites preparing a triumphal welcome for them at Grand Central Terminal in New York.

MacPhail went up to the 125th Street Station to greet the Dodgers and complete the journey with them. Durocher, however, had ordered the train to go on through, as he suspected some of the players would leave the train at 125th Street to duck the reception. So the train sped by, leaving Larry on the platform.

MacPhail and Durocher finally met at the Hotel New Yorker that night and Larry had some ideas on how the Dodgers should split up their World Series shares. Leo told him he wouldn't be admitted to the meeting. So irate did Durocher become that he refused to leave his room later in the night and pose with MacPhail for the newsreels.

That Leo was, Larry's kind of guy, there is no doubt. He hardly fills the bill as Branch Rickey's kind of guy, yet this will be his fifth season as a manager for Rickey as against four seasons managing for Larry.

An episode involving Durocher's tactics last season is revealing as to why he would please the ebullient MacPhail and might displease the conservative Rickey. The Dodgers were beating the Cubs, 2-0, but Kirby Higbe, the Brooklyn pitcher, was weakening in the closing innings. It was growing dark as the Dodgers came to bat and, if the Cubs could be prevented from getting their turn, the Dodgers would win.

"Lissen, you guys," snapped Durocher to his bench. "I'm gonna stir up a rhubarb!"

Mickey Livingston, the Chicago catcher, happened to be the nearest target, so Lippy took dead aim at him.

"Stay up there long enough, Stanky," shouted Durocher to the Dodger hitter, "and that bum will call for the wrong pitch and you'll get a hit."

Livingston, curious at this unwarranted blast, looked over at the Brooklyn bench.

"Yeah, you!" snarled Durocher. "Grimm never used you this year until the pennant race was over, did he? Couldn't take a chance with a bum like you when the chips were down!"

Mickey, not a guy to take a blast lying down, whipped off his mask and started toward the Dodger dugout, firing a return salvo. Umpire Beans Reardon, trying to save time, ordered Livingston to get behind the bat and catch. That got the Cub catcher mad at Reardon and they went at it, amid shouts from the Brooklyn bench.

Now out burst Charley Grimm from the Chicago dugout, to demand to know why Reardon was arguing with Livingston when the real culprit was Durocher. The wrangling went on, the shadows lengthened, the game was called, and the Dodgers won.

Durocher never hesitates to stoop to personal vituperation if it will help him gain his ends. Once last Summer he was abusing Murry Dickson, Cardinal pitcher, from the coaching box so violently that Umpire Lee Ballanfant begged him to lay off.

"Please, Leo," pleaded Ballanfant, "he's a nice kid—"

"I don't doubt it," interrupted Durocher, "and after the game, I'll be willing to buy Dickson a steak dinner with champagne trimmings and take him to a show. But right now I want to beat him any way I can, see?"

Joe DiMaggio is about as placid a ballplayer as I've encountered. Yet in the 1941 World Series between the Yankees and the Dodgers, Joe was jolted out of his customary calmness, because of the taunts hurled at him by Durocher from the Brooklyn bench.

In the fifth and final game of that Series, DiMaggio had words with Whitlow Wyatt, the Brooklyn pitcher, and it looked as if a first-class rhubarb was in the making. Joe and Whit were prevented from tangling, and later the pitcher visited the Yankee dressing room and he and Joe shook hands.

Behind it all was, of course, Durocher.

Naturally the riding handed out by Durocher from the bench is returned to him full force, but Leo has the hide of a rhinoceros. He doesn't mind being yelled at and takes all insults as part of the day's work. He expects to be ridden in return, and I have a sneaking suspicion he rather enjoys it.

Rickey, by the way, has a keener estimate of the peculiar talents which are Durocher's than Leo realizes. A top baseball executive once remarked to the Mahatma that Charley Dressen knew more inside baseball than Durocher.

As they were chatting they were seated in a hotel lobby where an artist was painting a beautiful mural.

"Dressen is a wonderful man for detail," admitted Branch, pointing toward the mural with his inevitable cigar. "See that painting? Well, it's conceivable that Charley might do one line of that picture even better than the artist."

"And Durocher?" probed Rickey's companion.

"Well," said Rickey, contentedly puffing his cigar, "Leo probably would get rid of the painter, grab the brush and palette, and stand in front of the mural in such a pose as to give you the impression he had done the thing!"

If you've known Durocher a long time, you gather the impression that a great many of the things he does grow out of boredom. Essentially a man of action, Leo rarely reads, not even the Western-action type of literature highly esteemed by many ballplayers. If he has to sit still, he insists on playing cards or taking a nap.

Although Durocher has literally hundreds of acquaintances, he has few close friends. There are only two men, outside of George Raft, with whom Leo is really close—Joe Herrick in St. Louis and Harry Lewine in New York. For a person who has the glittering baseball reputation that Durocher has, he is easily approachable and can keep conversation rolling at any social level. He's crazy about kids and kids go crazy over Leo.

Of his family or of his boyhood in West Springfield, Massachusetts, Durocher never talks.

The handout biography of the Dodgers is remarkably skimpy on Durocher's childhood. It records the fact that he was born at West Springfield on July 27, 1906, and comes to a dead stop between that date and the time he reached Hartford in the Eastern League some 19 years later.

Durocher's first job of record was fixing motorcycles and storage batteries at a repair shop. Leo was getting $60 a week but proved so proficient that he was taken into partnership. He took a two-week vacation to work out with Hartford, returning to the machine shop when he found he couldn't get the job away from the regular Hartford shortstop.

An injury to the regular shortstop forced the Hartford club to sign Durocher and once in the line-up, Leo, never looked back. The keen eye of Paul Krichell, Yankee scout, saw in Durocher possibilities far in excess of his anemic .220 batting average. Krich paid $7500 for Durocher, a fact which prompted Paul's boss, Ed Barrow, to ask him if he were losing his mind.

Krichell assured Barrow that Durocher could be a great shortstop and cited a long list of top major-league shortstops who were weak batters. Leo prepped for a year at Atlanta and another at St. Paul, and has never been in the minors since.

Although Durocher is the polished and urbane man-about-town now, at home anywhere from the New York "21" to Ciro's in Hollywood, with a stopover at the Pump Room in Chicago's Ambassador, he has changed but little from the rough, tough rookie who came up from St. Paul to make himself at home with the world-champion Yankees.

Then, as now, nothing fazed Durocher. In his early days with the Yankees, Leo would visit Jack Doyle's pool room after it had shut down for the night, with the regular customers gone home and the professionals playing among themselves—and for high stakes too.

Durocher is a remarkable pool player, although his habit of talking to his opponent when the latter is lining up a shot might not be considered ethical at the better billiard academies. As a matter of fact, most of Leo's talking, whether from the dugout in a ball park or in the midst of a poker game, is done for the express purpose of upsetting his competitors.

The willingness of The Lip to bet on anything was demonstrated during one of his early run-ins with Umpire George Magerkurth. One day in St. Louis, Mage told Durocher to go back into the dugout and button up his lip, two requests which Durocher to this day considers unreasonable.

"I'll give you 30 seconds by my watch or you're out of the game," roared Magerkurth.

"Why, you such-and-such," replied Leo, "I'll bet you haven't even got a watch."

Durocher was right. Magerkurth didn't have a watch and was forced to smile in spite of himself. The Lip escaped that rhubarb without penalty.

Joe Medwick used to tell a story about Durocher and Beans Reardon, an umpire who is almost as effervescent as Leo himself. It involved a double down the first baseline by Bill Nicholson of the Cubs, which was one of those hair-line things, and was called fair by Reardon.

Durocher delivered himself of a few thousand words, more or less well-chosen. Just when he sensed Reardon's patience had reached the breaking point, Leo turned to retire to the dugout, hurling one parting shot as he departed.

Since Durocher was walking away from Reardon and had his back turned when he uttered the last remark, Beans didn't quite hear what Leo said. But he had a good idea. He followed Leo to the bench.

"What did you just call me?" demanded Beans, in all of his umpirical dignity.

"Didn't you hear what I said?" demanded Durocher.

"No," said Reardon.

"Well, then," said Leo, "guess what I called you. You've been guessing all afternoon anyway."

His voice is—brassy, strident and rarely stilled. Leo never hesitates to express an opinion on any subject. And he never hesitates to pirate the opinions of others and palm them off as his own, assuming, of course, that he respects the intelligence of the person whom he first heard voice the opinion.

Very often somebody will use a word in conversation which Durocher has never heard before. If he likes it, Leo will be using it, and using it correctly, a few sentences later, a remarkable gift of observation.

When I was in Italy in the Winter of 1944–'45 on a USO-Camp Show tour with Durocher, Nick Etten, and Joe Medwick, I saw Leo give a remarkable demonstration of his powers of observation. Durocher had expressed a wish for an Italian pistol as a souvenir, an automatic known as a *Biretta*.

Sullivan brought the *Biretta* to Durocher and showed him how to strip the pistol down, an intricate process. Leo asked to watch it again, a little more slowly. He watched carefully, then took the pistol from Sullivan and proceeded to take it apart and put it together again as though he had been doing it all his life.

Durocher did a great deal of work for the USO during and after the war. He volunteered to go overseas in January, 1944, with Danny Kaye, another of his theatrical chums. Leo, toured with Kaye almost up to the day the Dodgers were scheduled to begin their Northern Spring training at Bear Mountain, a few miles up the Hudson River from New York City.

After the 1944 season ended, Durocher, in company with Etten, Medwick, and myself, toured North Africa and Italy. When the 1945 season was over, the war, too, was over, but Leo passed up the World Series and toured the Pacific, including the Philippines, Okinawa, and Japan with Kaye.

Durocher has the true actor's knack of winning an audience. One of his favorite tricks was to come on stage after I had introduced him and push the microphone away with disdain, bellowing: "Who ever heard of a guy from Brooklyn needing a mike?"

For all you may have read about red-necked ballplayers, baseball is not without its suave personalities. When he mellowed in his later years, John McGraw could fit in anywhere, with anybody. When Bill Terry chose to turn on the charm, he made a welcome guest in any drawing room.

Yet I doubt if anybody in baseball moves about as freely, in as many varied circles, as Durocher. On his USO tours, The Lip was equally at home with the enlisted man and the top brass.

Durocher has the knack of adapting himself to situations. That he learned this expediency the hard way there is no doubt, but it is a trait which has stood him in good stead. Leo's native intelligence, coupled with an amazing resiliency, makes him a hard man to keep down.

The more you see of Durocher through the years, the more you realize how rash it is to make any predictions about him. You wouldn't have given a nickel for his chances when Rickey succeeded MacPhail as the boss-man in Brooklyn, yet Leo is still there, as large as life and twice as noisy.

When Rickey came to Brooklyn, he was upset over reports that there had been a great deal of gambling on the club in the 1942 season, that there had been card games for high stakes, and much wagering on the ponies. The Mahatma made it plain that any gambling other than modest nickel-and-dime games must cease, instanter and forthwith.

Durocher hit the sawdust trail with a vengeance. In a mass interview with the press, immediately following Rickey's pronunciamento, The Lip declared that all gambling, other than for five-and-ten Woolworth stakes, was outlawed on the Brooklyn club as of that moment. He had hardly finished this virtuous declaration when he was called out of the conference room to answer a phone call.

As Leo left the room one of the writers remarked, "There goes a reformed man—pro tem."

PART FOUR

BOBBY THOMSON

The Day Bobby Hit the Home Run

Sports Illustrated   October 1960

Roger Kahn's depiction of the Giants–Dodgers final play-off game on October 3, 1951 has gone a long way toward etching Bobby Thomson's home run into the minds of baseball fans forever.

by Roger Kahn

S ome days—they come rarely—are charged with public events so unexpected, so shocking, so far beyond the limits of belief, that the events are not really public at all. Their impact thrusts them into the private lives of millions of people, who forever after remember these events in personal terms.

Pearl Harbor day was like that. ("I was listening to the radio, a football game, when I heard about the bombing.") There was the day President Roosevelt died. ("I was riding the subway and the conductor told me. He was crying.") And then there was the day in the most exciting of all baseball seasons, when Bobby Thomson hit his home run . . .

The night before nearly everyone slept well. Bobby Thomson was troubled because he had struck out with the bases full, but after a steak dinner and a few beers, he relaxed. Ralph Branca fell asleep quickly. He had pitched on Sunday, the last day of the regular season, and on Monday in the first game of the playoff. Tomorrow, October 3, 1951, would be Wednesday, and Branca did not expect that he would be called on to pitch again so soon.

Sal Maglie, who knew he was to start for the New York Giants, spent a comfortable night in his room at the Concourse Plaza Hotel. For all his intensity, Maglie had learned to control his nerves. So, to a degree, had Don Newcombe, who was to start for the Brooklyn Dodgers. "I can always sleep," Newcombe said, a little proudly. "I don't need to take pills like some guys do the night before they pitch."

Charley Dressen, who managed the Dodgers, went out to an Italian restaurant called Rocco's and ate a dinner of clams, mussels, lobsters and spaghetti with hot sauce. A few people asked him how he felt about tomorrow's game and Dressen told them he wasn't worried. "Our ball club is ready," he said.

One man who did feel restlessness was Andy Pafko, the Dodgers' new left fielder. The Dodgers had traded for Pafko at midseason, in a move the newspapers called pennant insurance and Pafko, reading the papers, was impressed. Now he felt that the pennant was almost his personal responsibility. Lying in his room at the Hotel St. George in Brooklyn, he thought of his wife, Ellen, in Chicago. He had sent her a ticket to New York so she could watch him play with the Dodgers in the World Series. Next year there would be time to find an apartment together in Brooklyn, but for the moment Andy Pafko was alone. Perhaps it was loneliness as much as pressure that depressed him.

Although New York City was bright with the quickening pace of autumn, none of the ballplayers went out on the town. Everywhere, harboring their energies, they went to bed at about 11 o'clock, and soon, everywhere, they slept.

These were two tough and gifted baseball teams. The Dodgers had been built around such sluggers as Duke Snider and Gil Hodges, and in Jackie Robinson they had the finest competitor in baseball. For months that year the Dodgers won big and won often. On the night of August 11 they had been in first place, a full 13 games ahead of the Giants, who were their closest competitors.

Under Leo Durocher the Giants were combative, strong in pitching and opportunism, concentrated in themselves. Bobby Thomson, like the other Giants, knew none of the Dodgers socially; the teams did not fraternize. He thought that Gil Hodges was a pleasant man but that the rest of the Dodgers were unpleasant. This was a sermon Durocher had preached ceaselessly throughout the last months of the season until finally the ballplayers came unquestioningly to believe their manager.

Durocher's Giants, jelling slowly, spent some of May in last place. It was only when Willie Mays was called up from Minneapolis and Thomson became the regular third baseman that the team began to show fire.

Then, from August 11 on, the Giants blazed, winning 37 games and losing only seven under demanding, unrelenting pressure.

The Dodgers, playing .500 ball as some of their sluggers slumped, were nonetheless uncatchable by all the traditions of baseball. But the Giants, establishing a new tradition, caught the uncatchable, forced them into a playoff and won the first game 3–1, defeating Ralph Branca at Ebbets Field. Then Clem Labine, a Dodger rookie, shut out the Giants at the Polo Grounds. The score was 10–0, but the game was close for some time and seemed to turn when Thomson, with bases full, struck out on a 3-and-2 pitch, a jumping curve that hooked wide of the plate.

No one expected the deciding game of the playoff to be easy, but no one, not Thomson, or Branca, or Durocher, or Dressen, felt any dramatic foreshadowing of what was ahead. The game would be tense, but they'd all been tense lately. That was all. It was against this background of tension, which the players accepted as a part of life, that everyone slept the night before.

Robert B. Thomson, brown-haired, tall and swift, said goodby to his mother a little before 10 a.m. and drove his blue Mercury to the Staten Island Ferry. The Thomsons lived on Flagg Place in New Dorp, once an independent village, now a community within the borough of Richmond. As he drove, Thomson thought about the game. "If I can just get 3 for 4," he mused, "then the old Jints will be all right." The thought comforted him. He'd been hitting well, and 3 for 4 seemed a reasonable goal.

Ralph T. Branca, black-haired, tall and heavy-limbed, said goodby to his mother in suburban Mount Vernon, N.Y., the town where he had grown up, and drove off in his new Oldsmobile. He felt a little stiff from all his recent pitching. It would take him a long time to warm up, should Dressen need him in relief.

It was a gray day, darkened with the threat of rain. The temperature was warm enough—in the high 60s—but the crowd, waiting for the gates of the Polo Grounds bleachers to open, was smaller than the one which had waited in bright sunshine the day before.

Most of the players arrived by car, but Andrew Pafko came by subway, an hour's ride from downtown Brooklyn. "I'll beat the crowd," he decided, "so there's no sense wasting money on a cab." The crowd, it was to develop, was scarcely worth beating; 34,320, some 15,000 under standing-room capacity.

As a ball park, the Polo Grounds was unique; oddly shaped and with clubhouses 600 feet from the dugouts. It was, actually, a football horseshoe and as such made strange demands upon pitchers. The foul line in right field ran only 250 feet until it reached the lower deck of the grandstands. The left-field line ran slightly longer, but in left a scoreboard was fixed to the façade of the upper deck, a façade that extended several yards closer to the plate than did the lower stands. A short fly, drifting down toward a fielder, could become a home run merely by grazing that projecting scoreboard.

Both walls fell away sharply, and the fence in center field was 485 feet out. The pitching rule was simply to make the batter hit to center, when distance didn't matter. The outfielding rule was to crowd the middle. The right and left fielders conceded drives down the line and tried to prevent hits from carrying into the deep all in left and right center. At the Polo Grounds, outfielders stood in a tightly bunched row, all seemingly about the same distance from home plate.

Back of center field stood an old green building which contained clubhouses, a dining room for press and an apartment for Horace Stoneham, the Giants' owner. Since both Durocher and Dressen believed in intensive managing, each team was gathered for a meeting in that green building shortly before noon. The announced purpose was to review hitters, although the two teams had played each other 24 times previously that season and there was nothing fresh or new to say about anyone.

"Jam Mueller on the fists," Dressen told Don Newcombe. "Keep the ball low and away to Thomson. Don't let him pull it." Dressen concluded, with more warmth than he customarily displayed: "Look, I know it's tough to have to play this game, but remember we did our best all year. So today, let's just go out and do the best we can."

"Don't give Hodges anything inside," Durocher told Maglie. Then, later: "We haven't quit all year. We won't quit now. Let's go get 'em."

During batting practice Branca was standing near the cage with Pee Wee Reese and Jackie Robinson. "You guys get butterflies?" a reporter asked.

"No matter how long you been playing, you still get butterflies before the big ones," Reese said. Robinson laughed and Branca nodded solemnly. Ralph's long face, in repose, was sad or, perhaps, deadpan. One never knew whether he was troubled by what was around him or whether he was about to laugh.

The game began badly for the Giants. Sal Maglie, who had won 23 games and beaten the Dodgers five times that season, walked Reese and Duke Snider in the first inning. Jackie Robinson came up and lined Maglie's first pitch safely into left field for a single. Reese scored, and the Dodgers were ahead 1–0.

Newcombe was fast but not untouchable, and in the second inning Lockman reached him for a single. Thomson followed with a sharp drive to left, his first hit, and briefly the Giants seemed to be rallying. But very briefly. Running with his head down, Thomson charged past first base and had almost reached second before he noticed that Lockman had stopped there. Thomson was tagged out in a rundown, an embarrassing end to the threat.

When the day grew darker and the lights were turned on as the third inning began, the ball park buzzed with countless versions of a joke: "Well, now maybe Thomson will be able to see what he's doing."

During the fifth Thomson doubled, his second hit, and Branca began to throw. Newcombe pitched out of the inning easily, but Branca threw a little longer. He wasn't snapping curves or firing fast balls. He was just working to loosen his arm, shoulder and back.

Branca threw again during the sixth inning, and when Monte Irvin doubled to left in the seventh, Branca began to throw hard. He felt loose by then. His fast ball was alive. Carl Erskine, warming up next to him, was bouncing his curve, but Branca had good control and good stuff.

With Irvin at second, Lockman pushed a bunt in front of the plate and Rube Walker, the Dodger catcher, grabbed the ball and threw to Billy Cox at third. Irvin beat the throw and now Thomson came to bat with the tying run at third base late in a 1–0 ball game.

Bearing down, Newcombe threw only strikes. After two, Thomson fouled off a fast ball. Then he hit another fast ball deep into center field and Irvin scored easily after the catch. As the eighth inning began, the score was 1–1.

"I got nothing left, nothing," Newcombe announced as he walked into the Dodger dugout. Jackie Robinson and Roy Campanella, who was not playing that day because he had pulled a thigh muscle, took Newcombe aside.

"My arm's tight," Newcombe said.

"Obscenity," Robinson replied. "You go out there and pitch until your obscene arm falls off."

"Roomie," Campanella said, "you ain't gonna quit on us now. You gonna hum that pea for us, roomie."

While the two built a fire under Newcombe, other Dodgers were making the inning miserable for both Maglie and Thomson. Reese and Snider opened with singles to right, and when Maglie threw a curve in the dirt and past Wes Westrum, Reese scored and Snider sped to third. Then Maglie walked Robinson, and the Dodgers, ahead 2–1, once again had runners at first and third.

Pafko pulled a bounding ball up the third-base line and Thomson, breaking nicely, reached backhand for it. The play required a delicate touch; the ball glanced off the heel of Thomson's glove and skidded away from him. Snider scored, making it 3–1 Brooklyn, and Pafko was credited with a single. Then Billy Cox followed with a fierce one-hopper, again at Thomson's sector.

One thought—"Get in front of it"—crossed Thomson's mind. He did, hanging recklessly. There were other times at third when Thomson had thought of hard smashes coming up and hitting him in the face. This time he didn't. He thought only of blocking the ball with his glove, his arm, his chest. But the ball bounced high and carried over his shoulder into left field. The Dodgers had their third run of the inning and a 4–1 lead.

Newcombe blazed through the eighth, his arm no longer tight, and Larry Jansen retired the Dodgers in the ninth. "Come on," Durocher shouted as the last of the ninth began. "We can still get 'em. Come on."

Newcombe threw two quick strikes to Alvin Dark. "Got to get my bat on the ball," Dark thought. "Just get my bat on it."

Newcombe threw again, and Dark tapped a bounder into the hole in the right side of the infield. Both Hodges and Robinson broke for the ball and Newcombe ran to cover first base. Hodges, straining, touched the ball with the tip of his mitt and deflected it away from Robinson. Perhaps if he had not touched it Robinson could have made the play. As it was, Dark reached first on a single.

It was then that Dressen made a curious decision. He let Hodges hold the bag on Dark, as though Dark as a base-runner were important. Actually, of course, Dark could have stolen second, third and home without affecting the game. The Giants needed three runs to tie, not one, and the Dodgers needed only outs.

Don Mueller, up next, quickly bounced a single through the right side —close to Hodges' normal fielding depth—and the Giants had runners at first and third. All around the Polo Grounds people stood up, but not to leave.

With Monte Irvin coming to bat, Dressen walked to the mound. Branca and Erskine were throwing in the bullpen, and Clyde Sukeforth, the bullpen coach, had told Dressen that Branca was fast and loose. But on the way to the mound the Dodger manager thought about catching, not pitching.

The right thing

Campanella had a way with Newcombe. He knew how to needle the big pitcher to fury, and this fury added speed to Newcombe's fast ball. Walking to the mound, Dressen wondered about replacing Rube Walker with Campanella. There was only one drawback. Foul territory at the Polo Grounds was extensive. A rodeo, billed as colossal, was once staged entirely in the foul area there. Campanella, with his bad leg, could catch, but he could not run after foul pops. Dressen thought of Hodges and Cox, both sure-handed, both agile. They could cover for Campanella to some extent. But there was all that area directly behind home plate where no one would be able to help Campy at all. Dressen thought of a foul pop landing safely, and he thought of the newspapers the next day. The second-guessing would be fierce, and he didn't want that. No, Dressen decided, it wouldn't be worth that. He chatted with Newcombe for a moment and went back to the dugout. When Irvin fouled out to Hodges, Dressen decided that he had done the right thing.

Then Newcombe threw an outside fast ball to Whitey Lockman, and Lockman doubled to left. Dark scored, making it 4–2, but Mueller, in easily at third, slid badly and twisted his ankle. He could neither rise nor walk. Clint Hartung went in to run for him, and action was suspended while Mueller, on a stretcher, was carried to the distant Giant clubhouse.

"Branca's ready," Clyde Sukeforth told Charley Dressen on the intercom that ran from dugout to bullpen.

"O.K.," Dressen said. "I want him."

Branca felt strong and loose as he started his long walk in from the bullpen. At that moment he had only one thought. Thomson was the next batter, and he wanted to get ahead of Thomson. Branca never pitched in rigid patterns. He adjusted himself to changing situations, and his thought now was simply to get his first pitch over the plate with something on it.

Coming into the infield, he remembered the pregame conversation with the newspaperman. "Any butterflies?" he said to Robinson and Reese. They grinned, but not very widely.

At the mound, Dressen handed Branca the ball and said: "Get him out." Without another word the manager turned and walked back to the dugout.

Watching Branca take his eight warmup pitches, Thomson thought of his own goal. He had two hits. Another now would give him his 3 for 4. It would also tie the score.

"Boy," Durocher said to Thomson, "if you ever hit one, hit one now." Thomson nodded but said nothing. Then he stepped up to the plate.

Branca's first pitch was a fast ball, hip-high over the inside corner. "Should have swung at that," Thomson told himself, backing out of the box.

"I got my strike," thought Branca. Now it was time to come up and in with a fast ball. Now it was time for a bad pitch that might tempt Thomson to waste a swing. If he went for the bad ball, chances were he'd miss. If he took it, Branca would still be ready to come back with a curve, low and away. Branca was moving the ball around, a basic point when pitching to good hitters.

The pitch came in high and tight, just where Branca had wanted it. Thomson swung hard and the ball sailed out toward left.

"Get down, get down," screamed Billy Cox as the line drive carried high over his head.

"I got a chance at it," thought Andy Pafko, bolting back toward the wall.

Then the ball was gone, under the overhanging scoreboard, over the high wall, gone deep into the seats in lower left. For seconds, which seemed like minutes, the crowd sat dumb. Then came the roar. It was a roar matched all across the country, wherever people sat at radio or television sets, a roar of delight, a roar of horror, but mostly a roar of utter shock. It was a moment when all the country roared and when an office worker in a tall building in Wall Street, hearing a cry rise all about her, wondered if war had been declared.

As the ball sailed into the stands, Thomson danced around the bases, skipping and leaping. The Giants crowded from their dugout to home plate. Ed Stanky, the second baseman, ran to Durocher, jumped on the manager's back, wrestled him to the ground and hugged him.

"It can't be"

In left, Pafko stood stunned. Then he started to walk slowly toward the clubhouse, telling himself over and over: "It can't be." Most of the Dodgers were walking before Thomson reached second base, but Jackie Robinson held his ground. He wanted to make sure that Thomson touched all bases before conceding that the Giants had won, 5–4, before conceding that the pennant race was over.

Clyde Sukeforth gathered gear in the bullpen, and nearby Carl Erskine turned to Clem Labine. "That's the first time I've ever seen a big fat wallet go flying into the seats," Erskine said.

As Thomson touched home plate, the Giants lifted him to their shoulders. Then, inexplicably, they lowered him, and everyone ran for the clubhouse. Champagne was waiting. "Gee whiz," Thomson said. "Gee whiz."

Wes Westrum and Clint Hartung grabbed Ed Stanky, who liked to boast that he had never been drunk, and pinned him to a rubbing table. Westrum poured champagne into Stanky's mouth. "You're gonna get drunk now," he shouted. Westrum turned to the rubbing table, where Mueller lay, ice packs at his ankle. "Hey, Don," he shouted and emptied a magnum over the injured leg.

"Isn't this the damndest thing you ever saw?" Durocher said.

"Gee whiz," Thomson said. "Gee whiz."

"How the hell did you go into second with Lockman there?" Coach Fred Fitzsimmons said to Thomson. "But the hell with that," he added, and kissed Thomson damply.

"Congratulations," Charley Dressen said to Durocher. "I told you we'd finish one-two. Well, we did, and I'm number two."

"Gee whiz," Thomson said.

In the Dodger dressing room, Branca wept a little, showered slowly and, after submitting to some questioning, asked reporters to leave him alone. Then he went to the Oldsmobile, where his fiancée, blonde Ann Mulvey, was waiting with Father Frank Rowley of Fordham.

"Why me?" Branca said inside the car. "I don't smoke. I don't drink. I don't run around. Baseball is my whole life. Why me?"

"God chose you," the priest said, "because He knew you had faith and strength enough to bear this cross."

Branca nodded and felt a little better.

Thomson went from the ball park to a CBS studio where he appeared on Perry Como's regular Wednesday night television show. Everywhere he went he was cheered, and always three thoughts ran through his mind. The old Jints had won. He had pushed his runs-batted-in total up over 100. He had got his 3 for 4.

When Thomson reached the house in New Dorp, his older brother, Jim, was waiting for him. "Do you know what you've done?" Jim said, all intensity and earnestness.

Only then, some six hours after the event, did Bobby Thomson realize that his home run was something that other people would remember for all the rest of his days.

Winning by Striking Out

*Walter Wellesley "Red" Smith holds the unique distinc-
tion of being both a member of the Baseball Hall of Fame
and winner of a Pulitzer Prize (in 1976, for commentary).
Here he shows why he deserved such honors, capturing the
quirky joys of both baseball and life in Brooklyn in a pair
of "Sports of the Times" columns.*

by Red Smith

It could happen only in Brooklyn. Nowhere else in this broad, untidy
universe, not in Bedlam nor in Babel nor in the remotest psycho-
pathic ward nor the sleaziest padded cell could The Thing be.

Only in the ancestral home of the Dodgers which knew the goofy
glories of Babe Herman could a man win a World Series game by striking
out.

Only on the banks of the chuckling Gowanus, where the dizzy-days of
Uncle Wilbert Robinson still are fresh and dear in memory, could a team
fling away its chance for the championship of the world by making four
outs in the last inning.

It shouldn't happen to a MacPhail!

As Robert W. Service certainly did not say it:

> Oh, them Brooklyn Wights have seen strange sights.
> But the strangest they ever did see,
> Today was revealed in Ebbets Field
> When Owen fumbled strike three!

Among all the Yankee fans in the gathering of 33,813 who watched the fourth game of the World Series, only one was smiling when Tommy Henrich faced Hugh Casey in the ninth inning with two out, nobody on base, the Dodgers in front by one run, and a count of three balls and two strikes on the hitter.

That one gay New Yorker was Jim Farley, whose pink bald head gleamed in a box behind the Dodger dugout. He sat there just laughing and laughing—because he hadn't bought the Yankees, after all.

Then The Thing happened.

Henrich swung at a waist-high pitch over the inside corner. He missed. So did Catcher Mickey Owen. Henrich ran to first. Owen ran after the ball but stopped at the grandstand screen.

That was Mickey's biggest mistake. He should have kept right on running all the way back home to Springfield, Missouri.

That way he wouldn't have been around to see and suffer when Joe DiMaggio singled, Charley Keller doubled, Bill Dickey walked, Joe Gordon doubled, and the Dodgers went down in horrendous defeat, 7 to 4.

Out of the rooftop press box in that awful instant came one long, agonized groan. It was the death cry of hundreds of thousands of unwritten words, the expiring moan of countless stories which were to have been composed in tribute to Casey.

For just as Owen has taken his place among the Merkles and Snodgrasses and Zimmermans and all the other famous goats of baseball, so now Casey belongs with the immortal suckers of all time.

The all-American fall guy of this series—round, earnest Casey—was only one pitch short of complete redemption for his sins of yesterday.

Remember that it was he whom the Yankees battered for the winning hits in the third game of the series. It was he whom Larry MacPhail castigated for failing, in MacPhail's judgment, to warm up properly before relieving Fred Fitzsimmons yesterday.

Now he was making all his critics eat their words. He was making a holy show of the experts who snorted last night that he was a chump and a fathead to dream that he could throw his fast stuff past the Yankees.

He was throwing it past them, one pitch after another, making a hollow mockery of the vaunted Yankee power as each superb inning telescoped into the one before.

No one ever stepped more cheerfully onto a hotter spot than did Casey when he walked in to relieve Johnny Allen in the fifth inning.

The Yankees were leading, 3 to 2, had the bases filled with two out, and the hitting star of the series, Joe Gordon, was at bat.

Casey made Gordon fly to Jim Wasdell for the final putout, and from there on he fought down the Yankees at every turn.

He made Red Rolfe pop up after Johnny Sturm singled with two out in the sixth. He breezed through the seventh despite a disheartening break when DiMaggio got a single on a puny ground ball that the Dodgers swore was foul.

Leo Durocher said enough short, indelicate words to Umpire Lary Goetz on that decision to unnerve completely anyone within earshot. But Casey, determined to hear no evil and pitch no evil, shut his ears and shut out the Yanks.

In the clutch, the great Keller popped up. The ever-dangerous Dickey could get nothing better than a puerile tap to the mound.

So it went, and as Casey drew ever closer to victory the curious creatures that are indigenous to Flatbush came crawling out of the woodwork. They did weird little dances in the aisles and shouted and stamped and rattled cowbells aloft and quacked derisively on little reedy horns.

Their mouths were open, their breath was indrawn for the last, exultant yell—and then The Thing happened.

Far into this night of horror, historians pored over the records, coming up at last with a World Series precedent for "The Thing."

It happened in the first game of the 1907 series between the Cubs and Detroit, when the Tigers went into the ninth inning leading, 3 to 1. With two out and two strikes against pinch-hitter Del Howard, Detroit's Wild Bill Donovan called catcher Charley Schmidt to the mound for a conference.

"Hold your glove over the corner," Donovan said, "and I'll curve a strike into it."

He did, but Schmidt dropped the strike, Howard reached base, and the Cubs went on to tie the score. The game ended in darkness, still tied after twelve innings, and the Cubs took the next four contests in a row.

That's about all, except that it should be said the experts certainly knew their onions when they raved about the Yankee power. It was the most powerful strikeout of all time.

Next to Godliness

by Red Smith

The game has been over for half an hour now, and still a knot of worshippers stands clustered, as around a shrine, out in right field adoring the spot on the wall which Cookie Lavagetto's line drive smote. It was enough to get a new contract for Happy Chandler. Things were never like this when Judge Landis was in.

Happy has just left his box. For twenty minutes crowds clamored around him, pushing, elbowing, shouting hoarsely for the autograph they snooted after the first three World Series games. Unable to get to Lavagetto, they were unwilling to depart altogether empty-handed. Being second choice to Cookie, Happy now occupies the loftiest position he has yet enjoyed in baseball. In Brooklyn, next to Lavagetto is next to godliness.

At the risk of shattering this gazette's reputation for probity, readers are asked to believe these things happened in Ebbets Field:

After 136 pitches, Floyd Bevens, of the Yankees, had the only no-hit ball game ever played in a World Series. But he threw 137 and lost, 3 to 2.

With two out in the ninth inning, a preposterously untidy box score showed one run for the Dodgers, no hits, ten bases on balls, seven men left on base, and two more aboard waiting to be left. There still are two out in the ninth.

Hugh Casey, who lost two World Series games on successive days in 1941, now is the only pitcher in the world who has won two on successive days. One pitch beat him in 1941, a third strike on Tommy Henrich, which Mickey Owen didn't catch. This time he threw only one pitch, a strike to Tommy Henrich, and this time he caught the ball himself for a double play.

Harry Taylor, who has had a sore arm half the summer, threw eleven pitches in the first inning, allowed two hits and a run, and fled with the bases filled and none out. Hal Gregg, who has had nothing at all this summer—not even so much as a sore arm—came in to throw five pitches and retired the side. Thereafter Gregg was a four-hit pitcher until nudged aside for a pinch hitter in the seventh.

In the first inning George Stirnweiss rushed behind second base and stole a hit from Pee Wee Reese. In the third Johnny Lindell caught Jackie Robinson's foul fly like Doc Blanchard hitting the Notre Dame line and came to his feet unbruised. In the fourth Joe DiMaggio caught Gene Hermanski's monstrous drive like a well-fed banquet guest picking his teeth and broke down as he did so. Seems he merely twisted an ankle, though, and wasn't damaged.

Immediately after that play—and this must be the least credible of the day's wonders—the Dodger Sym-phoney band serenaded Happy Chandler. The man who threw out the first manager for Brooklyn this year did not applaud.

In the seventh inning two Sym-phoney bandsmen dressed in motley did a tap dance on the roof of the Yankees' dugout. This amused the commissioner, who has never openly opposed clowning.

In the eighth Hermanski smashed a drive to the scoreboard. Henrich backed against the board and leaped either four or fourteen feet into the air. He stayed aloft so long he looked like an empty uniform hanging in its locker. When he came down he had the ball.

In the ninth Lindell pressed his stern against the left-field fence and caught a smash by Bruce Edwards. Jake Pitler, coaching for the Dodgers at first base, flung his hands aloft and his cap to the ground.

And finally Bucky Harris, who has managed major-league teams in Washington, Detroit, Boston, Philadelphia, and New York, violated all ten commandments of the dugout by ordering Bevens to walk Peter Reiser and put the winning run on base.

Lavagetto, who is slightly less experienced than Harris, then demonstrated why this maneuver is forbidden in the managers' guild.

Cookie hit the fence. A character named Al Gionfriddo ran home. Running, he turned and beckoned frantically to a character named Eddie Miksis. Eddie Miksis ran home.

Dodgers pummeled Lavagetto. Gionfriddo and Miksis pummeled each other. Cops pummeled Lavagetto. Ushers pummeled Lavagetto. Ushers pummeled one another. Three soda butchers in white ran onto the field and threw forward passes with their white caps. In the tangle Bevens could not be seen.

The unhappiest man in Brooklyn is sitting up here now in the far end of the press box. The *v* on his typewriter is broken. He can't writer either Lavagetto or Bevens.

JOE DiMAGGIO

The Streak of Streaks

Chance: New Directions for Statistics and
Computing   November 1989

*Of the recent numbers—happy baseball analysts, few are
as qualified as Stephen Jay Gould, professor of anthropol-
ogy at Yale University. Yet, after taking a statistician's
look at Joe DiMaggio's 56-game hitting streak, Gould reports that the feat shames any numerical characteriza-
tion.*

By Stephen Jay Gould

My father was a court stenographer. At his less than princely
salary, we watched Yankee games from the bleachers or high
in the third deck. But one of the judges had season tickets, so
we occasionally sat in the lower boxes when hizzoner couldn't attend.
One afternoon, while DiMaggio was going 0 for 4 against, of all people,
the lowly St. Louis Browns (now the even lowlier Baltimore Orioles), the
great man fouled one in our direction. "Catch it, Dad," I screamed. "You
never get them," he replied, but stuck up his hand like the Statue of
Liberty—and the ball fell right in. I mailed it to DiMaggio, and, bless
him, he actually sent the ball back, signed and in a box marked "insured." Insured, that is, to make me the envy of the neighborhood, and
DiMaggio the model and hero of my life.

I met DiMaggio a few years ago on a small playing field at the Presidio of San Francisco. My son, wearing DiMaggio's old number 5 on his Little League jersey, accompanied me, exactly one generation after my father caught that ball. DiMaggio gave him a pointer or two on batting and then signed a baseball for him. One generation passeth away, and another generation cometh: But the earth abideth forever.

My son, uncoached by Dad, and given the chance that comes but once in a lifetime, asked DiMaggio as his only query about life and career: "Suppose you had walked every time up during one game of your 56-game hitting streak? Would the streak have been over?" DiMaggio replied that, under 1941 rules, the streak would have ended, but that this unfair statute has since been revised, and such a game would not count today.

My son's choice for a single question tells us something vital about the nature of legend. A man may labor for a professional lifetime, especially in sport or in battle, but posterity needs a single transcendant event to fix him in permanent memory. Every hero must be a Wellington on the right side of his personal Waterloo; generality of excellence is too diffuse. The unambiguous factuality of a single achievement is adamantine. Detractors can argue forever about the general tenor of your life and works, but they can never erase a great event.

In 1941, as I gestated in my mother's womb, Joe DiMaggio got at least one hit in each of 56 successive games. Most records are only incrementally superior to runners-up; Roger Maris hit 61 homers in 1961, but Babe Ruth hit 60 in 1927 and 59 in 1921, while Hank Greenberg (1938) and Jimmy Foxx (1932) both hit 58. But DiMaggio's 56-game hitting streak is ridiculously and almost unreachably far from all challengers (Wee Willie Keeler and Pete Rose, both with 44, come second). Among sabermetricians (a happy neologism based on an acronym for members of the Society for American Baseball Research, and referring to the statistical mavens of the sport)—a contentious lot not known for agreement about anything—we find virtual consensus that DiMaggio's 56-game hitting streak is the greatest accomplishment in the history of baseball, if not all modern sport.

The reasons for this respect are not far to seek. Single moments of unexpected supremacy—Johnny Vander Meer's back-to-back no-hitters in 1938, Don Larsen's perfect game in the 1956 World Series—can occur at any time to almost anybody, and have an irreducibly capricious character. Achievements of a full season—such as Maris's 61 homers and Ted Williams's batting average of .406, also posted in 1941 and not equaled since—have a certain overall majesty, but they don't demand unfailing consistency every single day; you can slump for a while, so long as your average holds. But a streak must be absolutely exceptionless; you are not allowed a single day of subpar play, or even bad luck. You bat only four or five times in an average game. Sometimes two or three of these efforts yield walks, and you get only one or two shots at a hit. Moreover, as tension mounts and notice increases, your life becomes unbearable. Reporters dog your every step; fans are even more intrusive than usual (one stole DiMaggio's favorite bat right in the middle of his streak). You cannot make a single mistake.

Thus Joe DiMaggio's 56-game hitting streak is both the greatest factual achievement in the history of baseball and a principal icon of American mythology. What shall we do with such a central item of our cultural history?

Statistics and mythology may seem the most unlikely bedfellows. How can we quantify Caruso or measure *Middlemarch?* But if God could mete out heaven with the span (Isaiah 40:12), perhaps we can say something useful about hitting streaks. The statistics of "runs," defined as continuous series of good or bad results (including baseball's streaks and slumps), is a well-developed branch of the profession, and can yield clear —but wildly counterintuitive—results. (The fact that we find these conclusions so surprising is the key to appreciating DiMaggio's achievement, the point of this article, and the gateway to an important insight about the human mind.)

Start with a phenomenon that nearly everyone both accepts and considers well understood—"hot hands" in basketball. Now and then, someone just gets hot, and can't be stopped. Basket after basket falls in—or out as with "cold hands," when a man can't buy a bucket for love or money (choose your cliche). The reason for this phenomenon is clear enough: It lies embodied in the maxim, "When you're hot, you're hot; and when you're not, you're not." You get that touch, build confidence; all nervousness fades, you find your rhythm; swish, swish, swish. Or you miss a few, get rattled, endure the booing, experience despair; hands start shaking and you realize that you shoulda stayed in bed.

Everybody knows about hot hands. The only problem is that no such phenomenon exists. The Stanford psychologist Amos Tversky studied every basket made by the Philadelphia 76ers for more than a season. He found, first of all, that the probability of making a second basket did not rise following a successful shot. Moreover, the number of "runs," or baskets in succession, was no greater than what a standard random, or coin-tossing, model would predict. (If the chance of making each basket is 0.5, for example, a reasonable value for good shooters, five hits in a row will occur, on average, once in 32 sequences—just as you can expect to toss five successive heads about once in 32 times, or 0.5^5.)

Of course Larry Bird, the great forward of the Boston Celtics, will have more sequences of five than Joe Airball—but not because he has greater will or gets in that magic rhythm more often. Larry has longer runs because his average success rate is so much higher, and random models predict more frequent and longer sequences. If Larry shoots field goals at 0.6 probability of success, he will get five in a row about once every 13 sequences (0.6⁵). If Joe, by contrast, shoots only 0.3, he will get his five straight only about once in 412 times. In other words, we need no special explanation for the apparent pattern of long runs. There is no ineffable "causality of circumstance" (if I may call it that), no definite reason born of the particulars that make for heroic myths—courage in the clinch, strength in adversity, etc. You only have to know a person's ordinary play in order to predict his sequences. (I rather suspect that we are convinced of the contrary not only because we need myths so badly, but also because we remember the successes and simply allow the failures to fade from memory. More on this later.) But how does this revisionist pessimism work for baseball?

My colleague Ed Purcell, Nobel laureate in physics but, for purposes of this subject, just another baseball fan, has done a comprehensive study of all baseball streak and slump records. His firm conclusion is easily and swiftly summarized. Nothing ever happened in baseball above and beyond the frequency predicted by coin-tossing models. The longest runs of wins or losses are as long as they should be, and occur about as often as they ought to. Even the hapless Orioles, at 0 and 21 to start last season, only fell victim to the laws of probability (and not to the vengeful God of racism, out to punish major league baseball's only black manager).

But "treasure your exceptions," as the old motto goes. There is one major exception, and absolutely only one—one sequence so many standard deviations above the expected distribution that it should not have occurred at all: Joe DiMaggio's 56-game hitting streak in 1941. The intuition of baseball aficionados has been vindicated. Purcell calculated that to make it likely (probability greater than 50 percent) that a run of even 50 games will occur once in the history of baseball up to now (and 56 is a lot more than 50 in this kind of league), baseball's rosters would have to include either 4 lifetime .400 batters or 52 lifetime .350 batters over careers of 1,000 games. In actuality, only 3 men have lifetime batting averages in excess of .350, and no one is anywhere near .400 (Ty Cobb at .367, Rogers Hornsby at .358, and Shoeless Joe Jackson at .356). DiMaggio's streak is the most extraordinary thing that ever happened in American sports. He sits on the shoulders of two bearers—mythology and science. For Joe DiMaggio accomplished what no other ballplayer has done. He beat the hardest taskmaster of all, a woman who makes Nolan Ryan's fastball look like a cantaloupe in slow motion—Lady Luck.

A larger issue lies behind basic documentation and simple appreciation. For we don't understand the truly special character of DiMaggio's record because we are so poorly equipped, whether by habits of culture or by our modes of cognition, to grasp the workings of random processes and patterning in nature.

The old Persian tentmaker, Omar Khayyám, understood the quandary of our lives:

> Into this Universe, and Why not knowing,
> Nor Whence, like Water willy-nilly flowing;
> And out of it, as Wind along the Waste,
> I know not Whither, willy-nilly blowing.

> *(Rubaiyat of Omar Khayyám,*
> Edward Fitzgerald, tr.)

But we cannot bear it. We must have comforting answers. We see pattern, for pattern surely exists, even in a purely random world. (Only a highly nonrandom universe could possibly cancel out the clumping that we perceive as pattern. We think we see constellations because the stars are dispersed at random in the heavens, and therefore clump in our sight.) Our error lies not in the perception of pattern but in automatically imbuing pattern with meaning, especially with meaning that can bring us comfort, or dispel confusion. Again, Omar took the more honest approach:

> Ah, love! could you and I with Fate conspire
> To grasp this sorry Scheme of Things entire,
> Would not we shatter it to bits—
> and then
> Re-mould it nearer to the Heart's Desire!

We, instead, have tried to impose that "heart's desire" upon the actual earth and its largely random patterns:

> All Nature is but Art, unknown to thee;
> All Chance, Direction, which thou canst not see;
> All Discord, Harmony not understood:
> All partial Evil, universal Good.

> (Alexander Pope, *Essay on Man,*
> end of Epistle 1)

Sorry to wax so poetic and tendentious about something that leads back to DiMaggio's hitting streak, but this broader setting is the source of our misinterpretation. We believe in "hot hands" because we must impart meaning to a pattern—and we like meanings that tell stories about heroism, valor, and excellence. We believe that long streaks and slumps must have direct causes internal to the sequence itself, and we have no feel for the frequency and length of sequences in random data. Thus, while we understand that DiMaggio's hitting streak was the longest ever, we don't appreciate its truly special character because we view all the others as equally patterned by cause, only a little shorter. We distinguish DiMaggio's feat merely by quantity along a continuum of courage; we should, instead, view his 56-game hitting streak as a unique assault upon the otherwise unblemished record of Dame Probability.

Amos Tversky, who studied "hot hands" *(Chance,* Winter 1989), has performed a series of elegant psychological experiments with Daniel Kahneman. These long-term studies have provided our finest insight into "natural reasoning" and its curious departure from logical truth. To cite an example, they construct a fictional description of a young woman: "Linda is 31 years old, single, outspoken, and very bright. She majored in philosophy. As a student, she was deeply concerned with issues of discrimination and social justice, and also participated in anti-nuclear demonstrations." Subjects are then given a list of hypothetical statements about Linda: They must rank these in order of presumed likelihood, most to least probable. Tversky and Kahneman list eight statements, but five are a blind, and only three make up the true experiment:

> Linda is active in the feminist movement;
> Linda is a bank teller;
> Linda is a bank teller and is active in the feminist movement.

Now it simply must be true that the third statement is least likely, since any conjunction has to be less probable than either of its parts considered separately. Everybody can understand this when the principle is explained explicitly and patiently. But all groups of subjects, sophisticated students who ought to understand logic and probability as well as folks off the street corner, rank the last statement as more probable than the second. (I am particularly fond of this example because I know that the third statement is least probable, yet a little homunculus in my head continues to jump up and down, shouting at me—"but she can't just be a bank teller; read the description.")

Why do we so consistently make this simple logical error? Tversky and Kahneman argue, correctly I think, that our minds are not built (for whatever reason) to work by the rules of probability, though these rules clearly govern our universe. We do something else that usually serves us well, but fails in crucial instances: We "match to type." We abstract what we consider the "essence" of an entity, and then arrange our judgments by their degree of similarity to this assumed type. Since we are given a "type" for Linda that implies feminism, but definitely not a bank job, we rank any statement matching the type as more probable than another that only contains material contrary to the type. This propensity may help us to understand an entire range of human preferences, from Plato's theory of form to modern stereotyping of race or gender.

We might also understand the world better, and free ourselves of unseemly prejudice, if we properly grasped the workings of probability and its inexorable hold, through laws of logic, upon much of nature's pattern. "Matching to type" is one common error; failure to understand random patterning in streaks and slumps is another—hence Tversky's study of both the fictional Linda and the 76ers' baskets. Our failure to appreciate the uniqueness of DiMaggio's streak derives from the same unnatural and uncomfortable relationship that we maintain with probability. (If we understood Lady Luck better, Las Vegas might still be a roadstop in the desert, and Nancy Reagan might not have an astrologer friend in San Francisco.)

My favorite illustration of this basic misunderstanding, as applied to DiMaggio's hitting streak, appeared in a recent article by baseball writer John Holway, "A Little Help from his Friends," and subtitled "Hits or Hype in '41" *(Sports Heritage,* November/December, 1987). Holway points out that five of DiMaggio's successes were narrow escapes and lucky breaks. He received two benefits-of-the-doubt from official scorers on plays that might have been judged as errors. In each of two games, his only hit was a cheapie. In game 16, a ball dropped untouched in the outfield and had to be called a hit, even though the ball could have been caught, had it not been misjudged; in game 54, DiMaggio dribbled one down the third base line, easily beating the throw because the third baseman, expecting the usual, was playing far back. The fifth incident is an oft-told tale, perhaps the most interesting story of the streak. In game 38, DiMaggio was 0 for 3 going into the last inning. Scheduled to bat fourth, he might have been denied a chance to hit at all. Johnny Sturm popped up to begin the inning, but Red Rolfe then walked. Slugger Tommy Henrich, up next, was suddenly swept with a premonitory fear: Suppose I ground into a double play and end the inning? An elegant solution immediately occurred to him: Why not bunt (an odd strategy for a power hitter)? Henrich laid down a beauty; DiMaggio, up next, promptly drilled a double to left.

Holway's account is interesting, but his premise is entirely, almost preciously, wrong. First of all, none of the five incidents represents an egregious miscall. The two hits were less than elegant, but they were undoubtedly legitimate; the two boosts from official scorers were close calls on judgment plays, not gifts. As for Henrich, I can only repeat manager Joe McCarthy's comment when Tommy asked him for permission to bunt: "Yeah, that's a good idea." Not a terrible strategy either—to put a man into scoring position for an insurance run when you're up 3–1.

But these details do not touch the main point—Holway's premise is false because he accepts the conventional mythology about long sequences. He believes that streaks are unbroken runs of causal courage—so that any prolongation by hook-or-crook is an outrage against the deep meaning of the phenomenon. But extended sequences are no such thing. Long streaks always are, and must be, a matter of extraordinary luck imposed upon great skill. Please don't make the vulgar mistake of thinking that Purcell or Tversky or I or anyone else would attribute a long streak to "just luck"—as though everyone's chances are exactly the same, and streaks represent nothing more than the lucky atom that kept moving in one direction. Long hitting streaks happen to the greatest players—Sisler, Keeler, DiMaggio, Rose—because their general chance of getting a hit is so much higher than average. Just as Joe Airball cannot match Larry Bird for runs of baskets, Joe's cousin Bill Ofer, with a lifetime batting average of .184, will never have a streak to match DiMaggio's with a lifetime average of .325. The statistics show something else, and something fascinating: There is no "causality of circumstance," no "extra" that the great can draw from the soul of their valor to extend a streak beyond the ordinary expectation of coin-tossing models for a series of unconnected events, each occurring with the characteristic probability for that particular player. Good players have higher characteristic probabilities, hence longer streaks.

Of course DiMaggio had a little luck during his streak. That's what streaks are all about. No long sequence has ever been entirely sustained in any other way (the Orioles almost won several of those 21 games). DiMaggio's remarkable achievement—its uniqueness, in the unvarnished literal sense of that word—lies in whatever he did to extend his success well beyond the reasonable expectations of random models that have governed every other streak or slump in the history of baseball.

Cheating Death

Probability does pervade the universe—and in this sense, the old chestnut about baseball imitating life really has validity. The statistics of streaks and slumps, properly understood, do teach an important lesson about epistemology, and life in general. The history of a species, or any natural phenomenon that requires unbroken continuity in a world of trouble, works like a batting streak. All are games of a gambler playing with a limited stake against a house with infinite resources. The gambler must eventually go bust. His aim can only be to stick around as long as possible, to have some fun while he's at it, and, if he happens to be a moral agent as well, to worry about staying the course with honor. The best of us will try to live by a few simple rules: Do justly, love mercy, walk humbly with thy God, and never draw to an inside straight.

DiMaggio's hitting streak is the finest of legitimate legends because it embodies the essence of the battle that truly defines our lives. DiMaggio activated the greatest and most unattainable dream of all humanity, the hope and chimera of all sages and shamans: He cheated death, at least for a while.

Red Sox: 68 Years and Counting

Another in the line of columnists for the **New York Times***'s "Sports of the Times," column, George Vecsey looks at the most recent incarnation of the Boston Red Sox Jinx: the shocking sixth game loss to the New York Mets in the 1986 World Series.*

By George Vecsey

26 OCTOBER 86 LATE

The special agony of the Boston Red Sox continues for at least another day—or maybe another 68 years.

The collective pain of this franchise and the fans of New England was extended in excruciating and ghastly fashion early this morning, as the Mets scored three runs after two were out in the bottom of the 10th inning for a 6-5 victory that fans will talk about for years—certainly until the next time these two teams take the field, this evening, weather permitting.

The Red Sox and their fans might have thought they had seen everything since Babe Ruth helped pitch them to a World Series title in 1918 and was sold off a season later, but Bucky Dent's homer in the 1978 playoff, and Country Slaughter's mad dash home with the winning run of the 1946 World Series may now be equaled by this morning's terror.

The Sox began the bottom of the 10th with a 5-3 lead. With two outs, the Mets put together singles by Gary Carter, Kevin Mitchell and Ray

Knight for a run. Then it turned ghastly for New England, yet again. Bob Stanley, the relief pitcher, threw a wild pitch near Mookie Wilson's foot as Mitchell scored the tying run.

Bucky Dent and Country Slaughter were in the ozone as Wilson then hit a wobbly grounder down the first-base line. Bill Buckner, playing on grit with a ruined ankle, let it slither through him for the error that could haunt Boston for generations—the ultimate heartbreaker, at least until tonight.

Driving through New England during the last week, listening to the talk shows and the sports shows, was to hear open veins bleeding.

How could they pitch Nipper? Geez, Boggs is choking. Get that Buckner out of there. That Evans only hits in 9-1 games. Clemens hasn't been the same in a month. Same old Sawx.

New Englanders knew only too well the dreadful burden they carried, heightened by the grim, exacting heritage of the region. Last Tuesday, a fan in Fenway Park carried a banner that said: "I am a Calvinist. The Red Sox are predestined to win"—presumably a twinning of the relief pitcher, Calvin Schiraldi, and the theologian, John Calvin, who believed that redemption was not achieved through good works.

New Yorkers like to feel we know all about suffering, and of course we do, with our loonies loose on the street and vans running red lights and public officials dividing the loot out in Queens, but there is no one great focus of civic suffering that unites us the way the Red Sox unite Boston.

Not everybody in Boston lives and dies with the Red Sox, thank goodness. We need somebody to have enough psychic energy and civic responsibility to keep Boston the most European, the most civilized, of American cities.

But the tone of the city is set by Mickey the Fan and Ernie the Fan and Vinnie the Fan and Freddie the Fan, who have been letting the Red Sox break their hearts for so long that a great miasma of masochism hangs over the city. It's going to happen again, Boston fans have said, reflecting on the absence of a World Championship since 1918, when Babe Ruth was still a pitcher, when Babe Ruth was still a Red Sox. Betrayal is at the core of every Red Sox fan's psyche.

Four days in Boston convince a visitor that while New Yorkers have opinions and even passions about their sports teams, only Bostonians have complexes. They love their Red Sox so much that they fear the worst. They are jealous lovers.

This conclusion comes after a much-needed 24-hour break from the claustrophobic and often sterile environment of the World Series, described by Russell Baker in his column in Saturday's New York Times. He wrote of the massive overkill of journalists at the World Series, and he was exactly right. Cramped in between respected colleagues, all of them doing their best to fill space, is to bring out the Rabbit Angstrom in some of us.

Remember Rabbit's dashes for freedom in John Updike's "Rabbit Run"—the cathartic bolting for open space? More than two weeks of postseason baseball, no matter how exciting, can produce that feeling.

Not only a fidgety scribbler feels that way. Dave Johnson, the manager of the Mets, wisely canceled practice in Boston last Monday rather than subject his players to another day in public. They needed the sleep more than they needed the Greek chorus around the batting cage, enumerating their sins.

John McNamara got the point and declined to practice in Shea Stadium on the off day Friday, and Johnson also gave his troops the day off. They did not know it, or care, but they were also making life more livable for the poor drudges who report on this Series.

For this numbed Rabbit, the day off meant a liberating drive down to Cape Cod and then over to New York at the peak of the fall foliage season. As we drove along the Charles River, alongside crews and joggers and cyclists, the Boston radio stations were full of locals, daring to hope that the Red Sox could get appease the ghosts of Pesky and Yaz and Lonnie and Torrez.

Fans called in with that peculiar Boston-fan accent, that sounds like somebody being strangled while trying to sing "Take Me Out to the Ball Game" and eating a hot dog. These tortured souls picked apart the home team:

Get Buckner outta there; the poor guy's got guts but he can't move. Let Baylor hit against the lefty. The Sawx will never take the extra base; someday it's gonna kill 'em. Rawger better do it in the sixth because The Can will blow it in the seventh. If it rains on Sunday, they can go with Hurst in the seventh game.

These gargling sounds of fear and trembling stayed on the car radio all the way down to Provincetown, where there were still signs of Red Sox mania. Two elderly men sitting in the sun on a glorious afternoon discussed how the Red Sox had patiently forced Dwight Gooden to pitch into the strike zone in Thursday night's triumph.

People bought The Globe and The Herald and turned first to the sports pages crammed with Sox stories. Even in artsy-craftsy Provincetown, there were a few Red Sox caps. It is a region starving for redemption, carrying around a scarlet letter "B" for Bucky Dent.

As we drove back along the Cape, we could hear the news broadcasters, disk jockeys, weather persons, sports celebrities, all of them talking about how the Red Sox needed just one more to wrap it up. Just one more. One out of two. Fifty-fifty. Nobody sounded very confident. Red Sox fans have been carrying a lot of heavy baggage on their long pilgrimmage.

Now the pilgrimmage seems longer and more tortuous than ever, and the Sawx and their fans have only a few hours to recover from the brutal turnaround that matched anything Country Slaughter and Bucky Dent ever did to this haunted franchise.

PART FIVE

Mickey Mantle   Photo credit: TV Sports Mailbag/Photo File

MICKEY MANTLE

The Twilight of a Hero

Sport Magazine   August 1965

Arnold Hano captures the courage and determination of Mickey Mantle, struggling with the realization that he was now entering the twilight of his career.

By Arnold Hano

Ballplayers like to kid themselves. For a spell, they think they are immortal. Ask a ballplayer who is over 30 years old how long he expects to play, and he'll tell you he looks forward to five more good years. Ask him the same question a year later, and he'll give you the same answer. Five more good years. And ask him again in another year, and he'll tell you he expects five more good years. That kind of immortality. The postponement of mortality.

It is what Mickey Mantle has said in the past. He said it most recently in 1964. But when I asked him a few weeks ago in Chicago he shook his head.

"I'll never last another five years," he said. "If somebody would offer me the choice of three good years or take a chance on five, I'd settle for three good ones."

Attrition has done this to 33-year-old Mickey Mantle. The attrition has been overwhelmingly physical, but it has been mental and psychological, too. There is little or no cartilage in either knee. Johnny Keane sat in the coffee shop of the Bismarck Hotel, suffering the miseries of managing a once-great team mired at the moment in eighth place, and he said,

"When the cartilage is gone, you have a bone-on-bone situation. He'll always limp."

His thigh muscles and hamstrings and groin muscles are permanently weakened. In Boston on May 18 there'd been another injury. He struck out four times, and after the fourth strikeout, against Dave Morehead, he jammed his bat into the rack in the dugout, and then tried to snap off the handle of the bat with his right hand. He ended up straining a muscle in his neck. Add another item to the list. It is a list that would please only the masochist; you know them anyway, beginning with osteomyelitis when he was a high-school halfback right on through sprains and tears and fractures and dislocations and three knee operations. The picture of Mickey Mantle that lingers is the one that has him coming off the bench against Cincinnati in the 1961 World Series and banging a line drive to right field, and then limping off as blood from his abscessed butt soaked through the uniform. The hole was "the size of a golf ball," Clete Boyer said later.

Other pictures linger, and they are all pictures of decline. In Chicago the day I met with him Mantle ran out to his position in left field at the beginning of each inning, a high stiff trot, and he ran back to the bench when the Yankees came off the field, but after half a game he stopped trotting. In the sixth Mantle came up with two out, Joel Horlen shutting out the Yankees, and Mantle worked the count to three-and-one, and then swung and hit the ball straight up in the air. Ron Hansen caught the soft fly ball, and Mantle—0-for-3—walked slowly to left field, his head down, a man sunk in thought. He walked the rest of the evening, no more trotting, a silent, lonely appearing man limping back and forth in the cold windy Chicago night. Here is a man probably permanently crippled, playing major-league baseball in major-league style. He had eight home runs before June 1, most on the Yankees. Not the same man he was in 1956 and 1957, but still good enough every time he comes up that you hear a shuffling in the stands, a suspense-filled waiting as he uncoils and drives his pale bat through the air toward a speeding baseball. Still good enough, on crippled legs, that when he feels the team "needs" a base, he steals second. He .urt a hamstring early in May, and a week later the Yankees played Washington. Mantle singled off Phil Ortega in the middle inning of a tight ballgame. It was one out, and the count ran to 3-and-2 on Joe Pepitone, so Mantle looked over at Johnny Keane and gave him what Keane calls his "Shall-I-go?" look, and Keane gave back an "It's-up-to-You" shrug. Senator first-baseman Bob Chance was playing back, knowing Mantle couldn't run, not with his hamstring still mending, so Mantle stole second as Pepitone struck out, and a few minutes later he scored on Boyer's base hit.

"We needed the base," Mantle explains stiffly, but there is a sense of pride undercoating the accomplishment. They knew Mantle couldn't steal, so he stole.

Yet this, too, is part of the picture of decline. "I used to love to run," Mantle said softly, in his hotel room. "It was fun. Now it hurts to run." It hurts, and it is no longer fun, but he runs. By June 6 he had stolen four bases in four attempts.

On September 18, there will be a Mickey Mantle Day at the stadium. The Yankees are sensibly miserly about holding such days. They gave Ruth a day when he was dying, and Gehrig one when he was dying, and they gave DiMaggio a day and Berra a day, but they don't throw them around to every utility infielder and second-string catcher.

The chances are good the Day will embarrass Mantle, not only because he is essentially a shy person, but because the odds are likely he will not be playing up to his superstar par of the past. He was batting .248 in Chicago on May 28, and though he went four for ten in the series against the Sox, and then two for seven in a Memorial Day doubleheader against the Tigers, to climb above .250, the explosive days that used to mark Mantle's great years are coming less often. You ask him if he feels baseball has become a grind and he answers, "The only grind is those damn pitchers, those young pitchers. It's a whole new breed of pitching these days," and he shakes his head and whistles in awe when he speaks of Dean Chance and Joe Sparma and Dave Morehead. "And when you get one of them out, they bring in Radatz or Bob Lee."

These are the shadow days for Mickey Mantle, and it is fitting he is now the Yankee leftfielder. They have moved him out of the vast sunny expanse of Yankee Stadium's center field with its great distance to cover, into left field which is splotchy and crowded in by a curling fence, where a man does not have much running to do.

So let us give him his due, and quickly.

For one, despite injuries, Mantle has played a long and full career. He has now played more games than Hall of Famers Bill Terry, Bill Dickey, Mickey Cochrane, Hank Greenberg, and Joe DiMaggio. Only three men have played more games as a Yankee—Gehrig, Ruth, and Berra. If he plays another year he will pass Ruth and Berra. He came up the same year as Willie Mays, and going into 1965, he had one more home run than Mays, even though he'd batted 500 fewer times.

He has hit 18 home runs in the World Series, which leaves behind Ruth's former record of 15. He is the only current player to have hit 50 or more home runs in each of two seasons. As a fielder, when he was strong and swift, he covered as much ground as anyone, and one year he led the American League with 25 assists.

And when he could run, he'd come out of the box like a sprinter, toes blasting. They timed him going down those 90 feet in 3.1 seconds once.

There must be sprinters, great sprinters, who don't cover the first 30 yards in 3.1. He had, and has, a kind of rocking-chair slide, so when he stole bases and the catcher threw the ball away, he'd be up in a swift bound, and on his way.

In the years of his greatness, climaxed by the two seasons of 1956 and 1957, when he hit .353 and .365, he was the dominant ballplayer of the game. Nobody was close. Paul Richards was exaggerating, but only slightly, when he said back then: "He can hit better than anyone else, he can field better than anyone else, he can throw better and he can run better. What else is there?" And Marty Marion, when he was managing the Browns, said it all: "He can't throw lefthanded. Who's perfect?"

But the statistics and the quotes do not really do the job. There has been the quality of it all. A Mantle home run has always been the most splendid home run since Ruth's. A Mantle home run jumps off the bat, often at incredible velocity, to fly an even more incredible distance. He plays in Yankee Stadium where no man has driven a fair ball out of the park; but no man has come as close as did Mantle on Memorial Day ten years ago when he propelled a Pedro Ramos fastball on a rising line to right field the ball finally striking the facade, 18 inches below the roofline.

So these are the things he did, and how he did them. Pitchers literally quaked before his figure at the plate. Steve Hamilton, who is now with the Yankees, tells of the first time he faced the Yankees:

"I came up from Jacksonville, and joined the Senators in 1962, and we were beating the Yankees, 4-2, when I came in to pitch in the eighth. I got them out in the eighth. In the ninth, Maris doubled, and up came Mantle."

Hamilton shakes his head today, at the memory. He is terribly glad to be on the same team as Mantle, today. "Mickey looked enormous. He looked huge. No hitter ever looked bigger. I was scared."

Somehow, Hamilton got Mantle out, and the Senators won, 4-2, but the notion of Mantle looking so huge is the story. Steve Hamilton is six feet seven inches tall.

For all of this, it took Mantle years to win the acclaim he deserved. Perhaps one reason is his almost total lack of personal flair. Willie Mays had his high-pitched voice and infectious giggle those first years, his cap flying off, his intuitive genius for the right play, DiMaggio was ice-cold and solemn, the noblest Roman of them all. "He looked like a senator," Mantle once said of DiMaggio. Ruth had his huge, warm, wonderful personality, big and coarse, a brazen man who lived a loud and vulgar life. Duke Snider could snarl at the fans and call them "crummy" when they booed him. Ted Williams could wrist them. And Mantle?

They booed him the first year. What did Mantle think of that? Did it anger him?

"It puzzled me," he says, today.

No wrist gestures, no vocal outbursts. Just a quiet puzzlement.

He had other problems long in the working out. He came up in 1951 in a river of praise gushed forth by Yankee public-relations men and by an obliging press, and he was obviously going to be worth every superlative of it. Eventually.

He was declared to be too good, too soon, and the shrunken-chested fans who sat in the bleachers, the henpecked and the failures, saw this 19-year-old kid and took out on him all the hostility they felt at anybody who was better than they. And when he wasn't immediately what the publicity had said, they cackled their glee and hooted their derision.

Again, the press helped, picking up the notion that a great young ballplayer like Mantle should have been greater. The press fed the hostility until the American League's finest young prospect became one of the league's more disliked ballplayers.

So when you speak of decline, place this atmosphere of envy and resentment right up there with Mantle's right knee. Together, they ate at Mickey.

There is a standing gag on the Yankees: "When will you reach your potential, Mickey?" asks Joe Pepitone, and everybody grins. It is going out of style, because the fans have stopped hating Mantle, and the press has accordingly picked up its cue and stopped complaining that Mantle hadn't yet hit 60 home runs and batted .400 the same season. For years it epitomized Mantle. Wait until he *really* matures, people said. Then you'll see the greatest. We waited, and he had two seasons over .350, and two years over 50 home runs, and he won the Most Valuable Player award three times, which obviously wasn't enough for some people. Hitting 50 home runs only indicated what Mantle's potential was. Hitting .365 only indicated how high Mantle could hit, and what a nerve he had batting .275 one year! Who the hell did he think he was, knocking in only 94 runs? When would the guy reach his potential and stay there?

Yet when you look at Mantle over the years, the truth that has finally emerged is that few players have actually come closer to fulfilling their promise. What is the potential of a man afflicted by osteomyelitis, a natural righthanded hitter who hits three-fourths of the time lefthanded, an infielder converted to the outfield two years after he had entered pro ball. The potential of such a ballplayer must be measured by these limits. Sandy Koufax had a numb index finger and became a totally different physical specimen. What was his potential—30 wins or 14? What is the potential of a Whitey Ford whose pitching hand loses its feeling on a cold day? Ted Williams hit .406 one year, but later he broke his collarbone and played with steel pins drilled through the ends of the bone, and his potential obviously changed.

This new truth concerning Mantle has finally come through. After the 1963 season, Mantle underwent his third knee operation (two on the right, one on the left). During the 1964 season he suffered "minor" injuries to knee, thigh, shoulder and groin. Gimpy-legged, he was moved from centerfield to rightfield in some parks, and leftfield in others. Yet he hit .303 and knocked in 111 runs; in the '64 Series he hit .333, with three home runs and eight runs batted in. "I'm not griping about my legs, you understand," Mantle says, "I think I've been real lucky but I can't help wondering how far I'd have gone with two legs."

A second change has come about in the acceptance of Mickey Mantle. Not only do we now appreciate what he has done despite his injuries, but we have come to understand something—not all—of the Mantle temperament, so long an enigma to press and public.

Mantle is unsure of himself. He says, "I guess," and "I think," and "probably," when he is asked to venture an opinion. "When I come into a restaurant and I hear somebody say, 'Look, there's Mickey Mantle!' my head automatically goes down. I'm embarrassed. I'm shy as hell, I guess. It doesn't seem to get any easier. I'm about as shy as I ever was." When he returned home a hero after the 1952 World Series, Commerce, Oklahoma, threw him a big welcome, with 16 bands and 7500 people cramped into the town's seven blocks of main street. Mantle allowed how he "felt silly about the whole thing . . . What's so special about me?"

Recently, Mantle was quoted as saying, "I never could be a manager. All I have is natural ability." When he read the quote in the magazine, he was appalled.

"It's not right," he said to me in Chicago, "for me to be bragging on myself."

"But it's true you have natural ability," I said.

"Maybe so," he said, "but somebody else has to say it. Not me."

Fascinating. Other people might have been insulted by the suggestion he wasn't smart enough to manage. Mantle was embarrassed because there he was bragging on himself in public.

There have been slurs on Mantle's intelligence in the past. Mantle was quoted years ago on the subject: "I've heard how some of the folks rate me in the thinking league. I'm sorry some of 'em call me a dummy. But to tell you the truth, it doesn't bother me any more."

It took another ballplayer to put the intelligence question into perspective. Before a Yankee-Dodger World Series in the early 1950s, Jackie Robinson said, "Hell, we got plenty of guys that stupid. But we don't have anyone that good."

Rather than stupid, Mantle (who was a B and C student throughout high school) is a self-effacing man. A look at Mantle's background sheds some light on the why of this self-effacement, and how it affects his ballplaying.

Mickey Mantle was born, as every bubble-gum chewer knows, on October 20, 1931, in the tiny town of Spavinaw, Oklahoma, son of a zinc and lead miner, Elvin Mantle. Elvin, whom they called Mutt, was a ball fan and a semipro pitcher. So was Mickey's grandfather Charles Mantle. Mutt Mantle named his son Mickey, after a baseball idol, Mickey Cochrane.

Baseball became the boy's life. When he was six months old, Mickey wore a baseball cap knitted by his mother. When he was three, he had his own uniform tailored from a pair of Mutt's baseball pants. Today Mickey says, "I can't remember when I wasn't wearing a glove, throwing a tennis ball against a wall, or hitting a tennis ball with a bat." His father and grandfather pitched to him alternately; his father was righthanded and his grandfather lefthanded, and the converting of the boy into a switchhitter began when he was still a tot.

"Those early switchhitting lessons were tough," Mickey says today, "because I couldn't hit the ball as often or with as much power lefthanded in the beginning." But when you ask him whether the frustration of hitting unnaturally ever reduced him to angry tears, he looks at you as though you are crazy. All it "reduced" him to was a more dogged, silent effort to do what his father and grandfather wanted him to do.

Once, the frustration cracked through. In a sandlot game, facing a righthanded pitcher, Mickey decided not to switch, and instead batted righthanded. His father was in the stands. Mutt Mantle ordered the boy off the field and sent him home. He said to his son: "Don't you ever put on that baseball uniform again until you switch-hit like I taught you."

So he obeyed, giving up a piece of himself to his father's will. There is another reason he obeyed. He loved his father enormously, and respected him tremendously. In Mantle's book, *The Quality of Courage,* ghosted by Robert Creamer, the epitaph to Mutt Mantle reads: "He didn't die scared and he didn't live scared." In a story by Gerald Astor in *Look,* Mantle says of his father, who died of Hodgkin's Disease in 1952 at the age of 41: "I just wanted to please him more than anything else. I had so much respect for him. I could never take a drink or smoke in front of Dad."

Mutt Mantle didn't want his son to end up a miner, like himself, and like his own father, Charles Mantle, who also died young. It is, if you don't mind a little corn, the American way, pushing your own kin toward a better life than your own. Today, Mickey Mantle is helping his kid brother, Larry, through college. It is almost an obsession with the Mantles, to keep out of the mines. The day I arrived in Chicago, there was a headline on page 1 of the *Daily News,* "India Mine Blast/300

Feared Dead." I clipped the headline and shoved it at Mickey. He nodded and said, "I was in the mines."

So into baseball he came, sandlot, amateur leagues, semipro, high-school ball, until the day of his graduation from Commerce High in June of 1949, when he signed with the Yankees. He received an $1100 bonus and a salary of $140 a month to finish the 1949 season at Independence, in the Kansas-Oklahoma-Missouri League.

Harry Craft was his manager at Independence, where Mantle played shortstop. Mickey made 47 errors in 89 games, but he batted .313 and knocked in 63 runs. Craft wrote to his Yankee superiors: "Can be a great hitter. Exceptional speed . . . Attitude excellent. Will go all the way. He has everything to make a great ballplayer. I would like to see him shifted to third or outfield."

Despite the "attitude excellent," Craft later said Mickey's real weakness was "his temperament. He acted as if the whole world was coming to an end just because he booted one or struck out in the clutch."

Mantle laughed. "You should have seen me. I'd still have my head down two innings later when they'd hit a ground ball at me."

He had a very good year at Joplin, in 1950, and after the season ended, he joined the Yankees in September in St. Louis, working out with the team. After that 1950 season, Mantle returned home, to work in the mines for $33.90, take home. He joined the Yankees in 1951, switched to the outfield in spring training and batted .402 in the exhibition season. He stuck with the Yankees.

A draft physical in December, 1950, had found him unfit for military service, because of the arrested case of osteomyelitis in his left leg. Now, the public grumbled how come this healthy, husky blond lad could hit baseballs 500 feet and run so fast, and yet wasn't fit for Army duty. There was a second physical, a third, and a fourth. They all concurred. A man with osteomyelitis was a terrible risk for the Army. Had Mantle been a miner or a plumber, nobody would have known. But he wasn't.

His big-league career thus began under a faint cloud. Mantle recalls it: "When I first came up, there was all that publicity. I was supposed to be another Joe DiMaggio. Unfortunately, I wasn't. I wasn't going good, and the fans resented me. They started off booing me. I wondered what they wanted."

And when Mantle talks about the change in the fans' attitude, and in his own attitude toward the fans, he leaps from that first year of 1951 to the year 1961, when Ralph Houk became the Yankee manager. The first thing Houk did was announce: "As Mantle goes, so go the Yankees," which may have been obvious, but Mantle needed the praise and the attention.

"It made me feel good," he says today, "when Ralph Houk started bragging on me. How I would be the team leader and all that. It made me believe in myself. I found I could take the boos better."

The year, 1961, marked the year of Maris and Mantle's assault on Ruth, and Mantle, with his injuries, slipped into the role of underdog. This also helped. The fans began to root for him.

Before then, they booed him perhaps because of his publicized—and often misunderstood—temperament.

"The trouble with Mantle is Mantle," Casey Stengel, Mantle's first Yankee manager, once said. "Telling Mantle something is like telling him nothing."

Stengel said other things. Mantle would strike out and storm back to the dugout and belt the water cooler. "Son," Stengel would say, "it ain't the water cooler that's striking you out."

Mantle did his best and the boos and criticism bothered him, but he kept it all to himself. Which was part of his problem. He was, and is, a silent sufferer. Tom Tresh recently said to George Vass, a Chicago sportswriter: "What can I tell you? Nobody knows how much pain he (Mantle) goes through but himself, and he'll never tell. About the only way I know how he's feeling is when he drops a casual remark. Like one day he will say, 'My legs are feeling good.' Other times he'll tell me: 'Field everything you can get.' But he never says he's feeling bad."

Some people read his early silence differently. One man wrote of Mantle in 1953: "So far he has not demonstrated a willingness to work everlastingly hard to make himself the best. He seems to lack the inner spark of a DiMaggio—that burning desire to excel."

With these odd pressures, Mantle developed defenses. He became, at times, surly in the face of the press. He always had found it hard to talk to strangers; now on top of his usual shyness there was a wariness, a hostile suspicion. Again, there was reason. Con artists talked him into onesided business deals. The fans rushed him after a game in 1960, and in the melee, Mantle was punched on the jaw. Kids flipped ink on his clothes.

Today he is more tolerant of all this. "They flipped ink on everybody. Bob Cerv refused to sign any more. A drunk in Toots Shor's asked Stan Musial for his autograph and tore the autograph up in front of Musial."

Houk turned the key in Mantle and opened up the internal man. And all Houk did was let Mantle know somebody in authority thought he was a great ballplayer and a fine human being. As simple as that.

Unfortunately and ironically, with this change of attitude toward Mantle has come concurrently the deterioration of his skills by the succession of injuries and a lifetime of pain. Still, that's life, and a matured Mantle says, "I figure I got all the breaks in spite of my legs. Otherwise, I'd have been in the mines."

So that is where we are today. We've skipped over the 565-foot home run off Chuck Stobbs, the triple crown in '56, the home run off Barney Schultz in the ninth inning of a World Series game in 1964 ("my biggest thrill"), the time he hit a groundball in 1962 to Zoilo Versalles and tried to beat it out, but succeeded instead in tearing the adductor muscle in his thigh and going down like a shot rabbit. Running into a fence in Baltimore and breaking his foot. Setting his right foot on the rubber cover of a water drain in the second game of the 1951 World Series, and having his right knee pop out when the foot caught, and never being the same again. We've skipped the strikeouts and the tape-measure blasts.

And we come to 1965, Mantle in Chicago, Mantle struggling to hit, on a team struggling to come alive, a team hit by staggering injuries, not only to Mantle, but to Maris, Howard, Ford and Kubek. "Is it humiliating," Mantle was asked, "to be on a second-division team?"

"Yes," he said. "It is a bad feeling."

How did he assess the Yankee chances?

"A lot better than other people do. But we have to start right now." Right now was May 28, the Yankees in eighth, eight games behind the league-leading White Sox. "We can't wait another two weeks."

Mantle agreed the Yankee pitching was not as good as it had been, but, he said, that wasn't where the trouble lay. "It doesn't matter how good the pitching is if you don't get them some runs. We give the pitchers no breathing room. They're always pitching under a strain."

Naturally, he blamed himself as much as anybody, maybe more. He sat on his stool in the dressing room after each game, brooding. Charley Feeney, of the New York *Journal-American* wrote, "Mantle figures he must solve all Yank bat problems. It's an impossible task."

"I feel good," he said, "when I hit, and I still get a great kick out of hitting a home run, maybe a bigger kick than ever. The game is enjoyable when I am going good, but I am not going good. I hate to embarrass myself."

The pitching, Mantle felt, was the big change in baseball during his 14 years.

"In the early 1950s, when the count was 3-and-0 or 3-and-1, you could look for the fastball, because they didn't want to walk you. Now they throw the slider 3-and-0. I have even seen knucklers, 3-and-0."

Had he mellowed not only as a person, but as a ballplayer? Despite straining his neck in Boston, did he control his temper better?

"I still have to fight my temper. In a game the other day against Washington, the umpire called a strike on a pitch that was outside. He called a second strike on another outside pitch. He is the one umpire in the league I don't see eye to eye with. On the next pitch I took a half-hearted swing at a ball that was as far outside as from here to that ashtray." He pointed eight feet away.

What was he thinking when he went back to the dugout?

"All I did was hurt myself. I was mad at the umpire. I was mad at myself. I was thinking, 'You've wasted a time at bat.' "

How did he feel physically? How were his legs? It is the inevitable question.

"Actually my legs felt better last year than they had the past few years. They feel good this year. They get stiff when the weather is cold. They get *real* stiff when it's cold and wet."

How did he find left field?

"Yankee Stadium has the toughest left field by far. It is the toughest sun. It is hardest to pick up the ball. It has that circular wall so if balls get behind you they hug the wall and roll to deep left-center, for a home run inside the park or at least a triple. I used to say centerfield at Yankee Stadium was tough, but it's not anything like left field."

Did he get help from the other Yankee fielders? Mantle grinned and said, "You might say Tresh shades me a little. And Kubek comes out on pops."

Which brings up a facet of Mantle usually overlooked. He can be a very amusing man. Mantle's humor sometimes takes the form of folksy stories and sometimes is on the practical-joke side. When Phil Linz joined the Yankees, Mantle kept praising the boy until Linz was properly awed by the great man. So one evening Mantle and Ford saw Linz and Joe Pepitone eating in a restaurant in Detroit. Mantle walked over to the table and greeted the two youngsters. Linz tells the story:

"Mickey told us that he and Whitey rarely did this, but they'd like to show us around a bit after dinner. They told us to meet them and they gave us an address. Mickey said to ask for Mr. Mantle's table. We thought, 'Boy, they must really like us.' So Joe and I took a cab to the address."

Turned out to be a rundown striptease joint.

This is the other side of Mantle, the man with the broad boyish grin and the broader bent of humor. It is not, however, the typical Mantle.

The more typical Mantle is the man who earns $100,000 a year in salary, but is still concerned with his future. "I'm saving what I can, scraping together everything I can get my hands on," he said to me, "and putting it into an insurance company, the First Insurance Company of San Antonio. It's looking *real* good."

Mantle is not rich, for all the dollars per year. He takes care of himself and his family; he helps out his mother who is living with Mickey's sister, Barbara; he helps his brother, Larry. Mantle invested heavily in a bowling alley in Dallas, and a motel in Joplin, and though he did not lose in either operation, he also did not make anything and it tied up a lot of his money. Taxes make it tough, and he and his wife and their sons live fairly well. They own a house in Dallas, and then in the summer Merlyn and the boys come East after school is out and rent a house in Jersey, which means keeping up two places a good part of the year. Mantle owns a Cadillac, and he gets the free use of a Dodge from the Dodge Corporation ("Merlyn drives the Cadillac; I drive the Dodge," Mickey laughs), and though he does not really throw away his money on clothes, he is not the same boy who arrived from Oklahoma in 1951 wearing a straw hat and toting a $4 cardboard suitcase. His one recent splurge was a pair of $155 alligator shoes that are supposed to last a lifetime.

He and Merlyn recently received $7500, plus future residuals, for a Lifebuoy commercial on TV, and there is other money not infrequently coming Mantle's way.

Still, he is a ballplayer, and these are likely to be waning years, less productive years. Even if they are not, he will not be playing ball a decade from now. He will need what he gets. "The insurance company may do it," he says, speaking of a future comfort. "I hope so." He is a ballplayer, and that is all he has ever learned to do. When you ask him whether *he* thinks he is a courageous man (the whole world thinks he is, of course), he shakes his head and says, "No. The only thing I can do is play baseball. I *have* to play ball. It's the only thing I know. So it doesn't matter if my legs hurt. I've got to play. What else would I do?"

The thing he must do is play ball, and he will play until he cannot play well. Which is a future perhaps not far off. With Mantle, discussing the future is a slippery business. He has what other people have called "a tragic vision" of himself. His father died at 41, his grandfather before he was 45, and two uncles in their 40s. There is a story that Mantle was once asked what his goal was and he said, "Forty," and he didn't mean 40 home runs, but 40 years.

When he and I finished talking in his hotel room, I went to Comiskey Park to watch him play ball. It was one of those cold nights, the kind, he had earlier said, that make his legs feel stiff—cold and windy, though not wet. The temperature in Chicago was 47 at gametime, and it dropped four or five degrees during the game. A wind blew from left to right, making fly balls tricky. On the field before the game, Bobby Richardson said of Mantle: "He is our inspiration. He doesn't realize it!"

In the first inning, Linz singled to left, and with one out, Maris singled, and Mantle came up, runners on first and third. Immediately there was a conference, John Romano rushing out to talk to Horlen, while Mantle adjusted the dirt in the box with his spikes. Horlen threw a big curve, and Mantle swung and missed, and then Mantle hit a fastball down to Don Buford at second. Buford took an almost insolent amount of time feeding Hansen, who relayed to first for the double play. In the pressbox, everybody said, "If he had his legs, they wouldn't have got him."

In the fourth Mantle came up again. He took three balls, and looked down at coach Frank Crosetti, and then got back in. Horlen threw a ball on the inside corner, and Mantle began to swing and then checked, but the ball struck his bat and rolled slowly past Horlen down to Hansen, who fired in time. Again, in the pressbox, they said, "If he had his legs."

He popped up in the sixth, on a 3-and-1 count, and in the ninth he singled and came out for a runner, but the Yankees did nothing, and the Sox won, 2-0.

I went down to the Yankee dressing room. Mantle sat with his head down, his uniform on. No, he said, his legs hadn't bothered him. No, there was no reason he ran to his position the beginning of the game and walked the last innings. Then he looked up, with a brief flicker of anger, and he said evenly: "I'm through talking."

He loses hard, which is admirable, and even when the downcast Yankee dressing room started to take on life, Mantle sat still, head down, and then he began to unpeel the bandages from his legs.

There would be more moments like this in Mickey Mantle's twilight and there would be happier moments, too, moments of heroics, perhaps great heroics. And, for everyone, there would be memories. Like the memory of Al Kaline recently signing autographs in a Detroit department store and hearing from a young boy: "You're not half as good as Mickey Mantle."

"Son," said Kaline, *"nobody* is half as good as Mickey Mantle."

Sandy Koufax

Photo credit: UPI/Bettmann

SANDY KOUFAX

The Sophistication of Sandy Koufax

Sport Magazine   September 1963

*Bill Libby had a choice in which Sandy Koufax he pro-
filed: a pitcher reaching his overpowering potential; or a
man with a career record just over .500 and circulatory
problems in his pitching hand. Libby chose correctly,
spotting Koufax rounding into the form which won him
the National League's Most Valuable Player Award that
1963 season and shot him into the Hall of Fame after
three more blazing years.*

By Bill Libby

From the Dodger Stadium stands, the pitcher, Sandy Koufax,
seemed small, a single figure trapped by his destiny in a single spot
on the diamond, marked by the attention of each person in the
ballpark. Within the walls, Koufax pumped, and pitched, whipping his
left arm forward with the entire weight of his body behind it.

Harvey Kuenn hit the ball on a line to Frank Howard in right field.
Howard caught the ball, as the crowd cheered. The Dodgers led the
Giants, 4-0, in the seventh inning, but there was more to this 1963 night
game than that. Kuenn had been the 19th Giant to bat in the game and
the 19th Giant Koufax had retired.

Koufax pitched to Felipe Alou. Alou got under a fastball and hit a long fly to left. Tommy Davis drifted back toward the stands and caught the ball, and the crowd cheered again.

Dick Calmus, a rookie, came off his seat on the Dodger bench to applaud. Coach Leo Durocher superstitiously ordered him back to his seat.

Willie Mays now. Sandy coiled, uncoiled, pitched. Mays smashed the ball on a line toward left. Jim Gilliam stepped toward third and intercepted the ball in its flight. The crowd cheered as Sandy, his head lowered, walked slowly off the mound.

He sat in the dugout, alone, wiping his face with a towel. No one spoke to him. But a youngster sitting behind the dugout yelled, "Hey, Sandy, you gonna pitch me a no-hitter?"

And Sandy smiled and said to himself, I hope to God so.

Durocher made a face.

Presently it was the ninth inning, the perfect game gone (Ed Bailey had walked in the eighth), the no-hitter still alive. The Dodgers had scored four runs in their last at-bat and led, 8-0. Sandy pitched to Joey Amalfitano, then Jose Pagan, got them both out. Willie McCovey pinch-hit for the pitcher and Sandy walked him.

Sandy considered the situation. The big men coming up, a four-run lead to protect, he'd be in trouble if anyone else got on. He turned around to look at the scoreboard. Eight runs, he corrected himself. Lost in concentration on his no-hitter, he had forgotten the four extra runs.

Sandy pressed his lips together, hunched, and looked down at catcher John Roseboro. The tension was stifling. He felt as if he could not breathe, as if he wanted to shake. He stretched, glanced at McCovey, and pitched to Kuenn.

Kuenn bounced the ball slowly to the right of the mound. Sandy rushed over, grabbed the ball, threw it to Ron Fairly for the putout and followed the ball into Fairly's glove, jumping on the young first-baseman in his joy. The Dodgers swarmed over him in excitement as the fans stood, applauding and yelling.

Sandy was rushed into the dugout, out of reach of the crowd. He was brought in for post-game radio and television interviews, which were a letdown. He had to wait, bristling with excitement, while the announcer read a commercial message. Then he had to sit patiently through the interview, answering the questions with proper joy, restraint and modesty.

Finally, he was released, and he rushed to the dressing room. "Hiya tiger," he shouted to Don Drysdale, who grinned broadly at such unaccustomed emotion from his teammate. Drysdale replied with some profanity about players who stir up too much fuss, but rushed to Sandy as the room exploded around him. Almost immediately, however, newsmen pulled Sandy away. Reluctantly, but politely, he responded, saying all the right things:

"This has to be my greatest thrill . . . Johnny Roseboro called a brilliant game and kept encouraging me all the way . . . I'll never forget the ovation the wonderful Los Angeles fans gave me when I came to bat in the eighth. It was the greatest. They had been with me all the way. I'm very happy . . . very happy."

He was happier when they left, so he could return to his teammates, who, however, were mostly dressed by now, and beginning to leave the ballpark. Parties of various sizes and shapes were suggested to Sandy, who declined them with polite grins. He had a previous date—with an FM radio station he partially owns in Thousand Oaks in the San Fernando Valley. He had arranged an all-night charity fund-raising show for that night.

He showered, shaved and dressed. Already the excitement within him seemed to be subsiding. He moved out of the dressing room, rode the elevator up, squeezed past the excited fans who had waited long for him, signed a few autographs on the move, said a few smiling thank yous, and escaped to the darkened, quieting parking lot.

He got into his big car, turned out the Sunset Boulevard exit, turned onto the freeways, and drove to the station. He went on the air for a little while. When he'd done a sufficient stint, he left the station and drove home.

Sandy Koufax is, at his best, the greatest pitcher in baseball. "His fastball takes off like a jet fighter," says Dodger vice-president Fresco Thompson. "He shows just enough curves and changeups to keep the batters guessing. When he is working properly, the batters, trying to get their bats out front to outguess the fastball, are made to look stupid when he comes in with the curve."

He has pitched two no-hitters and two 18-strikeout games. Until he was stricken in 1962 with the circulatory ailment that caused him to be called the million-dollar arm with the ten-cent finger, he was on his way to as good a season as any pitcher has had in 30 years. And although sidelined by a sore shoulder early this season, he again appeared on his way at least to the truly outstanding year that has long been expected of him.

With good luck and improved health, he may sustain his greatness over a full season, and then over many seasons, to move ahead of the best of his contemporaries, and possibly even within reach of the best of his predecessors. If he does, he will be self-satisfied only to a point, because he will be more squarely in the spotlight than he even is now.

Koufax says he likes living alone, but his doing so in a big house mystifies many of his teammates. "He's a damned hermit. He vants to be alone," one of them says, with a mock Garbo accent. Although Sandy's doors are open to them, his teammates don't usually pass through them. Some of his teammates consider him a man apart.

"Why should Sandy get married?" a Dodger said recently. "Why should any big-league baseball player get married?"

"You did," a fellow said. "So did most of the rest."

"Sure," the Dodger said, grinning. "We all want to, sooner or later. Only with most of us, it's usually sooner."

"But not with Sandy?"

"Not with Sandy. He's not like the rest of us. He's *different.*"

Frankly, big-league ballplayers have open invitations from more women than most can handle. Their self-control in such situations seems satisfactory. Sandy's self-control is super-satisfactory. To put it mildly different, Koufax, a more important ballplayer than most, handsomer than most, young and unmarried, has no trouble getting dates. It is said they line up for him. However, Sandy prefers to pick his own, and he has as good taste in this as he does in other matters.

"He is a wonderful escort," says one of his former dates. "He is a real gentleman. But he is a very hard guy to get to know. He does not tell you much about himself. But, then, he does not ask you much about yourself. He does not let himself get to know you very well."

He dates discreetly and privately. He does not put his dates on display for his teammates, nor does he take them places to be seen. "Hell, he doesn't brag or nothing," one Dodger says. "He just won't discuss his dames around the clubhouse, like the rest of us do." Men among men, in service or on ballclubs, kiss and tell, indeed even tell of kisses where kisses have not been given, and their secrets are usually safe with each other, even among those outsiders who have clubhouse privileges. Sandy goes a step further, keeping his secrets to himself.

Last year Sandy was dating Linda Kennon, a beautiful 20-year-old secretary, who was already "Miss Los Angeles," and was in a contest for the title of "Miss Southern California." When she won the title, Sandy was on hand. She rushed into his arms, where they whispered affectionately to each other, until the press came between them.

Since then Sandy has avoided coming out into the open with other young ladies. The writers have left Sandy's romances in the dark, where Sandy would have them.

With the writers respecting his wishes for personal privacy, he has been able to keep a great deal to himself. "He is a real gentleman, a class guy," says one writer, who has been traveling with the club for years. "Most ballplayers recognize that we are just doing a job, a job that is tied in with theirs, and cooperate with us without a second thought. As long as you don't get personal, Sandy will go beyond that. He is one of the few ballplayers—Don Drysdale is another—who you can talk to when things are bad for them. Even when he's taken a beating, he grits his teeth and holds his head up, and answers your questions."

"He doesn't alibi and he doesn't put blame on others," another writer says. "I won't say he'll say a whole lot, he sure won't volunteer much, but he won't hide from you. Even when you can see he wishes he didn't have to talk to you, and he doesn't have to, he feels he should, so he does. Until you ask him about something outside the ballpark, that is. If he's in the right mood, he'll go along with it, maybe, up to a point, but only up to a point. Many times, he won't stand for it at all. Which is his privilege, I would think, and which I must respect, although it doesn't make it easy to write interestingly about him."

He will talk about his background. He was one of the least heralded "bonus babies" of all time. Born Sanford Koufax, December 30, 1935, in Brooklyn, he was raised in modestly comfortable circumstances in several neighborhoods around the Bensonhurst section. Smiling, he recalls his friends as a "varied group." A few were more interested in displaying their muscles in alleys than in ballparks. Sandy, himself, was more interested in basketball than in baseball, and admits becoming a professional baseball player was the farthest thing from his mind.

He prepped at the Jewish Community House and on the playgrounds, where young New York schoolboys mix with college and pro players, and at Lafayette High School. He did very well. At 6-2, he was an exceptional leaper and a steady scorer, and he received a scholarship to the University of Cincinnati.

Sandy saw the Dodgers play at Ebbets Field about once or twice a year, usually only on group outings. Originally, he played sandlot baseball only to be with his friends, and didn't go out for his high-school team until he was a senior. He was a first-baseman for awhile, and it is rather unlikely he ever would have been turned pro in this category.

"I was as good a hitter then as I am now," Sandy says, smiling. "Only the pitching is better now."

He'd be an architect now (he studied the subject at Cincinnati and later at Columbia University) if his sandlot manager, Milt Laurie, of the Parkviews of the Coney Island League, had not been impressed with how hard Sandy threw, and suggested he try his luck as a pitcher. A Brooklyn sportswriter, Jimmy Murphy, told the Dodgers that there was a 15-year-old sandlotter named Koufax who threw as hard as any youngster he'd seen, and the Dodgers kept an eye on him from then on.

In the fall of 1953, Sandy averaged ten points a game for the Cincinnati basketball team. The next spring he turned out for freshman baseball and was overpowering. He struck out 51 batters in 32 innings, 34 in two consecutive games. During vacation that June, the Giants took him to a Polo Grounds tryout. He was tense and frightened, and a wild pitcher to begin with. He threw with all his might and came closer to the early arrivals in the box-seats then he did to his catcher. The Giants lost interest.

Other clubs remained interested. Being wild is not exactly a rare trait in a kid lefty, and this kid could throw unusually hard. The Dodgers, Braves and Pirates indicated they would go after him. Al Campanis, the Dodger scout, felt he should act fast. On December 22, 1954, he offered Sandy a $14,000 bonus. Campanis also convinced Sandy's parents that a Brooklyn boy should play ball for Brooklyn.

As Campanis left the Koufax house, he met a Pittsburgh scout who was on his way inside, authorized by Branch Rickey to top the Dodger bid by $5000. Within a day Milwaukee, unaware Sandy had signed with the Dodgers, indicated it was ready to go higher. A few years after the signing, the Brooklyn team moved to Los Angeles. Walter O'Malley did not consult either Campanis or the Koufax family. Campanis has admitted, "I've always felt guilty in the Koufax signing."

When Sandy's bonus acquisition was announced, the unanimous reaction among Brooklynites and New York sportswriters was, "Who's he?" Not long after he had reported to spring training at Vero Beach, there seemed good reason to wonder if anyone outside of his parents and friends would ever know.

Sandy was so nervous and tense, he couldn't throw for a week. Then he tried to throw so hard, got a sore arm and couldn't throw for another week. When he resumed, he was so wild, Dodger pitching coach Joe Becker recalls taking him to warm up in isolation behind the barracks so "he wouldn't be embarrassed."

When he came out of hiding, the other players went in. "Taking batting practice against him is like playing Russian roulette with five bullets," one Dodger said. "You don't give yourself much of a chance."

Here was a youngster signed to a big-league bonus contract after having pitched no more than 15 or 16 games, perhaps 100 innings, in organized amateur competition, and who could not be farmed out to the minors because of prevailing bonus restrictions.

The club was patient but Sandy was not. The Dodgers were a good, pennant-contending team with solid pitching at the time. They could risk using the wild kid southpaw only infrequently, in one-sided games. In Becker's opinion, Sandy's development was seriously retarded. "He'd have been a top star twice as fast had he been able to pitch regularly in the minors, or with a weaker club in the majors," Becker says.

For his first six seasons in the big leagues, Koufax was on part-time employment. He averaged appearances in about two dozen games and decisions in about a dozen games each season, and usually had a medio-cre earned-run average that once soared as high as 4.88. He struck out almost 700 batters, but he also walked almost 400. He threw a lot of wild pitches, including a league-leading 17 in 1958. He had to struggle to break even. He won 36 games and lost 36 games in this span.

He had his moments. In August of his rookie year, with the Dodgers breezing, the club gambled on some starts for him. In his second start, Sandy pitched a two-hit, 14-strikeout shutout over Cincinnati, which he regards as his first big thrill in baseball. He came back to shut out the Pirates. Each time he seemed to be straightening out, however, he would relapse into scatter-armed ineffectiveness and would be returned to the bench.

Sandy's inner smouldering erupted to the surface during this period. "I want to pitch and I'm not getting a chance," he complained to general manager Buzzie Bavasi one day.

"How can you pitch when you can't get the side out?" Bavasi said.

"Who the hell can get the side out sitting in the dugout?" Koufax said.

He spent six months in the army during the winter of 1957 and began to get somewhat greater opportunities when he returned, but he did not respond until 1959. In June, 1959, he struck out 16 Phillies. On August 21, he struck out 18 Giants, breaking by one the National League record set by Dizzy Dean in 1933, tying the major-league record set by Bob Feller in 1943.

That fall he started and lost a 1-0 game to Bob Shaw of the Chicago White Sox in the fifth game of the World Series. During the off-season, the Dodgers offered Duke Snider and Johnny Podres to the Yankees for Elston Howard, but when the Yankees asked for Koufax instead of Podres, the Dodgers refused.

"From the time I broke in, I'd progress a little each year, but in 1960, the roof fell in," Sandy recalls. "I got pretty disgusted with myself. But I never thought of quitting. I was too young to quit. And, besides, I didn't know much else to do except play baseball."

Technical and spiritual imperfections were spoiling and smothering his raw talent. "He used to get upset. He'd rush," Becker says. "I told him, 'Nothing can start until you get damn good and ready to pitch. Whatever you do, don't rush.' I tried to get him to shorten his stride and to throw with an easy, natural rhythm. But he was overanxious."

He was "a silent temper case," says Bavasi. "He would get mad at himself and decide to overpower the hitter. His attitude was, 'Here it comes you dirty so and so, let's see you hit it.' Well, you can get away with that stuff from time to time, but not for a season. You keep defying major-league hitters to hit you and they will."

"I used to try to throw each pitch harder than the previous one,"

Sandy recalls. "There was no need for it. I found out that if I take it easy and throw naturally, the ball goes just as fast . . . I found that my control improved and the strikeouts would take care of themselves."

He credits this discovery to the advice of Norm Sherry, then a Dodger catcher. It is a fact of human nature that sometimes a person will stubbornly ignore expert advice, but listen to the casual words of a friend. Sitting on a bus alongside roommate Sandy one spring day in 1961, Sherry said, "You know what I think, Sandy?"

And Sandy said, "No, what do you think, Norm?"

And Norm said, "Sandy, I think your troubles would be solved if you would just throw easier, throw more changeups, just try to get the ball over."

Koufax mulled the matter over in his mind. He tried it and it worked. He won six of his first seven starts. The Dodger brass tripped over one another in an effort to determine which of their number had finally gotten through to their sterling young prospect. "If there was any magic formula," Koufax says, "it was getting to pitch every fourth day."

In 1961, Sandy was used in 42 games, pitched more than 200 innings for the first time in his career (256), pitched 15 complete games, won 18 games, lost 13, and had a 3.52 ERA. With his new, easy, rhythmic delivery, he struck out 269 batters, surpassing by two Christy Mathewson's 58-year-old National League record. Last season, mostly before his injury, Sandy worked 184 innings, pitched 11 complete games, won 14 games, lost seven, had a 2.52 ERA, struck out 216 men and walked only 57. He won the league ERA title.

On April 24, 1962, against the Chicago Cubs, he struck out 18 batters, becoming the only man ever to pitch two 18-strikeout games. On June 30, he pitched his first no-hitter, beating the Mets, 5-0. He struck out 13 Mets and walked five. He was simply overpowering. "Either he throws the fastest ball I've ever seen, or I'm going blind," Richie Ashburn said.

"I would have felt sick . . . I'd of shot myself . . . if someone had got a hit on an off-speed pitch," Sandy said later. "I guess a no-hitter is the dream, the ultimate ambition of every pitcher."

The closest thing to a hit was a hard grounder by Frank Thomas in the second inning. Shortstop Maury Wills ran into the hole to cut off the ball and throw out the batter. Wills also handled the final out, a twisting grounder. "I would have tripped that runner if I'd had to," Sandy said.

The injury, which sidelined Koufax from mid-July on, bothered him early in the year. Eventually it prevented him from throwing a curveball, but his fastball was enough for awhile. He had shut out the Giants and Mets in consecutive games when he finally had to give in to the injury.

At first, the tip of his left forefinger felt numb. Later it blistered. Sandy was bothered by it, but not deeply concerned. He thought the discomfort would pass and did not report it. Had he reported it earlier, treatment might have been more speedily effective. Had he reported it later, treatment might have been useless, and the finger might have had to be removed.

The finger was treated with expensive shots, drugs and ointments. The layers of dried skin peeled off the tip of the finger, which was left raw and sore. "I didn't mind when it was just numb," said Sandy, "but this is just intolerable. I can't touch anything. It's like I would be touching fire." He walked around with a glove on his left hand to keep his finger warm, while the Dodger pennant hopes went cold.

The origin of the ailment will forever be a mystery. It was the sort of thing which one might suffer catching a stinging throw barehanded. This might have happened to Sandy. Or he might merely have been squeezing the ball too hard when he pitched. He does remember getting hit on the left hand by a ball while batting.

Dr. Travis Winser, a cardiovascular specialist, discovered that Sandy had unusually large and thickly bunched muscles, and suggested that when Sandy drew his arm far back to pitch, these muscles temporarily blocked off the circulation of the blood to his hand. He suggested an operation on the shoulder. Sandy turned down the suggestion.

Some of Sandy's teammates do consider him "muscle bound," and he sometimes swings monkey-like from the dugout roof in an effort to loosen up before pitching. He has occasionally had shoulder and arm soreness which might be traced to this overmuscular development. In 1959 he had been taking injections for pains in his arms when he began to come back by working batting practice.

"How do you feel?" he was asked.

"Good."

"But you were grimacing every time you threw."

"That's nothing," Sandy said. "I usually cry."

There was real reason for tears in 1962. The ailment he suffered bears the quaintly impressive diagnosis of "The Reynaud Phenomenon," which will make a superb title for the mystery story yet to be written on how the Giants stole the pennant. Reynaud, a Frenchman who preferred soccer, discovered an arterial constriction or obstruction which limits the normal circulation.

In Sandy's case, the problem was centered in the fleshy part of his left palm between the knuckles and finger, and reduced passage of blood and oxygen to the forefinger by 85 percent, insufficient for 20-game winners. Four-Fingered Koufax proved considerably less adaptable than Three-Fingered Brown.

"I feel like Job," Sandy said. "I can't get mad at anybody except the Lord, and if I do that, I'm afraid things will get worse.

"What the hell could I have done about it, anyway?"

Off-season predictions on the 1963 National League pennant race were hung up in conjecture over Sandy's ability to regain his best form. The finger seemed healthy in spring training, although Koufax suffered a blood blister and a torn fingernail which were worth 150 interviews each.

Sandy waited no later than the second day of the season to steady the shaking hands and thumping hearts of his Dodger superiors by five-hitting the Cubs, 2-1, and two starts later he two-hit the Cubs, 2-0, striking out 14. Although he was keeping secret a stiffness in his shoulder, Koufax announced to the waiting world that his arm "feels as good as ever."

Whereupon Koufax was promptly stricken once again. "I have a pain in my left shoulder that keeps getting worse," he announced.

This ailment was found to be in the posterior capsule of his left shoulder, where the upper arm bone fits into the shoulder blade. Sandy had apparently stretched or torn the membrane which covers the muscles there and he was laid up two weeks.

He returned with a five-hit, 11-1 victory over St. Louis, whereupon he was able to joke. "I guess I'm just getting old," he said, "falling apart piece by piece." The Dodgers laughed nervously.

Sandy's next start, on May 11, was the Dodger Stadium no-hitter against the Giants. After his first no-hitter, the sparkle had been spoiled a bit by criticism of his weak-hitting victims, the Mets. Koufax admits the criticisms gave him added incentive as he pitched his no-hitter against the Giants. "There's not a weak spot in their lineup," he pointed out, permitting a rare boast.

As it stands, only Warren Spahn among other active pitchers has thrown two no-hitters. Only Bob Feller, Cy Young and Larry Corcoran among all pitchers have ever thrown three no-hitters. Possibly no pitcher in baseball history has been harder to hit when he was right than Feller, and Koufax is showing signs of being that type of pitcher.

During his career, Koufax has averaged more than nine strikeouts a game, which is an all-time record pace. Closest to him has been Herb Score, who, in his brief big-league career, averaged more than eight strikeouts a game. Feller averaged fewer than seven.

The question with Koufax would seem to be: is he another Score, or another Feller? A fastball pitcher's career is often limited and easily destroyed by sore arms or other injuries, if not by the passage of years alone. Pitching can be an old man's game. Many, as Feller did, and as Warren Spahn has been doing, lose little to the years. The extra hop goes off the fastball, but the repertoire increases and the pitches are thrown at various speeds to set up the batters, keep them off balance and retire them effectively.

Will Koufax be able to make the adjustment when he is no longer young and his arm is no longer strong? "It is impossible to tell how Koufax or any pitcher will do," says Becker. "It's inside them, in their hearts and in their minds. You can't predict it. Up to now, Sandy has overpowered the hitters. He hasn't pitched to spots, developed many pitches or used slow stuff much. He hasn't had to be a student of pitching. It may be very hard for him. On the other hand, he is intelligent, he has overcome a lot of problems up to now, and he has matured. He may be able to change himself over when the time comes."

"I don't know if I can make the change," Sandy says, reasonably. "I do know that I'm not yet ready to try. Why should I, as long as I have my speed?"

The question may be one of dedication. "I'm not sure I want to stay in baseball all my life," Sandy says. "Maybe I'd like to coach, but I have no managerial ambitions. I might go into business."

Sandy does work hard at his present trade. "If it is his turn to pitch and it is an off-day, he will come out to the ballpark and work," manager Alston says. "Not every pitcher will do that. Oh, he's had the natural ability all along, but he had to work very hard to make something of it. He's done just that and it reflects a lot of credit on him."

Sandy Koufax, says Birdie Tebbetts, "is an example of a pitcher who has worked at his trade since the time he left college and came directly to pitch in the majors. He has worked, and now look at him—he's the best in baseball."

"When I first saw Koufax," Leo Durocher says, "I thought he was going to be another Rex Barney, a speedballer who never quite finds himself. But gradually Sandy has developed a better rhythm. He isn't as tight now as he used to be, and his control is greatly improved."

There are no measurements to determine if Sandy approaches Barney, much less Feller, in velocity. Stan Musial, perhaps today's leading veteran expert, says, "I'd say Sandy throws just as fast as anyone around today. Feller was clocked at 100 miles-per-hour. I'd say Sandy's fastball is about the same."

Additionally, says Don Zimmer, "Koufax has the best lefthanded curveball I've ever seen. I'm a wild swinger. He's the only pitcher I know where when I expect the curveball, and I get the curveball, I still can't hit it. It's up so high, I hold back, and then it breaks down across the plate so blankety sharp and so blankety late, it's too late for me to swing at it."

Throwing hard, whether straight or crooked, Sandy regularly keeps the batters from hitting the ball well, if at all. In his own opinion, the 18-strikeout games represented more than the no-hitters. "You need luck to pitch a no-hitter," he has said. "The batters hit the ball and they must hit it to the right places, and you need the fielders behind you to make the outs. There is very little if any luck involved in strikeouts."

However, he seems disenchanted with strikeouts. "I'd rather get the batters out with one pitch," he says. "Wild-man Koufax tried to throw it by everyone. Older and wiser Koufax pitches the ball, anticipating it will be hit at someone. . . . Strikeouts are nice to have, particularly in a jam, and they're going to come to a pitcher who throws hard, but I wouldn't trade a 20-game season for all the strikeout records in the book."

On the night of a losing game, during which Sandy had passed the milestone of his 1000th strikeout, a reporter mentioned the fact to him. "So what?" Sandy snapped. "I lost, didn't I?"

He no longer loses very often, neither his temper, nor games. "It is an amazing thing to see him now," says Zimmer. "He used to fight himself, on the mound and off. He couldn't stand for anything to go wrong. You could see he couldn't stand it, you could actually see him fighting himself on the mound.

"He has incredible confidence," says Larry Sherry. "He should have, of course, he's that good, but it's more than that. He just doesn't seem to have any doubts at all. He knows, he just plain *knows*, he's going to get them out. When you mature as a player, you mature as a person. He has confidence in himself now, not only as a player, but also as a person."

Koufax has said, "When I get near the end of my career, I hope to have earned the respect of players and public that Gil Hodges commands. I like to pattern myself after him."

Mostly Sandy Koufax stays in quiet and complex character. He is a mental person leading a physical life. He is intelligent and articulate, but shy and quiet, celebrated but withdrawn. He is polite to people, but often he cannot be at ease with them, and thus warm with them. If he does not welcome them, it is hard for him to pretend he does. He brushes off slights, at least openly. He is grateful for favors and fair treatment.

After his second no-hitter, Koufax got a call from Dodger vice-president Buzzie Bavasi. The club, Bavasi said, was going to give him something extra as a reward. "You don't owe me a thing," Sandy said. "You've been too good to me already." Later, Sandy elaborated. "They paid me for 1963 just like I had pitched great ball all season long last year," he said. "My contract never has reflected the fact that I was hurt from July on. I won't forget what the club has done for me."

Overall, says Koufax, baseball has been good to him. "It's been my life, a good life," he says. "I know that. I owe it a lot and I intend to pay it back. I'll be as good a pitcher as I can be.

"As for the rest, well, I'll go my own way. Whatever I do off the field, outside of baseball, after baseball, is my own business, so long as I don't cause any trouble. If I live alone, well, so what? If I like to do something, who has to know? Who cares? I'm no different than anyone else. I figure my life is my own to live as I want.

"Is that asking too much?"

Roberto Clemente   Photo credit: National Baseball Library/Cooperstown, N.Y.

ROBERTO CLEMENTE

Man of Paradox

Sport Magazine   May 1965

Once again, **Sport** *is in the right place ahead of time, with a profile of Roberto Clemente a year before he won the National League's Most Valuable Player Award. Author Arnold Hano later produced a book-length biography of the great, often brooding outfielder shortly before Clemente's tragic death in 1972.*

By Arnold Hano

It was a good year, 1964.

For the second time in four years, Roberto Walker Clemente was the National League's leading hitter for average, batting .339. He'd hung tough while Willie Mays and Billy Williams threatened to tear the league apart, he'd passed them both with 2½ months to go, and he held on. In racing parlance, he won in hand.

Thirty years old and the league's finest hitter. Over the past five years, Roberto Clemente batted slightly over .328. To keep matters in perspective, over the same years, Hank Aaron hit .314. That's how good Clemente is.

And so he spoke from a pinnacle at the end of the 1964 season. He was 30 years old, with ten years in the majors behind him. Looking ahead, he pictured another ten years "at full speed." Then, he said, if he needed the money or felt he just had to play some more, "I would go three, four more years, slowed down a little." Baseball was in his blood. When he was finally through, he would coach or manage down in Puerto Rico, his home.

He was earning slightly over $50,000 a year in salary, plus a few extra dollars in testimonials and the like. Not too much extra, because Clemente is Latin and Clemente is dark-skinned, and somehow advertising agencies think that there's nothing quite like running a stainless blade over the pink cheek and fuzzy skin of a young white lad from Peoria.

"I look forward to a rest," he said. "No more winter ball. I play too much winter ball in the past. It makes me tired when I go to spring training. Last three winters, I just play half seasons in Puerto Rican league. Now, no more winter ball. In spring of 1965, I'll report strong. You see."

Confident, strong, assured, talented. Few worlds to conquer. Yes, he'd like to win a pennant with the Pirates. But he'd already been on one pennant winner and World Series winner, in 1960. Perhaps some year the writers who select the Most Valuable Players of each league would suddenly realize Clemente existed. But little else remained. Still, reporting strong for spring training in 1965 would mean a Clemente ready to belt the ball with all that savage joy he seems to lug up to the plate. A ball fan can ask for little else more exciting than watching a healthy Clemente club baseballs. And so we perched, waiting for spring training, for the new year, which to ball fans begins on March 1, when the players begin falling out on the grasses of Florida and Arizona and Palm Springs. Clemente, reporting strong, would be at Ft. Myers.

He almost didn't report at all. Weak or strong.

Roberto Walker Clemente is a paradox. For one, his middle name proves it. Walker. Nobody walks as seldom as Clemente. Swinger, they should call him. Vernon Law calls him Herschel, which is absurdly ludicrous, but not so ludicrous as a middle name of Walker.

He says things he means, and then he finds he is doing the opposite.

And he said no ball in the winter of 1964–65, in Puerto Rico. Absolutely. Finished. Clemente is an honest man, one of the most honest men we know. He is also an honorable man. When there are kids to see in hospitals, Clemente arranges it himself, and goes. No photographers tag along. "I do not go because the club wants me to go. I go because *I* want to go," he says. He is currently involved in a youth program in Puerto Rico to combat delinquency. Conscientious. He bought his folks a home in Carolina, Puerto Rico, nine years ago. "I do not think I am giving my parents something. I am trying to pay them back for giving me so much." Cornball and true. That is Roberto Clemente.

So he went home after the '64 season, and agreed to manage the San Juan club in the Puerto Rican league against such teams as Arecibo and

Santurce and the rest, a tough league, full of major-leaguers. But he wouldn't play winter ball. Never again.

Not at first.

Besides, he was a bridegroom. He'd married Vera Zabala, and moved into a new house in Rio Piedras, south of San Juan, a few miles west of Carolina, where his folks lived, and he settled down to the domestic life.

Too completely.

One afternoon in December he was mowing the lawn, as a good husband should. The blade of the mower hit a sharp rock, propelled it upward. It struck Clemente on the right thigh with shocking force.

By this time, of course, Clemente had started performing as a playing-manager. In a league that ran nearly three months, he played part-time in 15 games. Not too arduous. But 15 more games than he had planned. Back in Pittsburgh, the front office—alerted by the lawn mower accident—was biting its collective nails. "We would naturally prefer that Clemente rest," said a Pirate official during this past winter. "He can't improve any. He does not need to play. They put pressure on him to change his mind. The people in San Juan hounded him until he gave in to the popular demand."

Clemente had a slightly different version. "They want me to play, yes, and I want to help San Juan win the pennant, but I also do it to earn extra money."

Along came the Puerto Rican league All-Star game, and Clemente was prevailed upon to make a pinch-hitting appearance. "I could hardly walk," Clemente has since said. "I couldn't risk running." He batted, and hit a typical Clemente shot to right field, and he trotted slowly to first.

Not slowly enough. The leg crumpled. A ligament popped. He felt "something like water draining inside my leg." Not water. Blood. After the game, he was carried to a car, taken to a doctor.

The leg had started to swell. The next day he couldn't walk. The doctor said it was an internal hemorrhage. He gave it three days to stop of its own accord, and drain off. Each day the leg was bigger. Finally the doctor scheduled an operation in a San Juan hospital. The thigh was sliced open and the excess blood drained from the clotted bruise.

A ligament was torn in the right thigh. This is not terribly serious. Nearly every sprain involves a torn ligament. Ligaments heal quickly. Still, Clemente is a valuable piece of property. As the same Pirate official said candidly: "We can't afford to lose him." When word reached an already nervous Pittsburgh organization, general manager Joe L. Brown dispatched Caribbean scout Howie Haak to see Clemente and the doctor. Haak transmitted optimistic reports. But an item in the *Sporting News* of February 13, 1965, again cast a dark light on the injury. It quoted Clemente as saying the doctor "told me not to run much in spring training and that it would come around halfway through the season if I took care of it, which I will."

Brown was frantic. A Clemente partially disabled for half a season is a ball team deprived of its lone steady gun. He picked up the phone and called Clemente. And—relayed Pirate public relations man Jack Berger —once again Clemente painted a rosy picture. The reports were exaggerated. He was in good condition. His leg was fine. He'd report for spring training, ready to go full speed. Amen.

Clemente, of course, did not report to spring training ready to go at top speed. Clemente, in fact, was still in Puerto Rico when spring training opened. He was in a hospital with a malarial fever. Doctors said he had contracted a paratyphoid infection at a hog farm he operates. But the paradox before that was Clemente telling the *Sporting News,* the Pirates and me different things.

Roberto Clemente, man of paradox, is a man who has insisted through the years the only way a team can win a pennant is to be "a family team." To play as a family, not a bunch of individuals. In a family, as Clemente knows—he comes from a family of six children—it is all for one, one for all, and everybody protects everybody else. Yet the last words Clemente said to me over the phone from Puerto Rico short weeks before the 1965 season opened were: *"I* had a good season last year. Now *they* have to have a good season, too."

It is as close as you usually can get one man to criticize his teammates. Yet it is also the truth. And for a man who insists a winning team be a family, it must be recalled that as soon as Bill Mazeroski hit a home run off Ralph Terry to win the seventh game of the 1960 World Series, Bob Clemente turned his back on the post-Series victory celebration and instead rushed straight back to Puerto Rico. It is also Clemente who blasted writers for choosing teammate Dick Groat as the Most Valuable Player that 1960 season, and it is also an incredulous Clemente who was flabbergasted when teammate Don Hoak was No. 2 in the same poll.

He is blunt, honest, outspoken, critical. Yet he is also a man uneasy about his own public reputation. Teammate Alvin McBean, who is the resident intellectual on the Pirates, and for one season a roommate of Clemente, said last summer: "Robby loves his image. He takes good care of it. He is wary of being with people he does not approve of. He believes people know you by the company you keep, so he keeps careful company." Clemente does not like the Pittsburgh press—McBean says— "because he thinks the press doesn't like him and won't give him the publicity he deserves." McBean feels Clemente's gripe is justified. "If Robby were on the Yankees, Mickey Mantle would be nowhere. That's how good he is."

Which brings us back to high ground. He is a bridegroom, yes, a self-styled gardener, and a Puerto Rican manager; he is blunt, honest, and bitter. He talks family ball while worrying over his personal image.

There is a book out, in hardcover and papercover, titled: *Baseball's Greatest Players Today.*

Excluded is perhaps *the* greatest player today.

Bob Clemente.

It is an old story to Bob Clemente, this odd neglect. Nobody in base-ball is a better hitter, if for once we remember that a hitter's ability is not measured by the length of his foul drives or the kind of car he owns. We measure a hitter by the frequency of his base hits.

It has always been thus. Neglect, and a need to explain him away. A caption beneath a photo of Bob Clemente in a baseball yearbook after the 1963 season read:

"Roberto Clemente's .320 BA was second best in the NL, but he has yet to bat in 100 runs a season."

Second highest in the league, *but.* Always, they toss in a "but" after pinning praise on Clemente.

Praise of Clemente rarely sounds like praise. At the conclusion of one season, Stan Musial said, "He's a fine, all-around player, good defensively, good at bat, and getting better all the time." Musial might have been talking about Jerry Lumpe or Tony Gonzalez.

He was talking of Clemente, and he was talking right after the 1961 season. All Clemente did in '61 was hit .351. He also scored 100 runs, knocked in 89, belted 23 home runs.

He led his league in 1961. Nobody really noticed because this was the year an unknown named Norm Cash hit .361, and Roger Maris hit his 61 home runs. And anyway, the world champion Pirates finished sixth. Who cares what Clemente hit? So he again led the league in 1964, after being close in the interim 1962 and 1963 seasons. This time he led both leagues, and when *United Press-International* put together its 1964 All-Star team, it left off Clemente. Its outfielders were Mays, Mantle and Williams. The *UPI* writers must have thought this Williams was Ted, not Billy, and that Mays was Mays of 1954 not 1964, and that Mantle should be honored solely because he was still warm and breathing after the cruel ordeal of another year on his crippled legs.

The *Associated Press* set things right. It put Clemente on the team, and did not list Williams on the first or second squads. Because all you Williams fans will start writing letters with pointy sticks dipped in blood— yours, I hope—I hastily add that I think Williams is a fine and powerful hitter and a likeable human being, and when he begins to play a tighter game in left field, the *AP* will take more notice.

Neglect. Through the ten years of Clemente's National League career, experts have failed to applaud his hitting. What is far more incredible is the failure to recognize what a superb fielder he is. He may be the finest rightfielder of the past 35 years, or as far back as I can safely stretch my memory. He is All-Star on his fielding alone. But even if I am exaggerating, and Clemente is not a whit better defensively than Johnny Callison, who is a marvelous rightfielder, this ought to be enough. To hit like Clemente and field like Callison makes for a great performer. After the '64 season, Clemente, as usual, finished far back in the Most Valuable Player voting. Eighth, to be exact. Remove Clemente from the Pirate lineup and the Pirates would find themselves battling the Mets.

It has had its effect, this lack of acclaim. Clemente is pained by it. He wants to be noticed, appreciated, loved. And because he is not noticed—at least, not as much as he thinks he deserves—he feels there is a dark conspiracy operating against him. There is a Pittsburgh sportswriter, he says (and he names him), who has it against Clemente. "He makes propaganda against me," Clemente says. It has soured Clemente, embittered him.

"I have no goals," he said a trifle impatiently. "Have a good season. That is enough. Hitting for average is not the whole thing. My best year was 1960. I should have been voted Most Valuable Player."

Just like that. It happened four years before, but he still felt the blow.

"I was very bitter. I still am bitter. I carried the club all year." He says this, mind you, without meaning to be offensive, without wanting to sound conceited or rude. "I was the only batter to hit over .300 all year. Never under. The year 1961 was good."

You can get him away from the bitterness, but not for long. "Groat had a fine year," Clemente will inject, "but he was out a month." Bitterness has twisted a fact or two. There are things Clemente did that Groat did not do—such as knocking in 94 runs to Groat's 50—but you cannot belittle Groat's devotion to the game that season. He was not out a month, despite a broken wrist. Clemente played 144 games; Groat played 138. Clemente batted 570 times. Groat batted 573 times.

But Clemente's major point is correct. He was—again—unnoticed. When the Pirates went against the Yankees in the World Series that year, Yankee pitchers could scarcely believe their eyes. They had Bill Skowron on their own squad. Skowron was the wildest swinger an American Leaguer could imagine. But Clemente went beyond Skowron. Yankee pitchers could hardly wait. Now, Clemente did not break any hitting records in the '61 Series, but for a guy the Yankees just plain knew they could get out, he was the only Pirate to hit safely every game, going nine for 29. Clemente hit .310.

A hit every game, and as Clemente recalls today: "The only way you could find my name in the papers was with a magnifying glass." And when the Series ended on its high note, Clemente hustled out of the winning clubhouse and flew home. Today, instead of wearing the 1960 pennant or World Series ring, it is the 1961 All-Star ring Clemente wears and cherishes.

The 1961 All-Star Game was the game in Candlestick Park, won by the National League by one run in the tenth inning. Clemente was the star. He tripled to the right-center field fence in the second inning off Whitey Ford, and scored on a flyball by Bill White. In the fourth, with Mays on third, Clemente hit the sacrifice fly. And in the last of the tenth, with Mays on second and the score tied, Clemente singled and Mays scored the winning run.

After it was over, Clemente bubbled. (He did not yet know the newspapers would spend more time telling how the wind had blown Stu Miller off the mound.) "When I get big hit in the tenth inning," he said, "I feel better than good. But what really makes me feel most good is that Danny Murtaugh let me play the whole game . . . He pay me big compliment."

Getting pulled out of All-Star lineups after three innings happens to the best of players. To Clemente it would have been a blow to his pride, his manhood, his confidence. He cannot slough off such things.

Clemente is a feeling man. In early August of 1964, Clemente set an unofficial record for helmet punting. It was in Chicago, and it was hot. Clemente had planted himself in the batter's box the way he always does, which is to say slightly illegally. His rear foot, his right foot, was two or three inches out of the back of the box. The Cub catcher pointed this out to the plate umpire. Eventually the umpire told Clemente to get in the box.

"What's the matter?" Clemente asked sharply. "For ten years I bat this way. Where you been?" The batter's box was re-drawn, and a grumbling Clemente bounced out easily to short. Then he removed his helmet and from beyond first base, booted it into the Pirate dugout.

There is a grapevine in baseball, and along the vine traveled this latest juicy bit: Get Clemente back in the box. He turns so blind-mad he can't see the ball. So in Philadelphia on August 28, catcher Clay Dalrymple pointed to Clemente's feet, and umpire Chris Pelekoudas demonstrated his ability to draw a straight line. Clemente cramped himself into the new box, and promptly singled to right field.

Which puts it in perspective. He wears his emotions on his thin skin, yes, but he is not stupid. He grasped what was happening, and shrugged off the tiny battle of nerves.

He has won other battles of nerves. For many of the ten years Clemente has spent in the majors, he was the special pigeon of pitcher Bob Purkey. At one point last season, Clemente was hitting .176 lifetime against Purkey, ten hits in six years. Clemente looked back through that six-year drought.

"Lots of pitchers give me trouble. Drysdale, Marichal, Maloney. Last year Maloney pitched a game against us, nobody could see the ball. It was the fastest I ever saw anybody. But Purkey was the worst. He threw lots of bad balls. I hit pitches I like, no matter where they are. But I couldn't hit Purkey's bad pitches. Then one day I said to myself, 'You win, Purkey.' I decided to stop swinging at his bad balls."

They got together, Purkey and Clemente, once in Cincinnati and once in Pittsburgh, and the first time since resolving the matter in his mind, Clemente walloped Purkey for three hits. One of them kangarooed over the center-field fence on one bounce. The next time, in Pittsburgh, Clemente again laid off until a now-surprised Purkey was forced to come in, and Clemente bombed him for three more hits. Six hits in two games, after ten hits in six years.

But raking opposing pitchers is an old story; it is almost the only story the public seems to know of Clemente, probably the finest ballplayer alive.

There is more.

Roberto Clemente was born in Puerto Rico in the depression year of 1934. He was the youngest of six kids, one girl, five boys. Later, the sister and one brother died. But even in the depression, with six little ones to feed, it was never bad.

Clemente's father was the foreman of a sugar plantation. Not wealthy, no, but never poor. Always working, always well able to take care of himself, his wife, and the kids. Perhaps if there is a fault to be found in Clemente's youth, it lies in Clemente's youth. He was the youngest—the baby—and it was never very difficult for any of them, particularly the baby. Spoiled, is what we call it here. Loved, is what Clemente calls his boyhood.

"We lived in a big wooden house, with a large front porch," he says. "Five bedrooms, living room, dining room, kitchen. Indoor bathroom." The elder Clemente also owned trucks, and took on shipping jobs. During the summers Roberto occasionally helped out, loading and unloading sand. An easy life, mildly indolent, under the warm sun.

"When I was a kid, I realized what lovely persons my mother and father were. I was treated real good. I learned the right way to live. I never heard any hate in my house. Not for anybody. I never heard my mother say a bad word to my father, or my father to my mother. During the war, when food all over Puerto Rico was limited, we never went hungry. They always found a way to feed us."

Roberto played ball every day. Mainly, softball. He played shortstop. He pitched. He played hard ball in high school, in his home town of

Carolina. When not playing he squeezed a hard rubber ball, to strengthen his arm muscles. He went out for track in high school. Soon he threw the javelin 195 feet, high-jumped six feet, broke 45 feet in the triple jump, and was considered a shoo-in for a place on the 1956 Olympic squad.

But that was the future. Clemente went to high school and wanted to continue at the university, studying engineering. It was not to be. Baseball got in the way.

His first formal fan was his high-school history teacher, Roberto Marin, who saw the youngster play softball, and passed the word to Pedro Zorilla, owner of the Santurce team.

Zorilla shrugged off the unsolicited advice. Later, Zorilla took in a double-A baseball game in the town of Manati, where he lived. There was a 17-year-old centerfielder who that day hit a 390-foot line drive and threw out a runner at third.

In the stands, Zorilla asked, "Who is he?"

"His name is Roberto Clemente," said a fan.

"Sounds familiar," said Zorilla.

Zorilla approached the boy he once could have had for nothing. This time he offered a bonus of $300. Elated, Roberto went home, but to his astonishment his parents said, "Not enough."

Zorilla agreed to pay Clemente a $500 bonus, plus $60 a month, and the boy began to play for Santurce during the winters on the same team as Willie Mays, Orlando Cepeda, Ruben Gomez and others.

During his youth Clemente had no notion he would ever play bigleague ball. "I thought Stateside players were better than Latin players," he said. "I thought you had to be Superman to make it. But when Minoso and Avila made it big, I realized others could do it, too."

Big-league scouts began to tail Clemente. Al Campanis, of the Dodgers' scouting office, organized a clinic in Puerto Rico. Clemente was one of 100 prospects invited. "Campanis asked me to do everything," says Clemente. "Run, hit, field, throw. Nobody else did anything." When the one-man show ended, Campanis suggested the boy join the Dodger farm system. Clemente's father turned down the idea. He wanted Roberto to finish high school.

More big-league scouts tailed Clemente. During his senior year of high school in 1953, nine teams approached Clemente. They held fire until graduation. Then the Dodgers made a concrete offer: a $10,000 bonus for signing. It was one of the largest bonuses paid a Latin boy. Clemente agreed verbally. Later that same day, Milwaukee came along with a bonus of close to $40,000.

The confused boy brought the dilemma home to his folks.

His mother said sternly: "If you give the word, you keep the word."

He signed with the Dodgers.

Clemente went to Montreal for the 1954 season and when the Dodgers left him unprotected in the draft, the Pirates claimed him. "I did not even know where Pittsburgh was," he says.

He had other problems. "I had studied English in school, but I was not able to speak until I began to talk to players up here. Not speaking the language is a terrible problem." There was the matter of race. "At Montreal, when we went on the road, I could not stay with the white players in Richmond, Virginia. I felt it was childish." There were other racial difficulties. "The first thing the average white Latin American player does when he comes to the States is associate with other whites. He doesn't want to be seen with Latin Negroes, even ones from his own country, because he's afraid people might think he's colored." So Clemente was cut off this second way, as well.

It got a little worse, a little more open later. He joined the Pirates for '55 and, says Clemente, "there was trouble with the players. They make smart remarks—about Negroes—to me. I make them back to them. Not behind my back. Right to my face."

The first year up was difficult all around, Clemente says. "Latin Americans need time to get adjusted. We lead different lives in the U.S. We're always meeting new people, seeing new faces. Everything is strange. The language barrier is great at first. We have trouble ordering food in restaurants. You have no idea how segregation held some of us back. We Latins are people of high emotions, and coming to this country we need time to settle down emotionally. Once we're relaxed and have no problems, we can play baseball well. The people who never run into these problems don't have any idea at all what kind of ordeal it can be."

In 1955, Clemente, who had the terrible habit of bobbing his head when he swung, batted an indifferent .255, in 124 games. Nor was there much power. Five home runs, 47 RBI. Also, he had a habit of swinging at bad balls and he walked only 18 times in 474 at-bats. Coach George Sisler corrected the bobbing head. He also informed Clemente the only way he would make it would be to lay off bad balls, to force the pitcher to come in with the pitch Clemente liked. Clemente nodded soberly, and in 1956, in 70 more at-bats, he walked five times fewer.

But he also hit .311. Clemente had indeed forced the pitcher to come in with the pitches he liked. He just liked them all.

Good years alternated with lean. He hit .255 his first year, raised it to .311, plunged to .253, and bounced back to .289. But there were reasons for this Yo-Yo hitting. Clemente bears other tags than bargain-basement price tag. He is injury prone; worse, he is considered by many baseball people to be one of the game's true hypochondriacs.

Injuries kept him out of 30 games in 1955. Injuries kept him out of 43 games in 1957. Later, he sat out 49 games in 1959. He missed 143 games in his first five full years.

In 1953, in the Puerto Rican league, Clemente tried to solve his failure to hit home runs by switching to a lighter bat, a la the big-leaguers. "I swung so hard I spun around and hurt my back." The sore back was aggravated in 1954. Clemente had just paid a visit to his brother, dying of a brain tumor in a Puerto Rican hospital, and was driving back to the park. At an intersection, a drunk smashed into him at 60 miles an hour. Three spinal discs were jarred loose. The back bothered Clemente off and on for years. Then a six-month spell in the Marines at Paris Island and Camp Lejeune in the winter of 1957–58 mysteriously eased out the kinks. Clemente explains it cryptically: "I worked like hell."

Other ills. Clemente made a sidearm throw in 1958 and cracked his right elbow. The condition was worsened in 1961 when a stray pitch by Don Drysdale caught Clemente on the elbow. That winter he underwent surgery to remove a bone chip.

Clemente has been beset with colds and flu attacks and nervous stomach spasms. And now malaria. Teammates say not a day goes by that Roberto does not have some complaint. Teammate McBean has "psyched" Clemente this way:

"Robby likes to talk about the way he feels. He complains a lot. He wants you to talk to him, make him feel good. When he says he feels terrible, I tell him he feels good, that he can really hit the pitcher going against us, that he'll go four-for-four. He will say he has diarrhea or he feels weak. I tell him he is fine. He has his own routine for keeping up his strength. He gets up late, has breakfast, takes maybe a 30-minute walk, and then he goes back to bed. He used to say to me, 'The more you rest, the prettier you become.' "

Clemente agrees he likes lots of sleep. "Because of the schedule and all the travel, it is tough getting the sleep you need," he says. "I do not believe in slumps. I believe a batter gets tired, and he can't swing the way he should. If I feel strong, I know I will hit. So I must sleep and rest."

Clemente knows what is said about him. "They think it is an act. When I said I had back trouble, they call me, 'Mama's Boy.' 'Goldbrick.' When my elbow was swollen big as a softball, they say it was in my head." Then he zeroes in. "If I am sick, I do not deny. If my back is hurting me and I am forced to punch at the ball, with no power, I tell the truth. I tell them I am hurting."

In 1963 this clash between Clemente and his doubters over his health reached its peak. "The Pittsburgh press had me at odds with Danny Murtaugh. They never said it exactly that way, but they know how to say it other ways. They are so slick. I caught the flu in San Francisco. Then we flew to Los Angeles, and we had shrimp and steak on the plane. I got sick in my room at three a.m. I began to sweat. I had the shakes. I called the doctor at six. His nurse told me to put hot towels on my stomach. Later that morning, they pumped out my stomach. I went to the ballpark. Murtaugh asked me how I felt.

"How do you think I feel?" Clemente answered. "Very bad."

Murtaugh told Bill Mazeroski, the team captain, to look over Clemente. Mazeroski asked Clemente how he felt.

"Bad," Clemente said.

"Stick around," Maz said, and reported back to Murtaugh that he thought Clemente could play.

"Drysdale struck me out twice that day," Clemente recalls. "I had no swing at all. You can imagine." But Clemente also had a hit that day.

The next day was a doubleheader in Houston. Clemente spent 40 minutes on the rubbing table, feeling dizzy. Murtaugh tried his own special brand of psychology.

"I think you're the best in the league," he told his rightfielder. "You make good money. You have to put out."

"I can't play like this," Clemente protested. In disgust, Murtaugh walked away.

So Clemente sat out the next three games, which gave the Pittsburgh press a chance to suggest that the star and his manager were not getting along, that Murtaugh was "tired" of Clemente's attitude.

Having said all this, the name is still baseball, not psychosomatics. Sick or well or both, he has managed to drag his body to the plate and cream baseballs. Clemente began hitting with greater authority in the pennant year of 1960. He had 16 home runs. All season long he came up with Virdon and Groat on base, and line drives drilled them home. In the field he made his patented catches—racing far to left or right, leaving his feet in a leap toward the stars, and gaffing baseballs with the fingers of his glove. He threw bullets from the base of Forbes Field's distant right-field fence to cut down would-be stretchers at second. He caught flies hit straightaway with his basket catch, a la Mays. (And, as always, he was infuriated when anybody suggested he stole the style from Mays.)

Even running the bases had extra drama. A moment that well symbolizes Clemente came on the day the 1960 pennant was clinched. He stood in the batter's box while the public-address announcer told the crowd that the Cubs had beaten the Cardinals. And Pittsburgh was the National League champion. A jubilant Clemente nailed Warren Spahn's fastball for a base hit. Then Hal Smith doubled, and Clemente ran through coach Frank Oceak's signal at third, to score in a belly-whooping cloud of dust.

"Stop at third?" he said later, incredulous. "I want to get to the bench quick, and talk about winning the pennant."

Another time he scored from first on a single to break up the game with the Dodgers. "I had a sore foot," he said happily. "I wanted to end the game and rest it."

This was Roberto Clemente in 1960, 25, going on 26 years old, strong and lean and happy and on a pennant winner. "We were a family team," he says today.

But the family-ness vanished. The Pirates won the pennant, and what Clemente remembers of the Series is the newspaper version. "When the papers describe all the Pirates before the World Series starts," he once said, "you know what they say about me? 'Good fielder and good runner.' That was supposed to be my contribution. What about my hitting and the runs I batted in?" He hit .314, fourth best in the league, but he felt cheated somehow, so he rushed straight home when Maz hit his home run, and today he wears his All-Star ring, not his Series ring.

But 1960 ushered in a new decade, and it has brought to fruition this most talented hitter. The next year he batted an enormous .351. He had 201 hits for the season, which reminded everybody of the Pirates' last 200-plus hitter, Paul Waner, and only served to embitter Clemente more. "They say the only thing Waner could do better was hit singles," he says. "They say he was only an average fielder."

In 1961 he pounded the ball. Twenty-three home runs, 319 total bases. Four-for-four against the Dodgers May 6; four-for-five against Jim O'Toole on June 14; seven-for-nine in a doubleheader against the Cubs, including five hits in the opener. Four-for-four against Milwaukee, July 8, and the big one, five straight hits against the Cards, on August 3, every hit coming with two strikes. Nobody could get him out. You couldn't waste anything; he hit waste pitches. You couldn't outguess him. He seldom guessed. He just swung and got on base.

And not just hitting. The year before he had led both leagues with 19 outfield assists. In 1961 he made it an unbelievable 23 assists, and five double plays. That's throwing.

It's been that way ever since, .312 and .320 the next two years, and .339 last year, with 211 hits and 87 runs batted in. Lifetime, he has over 1600 hits; he could reach 2000 by the end of 1966. Three thousand hits is within reason. He checks in at 185, tries to stay around 180, and ends up closer to 170. Still, at 5-11, big enough. He does not smoke and he drinks only an occasional beer.

He is at a point in his career where the past and the future are evenly balanced. He looks back ten years and for all the bitterness, he sees them as reasonably good years. He says he expects to get along, in the immediate future, with Harry Walker. "I always get along with my manager," he says.

And does he have any word for other kids, coming out of the sugar fields and mills of Latin America?

"Lead a clean life. Be strong. Work hard. If he is a good player, someone will find him. He does not have to look for someone to tell him he is good."

This is what matters, to Bob Clemente. He is at the halfway point in his career; he has behind him racial slurs and the unhappiness of a stranger in a new land; he has brought with him a burden of pain, some perhaps imagined, but much of it real. He says he has been a man since he was 17 years old, but he still craves the pat on the back, the word of praise, someone coming along to tell him he is good. He is very likely the finest ballplayer alive, when he is right, in mind and body, but one person continues to doubt it and continues to insist it be proved over and over.

Roberto Clemente.

PART SIX

Baseball and the American Character

October 17, 1985

Three years before becoming baseball's 7th commissioner, A. Bartlett Giamatti offers up his view
—as a outsider, Yale University president, and
historian—about what baseball means to society.
This speech was given to the Massachusetts Historical Society and has never before been published.

By A. Bartlett Giamatti

I thank the Massachusetts Historical Society, its speakers committee
and particularly its gracious and learned Director, Mr. Tucker, for
the invitation to speak to you tonight. I sense keenly my unworthi-
ness to address the topic set me—"Baseball and the American Character"—because while an enthusiast about both, I am no expert on baseball, or the American character. I could not, however, resist Mr.
Tucker's invitation which opened by asking "Can we lure you back to
your native city this fall . . ." For what is baseball, and indeed so much
of the American experience, about but looking for home? *Nostos,* the
desire to return home, gives us a nation of immigrants always migrating
in search of home; gives us the American desire to start over in the great
green garden, Eden or Canaan, of the New World; gives us the concept of
a settled home-base and thus, the distance to frontiers; gives us a belief in
individual assertion that finds its fulfillment in aggregation, a grouping

with the like-minded and similarly driven; gives us our sentimental awe of old ways. The hunger for home makes the green geometry of the baseball field more than simply a metaphor for the American experience and character; the baseball field and the game that sanctifies bounderies, rules and law and appreciates cunning, theft and guile; that exalts energy, opportunism and execution while paying lip service to management, strategy and long-range planning, is closer to an embodiment of American life than to the mere sporting image of it.

In all its complementary contradictions, its play of antitheses, baseball captured a continent bounded to east and west by oceans, laced by mountains and rivers, dry, fertile, wet, wooded and at its heart, or stomach, endlessly flat. America is a topographly mythologized by its inhabitants as they crossed and re-crossed it into an image of themselves, diverse, demanding, unified by common acts of consent to a government of themselves, a government consciously checked and balanced, the formal antitheses of the state reflecting and shaping the inclusive ideals and isolationist tendencies of a people receptive and wary. It is a land simultaneously perceived as a field and a park, as a wilderness and a paradise, as raw material endlessly available and an enclosure infinitely significant. The inhabitants of such a land produce high principle easily and endlessly, as a form of native handicraft. We are capable of investing any principle with the systematic coherence, spiritual luminosity and transcendent character of a religious belief as long as it seems to promise to bind us up so that we may go our separate ways.

In *Democracy in America,* De Tocqueville implicitly characterizes this capacity when he shrewdly says, "The Americans have combated [sic] by free institutions the tendency of equality to keep men asunder and they have subdued it" (I. 589). He leads us to an understanding of our America's moral hunger for egalitarian collectivity, which impells us as individuals to aggregate and then to invest the aggregation with numinous meaning, over and over again, as if for the first time every time. This American capacity for religious awe, especially when applied to our social and political structures, at first enchants and then appalls those from other cultures. They find it difficult to comprehend how so many different institutions can be laden with significance akin to religious value merely in order to expunge class and other distinctions and to promote and protect egalitarian diversity.

If such may be at least suggested by the briefest look at a sympathetic French observer in the 1830's and 1840's, what can we learn of ourselves from an observer who did not visit and leave, but who left and visited? In 1877, Henry James published *The American.* The hero is Christopher Newman and we meet him in the Louvre. The year is 1868. The confrontation between the new American man and the old world, urban and aesthetic in its values, is initially less striking than the contraries embodied in Newman himself. "His eye . . ." says James, "was full of contradictory suggestions: and though it was by no means the glowing orb of romance you could find in it almost anything you looked for. Frigid yet friendly, frank yet cautious, shrewd yet credulous, positive yet sceptical, confident yet shy, extremely intelligent and extremely good-humored, there was something vaguely defiant in its concessions and something profoundly reassuring in its reserves" (Boston, 1907, p. 4).

James sees all the contradictions in his American, from frank oppositions yoked by "yet," "yet" to subtle blends of "defiant . . . concessions" and "reassuring . . . reserves." In this eye, this Ego Americanus, there are contraries more complex and tensions more clear than in the generalizing characterizations of De Tocqueville. But our French visitor wrote in the 1830's and 1840's when institutional coherence promised to subdue the centripedal force of equality. James writes in the 1870's. By then the promise of a more perfect Union had been broken by a savage Civil War. Now America would, once again, be compelled to compose or re-compose herself in the aftermath of division and upheaval; once again, free institutions would have to play the role of subduing the tendency equals have to be asunder. Now there was no escaping the gap between America's promises and her execution of them. Post-Civil War America was complex in darker and subtler ways than De Tocqueville could have foreseen. The matter of race would now forever claim the American conscience, if not its consciousness, and that compound whose mix forms the American character—of moral energy and pragmatic efficiency, optimism and guile, respect for law, admiration for the maverick and love of the underdog—would be forever flecked with race-auxilty.

But where in all this is baseball? It is amidst it all. Baseball spans the nineteenth century, its origins and first examples Ante-Bellum, its growth and first golden age coterminous with Reconstruction and the period through the First World War. Baseball grew in the surge to fraternalism, to fraternal societies, sodalities, associations and aggregations, that followed the fratricide. Baseball showed who had won the War and where the country was building, which was in the industrial cities of the North. It was a conservative game, remembering its origins or even making up origins (as in the myth of Abner Doubleday and the invention of the game in 1839 in Cooperstown, a legend created at a banquet at Delmonico's in New York City in 1889). In a fashion typically American, baseball carried a lore at variance with its behaviour; it promoted its self-image as green game while it became a business. That gap in baseball between first promise and eventual execution is with us to this day, as it is with us in so many other ways.

Baseball was Janus, looking both ways by the 1860's. One face looked back at all the varied and original images of the country as a wilderness becoming a garden. This imagery, superbly elucidated by George H. Williams in *Paradise and Wilderness in Christian Thought,* runs through New England Puritanism, German Pietism, Quakerism, Mormonism, Black American spirituals and the great debates on wilderness vs. conservation; it has been addressed in various contexts by such scholars as Henry Nash Smith, Leo Marx and Roderick Nash, to mention a few. One cannot underestimate the impact on the American mind of the image, whether derived from the Bible or the classics, of the contained green space (reified as well in such variety, from the same sources and with the same impact, on our campuses). The force of such imagery may be one reason why now some forty-five million people a summer flow to baseball parks in the midst of urban wilderness, flow in big cities to places which recall in some distant way the place that promised perfection, whose name we derive from the enclosed park of the Persian King, paradise.

Do other American games, also played on green fields, have the same hold? In part, they do; in part, they cannot because they do not reach back to our origins the way baseball does. On April 17, 1778, George Ewing, soldier in the Continental Army at Valley Forge, records in his diary that he played in a game of "base." In 1786, a Princeton student describes a game of "baste ball" on the campus. How could it be? Because in 1744 John Newberry published in London *A Little Pretty Pocket-Book* that contained a rhymed description of "base-ball" and a woodcut showing three boys standing at posts arranged in a diamond shape. Newberry's book was reprinted in America up to 1787. Americans played other ball games, Dutch "stool-ball," Old Cat, Towne-ball, round-ball, and, derived from English rounders, what were called the "New York" and "Massachusetts" games. "By the early nineteenth century," says Harold Seymour in his excellent history of baseball, to which I am throughout indebted, "these simple, informal ballgames were a common sight on village greens and college campuses, especially in the more settled areas of New York and New England, for it was only when communities became established and enjoyed a certain amount of leisure that ball games could flourish."

In 1834, Robin Carver published for children *The Book of Sports* (Boston) and called the game "Base, or Goal Ball"; in 1835, *The Boys and Girls Book of Sports* (Providence) established that a "feeder" tossed a ball underhand to a "striker"; if the striker missed three times with his hoe handle or stick, he was out; if he hit the ball behind him, he was out; if he hit the ball and it was caught, he was out; if he was hit by a thrown ball while running the bases, he was out. The striker ran the bases clockwise. In 1839, the rule became fixed that one runs counter-clockwise.

Thus, people were playing something called base-ball before the birth of the Republic. Within ten years of Jefferson's death, the early outlines of the game and some of its fearful symmetry (3 bases, 3 strikes) were in existence. Within fifty more years, the modern game in most its essentials was set. But back there, before the Civil War, the new country was creating the game.

On June 19, 1846, Alexander Cartwright led his Knickerbocker Base Ball Club of New York to play the New York Nine. We should regard this as the first modern baseball game. The Knickerbockers were a social club of young men in various professions and trades who were as interested in dining well as in playing well and who had elaborate rules for socializing and for baseball. Because their rules for playing baseball were widely imitated, they are responsible for the New York game becoming modern baseball. As Seymour sums up the Knickerbocker's contribution, they established: "The four-base diamond; 90-foot basepaths; three out, all out; batting in rotation; throwing out runners or touching them; nine-man teams, with each player covering a defined position; the location of the pitcher's box in relation to the diamond as a whole" and they established the absolute authority of the umpire (I, 18; 19–20). On June 19, 1846, the Knickerbockers lost 23–1; the contest lasted only four innings. But the game was permanently shaped. And given my view of the congruence between America's deepest dreams and baseball, I never cease to marvel that by some splendid serendipity (or is it Providence?) the lovely, open tract fronting the Hudson and surrounded by woods, in Hoboken, where the Knickerbockers played on that June day, and always played, was called Elysian Field. The Biblical imagery of wilderness and garden from Genesis, the Canticles, Revelation 12 is caught up in the image of Elysium. It is meet and right that this place is the birthplace of our game.

After the Civil War, baseball exploded. Between 1876 and 1902, there were five, perhaps six, major league circuits—The National League (including from '92–'99 the consolidated 12-Club League), The American Association (1882–1892), Union Association (1884), Players' League (1890) and the American League. There, was, therefore, at least one major league club in Altoona, Baltimore, Boston, Brooklyn, Buffalo, Chicago, Cincinnati, Cleveland, Columbus, Detroit, Hartford, Indianapolis, Kansas City, Louisville, Milwaukee, New York, Philadelphia, Pittsburgh, Providence, Richmond, Rochester, St. Louis, St. Paul, Syracuse, Troy, Washington, Wilmington and Worcester. With few exceptions, to the victors of the War belonged the game.

Baseball became professional, gaudy, rowdy and exciting. Skill developed, playing fields appeared everywhere, it swept the country and in-

vaded the Caribbean and Central America. Cartwright took the game to
Hawaii. The Clergy approved, the President and Congress discovered
they were fans, and the average person could not get enough. Harper's
Magazine, 1886: ". . . the fascination of the game has seized upon the
American people, irrespective of age, sex, or other condition." Sporting
News, 1891: "No game has taken so strong a hold on Americans as
baseball." Why? What accounts for this love affair between America and
baseball that has matured and changed but never died?

Mark Twain hints at something when he says of baseball that it had
become "the very symbol, the outward and visible expression of the drive
and push and rush and struggle of the raging, tearing, booming nineteenth century" (Seymour, I. 345). Baseball became business as Business
and wealth and population boomed across the country, as millions of
immigrants poured in, as the tempo of life quickened and the country
flexed its muscles. Baseball, increasingly played with increasing skill,
caught the mood of America and rode it. But still one asks—why?

I think the answer lies in the convergence of many points we have
touched upon. For those native to America, particularly in cities, the
game, whether watched or played, recalled the earlier, rural America, a
more youthful, less bitterly knowing country; for the immigrant, the
game was another fraternal organization, a common language in a
strange land. For so much of expanding and expansive America, the
game was a free institution with something for everyone.

To the working man, it was cheap to watch, cheap to play. One did not
need to own property or a horse or a shell to participate. The players
themselves tended to come from working America, and the game became
rough, profane, strenuous, more exciting and so did the crowds. But
baseball had genteel origins, at least in its pre-Civil War version; the
young gentlemen of the Knickerbocker Base Ball Club, the New York
Nine and their host of imitators did not often play professional ball but
they played in schools and colleges, with clubs and associations; and the
educated or well-to-do never lost their taste for baseball.

Baseball was not dangerous, like prizefighting or football. As we know
from the early game books, girls and boys could play; indeed, anyone
could, for you did not have to be extra big or extra strong or extra fast.
Nor was it especially difficult. No arcane skill was required. In fact, to
watch or play the only requirement was desire, desire to participate, to be
part of the throng, the singing, the shouting, the swearing, the camarade-
rie, the noise, the sunshine. It was neither *chic* nor *déclassé* to care about
baseball. It was simply part of being an American, for no one else had a
game anything like it, any more than they had a country as raw, promising and strong as America.

If you did not watch or play baseball, you could read about it. As

Seymour tells us, newspapers grew with the sport, sports papers came into existence. Sports writing flowered as baseball enriched the language and the language developed a vast sub-continent of circumlocutions, euphemisms and new coinages for baseball. Vivid, opinionated, salty, redolent journalism matched the game. The reader found the box score; the box score provided the diamond in the mind, and, more importantly gave statistics, data, arithmetic permutation, lore masquerading as quantifiable reality, history that the mind could encompass and retain. Baseball as scriptive was born and developed. Then as now, intellectuals could moralize about baseball; writers and poets could rhapsodize and mythologize; journalists could cover a story with a beginning, middle and end, and a world of colorful characters, nicknames only matched by mobsters, and communal significance. No one who wanted to be in, was left out. As America opened her arms to the foreign born and healed the wounds of the war, baseball embraced all classes, conditions, regions.

Never was a game better matched to its season, or better, never was a season—from spring to early autumn—better matched by a game. The game was outdoors, on grass, in the sun. It began at winter's end, and ended before frost. It made the most of high skies, clement weather and the times of planting and growth. Until the advent of lights, then domed stadia and artificial turf, baseball was earthbound in the sense of using the earth and climate to advantage and the rhythms of light, shadow and dusk and spring, summer and early fall as part of itself. To be earthbound in such a fashion is, to me, pure heaven.

Baseball did not defy the elements. Excessive rain was respected; high wind was lamented; snow eschewed. Unlike football, whose industrial origins and organization force it to pretend to ignore Nature, baseball in its true state respects natural occurences and has adapted itself to Nature's deep cycles of renewal. Baseball is at home in the natural world, mindful of its own fragility, respectful of the elements, almost civilized in its regard for the safety of its player, careful as it can be of the comfort of spectators.

Genteel in its American origins, proletarian in its development, egalitarian in its demands and appeal, effortless in its adaptation to nature, raucous, hard-nosed and glamorous as a profession, expanding with the country like fingers unfolding from a fist, image of a lost past, evergreen reminder of America's best promises, baseball fits America. Above all, it fits so well because it embodies the interplay of individual and group that we so love, and because it conserves our longing for the rule of law while licensing our resentment of law givers.

Baseball, the opportunist's game, puts a tremendous premium on the individual, who must be able to react instantly on offense and defense and who must be able to hit, run, throw, field. Specialization obviously exists but in general baseball players are meant to be skilled generalists. The "designated hitter" is so offensive precisely because it violates this basic characteristic of the game. Players are also sufficiently physically separated on the field so that the individual cannot hide from clear responsibility in a crowd, as in football or Congress. The object, the ball, and what the individual must do are obvious to all, and each player's skill, initiative, zest and poise are highlighted.

Individual merit and self-reliance are the bed-rock of baseball, never more so than in the fundamental acts of delivering, and attempting to hit, the ball. Every game recommences every time a pitcher pitches and a batter swings. But before a swing or not-swing can trigger the vast grid of mental and physical adjustments that must proceed with every pitch, there is the basic confrontation between two lone individuals. It is primitive in its starkness. A man on a hill prepares to throw a rock at a man slightly below him, not far away, who holds a club. First, fear must be overcome; no one finally knows where the pitched ball, or hit ball, will go. Most of the time control, agility, timing, planning avert brutality and force sport. Occasionally, suddenly, usually unaccountably, the primitive act of throwing or of striking results in terrible injury. The fear is never absent, the fear that randomness will take over. If hitting a major league fastball is the most difficult act in organized sport, the difficulty derives in part from the need to overcome fear in a split second.

The batter is, they say, on offense yet batting is essentially a deeply reactive and defensive act. The pitcher is, they say, on defense, yet the pitcher initiates play and controls the game ("Pitching is 75% of the game"). It is not clear, at least to me, finally who is on offense and who is on defense in baseball. Consider the catcher, who may actually control the game. The catcher is the only defensive player in any sport I know of whose defined position requires him to adopt the perspective, if not the stance, of the player on offense. Part of what a batter must overcome, part of the secretive, ruthless dimension of baseball, is the batter's knowledge that an opposing player, crouching right behind him, signals wordlessly in order to exploit his weaknesses. Is it so clear who is the defense, who is the offense? I think it is clear that part of the appeal of baseball is that at the outset it focusses on the individual with such clarity in such ambiguous circumstances.

If the game flows from the constantly re-iterated, primitive confrontation of an individual with the world, represented by another solitary individual, nothing that ensues, except a home-run—the dispositive triumph of one over the other, the surrogate kill—fails to involve the team. A strikeout involves the catcher and anything else brings the community, either on the bench or in the field, into play. And while the premium on individual effort is never lost, eventually the communal choreography of a team almost always takes over. Every assigned role on the field potentially can and often does change with every pitch, and with each kind of pitch, or each ball hit fair. The subsequent complexities and potential interactions among all the players on the field expand in uncalculable ways. When in the thrall of its communal aspects, hitting, stealing and individual initiative give way to combined play-making, acts of sacrifice or cooperation, and obedience to signs and orders. Whether on offense or defense, the virtuoso is then subsumed into the ensemble. The anarchic ways of solo operators are subdued by a free institution.

The ambiguities surrounding being an offense or defense, surrounding what it means to stand where you stand, endlessly recreate the American pageant of individual and group, citizen and country. In baseball and daily life, Americans do not take sides so much as they change sides in ways checked and balanced. Finally, in baseball and daily life, regardless of which side you are on and where you stand, shared principles are supposed to govern.

Law, defined as a complex of formal rules, agreed upon bounderies, authoritative arbiters, custom and a system of symmetrical opportunities and demands, is enshrined in baseball. Indeed, the layout of the field shows baseball's essential passion for and reliance on precise proportions and clearly defined limits, all the better to give shape to energy and an arena for equality and expression. The pitcher's rubber, 24 inches by 6 inches, is on a 15 inch mound in the middle of an 18 foot circle; the rubber is 60 feet 6 inches from home plate; the four base paths are 90 feet long; the distance from first base to third, and home plate to second base, is 127 feet 3⅜ inches; the pitcher's rubber is the center of a circle, described by the arc of the grass behind the infield from foul line to foul line, whose radius is 95 feet; from home plate to backstop, and swinging in an arc, is 60 feet. On this square tipped like a diamond containing circles and contained in circles, built on multiples of 3, nine players play nine innings, with 3 outs to a side, each out possibly composed of 3 strikes. Four balls, four bases break (or is it underscore?) the game's reliance on "threes" to distribute an odd equality, all the numerology and symmetry tending to configure a game unbounded by that which bounds most sports, and adjudicates in many, Time.

The game comes from an America where the availability of sun defined the time for work or play—nothing else. Virtually all our other sports reflect the time clock, either in their formal structure or their definition of a winner. Baseball views time as daylight and daylight as an endlessly renewable natural resource; it may put a premium on speed, of throw or foot, but it is unhurried. Daytime, like the water and forests, like the land itself, will be ever available.

The point is, symmetrical surfaces, deep arithmetical patterns and a vast, stable body of rules designed to ensure competitive balance in the game, show forth a country devoted to equality of treatment and opportunity; a country whose deepest dream is of a divinely proportioned and peopled (the "threes" come from somewhere) green garden enclosure; above all, a country whose basic assertion is that law, in all its mutually agreed-upon manifestations, shall govern—not nature inexorable, for all she is respected, and not humankind's whims, for all that the game belongs to the people. Baseball's essential rules for place and for play were established, by my reckoning, with almost no exceptions of consequence, by 1895. By today, the diamond and the rules for play have the character of Platonic ideas, of pre-existent inevitabilities which encourage activity, contain energy and, like any set of transcendent ideals, do not change.

Symbolic of this sensibility, the umpire in baseball has unique stature among sport's arbiters. Spectator and fan alike may, perhaps at times must, object to his judgment, his interpretation, his grasp of precedent and relevant doctrine. Such dissent is encouraged, is valuable and rarely, if ever, is successful. As instant replay shows, very rarely should it be. The umpire is untouchable (there is law protecting his person) and infallible. He is the much maligned, indispensible, faceless figure of Judgement, in touch with all the codes and lore and with nature's vagaries, for he decides when she has won. He is the Constitution and Court before your eyes. He is also the most durable figure in the game for he, alone, never sits, never rests. He has no side, he is on every side. His sole obligation is to dispense justice speedily.

So much does our game tell us, about what we wanted to be, about what we are. Our character and our culture are reflected in this grand game. It would be foolish to think that all of our national experience is reflected in any single institution, even our loftiest, but it would not be wrong to claim for baseball a capacity to cherish individuality and inspire cohesion in a way which is a hallmark of our loftiest free institutions. Nor would it be misguided to think that, however vestigial the remnants of our best hopes, we can still find, if we wish to, a moment called a game when those best hopes, those memories for the future have life, when each of us, those who are in and those out, has a chance to gather, in a green place around home.

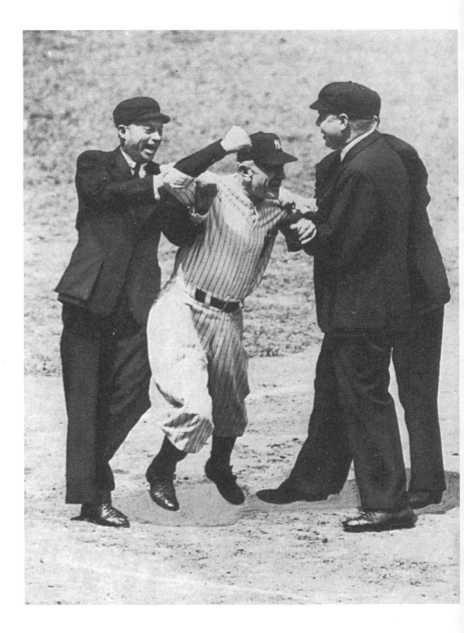

Casey Stengel

Photo credit: UPI/Bettmann

HEARINGS BEFORE THE SUBCOMMITTEE ON ANTITRUST AND MONOPOLY OF THE COMMITTEE ON THE JUDICIARY UNITED STATES SENATE

July 1958

Here's an extended example of "Stengelese": The Ol' Professor's testimony before a Congressional committee investigating baseball's antitrust exemption. Incidentally, it's also a perceptive discussion of baseball history from a man who spent over 60 years in the game. And don't miss the surprise testimony from Mickey Mantle at the finish.

By Casey Stengel

STATEMENT OF CASEY STENGEL, MANAGER OF THE NEW YORK YANKEES

Mr. STENGEL. Well, I started in professional ball in 1910. I have been in professional ball, I would say, for 48 years. I have been employed by numerous ball clubs in the majors and in the minor leagues.

I started in the minor leagues with Kansas City. I played as low as class D ball, which was at Shelbyville, Ky., and also class C ball, and class A ball, and I have advanced in baseball as a ballplayer.

I had many years that I was not so successful as a ballplayer, as it is a game of skill. And then I was no doubt discharged by baseball in which I had to go back to the minor leagues as a manager, and after being in the minor leagues as a manager, I became a major league manager in several cities and was discharged, we call it "discharged", because there is no question I had to leave. [Laughter.]

And I returned to the minor leagues at Milwaukee, Kansas City, and Oakland, Calif., and then returned to the major leagues.

In the last 10 years, naturally, in major league baseball with the New York Yankees, the New York Yankees have had tremendous success and while I am not the ballplayer who does the work, I have no doubt worked for a ball club that is very capable in the office.

I must have splendid ownership, I must have very capable men who are in radio and television, which no doubt you know that we have mentioned the three names—you will say they are very great.

We have a wonderful press that follows us. Anybody should in New York City, where you have so many million people.

Our ball club has been successful because we have it, and we have the spirit of 1776.

We put it into the ball field and if you are not capable of becoming a great ballplayer since I have been in as the manager, in 10 years, you are notified that if you don't produce on the ball field, the salary that you receive, we will allow you to be traded to play and give your services to other clubs.

The great proof of that was yesterday. Three of the young men that were stars and picked by the players in the American League to be in the all-star game were Mr. Cerv, who is at Kansas City; Mr. Jensen who was at Boston, and I might say Mr. Triandos that caught for the Baltimore ball club, all three of those players were my members and to show you I was not such a brilliant manager they got away from me and were chosen by the players and I was fortunate enough to have them come back to play where I was successful as a manager.

If I have been in baseball for 48 years there must be some good in it. I was capable and strong enough at one time to do any kind of work but I came back to baseball and I have been in baseball ever since.

I have been up and down the ladder. I know there are some things in baseball, 35 to 50 years ago that are better now than they were in those days. In those days, my goodness, you could not transfer a ball club in the minor leagues, class D, class C ball, class A ball.

How could you transfer a ball club when you did not have a highway? How could you transfer a ball club when the railroads then would take you to a town you got off and then you had to wait and sit up 5 hours to go to another ball club?

How could you run baseball then without night ball?

You had to have night ball to improve the proceeds, to pay larger salaries and I went to work, the first year I received $135 a month.

I thought that was amazing. I had to put away enough money to go to dental college. I found out it was not better in dentistry, I stayed in baseball.

Any other questions you would like to ask me?

I want to let you know that as to the legislative end of baseball you men will have to consider that what you are here for. I am a bench manager.

I will speak about anything from the playing end—in the major or minor leagues—and do anything I can to help you.

Senator KEFAUVER. Mr. Stengel, are you prepared to answer particularly why baseball wants this bill passed?

Mr. STENGEL. Well, I would have to say at the present time, I think that baseball has advanced in this respect for the player help. That is an amazing statement for me to make, because you can retire with an annuity at 50 and what organization in America allows you to retire at 50 and receive money?

I want to further state that I am not a ballplayer, that is, put into that pension fund committee. At my age, and I have been in baseball, well, I will say I am possibly the oldest man who is working in baseball. I would say that when they start an annuity for the ballplayers to better their conditions, it should have been done, and I think it has been done.

I think it should be the way they have done it, which is a very good thing.

The reason they possibly did not take the managers in at that time was because radio and television or the income to ball clubs was not large enough that you could have put in a pension plan.

Now I am not a member of the pension plan. You have young men here who are, who represent the ball clubs.

They represent them as players and since I am not a member and don't receive pension from a fund which you think, my goodness, he ought to be declared in that too but I would say that is a great thing for the ballplayers.

That is one thing I will say for the ballplayers they have an advanced pension fund. I should think it was gained by radio and television or you could not have enough money to pay anything of that type.

Now the second thing about baseball that I think is very interesting to the public or to all of us that it is the owners' own fault if he does not improve his club, along with the officials in the ball club and the players.

Now what causes that?

If I am going to go on the road and we are a traveling ball club and you know the cost of transportation now—we travel sometimes with three pullman coaches, the New York Yankees and remember I am just a salaried man and do not own stock in the New York Yankees, I found out that in traveling with the New York Yankees on the road and all, that it is the best, and we have broken records in Washington this year, we have broken them in every city but New York and we have lost two clubs that have gone out of the city of New York.

Of course we have had some bad weather, I would say that they are mad at us in Chicago, we fill the parks.

They have come out to see good material. I will say they are mad at us in Kansas City, but we broke their attendance record.

Now on the road we only get possibly 27 cents. I am not positive of these figures, as I am not an official.

If you go back 15 years or if I owned stock in the club I would give them to you.

Senator KEFAUVER. Mr. Stengel, I am not sure that I made my question clear. [Laughter.]

Mr. STENGEL. Yes, sir. Well that is all right. I am not sure I am going to answer yours perfectly either. [Laughter.]

Senator KEFAUVER. I was asking you, sir, why it is that baseball wants this bill passed.

Mr. STENGEL. I would say I would not know, but I would say the reason why they would want it passed is to keep baseball going as the highest paid ball sport that has gone into baseball and from the baseball angle, I am not going to speak of any other sport.

I am not in here to argue about other sports, I am in the baseball business. It has been run cleaner than any business that was ever put out in the 100 years at the present time.

I am not speaking about television or I am not speaking about income that comes into the ball parks. You have to take that off. I don't know too much about it. I say the ballplayers have a better advancement at the present time.

Senator KEFAUVER. One further question, and then I will pass to the other Senators.

How many players do the Yankees control, Mr. Stengel?

Mr. STENGEL. Well, I will tell you: I hire the players and if they make good with me I keep them without any criticism from my ownership.

I do not know how many players they own as I am not a scout and I cannot run a ball club during the daytime and be busy at night, and up the next day and find out how many players that the Yankees own.

If you get any official with the Yankees that is here, why he could give you the names.

Senator KEFAUVER. Very well.

Senator Langer?

Senator LANGER. Mr. Stengel?

Mr. STENGEL. Yes, sir.

Senator LANGER. What do you think is the future of baseball? Is it going to be expanded to include more clubs than are in existence at the present time?

Mr. STENGEL. I think every chamber of commerce in the major league cities would not change a franchise, I think they will be delighted because they have a hard time to put in a convention hall or to get people to come to your city and if it is going to be like Milwaukee or Kansas City or Baltimore, I think they would want a major league team.

But if I was a chamber of commerce member and I was in a city I would not want a baseball team to leave the city as too much money is brought into your city even if you have a losing team and great if you have a winning ball team.

Senator LANGER. You look forward then, do you not, to, say, 10 years or 20 years from now this business of baseball is going to grow larger and larger and larger?

Mr. STENGEL. Well, I should think it would.

I should think it would get larger because of the fact we are drawing tremendous crowds, I believe, from overseas programs in television, that is one program I have always stuck up for.

I think every ballplayer and everyone should give out anything that is overseas for the Army, free of cost and so forth.

I think that every hospital should get it. I think that because of the lack of parking in so many cities that you cannot have a great ball park if you don't have parking space.

If you are ancient or 45 or 50 and have acquired enough money to go to a ball game, you cannot drive a car on a highway, which is very hard to do after 45, to drive on any modern highway and if you are going to stay home you need radio and television to go along for receipts for the ball club.

Senator LANGER. That brings us to another question.

Mr. STENGEL. Yes, sir.

Senator LANGER. That is, what do you think of pay-as-you-go television?

Mr. STENGEL. Well, to tell you the truth, if I were starting in it myself I would like to be in that line of business as I did not think they would ever have television and so forth here but they have got it here now. [Laughter.]

Forty years ago you would not have had it around here yourself and you would not have cameras flying around here every 5 minutes but we have got them here and more of them around here than around a ball field, I will give you that little tip.

Senator LANGER. You believe the time is ever going to come when you will have pay-as-you-go in the world series, which would be kept from the public unless they had pay-as-you-go television in their homes?

Mr. STENGEL. I think you have got a good argument there and it is worthy of you to say that.

I am thinking myself of anybody that is hospitalized and anybody who cannot go to a ball park, I should think if they could pass that they should try to pass it.

But I don't think they will be able to do it because they have gone in television so far that they reach so many outside people, you have to have a sponsor for everything else you do, go pay television and that is going to run all the big theaters out of business where you have to use pay television.

All the big theaters and all the big movie companies went broke. We know that. You see that now or you would not have a place to hold a television for pay.

I don't know how they would run that of course. I am not on that side of the fence. I am paid a salary——

Senator LANGER. Just one further question. You do not have to answer it unless you want to. That is, is there any provision made whereby the team owners can keep a racketeer out of the baseball business?

Mr. STENGEL. Well, sir——

Senator LANGER. Can the owners of the New York Yankees, for example, sell out to anyone who may want to buy the club at a big price without the consent of the other owners?

Mr. STENGEL. That is a very good thing that I will have to think about but I will give you an example.

I think that is why they put in as a commissioner Judge Landis, and he said if there is a cloud on baseball I will take it off, and he took the cloud off and they have only had one scandal or if they had it is just one major league city.

How can you be a ballplayer and make 25 ballplayers framed without it being heard?

It is bound to leak, and your play will show it.

I don't think, an owner possibly could do something but he can't play the game for you. It is the most honest profession I think that we have, everything today that is going on outside——

Senator LANGER. Mr. Chairman, my final question. This is the Antimonopoly Committee that is sitting here.

Mr. STENGEL. Yes, sir.

Senator LANGER. I want to know whether you intend to keep on monopolizing the world's championship in New York City.

Mr. STENGEL. Well, I will tell you, I got a little concerned yesterday in the first 3 innings when I say the 3 players I had gotten rid of and I said when I lost 9 what am I going to do and when I had a couple of my players. I thought so great of that did not do so good up to the sixth inning I was more confused but I finally had to go and call on a young man in Baltimore that we don't own and the Yankees don't own him, and he is doing pretty good, and I would actually have to tell you that I think we are more the Greta Garbo type now from success.

We are being hated I mean, from the ownership and all, we are being hated. Every sport that gets too great or one individual—but if we made 27 cents and it pays to have a winner at home why would not you have a good winner in your own park if you were an owner.

That is the result of baseball. An owner gets most of the money at home and it is up to him and his staff to do better or they ought to be discharged.

Senator LANGER. That is all, Mr. Chairman. Thank you.

Senator KEFAUVER. Thank you, Senator Langer.

Senator O'Mahoney?

Senator O'MAHONEY. May I say, Mr. Stengel, that I congratulate you very much for what happened on the field at Baltimore yesterday. I was watching on television when you sent Gil McDougald up to bat for Early Wynn. I noticed with satisfaction that he got a hit, knocking Frank Malzone in with the winning run. That is good management.

Mr. STENGEL. Thank you very much. [Laughter.]

Senator O'MAHONEY. Did I understand you to say, Mr. Stengel, at the beginning of your statement that you have been in baseball for 48 years?

Mr. STENGEL. Yes, sir; the oldest man in the service.

Senator O'MAHONEY. How many major league teams were there in the United States when you entered baseball?

Mr. STENGEL. Well, there was in 1910—there were 16 major league baseball teams.

Senator O'MAHONEY. How many are there now?

Mr. STENGEL. There are 16 major league clubs but there was 1 year that they brought in the Federal League which was brought in by Mr. Ward and Mr. Sinclair and others after a war, and it is a very odd thing to tell you that during tough times it is hard to study baseball. I have been through 2 or 3 depressions in baseball and out of it.

The First World War we had good baseball in August.

The Second World War we kept on and made more money because

everybody was around going to the services, the larger the war, the more they come to the ball park, and that was an amazing thing to me.

When you were looking for tough times why it changed for different wars.

Senator O'MAHONEY. How many minor leagues were there in baseball when you began?

Mr. STENGEL. Well, there were not so many at that time because of this fact: Anybody to go into baseball at that time with the educational schools that we had were small, while you were probably thoroughly educated at school, you had to be—we had only small cities that you could put a team in and they would go defunct.

Why, I remember the first year I was at Kankakee, Ill., and a bank offered me $550 if I would let them have a little notice. I left there and took a uniform because they owed me 2 weeks' pay. But I either had to quit but I did not have enough money to go to dental college so I had to go with the manager down to Kentucky.

What happened there was if you got by July, that was the big date. You did not play night ball and you did not play Sundays in half of the cities on account of a Sunday observance, so in those days when things were tough, and all of it was, I mean to say, why they just closed up July 4 and there you were sitting there in the depot.

You could go to work some place else but that was it.

So I got out of Kankakee, Ill., and I just go there for the visit now. [Laughter.]

I think now, do you know how many clubs they have?

Anybody will start a minor league club but it is just like your small cities, the industries have left them and they have gone west to California, and I am a Missourian—Kansas City, Mo.—but I can see all those towns and everybody moving west and I know if you fly in the air you can see anything from the desert, you can see a big country over there that has got many names.

Well, now why wouldn't baseball prosper out there, with that many million people?

Senator O'MAHONEY. Are the minor leagues suffering now?

Mr. STENGEL. I should say they are.

Senator O'MAHONEY. Why?

Mr. STENGEL. Do you know why?

I will tell you why. I don't think anybody can support minor league ball when they see a great official, it would be just like a great actress or actor had come to town. If Bob Hope had come here or Greta Garbo over there half of them would go to see Greta Garbo and half Bob Hope but if you have a very poor baseball team they are not going to watch you until you become great and the minor leagues now with radio and television will not pay very much attention to minor league ballplayers. Softball is interesting, the parent is interested; he goes around with him. He watches his son and he is more enthusiastic about the boy than some stranger that comes to town and wants to play in a little wooden park and with no facilities to make you be interested. You might rather stay home and see a program.

Senator O'MAHONEY. How many baseball players are now engaged in the activity as compared to when you came in?

Mr. STENGEL. I would say there are more, many more. Because we did not have as many cities that could support even minor league baseball in those days.

Senator O'MAHONEY. How many players did the 16 major league clubs have when you came in?

Mr. STENGEL. At that time they did not have as many teams. They did not have near as many teams as below.

Later on Mr. Rickey came in and started what was known as what you would say numerous clubs, you know in which I will try to pick up this college man, I will pick up that college boy or I will pick up some corner lot boy and if you picked up the corner lot boy maybe he became just as successful as the college man, which is true.

He then had a number of players.

Now, too many players is a funny thing, it costs like everything. I said just like I made a talk not long ago and I told them all when they were drinking and they invited me in I said you ought to be home. You men are not making enough money. You cannot drink like that. They said, "This is a holiday for the Shell Oil Co.," and I said "Why is it a holiday?" and they said, "We did something great for 3 years and we are given 2 days off to watch the Yankees play the White Sox," but they were mostly White Sox rooters.

I said, "You are not doing right."

I said, "You can't take all those drinks and all even on your holidays. You ought to be home and raising more children because big league clubs now give you a hundred thousand for a bonus to go into baseball." [Laughter.]

And by the way I don't happen to have any children but I wish Mrs. Stengel and I had eight, I would like to put them in on that bonus rule. [Laughter.]

Senator O'MAHONEY. What I am trying to find out, Mr. Stengel, is how many players are actively working for the major league teams now as was formerly the case?

How many players do you suppose——

Mr. STENGEL. You are right, I would honestly tell you they naturally have more and they are in more competition now.

You have to buck now a university—anyone who wants to be a hockey player——

Senator O'MAHONEY. Let's stick to baseball for a minute.

Mr. STENGEL. I stay in baseball. I say I can't name them. If you want to know you get any executive, you have got any names, bring any executive with the Yankees that is an official in the ball club and he will tell you how many players the Yankees have.

And there is his jurisdiction—every ball club owner can tell you he is an official, they have enough officials hired with me with a long pencil, too.

Senator O'MAHONEY. I recently saw a statement by a baseball sports writer that there were about 400 active ball players in the major leagues now.

Would you think that is about correct now?

Mr. STENGEL. I would say in the major leagues each club has 25 men which is the player limit.

There are 8 clubs in each league so you might say there are 400 players in the major leagues, you mean outside of it that they own two or three hundred each individual club, isn't that what you have reference to?

Senator O'MAHONEY. I was coming to that, but is that the fact?

Mr. STENGEL. Well, I say that is what you would say [laughter] if you want to find that out you get any of those executives that come in here that keep those books. I am not a bookkeeper for him. But I take the man when he comes to the big league. They can give it to you and each club should.

That does not mean and I would like to ask you, How would you like to pay those men?

That is why they go broke.

Senator O'MAHONEY. I am not in that business.

Mr. STENGEL. I was in that business a short time, too; it is pretty hard to make a living at it.

Senator O'MAHONEY. But the stories that we read in the press——

Mr. STENGEL. That is right.

Senator O'MAHONEY. Are to the effect that the minor leagues are suffering. There are no more major league teams now than there were when you came into baseball, and what I am trying to find out is, What are the prospects for the future growth of baseball and to what extent have the 16 major league teams, through the farm system, obtained, by contract or agreement or understanding, control over the professional lives of the players?

Mr. STENGEL. That is right.

If I was a ballplayer and I was discharged, and I saw within 3 years that I could not become a major league ballplayer I would go into another profession.

That is the history of anything that is in business.

Senator O'MAHONEY. Do you think that the farm system keeps any players in the minor leagues when they ought to be in the majors?

Mr. STENGEL. I should say it would not keep any players behind or I have been telling you a falsehood.

I would say it might keep a few back, but very few.

There is no manager in baseball who wants to be a success without the ability of those great players and if I could pull them up to make money in a gate for my owner and for myself to be a success, I don't believe I would hold him back.

Senator O'MAHONEY. The fact is, is it not, Mr. Stengel, that while the population of the United States has increased tremendously during the period that you have been engaged in professional baseball, the number of major-league teams has not increased; it remains the same as it was then. The number of players actually engaged by the major-league teams is approximately the same as back in 1903, and there is now, through the farm system, a major league control of the professional occupation of baseball playing. Is that a correct summary?

Mr. STENGEL. Well, you have that from the standpoint of what you have been reading. You have got that down very good. [Laughter.]

But if you are a player——

Senator O'MAHONEY. I am trying to get it down from your standpoint as a 48-year man in baseball.

Mr. STENGEL. That is why I stayed in it.

I have been discharged 15 times and rehired; so you get rehired in baseball, and they don't want a good ballplayer leaving, and I always say a high-priced baseball player should get a high salary just like a moving-picture actor.

He should not get the same thing as the 25th man on the ball club who is very fortunate he is sitting on your ball club, and I say it is very hard to have skill in baseball.

Senator O'MAHONEY. You are not changing the subject; are you, sir?

Mr. STENGEL. No. You asked the question and I told you that if you want to find out how minor league baseball is; it is terrible now.

How can you eat on $2.50 a day when up here you can eat on $8 or better than $8?

Now how can you travel in a bus all night and play ball the next night to make a living?

How can you, a major league man, make it so that you can't?

Is he going to fly all of them to each place?

Senator O'MAHONEY. I am not arguing with you, Mr. Stengel.

Mr. STENGEL. I am just saying minor league ball has outgrown itself, like every small town has outgrown itself industrially because they don't put a plant in there to keep the people working so they leave.

Senator O'MAHONEY. Does that mean in your judgment that the major league baseball teams necessarily have to control ball playing?

Mr. STENGEL. I think that they do.

I don't think that if I was a great player and you released me in 4 years, I think it would be a joke if you released a man and he made 1 year for you and then bid for a job and then played the next year, we will say, out of Washington, he played in New York the third year, he would play in Cleveland and put himself up in a stake.

I think they ought to be just as they have been.

A man who walks in and sees you get fair compensation and if you are great be sure you get it because the day you don't report and the day you don't open a season you are hurting the major league and hurting yourself somewhat, but you are not going to be handicapped in life if you are great in baseball.

Every man who goes out has a better home than he had when he went in.

Senator O'MAHONEY. Did I understand you to say that in your own personal activity as manager, you always give a player who is to be traded advance notice?

Mr. STENGEL. I warn him that—I hold a meeting. We have an instructional school, regardless of my English, we have got an instructional school.

Senator O'MAHONEY. Your English is perfect and I can understand what you say, and I think I can even understand what you mean.

Mr. STENGEL. Yes, sir. You have got some very wonderful points in. I would say in an instructional school we try you out for 3 weeks and we clock you, just like—I mean how good are you going to be in the service; before you go out of the service we have got you listed.

We know if you are handicapped in the service and we have got instructors who teach you. They don't have to listen to me if they don't like me.

I have a man like Crosetti, who never has been to a banquet; he never would. He does a big job like Art Fletcher; he teaches that boy and teaches his family; he will be there. I have a man for first base, second base, short; that is why the Yankees are ahead.

We have advanced so much we can take a man over to where he can be a big league player and if he does not, we advance him to where he can play opposition to us.

I am getting concerned about opposition. I am discharging too many good ones.

Senator O'MAHONEY. Mr. Chairman, I think the witness is the best entertainment we have had around here for a long time and it is a great temptation to keep asking him questions but I think I had better desist.

Thank you.

Senator KEFAUVER. Senator Carroll.

Senator CARROLL. Mr. Stengel, I am an old Yankee fan and I come from a city where I think we have made some contribution to your success—from Denver. I think you have many Yankee players from Denver.

The question Senator Kefauver asked you was what, in your honest opinion, with your 48 years of experience, is the need for this legislation in view of the fact that baseball has not been subject to antitrust laws?

Mr. STENGEL. No.

Senator CARROLL. It is not now subject to the antitrust laws. What do you think the need is for this legislation? I had a conference with one of the attorneys representing not only baseball but all of the sports, and I listened to your explanation to Senator Kefauver. It seemed to me it had some clarity. I asked the attorney this question: What was the need for this legislation? I wonder if you would accept his definition. He said they didn't want to be subjected to the ipse dixit of the Federal Government because they would throw a lot of damage suits on the ad damnum clause. He said, in the first place, the Toolson case was sui generis, it was de minimus non curat lex.

Do you call that a clear expression?

Mr. STENGEL. Well, you are going to get me there for about 2 hours.

Senator CARROLL. I realize these questions which are put to you are all, I suppose, legislative and legal questions. Leaning on your experience as a manager, do you feel the farm system, the draft system, the reserve-clause system, is fair to the players, to the managers, and to the public interest?

Mr. STENGEL. I think the public is taken care of, rich and poor, better at the present time than years ago. I really think that the ownership is a question of ability. I really think that the business manager is a question of ability. Some of those men are supposed to be very brilliant in their line of work, and some of them are not so brilliant, so that they have quite a bit of trouble with it when you run an operation of a club in which the ownership maybe doesn't run the club.

I would say that the players themselves—I told you, I am not in on that fund, it is a good thing. I say I should have been, to tell you the truth. But I think it is a great thing for the players.

Senator CARROLL. I am not talking about that fund.

Mr. STENGEL. Well, I tell you, if you are going to talk about the fund you are going to think about radio and television and pay television.

Senator CARROLL. I do not want to talk about radio and television, but I do want to talk about the draft clause and reserve systems.

Mr. STENGEL. Yes, sir. I would have liked to have been free four times in my life; and later on I have seen men free, and later on they make a big complaint "they wuz robbed," and if you are robbed there is always some club down the road to give you an opportunity.

Senator CARROLL. That was not the question I asked you, and I only asked you on your long experience——

Mr. STENGEL. Yes, sir. I would not be in it 48 years if it was not all right.

Senator CARROLL. I understand that.

Mr. STENGEL. Well, then, why wouldn't it stay that?

Senator CARROLL. In your long experience——

Mr. STENGEL. Yes.

Senator CARROLL. Do you feel—you have had experience through the years——

Mr. STENGEL. That is true.

Senator CARROLL. With the draft system, and the reserve clause in the contracts. Do you think you could still exist under existing law without changing the law?

Mr. STENGEL. I think it is run better than it has even been run in baseball, for every department.

Senator CARROLL. Then I come back to the principal question. This is the real question before this body.

Mr. STENGEL. All right.

Senator CARROLL. Then what is the need for legislation, if they are getting along all right?

Mr. STENGEL. I didn't ask for the legislation. [Laughter.]

Senator CARROLL. Your answer is a very good one, and that is the question Senator Kefauver put to you.

Mr. STENGEL. That is right.

Senator CARROLL. That is the question Senator O'Mahoney put.

Mr. STENGEL. Right.

Senator CARROLL. Are you ready to say there is no need for legislation in this field, then, insofar as baseball is concerned?

Mr. STENGEL. As far as I am concerned, from drawing a salary and from my ups and downs and being discharged, I always found out that there was somebody ready to employ you, if you were on the ball.

Senator CARROLL. Thank you very much, Mr. Stengel.

Senator KEFAUVER. Thank you very much, Mr. Stengel. We appreciate your testimony.

Senator LANGER. May I ask a question?

Senator KEFAUVER. Senator Langer has a question. Just a moment, Mr. Stengel.

Senator LANGER. Can you tell this committee what countries have baseball teams besides the United States, Mexico, and Japan?

Mr. STENGEL. I made a tour with the New York Yankees several years ago, and it was the most amazing tour I ever saw for a ball club, to go over where you have trouble spots. It wouldn't make any difference whether he was a Republican or Democrat, and so forth.

I know that over there we drew 250,000 to 500,000 people in the streets, in which they stood in front of the automobiles, not on the sidewalks, and those people are trying to play baseball over there with short fingers [laughter], and I say, "Why do you do it?"

But they love it. They are crazy about baseball, and they are not worried at the handicap. And I'll tell you, business industries run baseball over there, and they are now going to build a stadium that is going to be covered over for games where you don't need a tarpaulin if it rains.

South America is all right, and Cuba is all right. But I don't know, I have never been down there except to Cuba, I have never been to South America, and I know that they broadcast games, and I know we have players that are playing from there.

I tell you what, I think baseball has spread, but if we are talking about anything spreading, we would be talking about soccer. You can go over in Italy, and I thought they would know DiMaggio everyplace. And my goodness, you mention soccer, you can draw 50,000 or a hundred thousand people. Over here you have a hard time to get soccer on the field, which is a great sport, no doubt.

Senator LANGER. What I want to know, Mr. Stengel, is this: When the American League plays the National League in the world series and it is advertised as the world championship——

Mr. STENGEL. Yes, sir.

Senator LANGER. I want to know why you do not play Mexico or Japan or some other country and really have a world championship.

Mr. STENGEL. Well, I think you have a good argument there. I would say that a couple of clubs that I saw, it was like when I was in the Navy, I thought I couldn't get special unless they played who I wanted to play. So I would look over a team. When they got off a ship I would play them, but if they had been on land too long, my team couldn't play them.

So I would play the teams at sea 6 months, and I would say, "You are the club I would like to play." I would like to play those countries, and I think it should be nationwide and governmentwide, too, if you could possibly get it in.

Senator LANGER. Do you think the day is ever going to come, perhaps 5 years from now or 10——

Mr. STENGEL. I would say 10 years, not 5.

Senator LANGER. When the championship team of the United States would play the championship team of Mexico?

Mr. STENGEL. I really think it should be that way, but I don't think you will get it before 10 years, because you have to build stadiums and you have to have an elimination in every country for it, and you have to have weather at the same time, or how could you play unless you would hold a team over?

Senator LANGER. Do you not think these owners are going to develop this matter of world championship of another country besides the United States?

Mr. STENGEL. I should think they would do that in time. I really do. I was amazed over in Japan. I couldn't understand why they would want to play baseball with short fingers and used the same size ball, and not a small size, and compete in baseball. And yet that is their great sport, and industries are backing them.

Senator LANGER. In other words, the owners some day, in your opinion, Mr. Stengel, are going to make a lot of money by having the champions of one country play another country and keep on with eliminations until they really have a world championship?

Mr. STENGEL. That is what I say. I think it is not named properly right now unless you can go and play all of them. You would have to do that.

Senator LANGER. That is all, Mr. Chairman.

Senator KEFAUVER. Mr. Stengel, one final question. You spoke of Judge Landis and the fact that he had rather absolute control over baseball. There was a clause in Judge Landis' contract which read:

> We, the club owners, pledge ourselves to loyally support the commissioner in his important and difficult task, and we assure him that each of us will acquiesce in his decisions even when we believe they are mistaken, and that we will not discredit the sport by criticism of him or one another.

This same clause was in Mr. Chandler's contract, but we do not understand it to be in Mr. Frick's contract. Do you think the commissioner needs to have this power over the management?

Mr. STENGEL. I would say when there was a cloud over baseball, like any sport, you have to have a man that has the power to change things.

Now when Landis was in, that was the situation with baseball. You were bucking racetracks. We don't have a tote board. We are playing baseball for admission fees.

Now, we don't want a tote board in baseball. Who would? That would be great, if you have that out there, and you could go out there and, you know, use a tote board and say, "Does he get to first or won't he get to first?" and so forth.

Now Landis was an amazing man. I will give you an example of him. It is a good thing you brought him in. I was discharged one year, and I was the president of a ball club at Worcester, Mass., so I discharged myself, and I sent it in to Landis and he O. K.'d it.

Why was I president? Then I could release my player, couldn't I? And I was the player. So I was the only player ever released by the president, and that was in Worcester, Mass., so I got discharged.

Senator KEFAUVER. Do you think the present commissioner ought to have the same power?

Mr. STENGEL. There are 16 men in baseball who own ball clubs. We will say that an individual can hardly make it any more unless he is wealthy. That is how it has grown. I would say the biggest thing in baseball at the present time now, and with the money that is coming in, and so forth, and with an annuity fund for the players, you can't allow the commissioner to just take everything sitting there, and take everything insofar as money is concerned, but I think he should have full jurisdiction over the player and player's habits, and the way the umpires and ball clubs should conduct their business in the daytime and right on up tight up here.

Senator KEFAUVER. Thank you very much, Mr. Stengel. We appreciate your presence here.

The committee is very glad that Senator Mundt is interested and is present. We will be glad to have any Senators testify or participate in the hearing.

Mr. Mickey Mantle, will you come around?

Mr. Mantel, I am sure all of us saw you play yesterday, either in the sunshine and hot weather in Baltimore, or on television.

Will you very briefly give your baseball experience? Of course you are from Oklahoma.

STATEMENT OF MICKEY MANTLE, NEW YORK YANKEES

Mr. MANTLE. I started playing baseball in 1949 with the Independence, Kans., class D league; and in 1950 I went to Joplin, Mo., a class C league; and in 1951 I came with the Yankees.

Senator KEFAUVER. How many years is that, altogether, that you have been in baseball?

Mr. MANTLE. Well, this would be my 10th year.

Senator KEFAUVER. Mr. Mantle, do you have any observations with reference to the applicability of the antitrust laws to baseball?

Mr. MANTLE. My views are just about the same as Casey's. [Laughter.]

Senator KEFAUVER. If you will redefine just what Casey's views were, we would be very happy. Let us get at it another way. What was your first team, Mr. Mantle?

Mr. MANTLE. I didn't quite hear that.

Senator KEFAUVER. Who did you play with first? What was the name of the team?

Mr. MANTLE. Independence, Kans., the Independent Yankees.

Senator KEFAUVER. And that is a Yankee farm team?

Mr. MANTLE. That is right, class D team.

Senator KEFAUVER. Then how long did you stay with that club?

Mr. MANTLE. I got out of high school in the middle of the season, and I just finished up the year with Independence.

Senator KEFAUVER. Were you a minor when you first signed the contract?

Mr. MANTLE. I was 17 years old.

Senator KEFAUVER. How long were you under that contract?

Mr. MANTLE. I am still under it. I signed up with the Yankees, and I belong to them now.

Senator KEFAUVER. Do you think the unlimited reserve clause in your contract is a fair thing for the players?

Mr. MANTLE. Well, I don't have any gripes. I have been very fortunate.

Senator KEFAUVER. Under that clause, of course, they can do anything with you they want to; is that right.

Mr. MANTLE. If they don't do anything different, I don't care what they do. [Laughter.]

Senator KEFAUVER. In other words, you are well satisfied with what happened to you?

Mr. MANTLE. Yes, I am.

Senator KEFAUVER. But what if some manager did not think you were as good as you think you are, and sent you somewhere else?

Mr. MANTLE. Well, it's like Casey said. I have twin brothers that signed with the Yankees just like I did, and they didn't do too good, so they just quit baseball, and I think that is probably what you should do. If you play 2 or 3 years and you think you are not advancing like you should, I think you should quit.

Senator KEFAUVER. Do you think there should be any limit on the number of years you are held under the reserve clause?

Mr. MANTLE. I don't know. I don't think about this stuff very much. [Laughter.]

Senator KEFAUVER. How long have you been under contract with the Yankees?

Mr. MANTLE. Well, since 1949. I never have been under contract with anybody else.

Senator KEFAUVER. You were 17 years old then. Do you think a contract should be binding on a minor?

Mr. MANTLE. Against a minor?

Senator KEFAUVER. Yes. You were 17 years old.

Mr. MANTLE. Well, I don't know.

Senator KEFAUVER. What did you get paid when you signed?

Mr. MANTLE. I got $150 a month.

Senator KEFAUVER. Would you mind telling us what you make now? I do not want to ask you unless you want to tell us.

Mr. MANTLE. I don't guess so.

Senator KEFAUVER. You would rather not?

Mr. MANTLE. No.

Senator KEFAUVER. Do you players think you should have any voice in the selection of the commissioner of baseball?

Mr. MANTLE. I have never thought about that, either. I just—we have club representatives, you know, and they take care of all this kind of stuff. You vote for them. [Laughter.]

Senator KEFAUVER. Mr. Mantle, who is your club representative?

Mr. MANTLE. Bob Turley.

Senator KEFAUVER. Do you have any opinion about why minor-league baseball is having a rough time, why it is not doing so well, as a lot of people in smaller cities would like it to do?

Mr. MANTLE. Well, I think that if you have a good team you have to win in the minor leagues. If you are on a loser, you don't draw very many people.

In 1950, when we had a real good team at Joplin, Mo., we still didn't draw, so I think it's just—people, like Casey said, don't like to go out to a wooden ball park when they can watch—their kids are all playing little league now, and they would just as soon see their own kids play little-league ball than go out to a ball park and watch somebody they don't know or major leaguers.

Senator KEFAUVER. All right.

Senator Langer, any questions?

Senator LANGER. One question.

Supposing, Mr. Mantle, you became permanently disabled as a result of playing baseball. What pension would you get and how long would it last?

Mr. MANTLE. I don't know. I don't know. I think that you have to be 50 years old, I think, to get a pension. They probably—I don't know.

Senator LANGER. We will get that testimony from the owners, Mr. Chairman. That is all.

Senator KEFAUVER. Yes; we will get it from them.

Senator O'Mahoney?

Senator O'MAHONEY. No questions.

Senator KEFAUVER. Senator Carroll?

Senator CARROLL. Supposing you were injured in a baseball game. Is there any provision in the contract or is there any collective bargaining done by players to protect themselves?

Mr. MANTLE. I think if you get injured during the season you probably get paid the rest of the year.

Senator CARROLL. We will go into that later.

I think that is all, Mr. Chairman. Thank you.

Senator KEFAUVER. Thank you very much, Mr. Mantle.

Mr. Ted Williams, will you come around?

Mr. Williams, will you give your background and tell us when you started in baseball?

STATEMENT OF TED WILLIAMS, BOSTON RED SOX

Mr. WILLIAMS. I started to play baseball when I was 16 years of age, out of high school, in 1936. I signed with the local team in San Diego, Calif., where I was born. I was there a year and a half, and the Boston Red Sox picked up my contract, and I played a year in Minneapolis, which was a farm team of the Red Sox. That was in 1939.

I went to the Red Sox, and I have been there ever since, except for a couple of interruptions, military, militarywise, and injuries.

Senator KEFAUVER. You started in San Diego. With whom did you have a contract?

Mr. WILLIAMS. With the San Diego club. And Mr. Collins of the Red Sox went out and requested first chance to buy me from the San Diego club, and in 1937 he did buy the contract from the San Diego club.

I went to the Red Sox in spring training, and they farmed me out to Minneapolis.

Senator KEFAUVER. When the Red Sox bought you from the San Diego club, did you get part of the purchase price?

Mr. WILLIAMS. No, I didn't. I didn't make provision for that when I signed up. In fact, I signed up with the San Diego club at $150 a month. And when the Red Sox did buy my contract from San Diego, I tried to get a bonus. We were very poor, and I tried to get a bonus, and later did get a little bit of a bonus from the club as I signed a Red Sox contract.

Senator KEFAUVER. Do you think a player ought to get a part of the purchase price?

Mr. WILLIAMS. I think a player who signs up with an individual club, I think he ought to make provisions for that. I think if he becomes good enough to be bought by a big league club, I think he should be smart enough to stipulate that he gets a percentage of it, and I think most clubs work along that way.

Senator KEFAUVER. Do you have any right to get a percentage in the absence of willingness to pay it to you?

Mr. WILLIAMS. Well, I think that a big league club, I think that if they want you bad enough and you have made any kind of an agreement that you are going to get your dough, because I think most of them have got dough, and I don't think there will be too much of an argument that way.

Senator KEFAUVER. How much did the Boston Red Sox pay for your contract?

Mr. WILLIAMS. I think it was around $25,000 and 5 minor league players.

Senator KEFAUVER. They gave $25,000 and 5 minor league players?

Mr. WILLIAMS. Yes, sir.

Senator KEFAUVER. Do you think you should have gotten part of that $25,000?

Mr. WILLIAMS. Well, at the time, I wasn't smart enough or have the right advice to try to have an agreement with the San Diego club. I am sure if I had said, "When the time comes I am sold to a big league club," if I had foreseen that in the future and thought enough about my own ability and would be bought by a big league club, I am sure I would have arranged for it, because I think that is a little incentive for anybody who is——

Senator KEFAUVER. You were 17½ years old when you were sold to the Boston Red Sox. Who acted for you?

Mr. WILLIAMS. Well, my mother. I mean, I didn't do anything without the advice of my high-school coach, who I was very close to, and my mother, of course, had to be with me when I signed the contract, my dad, and I think that is the way they generally work.

I don't think a young fellow under 21 goes right into a baseball negotiation without having advice from a parent or guardian, or something.

Senator KEFAUVER. They were not a party to the contract. They just advised you about it; is that right.

Mr. WILLIAMS. Yes, sir.

Senator KEFAUVER. What would happen if you did not want to go with the Boston Red Sox?

Mr. WILLIAMS. Well, I have never heard of that happening, that anybody who had a chance to go from the minors to the big league didn't want to go. I never have. Maybe you have. I was excited about it, and I couldn't wait to get there.

Senator KEFAUVER. Did you have any opportunity to refuse?

Mr. WILLIAMS. No. At the time, I was not particularly happy about going to the Red Sox. I certainly wanted to go with some club who were up there during those years, Detroit or the Yankees or some club that I felt was going to be a better ball club. At that time the Red Sox weren't very high in the standings, and wasn't particularly attractive to me at the time.

Senator KEFAUVER. You say you were not very interested in going at the time. Suppose you had hoped that you might go to the Yankees or some other club, and you had refused to go to the Boston Red Sox, would you have been through with baseball?

Mr. WILLIAMS. Well, I think that I had signed up with the San Diego team. I think that if I hadn't after another club had bought my contract and I didn't go, I think possibly I would have—they wouldn't have wanted to—they wouldn't want, I think, to fool around with a boy who wouldn't live up to an obligation.

After all, when you sign up in baseball, as I understand it, you are their property then until they sell you, trade you, or release you, and I think once you sign that, why, that's the way it goes for a ballplayer.

Afterword

By Peter Golenbock

In today's age of advancing technology, generations turn over every two or three years. The new becomes old quickly, and too soon we ignore our past. Heroes remain heroes for only a short period of time. Childhoods end so quickly. There is so much information piled on information that the past disappears in a flurry of new names, new dates, new places. So it is with baseball.

The early gods of America's Pastime have become mere names. The characters and personalities of The Bambino, The Georgia Peach, The Big Train, The Dutchman, Old Pete, and their contemporaries have been lost to us as time marches on and we concentrate on our newest heroes. David Gallen has been charged with the task of bringing these men back to life, and with his collection of portraits of the men who built the game, he proves that Ruth, Cobb, and company were not only supremely talented, but human, complex, and fascinating each in his own right.

We discover that Lou Gehrig, a player with a reputation for being an iron man, was so shy with women he loved romantic movies, where he could get the experience secondhand.

We learn that Gehrig, who grew up in poverty, was trapped by his "poignant sense of his personal inadequacy." And thus he was driven to play in 2,130 games over a fourteen-year period as much by his fear that another player might take his job if he sat out as anything else. We see that Joe Jackson, who reportedly was a broken man after he was barred from baseball by Judge Landis for being part of the Black Sox scandal in 1919, eloquently refused to see himself as a tragic figure and proved himself not to be the dummy the writers made him out to be. After reading Furman Bisher's moving interview, you aren't quite so convinced of the truth of the story of the youngster who supposedly said to him, "Say it ain't so, Joe."

Jackson denied that any kid said that and repudiated any involvement in throwing the 1919 World Series. He admitted only to having great financial success after baseball.

"Everything I've done has turned to money," Jackson said late in his life. "I'm willing to let the Lord be my judge."

Walter Johnson, the Big Train, was known for his great fastball and his lack of emotion. But then you discover his wife died when he was thirty-six and left him with five young children, and that his career came to an end when his teammate in spring training hit him with a line drive that broke his leg. Moreover, as a manager Johnson was surly and stubborn and was fired in Cleveland after his players complained about his whining and nagging. Even the greatest can be grumpy.

Pete Alexander was reputed to be a drunk. It was a reputation he earned. "He drank like a fool," said his saintly wife Aimee.

But *why* was he a drunk? Shell shock. Terror. World War I eventually killed Christy Mathewson, who was gassed, contracted tuberculosis, and ultimately died at a young age. When Alexander returned from that same war, he was deaf in one ear from the roar of the guns, suffered from epilepsy, and lived from then on unable to face everyday life.

When he left the game in 1931, he had little to live for. Nothing could curtail his chronic drinking. Can you imagine that after Pete was elected into the Hall of Fame in 1938, he was given a job at the Cooperstown shrine as a guard? How that must have hurt his great pride. He didn't hold the post long. One of the great pitchers in the game's history drank until he could no longer stand; as he waited to die.

If Alexander's job at Cooperstown guarding his own plaque wasn't strange enough, what about Elmer Dean, the brother of Dizzy and Paul Dean, pitchers for the St. Louis Cardinals. Elmer wanted to be near his brothers so badly he took a job as a peanut vendor in Sportsman Park.

After Dizzy, who loved baseball more than anything, retired, he used to travel the countryside, and if he saw kids playing a ball game, would get out of his car and join them.

Then there was Satchel Paige. We will never fully know his pain. He may have been greater than any pitcher, but his skin color denied him the chance to play major-league baseball until he was in his mid-forties.

One year when he was in the Negro Leagues, Paige played in Bismarck, North Dakota. Because he was black, no one would rent him a room. He spent the season sleeping in a boxcar. To eat, he shot rabbits with a shotgun. How great was he? One year he was 43–2. His team was 97–5. The Sioux Indians of North Dakota honored him by naming him, "The Long Rifle."

When he reached the St. Louis Browns in 1948, he was the highest paid player on the team, earning twenty-five thousand dollars a season. He was 6–1 with a 2.47 ERA. At age forty-five, he was the American League's Rookie of the Year. Imagine.

In *The Baseball Chronicles* we discover that two of the fiercest men ever to play the game, John McGraw and Ty Cobb, each defied their fathers to become baseball players. The great McGraw left the game after suffering from rage and melancholy. He rode players so hard, they quit the team in protest.

Ty Cobb was a man who loved to hate. He even hated Lou Gehrig. Cobb was vengeful. Show him up, and he'd try to make you look bad. He was mean. But he'd come home from second on a fly ball and was known to score from first on a hit-and-run single. He was a driving force in every game. If you loved Pete Rose, you must get to know Ty Cobb.

And then there was the Babe. "Everything Babe did was fabulous," wrote teammate Waite Hoyt. When asked the secret to Hoyt's success, he replied, "Having Babe Ruth on my side."

But even the great Babe Ruth suffered disappointment. When he retired, he wanted to manage, but no one would give him that chance. He never got over it.

This is a book of deeds, emotions, heroism, human frailty. There are tiny tidbits scattered throughout that fascinate. I always wondered what Bobby Thompson said after hitting his historic home run to win the 1951 National League pennant. According to Roger Kahn, it was, "Gee whiz, gee whiz."

Satch Paige wore a red beard when playing for the House of David. Dizzy Dean hated his catcher Virgil Davis so much he refused to pitch to him. Grover Cleveland Alexander once had important friends, General Pershing and John Barrymore as two examples. There is so much here that fascinates. Names turn into flesh and blood.

When you read the graceful prose of A. Bartlett Giamotti back to back with the eccentric meanderings of Charles Dillon Stengel, you begin to see that the average man can't understand much of what either man is saying but knows instinctively that each is a genius. I had the pleasure of meeting both men, and I can tell you that baseball misses both of them terribly.

As we do Roberto Clemente. While he was alive, he was the greatest right fielder in the game, but he got little ink. Only after he was killed in a plane crash was he placed upon the pedestal he always deserved.

Most of the legends in this book have passed away, but you can hardly say that any of them are dead. These are the men and some of the moments that have made the game of baseball so special. These are the men who have graduated into the status of legends. And in this volume, thanks to David Gallen's research, they indeed do come alive. O tempore. O mores.

Always remember these men. They made today possible.